James Martineau

Endeavors After the Christian Life

James Martineau

Endeavors After the Christian Life

ISBN/EAN: 9783337164362

Printed in Europe, USA, Canada, Australia, Japan

Cover: Foto ©Lupo / pixelio.de

More available books at **www.hansebooks.com**

ENDEAVORS

AFTER THE

CHRISTIAN LIFE.

𝔇𝔦𝔰𝔠𝔬𝔲𝔯𝔰𝔢𝔰

BY

JAMES MARTINEAU.

" Je sais que Dieu a voulu que les vérités divines entrent du cœur dans l'esprit et non pas de l'esprit dans le cœur. Et de là vient qu'au lieu qu'en parlant des choses humaines, on dit qu'il faut les connaître avant que de les aimer; les Saints, au contraire, disent, en parlant des choses divines, qu'il faut les aimer pour les connaître, et qu'on n'entre dans la vérité que par la charité. — PASCAL: *Pensées.*

REPRINTED FROM THE SIXTH ENGLISH EDITION.

BOSTON:

AMERICAN UNITARIAN ASSOCIATION.

1881.

UNIVERSITY PRESS: JOHN WILSON & SON,
CAMBRIDGE.

TO

REV. JOHN HAMILTON THOM,

THIS VOLUME, THE EXPRESSION OF A HEART ENLARGED BY HIS FRIEND-

SHIP AND OFTEN AIDED BY HIS WISDOM,

IS DEDICATED,

IN MEMORY OF MANY LABORS LIGHTENED BY PARTNERSHIP, PURPOSES

INVIGORATED BY SYMPATHY, AND THE VICISSITUDES OF YEARS

BALANCED BY CONSTANCY OF AFFECTION.

PREFACE

TO THE FIRST SERIES.

In a little work* published seven years ago, the Author of the following Discourses intimated a desire to work out for himself and present to his readers, a distinct answer to the question, "What is Christianity?" and the work then put forth was designed as a mere preliminary to another, in which this great inquiry should be prosecuted. The purpose then announced still remains, and the materials for its execution are for the most part prepared. The present volume, however, is not offered as any part of its fulfilment; but rather in temporary apology for its non-fulfilment.

Of his reasons for withholding for a time that promised volume, this is not the proper place to speak at any length. A change in some of his views, and the consciousness of immaturity in others, have certainly

---

* The Rationale of Religious Enquiry; or the Question stated of Reason, the Bible, and the Church.

had a share of influence in producing the postponement. But it has been occasioned chiefly by his desire
to lay aside for a while the polemical character, which
necessity, not choice, has impressed upon his former
writings ; and which, until relieved by some task of
higher spirit, misrepresents the order of his convictions,
— engaging him upon the outward form of Christian
belief, while silent of the inner heart of human life
and faith.

Of his reasons for presenting this unpromised volume, the Author has but few words to say. As its
contents were written, so are they now published,
because he takes them to be true, and good to be
recognized as true by the consciousness of all men:
and not having been produced as taskwork, but out
of an earnest heart, they may possibly find a reader
here and there, to whom they speak a fitting and
faithful word. Should the book avail for this, it
will sufficiently justify its appearance : should it not,
it will speedily disappear, and at least no harm be
done.

No formal connection will be found among the several discourses in this volume. Prepared at different
times, and in different moods of meditation, they are
related to each other only by their common direction
towards the great ends of responsible existence. The
title, indeed, expresses the spirit, more than the matter

of the book ; — which " endeavors " to produce, rather than describe, the essential temper of the " Christian life."

The Author would have introduced a larger number of discourses having direct reference, in word as well as in spirit, to the divine ministry of Christ, did he not hope to follow up the present volume by another devoted especially to this subject, and a third on the Christianity of Paul. In the meanwhile, he trusts that those who, in devout reading of books and men, look for that rather which *is* Christian, than which *talks of* Christianity, will find in this little volume no faint impression of the religion by which he, no less than they, desires to live and die.

LIVERPOOL, June 20, 1843.

PREFACE

———

A GLANCE at the contents of this volume will show that it does not fulfil the intentions avowed in the preface to the former volume. It does not refer specially to the ministry of Christ, or to the Pauline gospel: much less does it pretend to investigate the proper definition of Christianity. The hope of treating these subjects, in a manner at all suitable to my estimate of them, still recedes into the distance. The materials indeed are not wholly unprovided; or I should not have ventured on the pledge which still waits to be redeemed: but a growing sense of their inadequacy makes me wonder that I could ever think them worthy of my readers' acceptance; and induces me to withhold them, till the deficiencies can be in some measure supplied. Should the needful leisure never arrive, or should I finally esteem myself not qualified for the task to which, perhaps with presumptuous earnestness, I once aspired, I shall indeed regret my inconsiderate promise, but be clear of reproach for less considerate performance.

Though however the present volume, like its predecessor, is altogether practical and unsystematic, there is a sense in which it may be regarded as a step towards the completion of the original design. The prevalent differences of belief on questions of theology have their secret foundation in different philosophies of religion: and these philosophies are the product of moral experience and self-scrutiny, so as always to reflect the conception of human nature most familiar to the disciple's mind. Hence, controversies apparently historical cannot be settled by appeal to history alone: nor metaphysical disputes, by metaphysics only; but will ultimately resort for their answer to the sentiments and affections wakened into predominant activity by the literature, the teachings, and the social conditions of the age. No one can observe the changes of faith and the causes which determine them, without discovering, that the order of fact reverses the order of theory; that the feelings of men must be changed in detail, their perceptions be awakened in fresh directions, their tastes be drawn by new admirations, before any reasoning can avail to establish an altered system of religious thought. Who can suppose that the different estimates made of the authority of Scripture are really the result of historical research, and are simply so many varieties of critical judgment? Is it not obvious that the sacred writings are, in every case, allowed to retain precisely the residue of authority which, according to the believer's view of our nature and our life, is unsupplied from any other source? If this be so, the psychology of religion must have precedence — I do not say in dignity, but in time — of its documentary criticism: and every word faithfully spoken from the consciousness of a living man contributes a preliminary to the inquiry as to the inspiration of ancient books. I am not ashamed to confess, that extensive and, in the end, systematic changes in the opinions I derived from sect and education, have had no higher origin than self-examination and reflection, — a more careful interrogation of that internal experience, of which the superficial interpretation is so seductive to indolence and so prolific in error. And possibly, a volume like the present, should it at all awaken in others the sentiments from which it proceeds in myself, may indirectly lead to the recognition, on their proper evidence of consciousness, of those very truths, which, in a more systematic work, I could only aim to protect from the objections of philosophy, and reconcile with the results of criticism.

I have preserved what I have to say in its original form of discourses prepared for the pulpit. I have always felt indignant with those preachers who, when

they resort to the press, seem ashamed of their voca-
tion, and disguise, under new shapes and names, the
materials originally embodied in sermons. I should
as soon think of turning a sonnet into an epistle,
a ballad into a review, or a dirge into an obituary.
It must be a bad sermon that can be made into a
good treatise or even a good "Oration." In virtue
of the close affinity, perhaps ultimate identity, of
religion and poetry, preaching is essentially a lyric
expression of the soul, an utterance of meditation in
sorrow, hope, love, and joy, from a representative of
the human heart in its divine relations. In proportion
as we quit this view, and prominently introduce the
idea of a preceptive and monitory function, we retreat
from the true prophetic interpretation of the office back
into the old *sacerdotal :* — or (what is not perhaps so
different a distinction as it may appear) from the properly *religious* to the simply *moral.* A ministry of mere
instruction and persuasion, which addresses itself primarily to the understanding and the will, which deals
mainly with facts and reasonings, with hopes and fears,
may furnish us with the expositions of the lecture-
room, the commandments of the altar, the casuistry of
the confessional: but it falls short of that true " testimony of God," that personal effusion of conscience and
affection, which distinguishes the reformed *preaching*
from the catholic *homily.* Were this distinction duly

apprehended, there would be a less eager demand for extemporaneous preaching ; which may be the vehicle of admirable disquisitions, convincing arguments, impressive speeches ; but is as little likely to produce a genuine sermon, as the practice of improvising to produce a great poem. The thoughts and aspirations which look direct to God, and the kindling of which among a fraternity of men constitutes social worship, are natives of solitude : the spectacle of an assembly is a hindrance to their occurrence ; and though, where they have been devoutly set down beforehand, they may be re-assumed under such obstacle, they would not spontaneously rise, till the presence of a multitude was forgotten, and by a rare effort of abstraction the loneliness of the spirit was restored. The faculty of fluent speech is no doubt worthy of cultivation for various civic and moral ends: but if it were once adopted as the instrument of preaching, I am persuaded that the pulpit would exercise a far lower, though perhaps a wider, influence ; would be a powerful agent of theological discussion, of social criticism, of moral and political censorship, but would lose its noblest element of religion. The devout genius of England would have occasion deeply to lament a change, which would reduce to the same class with the newspaper article a form of composition, enabling us to rank the names of Taylor, Barrow, Leighton, Butler,

with the poets and philosophers of our country. At
all events, he who finds room under the conditions of
the sermon, to interest and engage his whole soul,
would be guilty of affectation, were he to disown the
occasion which wakes up his worthiest spirit, and
which, however narrow when measured by the capacities of other men, is adequate to receive *his* best
thoughts and aspirations. I am therefore well content
to mingle with the crowd of sermonizers.

It would be ungrateful, were I not to acknowledge,
as one of the results of the former volume of this
work, the delightful and unsought-for intercourse it
has opened to me with persons, whom it is an honor
to know, of various religious denominations. In the
divided state of English society, a work which touches
any springs of religious affection common to several
classes, performs at least a seasonable, though very
simple and natural, office. It is happily an office
which every day renders easier to earnest men. For
there is undoubtedly an increasing body of persons in
this country, who are rapidly escaping from the restraints of sects; who are not unaware of the new conditions under which the Christianity of the present
day exists; and who are ready to join hand and heart
in order to give free scope to the essential truths and
influences of our religion, in combination with the
manly exercise of thought, and just concessions to mod-

ern knowledge. To find one's-self in sympathy with such men is a heartfelt privilege, superior to all personal distinction: it is to share in an escape from the worst prejudices of the present, and in the best auguries of the coming age.

LIVERPOOL, September 2, 1847.

PREFACE

TO THE FOURTH EDITION.

————

BOTH Series of the " Endeavors after the Christian Life " being out of print at the same time, I have availed myself of the opportunity, in reproducing and revising them, to throw them together into a single volume : and I am glad to seek entrance for them to a' new class of readers by a reduction of price which their more assured place now renders possible.

It was not without uneasiness that I began to correct the proofs of this new edition. The twenty years which had elapsed since the sheets passed under my eye had been marked by momentous changes in theological feeling and belief, to which, in common with my contemporaries, I could not pretend to have been insensible. And it was natural to fear that a book produced at the other end of that interval, must now be out of date. I was relieved and surprised to find how little it had been thrown out of tune by

b

the altered pitch of thought and sentiment; how much less indeed it has to apprehend to-day from any jar against the prevailing tone of religion, than at the hour of its first appearance. It would have been far otherwise, had it treated of subjects whose interest is critical or speculative, and which take new aspects with the shifting light. But appealing mainly to the simplest trusts and aspirations of the human heart, it is compensated for having nothing new upon its page, by having so much the less that is liable to grow old; and, while not pretending to trace any line of progress in religion, gains a little shelter from its permanence. To heal the broken unity of Christendom, the scholar may rely on the ultimate establishment of his critical results; the ecclesiast may plan treaties of peace and fusions of doctrine between Church and Church; but, meanwhile, those who find it more congenial to pass behind the whole field of theological divergency, and linger near the common springs of all human piety and hope, may perhaps be preparing some first lines of a true *Eirenikon.*

LONDON, November 22, 1866.

CONTENTS.

DISCOURSES.

I.

THE SPIRIT OF LIFE IN JESUS CHRIST.

ROMANS VIII. 2.

THE LAW OF THE SPIRIT OF LIFE IN JESUS CHRIST.

" A MAN," says the Apostle Paul, "is the image and glory of God." And truly, it is from our own human nature, from its deep experiences and earnest affections, that we form our conceptions of Deity, and become qualified to interpret the solemn intimations which creation and Scripture afford to us respecting him. Without the stirring of divine qualities within us, without some consciousness of that which we ascribe to the All-perfect, the names and descriptions by which he is made known to us would be empty words, as idly sent to us as treatises of sound to the deaf, or some "high discourse of reason" to the fool. All that we believe without us, we first feel within us; and it is the one sufficient proof of the grandeur and awfulness of our nature, that we have faith in God; for no merely finite being can possibly believe the infinite. The universe of which each man conceives, exists primarily in his own mind; *there* dwell the angel he enthrones in the height, and the demon he covers with the deep; and vainly would *he* talk of shunning hell, who never felt its fires in his bosom; or *he* converse of heaven, whose soul was never pure and green as Paradise.

In virtue of this resemblance between the human and

1

the divine mind, Christ is the representative and revealer of both. God, by the very immensity of his nature, is a stationary being,—perfect, and therefore unchangeable : and so far as Jesus Christ was " the same yesterday, to-day, and for ever ;" so far as one uniform mind and power possessed him, as one sacred purpose was impressed upon his life,—so far is he the emblem of Deity; affording us, in speech, in feeling, in will, in act, an idea of God, which nothing borrowed from the material creation or mortal life can at all approach. His unity of soul, the unalterable spirit pervading all his altering moods of thought,—in short, his identity with himself, is altogether divine. In so far, on the other hand, as he underwent vicissitudes of emotion ; in so far as he spake, thought, acted differently in different periods of his career, and a changed hue of soul came over him, and threw across the world before him a brighter or a sadder shade,—so far is he the ideal and picture of the mind of man. His self-variations are altogether human.

The casual vicissitudes of feeling in Christ, his alternations of anxiety and hope, of rejoicing and of tears, have often been appealed to, as traces of his having had a like nature with our own. The appeal is just; and shows us that he was impressed, as we are, by those outward incidents which may make the morning happy and the evening sad. But besides these accidental agitations, which follow the complexion of our external lot, there is a far more important set of changes, which the affections and character undergo from internal causes ; which occur in regular succession, marking and characterizing the different periods of mental, if not of physical life ; and constitute the stages of moral development through which the noblest minds visibly pass to their perfection. The incidental fluctuations of emotion, raised by the good or evil tidings of the hour, are but as the separate waves which the passing wind may soothe to a ripple or press into a storm: but the seasonal changes of character, of which I now speak, are rather the great tidal movements of the deep within us, depending on less capricious forces than the transient gale, and bearing on their surface the mere film of tempest or of calm. The succession is distinctly traceable in the mind of Christ, making his life a model of moral progression the most impressive and sublime. He thus becomes in a new sense the representative of our duty, our visible and outward conscience : revealing to us not only the end to which we must attain, but the successive steps by which our nature reaches it ; the process as well as the result; the natural history of the affections which belong to the true perfection of the will. He is the type of the pure religious life; all its developments being crowded, by the rapid ripening of his soul, into his brief experience : and we read in the gospel a divine allegory of humanity, symbolical of those profound and silent changes, of passion and speculation, of faith and love, through which a holy mind rises to its most godlike power.

I propose to follow Jesus through the several periods, so far as they appear, of his outward and inward history ; and to show the correspondence between their order and the successive stages of growth in a religious and holy soul.

The only incident recorded of the childhood of Jesus strikingly commences the analogy between his nature and ours, and happily introduces him to us as the representative of the great ideas of duty and God within the 'soul. The annual pilgrimage from his village to the holy city, which had hitherto been the child's holiday, full only of the wonder and delight of travel, seized hold, on one occasion, of deeper feelings, which absorbed him with their new intensity. The visit which had become conventional with others appeared at once with its full meaning to him : and with the surprise of a fresh reverence he turned from the gay streets, and the sunny excursion, and the social entertainment, to the quiet courts of the temple, where the ancient story of miracle was told, and the mystery of prophecy explained. Eager to prolong this new and solemn interest, he missed, you will re-

member, the opportunity of travelling back with the caravan
of Nazareth: and when told by his parents, on their return
in quest of him, " Thy father and mother have sought thee
sorrowing," he replied, with a tone not altogether filial,
" Know ye not that I must be about my Father's business ? "

The answer is wonderfully expressive of the spirit of
young piety, taking its first dignity as an independent principle of action in the mind. The lessons of devotion are,
for a long time, adopted passively, with listening faith ; the
great ideas dwindling, as they fall from the teacher's lips,
to the dimensions of the infant mind receiving them. When
the mother calls her children to her knees to speak to them
of God, she is *herself* the greatest object in their affections.
It is by her power over them that God becomes Venerable ;
by the purity of her eye that he becomes Holy ; by the
silence of the hour that he becomes Awful ; by the tenderness of her tones that he becomes Dear. That the parents
bend, with lowly look and serene result, before some invisible
Presence, is the first and sufficient hint to the heart's latent
faith ; which therefore blends awhile with the domestic sympathies, simply mingling with them an element of mystery,
and imparting to them a deeper and less earthy coloring.
But the thoughts which constitute religion are too vast and
solemn to remain subordinate. They are germs of a growth,
which, with true nurture, must burst into independent life,
and overshadow the whole soul. When the mind, beginning to be busy for itself, ponders the ideas of the infinite
and eternal, it detects, as if by sudden inspiration, the
immensity of the relations which it sustains to God and
immortality : the old formulas of religious instruction break
their husk, and give forth the seeds of wonder and of love ;
every thing that before seemed great and worthy is dwarfed ;
and human affinities and duties sink into nothingness compared with the heavenly world which has been discovered.
There is a period when earnest spirits become thus possessed; disposed to contrast the grandeur of their new

ideal with the littleness of all that is actual; and to look
with a sublimated feeling, which in harsher natures passes
into contempt, on pursuits and relations once sufficient for
the heart's reverence. At such a crisis it was that Jesus
gave the answer to his parents; when his piety first broke
into original and self-luminous power, and not only took the
centre of his system, but threatened to put out those minor
and dependent lights which, when their place is truly understood, appear no less heavenly. He spake in the entranced
and exclusive spirit of young devotion. Well then may we
bear with the rebukes which this earnest temper is sometimes impelled to administer : for, by a mental necessity, all
strong feeling must be exclusive, till wisdom and experience
have trained it; till the worth of many things has been
ascertained; till God is seen, not sitting aloof from his
creation to show how contemptible it is, but pervading
it to give it sanctity; till it is found how much that is
human is also divine. None learned this so soon or so
profoundly as Jesus. And even now, the very sight of
home restored his household sympathies again : for when
he went to Nazareth with his parents, " he was obedient
unto them; and increased in favor " with " man," as well as
" God."

Nearly twenty years elapsed. Boyhood passed without
events. The slight flush of the youthful soul had fled.
Vainly did Mary notice how a light, as from within, came
upon his features as he bent over his daily toil, or forced
him to pause, as if in some secret and ineffable colloquy.
Though the life of God within him was strong enough to
win the world, and give direction to its reverence for ever,
he was a villager still, serving the same necessities, and
pacing the same track of custom as others. It was inevitable that the spiritual force within him should make insurrection against the narrow and cramping conditions by which
it was confined; that it should strive to burst its fetters,
and find or create a career worthy of itself : in short, that

we should find Jesus no longer at Nazareth, but in the wilderness; led thither, in spite of himself, of interest and comfort, of habit and home, by the beckoning of the divine image in his heart. That solitude he was impelled to seek, that he might grapple face to face with the evil and earthly spirits that beset our path, disengage himself from the encumbrances of usage and of doubt, and struggle into a life befitting one who stands in immensity and dwells with God. To the eye of the outward observer he may appear altogether quiet, sitting on the bleak rock in the collapse of feebleness and rest. Nevertheless, in that still form is the most terrible of conflicts; an exchange of awful defiances between heaven and hell; a heaving and wrestling of immortal powers, doing battle for the mind of Jesus, and suspending on that moment the souls of millions and the destinies of the world. His holy spirit won the victory; the angels of peace and power led him forth; and the transition was made from the obscurity of ordinary toil to the glory of his everlasting ministry.

Now in the development of all earnest and noble minds there is a passage corresponding with this scene. There is a time when their image of duty grows too large for the accidental lot in which it is encased, and seeks to burst it; when human life changes its aspect before the eye; and custom can no longer show it to us as a flat dull field, where we may plough and build and find shelter and sleep; but it swells into verdant slopes around the base of everlasting hills, whose summit no man can discern, passing away as a dim shape into the blue infinite above the lingering clouds. There is a crisis when every faithful son of God is agitated by a fierce controversy between the earthly and the divine elements of his nature. Self and the flesh seductively whisper, "Thou hast a life of many necessities; earn thy bread and eat it; and pay thyself for all thy trouble with a warm hearth and a soft bed." •The voice of God thunders in reply, "Thy life is short, thy work is great, thy God is near, thy heaven is far; do I not send thee forth, armed with thought and speech, and a strong right hand, to contend with the evil and avenge the good? Indulge no more, or I shall leave thee: do thy best, and faint not: take up thy free-will, and come with me." By some such conflict does every great mind quit its ease to serve its responsibilities; part, if need be, with the sympathy of friends and the security of neighborhood, in fidelity to duty; and suffer wasting and loneliness, as in the bleakest desert, till temptation be vanquished, and hesitancy flung aside.

The course of Jesus was now taken. The peasant had assumed the prophet's mantle and Messiah's power. How calm and free his mind had thus become, how unembarrassed it dwelt in the pure atmosphere of its own convictions, is evident from this, that to his own village he went and announced the change. In the very synagogue where parents and neighbors worshipped, and aged knees to which he had clung in infant sport were bent in prayer; where his ear had first heard the music, and his soul felt the sublimity of ancient prophecy,— *there* " He opened the book, and found the place where it was written, 'The Spirit of the Lord is upon me, because he hath anointed me to preach glad tidings to the poor: he hath sent me to proclaim liberty to the captives, and recovery of sight to the blind; to let the oppressed go free, to proclaim the acceptable year of the Lord.'" No wonder that as he spake in comment worthy of such a text, his hearers "were astonished at the gracious words that proceeded from his lips." The moment introduced, and fitly represents, the first era of his ministry; during the whole of which a *joyous* inspiration was on him. No sad forebodings visited him: no doubts restrained his freedom: no tears gushed forth to check his voice of mercy and delay his word of power. It was a hopeful and vigorous career; crowded with blessed deeds, and flushed with countless benedictions that only kindled him to an alacrity more godlike. Nay, it seemed impossible for him to bear his own

messages of love fast enough : and first the Twelve, and
then the Seventy, were sent successively forth on a systematic mission, to multiply his power, and make ready the
paths of peace. The report of the Seventy, on their return,
declares the triumph of his name and spirit, not only in the
conquest of disease, but in the attachment of the poor and
the oppressed ; and with the glow of glad devotion that
marks this period Jesus exclaimed, " I beheld Satan, as
lightning, fall from heaven." The Twelve brought far different tidings, which changed again the colors of his life.

Who does not discern, in the history of every faithful
mind, a period like this ? — a period immediately following
the solemn league and covenant which we make with duty.
Through sore and dark temptations the Christian first
emerges into the free-will, by which he stands up and lives
in the likeness of God ; and then, in the joy of his freedom
and sincerity, he springs, with self-precipitation, into the
mission Heaven assigns. That which he speaks — is it not
true ? that which he feels is holy ; that which he desires is
great and good. He loves the souls he would convert, and
knows them of the same family with his own. He has conquered in himself the weakness and the ills with which he
wars in others ; and shall he not have faith? God is vaster
than the most gigantic wrongs ; and *His* righteousness,
which is as the great mountains, will speedily suppress them
in the abyss. In the power of this glorious faith, the true
servant and prophet of the Lord goes forth ; makes a generous and confident rush upon evil ; and — since it is the
immortal against the perishable — he trusts to sweep it off
and triumph in its flight. But, alas ! the time is short, the
conflict long ; and, faint and bleeding, he discovers that he
must fall, before the cry of victory.. And yet was that faith
of his most true. Its computation of forces was most unerring, for always shall evil be overcome by good, — with
mistake, you will say, in its dates ; but that is only the
prophet's mistake, that sees the future as the present, and

considers the certainties of God superior to time. This right-souled man has uplifted his arm, and done a faithful work : and the efforts of the wise and holy are not mere momentary strokes dissipated and lost ; but an everlasting pressure upon ill, with tension increasing without end, till it drives the monstrous mass across the brink of annihilation.

Sad, however, is the hour when generous hope receives its first check; and with mournful attention Jesus hears, on the return of the Twelve, tidings of hostility and danger, forcing on him the conviction that he must die; tidings especially of the vigilance of Herod, recent murderer of John the Baptist. The shock was somewhat sudden. He retreated into solitude among the hills, that he might feel awhile without obstruction the refuge of his disciples' friendship and his Father's power. And soon in the Transfiguration, where his mind conversed with prophets of an elder age, the impression of his decease as the penalty of his faithfulness becomes finally fixed. Thenceforth, as it seems to me, not only did his views and expectations undergo a great change and receive a large accession of truth, but the spirit and moral tone of his ministry was different. Steadfast as before, even to " set his face to go to Jerusalem," he is less joyous and more serene ; more earnest and lofty, as if his great aims had become sublimer for the distance to which they had receded, and dearer for the price at which they must be gained ; more prone to tears, when asked for by the griefs of others, more driven to prayer in wrestling with his own. If his deeds of power — which by their nature must be self-repetitions — are less frequent, he gives himself more to speech, varying ever those words of eternal life from which all ages learn divinest wisdom. And so he passes on to his crucifixion : numbering the days only by the duties that remain ; devoting himself to the crowds of Jerusalem by day, and to the family of Bethany at even ; in the morning teaching in the temple, and predicting its fall at night ; blessing the widow's charity, laying bare the

priest's hypocrisy; found by his conspirators at midnight
prayer; in the trial, concerned for Peter; in the hall, con-
vulsing the conscience of Pilate; on the fatal road, turning
with pity to the daughters of Jerusalem; and not exclaim-
ing, "It is finished," till from the cross he looked on a
mother for whom he found a home, and a disciple whom he
made blessed by his trust.

And even this last change in Christ appears to be not a
mere external modification, but an internal ripening of his
perfect character, the last unfolding of its progressive
beauty: to which also there is a corresponding stage,
wherever the true religious life fulfils its course. When
the first sanguine enterprises of conscience seem to fail
(though fail they cannot, except to live as fast as our impatient fancies); when a cloud, like that which fell upon
Christ's future, descends upon the prospects of the good;
when the evils against which he has taken up his vow, withstand the siege of his enthusiasm, and years ebb away, and
strength departs, with no visible impression made; and
friends become treacherous, and foes alert, and God's good
providence seems tedious and cruel, — then weak spirits
may succumb, able to keep faith alive no more; and even
the man mighty of heart may find the controversy great,
whether to go on and bear up against such sorrow of the
soul. But if he be wise, he clings more firmly to his fidelity,
and thinks more truly of his mission, wherein he is appointed
not to do much, but to do well. He too takes counsel of
the prophets of old, — the sainted spirits of the good, who
rebuke his impatience, and tell him that *they* followed each
other at intervals of centuries, and, as they found, so after
true service still left, the mighty work of good undone; that
the fruits of heaven will not ripen in some sunny hour, but
every noble mind must lend its transitory ray: and then,
when the full year of Providence has gone its round, perchance the collective sunshine of humanity may have
matured the produce of the tree of life. Such communion

does indeed speak to him of his " decease which he must
accomplish ; " asks him to join the glorious *succession* of the
good ; sends him with transfigured spirit back into the
field of duty ; gives him a sadder but more enduring wisdom, by which, with or without hope, in or out of peril, he
lives and labors on ; renouncing power and success, yet
winning their divinest forms ; and through self-crucifixion
gifted with immortality.

II.

THE BESETTING GOD.

———◆———

PSALM CXXXIX. 5.

THOU HAST BESET ME BEHIND AND BEFORE, AND LAID THINE HAND
UPON ME.

PERHAPS it is impossible for us to represent God to our minds under any greater *physical* image than that of his diffused presence through every region of space. Certainly, to feel that He lives, as the percipient and determining agent throughout the universe, conscious of all things actual or possible from the vivid centre to the desert margin of its sphere, excluded from neither air, nor earth, nor sea, nor souls, but clad with them as a vestment, and gathering up their laws within his being, is a sublimer and therefore a truer mode of thought, than the conception of a remote and retired mechanician, inspecting from without the engine of creation to see how it performs. Indeed, this mechanical metaphor, so skilfully elaborated by Paley, appears to be, of all representations of the divine nature, the least religious; its very clearness proclaiming its insufficiency for those affections which seek not the finite, but the infinite; its coldness repelling all emotions, and reducing them to physiological admiration; and its scientific procedure presenting the Creator to us in a relation quite too mean, as one of the causes in creation, to whom a chapter might be devoted in any treatise on dynamics, and on evidence quite below the real, as a highly probable God. The true natural language of devotion speaks out rather in the poetry of the

Psalmist and the prayers of Christ; declares the living contact of the Divine Spirit with the human, the mystic implication of his nature with ours, and ours with his; his serenity amid our griefs, his sanctity amid our guilt, his wakefulness in our sleep, his life through our death, his silence amid our stormy force; and refers to him as the absolute basis of all relative existence; all else being in comparison but phantasm and shadow, and He alone the real and essential Life.

Were we to insist on philosophical correctness of speech in matters transcending all our modes of definition, we should reject, as irrational and in truth unmeaning, the question respecting any spiritual being, "*where is he?*" Local position, physical presence, is a relation of material things, and cannot be affirmed of mind without confounding it with body. Thought, will, love, which have no size and take up no space, can be in no spot, and move to none; and to the souls of which these are attributes we can ascribe neither habitation nor locomotion. It is only the bodily effects and outward manifestations of mental force, — the gestures of the visible frame and the actions of the solid limbs, — to which place can be assigned: and when we say that we are *here* and not *there*, it is to this organic system connected with our spiritual nature, and to this alone that we refer. Were we to press the notion further, and endeavor to settle the question where our minds are, the intrinsic impropriety of the question would leave us altogether at a loss. There would be no more reason to attribute to the soul a residence within the body, than in the remotest station of the universe; for God could as well establish a constant relation between the mind and the organism on which it was to act, at a distance thus vast, as in the nearest proximity: and there would be no more wonder in the movement of my arm on earth complying with my will at the confines of the solar system, than in the constant rush of our world on its career, in obedience to a sun separated by distance so immense. It may be, after all, but figuratively that we speak of any *migration* of the soul in death. When the body appropriated to it as its instrument and expression falls, we cannot say that the mind is here; we dream of what we know not, if we fancy it to require removal in order to present itself manifestly in a higher region. One order of physical relations being dropped here, another may on the instant be assumed elsewhere, revealing the spirit to a new society, and giving it the apparition of fresh worlds.

If we are unable to speak, otherwise than in figures, of the place of our own minds, it is not surprising that God's presence is quite ineffable, and that we bow with reverent assent to the poet's admission, "such knowledge is too wonderful for me." But the confession of our ignorance once made, we may proceed to use such poor thought and language as we find least unsuitable to so high a matter; for it is the essence and beginning of religion to feel that all our belief and speech respecting God is untrue, yet infinitely truer than any non-belief and silence. In whatever sense, then, and on whatever grounds, we affirm the tenancy of our own frame by the soul that governs it, must we fill the universe with the everlasting Spirit of whose thought it is the development. His agency is all-comprehending, and declares itself alike before us, from whichever side of the world's orbit, from whichever phase of life we survey the spectacle of the heavens or the phenomena of human history; nor can we help regarding the physical laws of creation (the same in all worlds) as his personal habits; the moral order of Providence as the unfolding of his character, the forms and flush of the universal beauty as the effusion of his art; the griefs and joys, the temptations, lapses, and triumphs, and all the glorious strife of responsible natures, as the energy of his moral sentiments, and his profuse donation of a divine free-will. It is true we do not everywhere alike discern him; but this is our blindness and not his darkness. In the nar-

row ways of common life, amid the din of labor and traffic,
he seems to pass away; though it were well that his sanctity should be nigh, to cool the heats and guard the purity
of our toiling and tempted hours. But we acknowledge
space and silence to be his attributes; and when the evening dew has laid the noon-day dust of care, and the vision
strained by microscopic anxieties takes the wide sweep of
meditation, and earth sleeps as a desert beneath the starry
infinite, the unspeakable Presence wraps us close again, and
startles us in the wild night-wind, and gazes straight into
our eyes from those ancient lights of heaven.

And to the same Omnipresence which the individual
thinker thus consciously realizes, the collective race of men
is perpetually bearing an unconscious testimony. As if in
acknowledgment of the mystery of God, as if with an instinctive feeling that his being is the meeting-place of light
and shade, and that in approaching him we must stand on
the confines between the seen and the unseen; all nations
and all faiths of cultivated men have chosen the *twilight*
hour, morning and evening, for their devotion; and so
it has happened, that all round the earth on the bordering circle between the darkness and the day, a zone of
worshippers has been ever spread, looking forth for the
Almighty Tenant of space, one-half towards the east, brilliant with the dawn, the other into the hemisphere of night,
descending on the west. The veil of shadow, as it shifts,
has glanced upon adoring souls, and by its touch cast down
a fresh multitude to kneel; and as they have gazed into
opposite regions for their God, they have virtually owned
his presence "besetting them behind and before." Our
planet, thus instinct with devout life, girded with intent
and perceptive souls, covered over, as with a divine retina,
by the purer conscience of humanity, is like a living eye,
watching on every side the immensity of Deity in which it
floats, and grateful for the rays that relieve its native gloom.
We sometimes complain of the conditions of our being as

unfavorable to the discernment and the love of God; we speak of him as veiled from us by our senses, and of the world as the outer region of exile from which he is peculiarly hid. In imagining what is holy and divine, we take flight to other worlds, and conceive that there the film must fall away, and all adorable realities burst upon the sight. Alas! what reason have we to think any other station in the universe more sanctifying than our own? There is none, so far as we can tell, under the more immediate touch of God; none whence sublimer deeps are open to adoration; none murmuring with the whisper of more thrilling affections, or ennobled as the theatre of more glorious duties. The dimness we deplore, no travelling would cure; the most perfect of observatories will not serve the blind; we carry our darkness with us; and instead of wandering to fresh scenes, and blaming our planetary atmosphere, and flying over creation for a purer air, it behooves us in simple faith to sit by our own wayside and cry, " Lord, that we may receive our sight." The Psalmist found no fault with this world as setting God beyond his reach; but having the full eye of his affections opened in perpetual vigil, he rather was haunted by the Omniscient more awfully than he could well bear, and would fain have found some shade, though it were in darkness or the grave, from a presence so piercing and a light so clear. Those to whom the earth is not consecrated will find their heaven profane.

God "besets us behind and before" in another sense. He pervades the successions of time as well as the fields of space, and occupies eternity no less than immensity. The imagination faints beneath the weight of ages which crowd upon it in the simplest meditation on his being, and in the utterance of the most familiar of our prayers. We call him the " *God of our fathers;* " and we feel that there is some stability at centre, while we can tell our cares to One listening at our right hand, by whom theirs are remembered and were removed; who yesterday took pity on their quaint

perplexities, and smiles to-day on ours, not wiser yet, but
just as bitter and as real; and who accepts their strains of
happy and emancipated love, while putting into our hearts
the song of exile and the plaint of aspiration. We invoke
him as the " *God of Jesus;* " and so doing we have contact
with a Mind yet conscious of every scene in the tragedy of
Palestine, wherein the shadows of the lake-storm are unef-
faced, and the cry of the Crucifixion is ringing still. We
speak to him as the " *Ancient of days;* " and so converse
with One who feels not the gradations of intensity that
make difference to us between the present and past, with
a consciousness that has no perspective; and we rest on the
surface of an unfathomable nature, comprising without confusion the undulation of all events, be it the tidal sweep of
centuries, or the surges of a nation's rage, or the small and
vivid ripplings of private grief. Nay, we pray to him as
having abode " *in heaven;* " and we cannot lift our eye to
that pure vault without thinking how old are those stars
amid which our imagination enspheres him; how they
watched over patriarchs in the plain of Mamre, and paced
the night in the same order and with like speed as yesterday; how they were ready there to meet the first human
sight that was turned aloft to gaze; and witnessed those
primeval revolutions that, having prepared the earth for
man, left their grotesque and gigantic vestiges as hiero-
glyphic hints to carry him back into the waste places of
eternity, and measure for him God's most recent step out
of the everlasting. How do the most vehement forms of history, the tempestuous minds that from any other point of
view would terrify us by their might, — the savage hordes
that have swept as a whirlwind over the patient structure
of civilization, — how do they all, in this contemplation,
dwindle into momentary shapes, angel or demon spectres,
vividly visible and suddenly submerged! By the granite
pillars of God's eternity, deep-rooted in the abyss, we all in
turn climb to the surface for a moment, to slip again into

the night. But during the moment we are there, if we use that moment well, we all see the same presence; turning this way and that, we perceive only that he "besets us behind and before." The Psalmist came up at a very different point of eternity from ourselves; and as he looked fore and aft he could see only God. We, who are presented at a station where the Hebrew poet himself is quite invisible, discern on every side the same immensity which he adored. Well may we fall down and worship with every creature, "Great and marvellous are thy works, O Lord God Almighty! who art, and wast, and art to come."

There is yet another sense in which we must confess that God "besets us behind and before." His physical agency in all places is a great and solemn certainty; his ceaseless energy through all time presents us with sublimer thoughts; but there is a *moral* presence of his Spirit to our minds, which places us in relations to him more intimate and sacred. Surely there occur to every uncorrupted heart some stirrings of a diviner life; some consciousness, obscure and transient it may be, but deep and authoritative, of a nobler calling than we have yet obeyed; a rooted dissatisfaction with self, a suspicion of some poison in the will, a helpless veneration for somewhat that is gazed at with a sigh as out of reach. It is the touch of God upon us; his heavy hand laid upon our conscience, and felt by all who are not numb with the paralytic twist of sin. Even the languid mind of self-indulgence, drowsy with too much sense, complacent with too much self, scarcely escapes the sacred warning. For though it is quite possible that such a one may have no compunctions in the retrospect which he takes from the observatory not of conscience but of comfort; though he may even have lapsed from all knowledge of remorse, so that God has ceased to "beset him *from behind*," — yet the future is not securely shut against contingencies; and a moment of alarm, a shock of death, a night of misery, may burst the guilty slumber, and wake the poor mortal, as on a morning breaking in tempest, with the flash of conviction, Behold! 'tis God! To most, I believe, there comes at least the casual misgiving that there is a destiny in reserve for them to which no justice of the heart has yet been done; and to each, there is the anticipated crumbling away of all his solid ground in death; which even to the sternest unbelief is a lapsing into the dark grasp of an annihilating God. So that the Almighty Spirit besets even these most lonely of his children "*from before.*" And as for minds that are awake and at all in quest of him, he haunts them every way. Oh that we could but know how false it is that "the good man is satisfied from himself"! When was there ever one of us who did not feel his recollections full of shame and grief, and find in the past the cup that overflowed with tears? When, one that did not look into the future with resolves made timid and anxious by the failures of experience, and distrust that breaks the high young courage of the heart, and prayers that in utterance half expect refusal? Which of us can stand this day at the solemn meeting-point of past and future, without abasement for the one, and trembling for the other?— without being beset by the Divine Spirit in penitent regrets from behind, and in passionate aspirations from before? And herein we should discover only this; that he has laid his hand upon us,—has resolved to claim us to the uttermost, and will haunt us with his rebukes, though they wither us with sorrow, till we surrender without terms.

It is not apparently the design of Heaven that we should be permitted to seek rest and to desire ease in this aspiring life; and it is the vain attempt to make compromise between duty and indulgence, that creates the corrosions of conscience, and the perpetual disquietudes of spirit, and disappoints our own ideal from day to day and from year to year. There is no way to the peace of God but by absolute self-abandonment to his will that whispers within us, without reservation of happiness or self. Then, the relinquishment once made,

— our whole nature given up to any high faith within the heart, — the sorrows of mortality, its reproaches, its fears, will soon vanish, and even death be robbed of its terrors; for, to quote the noble words of Lord Bacon, " He that dies in an earnest pursuit is like one that is wounded in hot blood, who for the time scarce feels the hurt ; and therefore a mind fixed and bent upon somewhat that is good, doth best avert the dolors of death."

III.

GREAT PRINCIPLES AND SMALL DUTIES.

—◆—

JOHN XIII. 14.

IF I THEN, YOUR LORD AND MASTER, HAVE WASHED YOUR FEET, YE OUGHT
ALSO TO WASH ONE ANOTHER'S FEET.

EVERY fiction that has ever laid strong hold on human belief
is the mistaken image of some great truth; to which reason
will direct its search, while half-reason is content with
laughing at the superstition, and unreason with believing it.
Thus, the doctrine of the Incarnation faithfully represents
the impression produced by the ministry and character of
Christ. It is the dark shadow thrown across the ages of
Christendom by his mortal life, as it inevitably sinks into
the distance. It is but the too literal description of the
real elements of his history; a mistake of the morally for
the physically divine; a reference to celestial descent of
that majesty of soul which, even in the eclipse of grief,
seemed too great for any meaner origin. Indeed, how
better could we speak of the life of Jesus than in the language of this doctrine, as the submission of a most heavenly
spirit to the severest burden of the flesh, — the voluntary
immersion within the shades of deep suffering of a godlike
mind, visibly radiant with light unknown to others, and
betraying its relation to eternity, while making the weary
pilgrimage of time? It was the peculiarity of his greatness
that it — stooped, I will not say, but — penetrated without
stooping, to the humblest wants; not simply stepped casu-
ally aside to look at the most ignominious sorrows, but went

directly to them, and lived wholly in them; scattered glorious miracles and sacred truths along the hidden by-paths
and in the mean recesses of existence; serving the mendicant and the widow, blessing the child, healing the leprosy
of body and of soul, and kneeling to wash even the traitor's
feet. In *himself* was the serene and unapproachable dignity
of a higher nature, a mind at one with the universe and its
Author; in his *acts*, a frugal respect for the most neglected
elements of human life, declaring that he came not to be
ministered unto but to minister. What wonder that, when
he had been ensphered in the immortal world, he appeared
to the affectionate memories of men as a divine being who
had disrobed himself of rightful glory to take pity on their
sorrows, and had put on for the gladness of praise the
garment of heaviness? The conception is at least in close
kindred with a noble truth, — *that a soul occupied with
great ideas best performs small duties;* that the divinest
views of life penetrate most clearly into the meanest emergencies; that so far from petty principles being best proportioned to petty trials, a heavenly spirit taking up its
abode with us can alone sustain well the daily toils, and
tranquilly pass the humiliations of our condition ; and that,
to keep the house of the soul in order due and pure, a god
must come down and dwell within, as servant of all its
work.

Even in intellectual culture this principle receives illustration; and it will be found that the ripest knowledge is
best qualified to instruct the most complete ignorance. It
is a common mistake to suppose that those who know little
suffice to inform those who know less: that the master who
is but a stage before the pupil can, as well as another, show
him the way ; nay, that there may even be an advantage
in this near approach between the minds of teacher and of
taught; since the recollection of recent difficulties, and the
vividness of fresh acquisition, give to the one a more living
interest in the progress of the other. Of all educational

errors, this is one of the gravest. The approximation required between the mind of teacher and of taught is not that of a common ignorance, but of mutual sympathy; not a partnership in narrowness of understanding, but that thorough insight of the one into the other, that orderly analysis of the tangled skein of thought, that patient and masterly skill in developing conception after conception, with a constant view to a remote result, which can only belong to comprehensive knowledge and prompt affections. With whatever accuracy the recently initiated may give out his new stores, he will rigidly follow the precise method by which he made them his own; and will want that variety and fertility of resource, that command of the several paths of access to a truth, which are given by a thorough survey of the whole field on which he stands. The instructor needs to have a full perception, not merely of the internal contents, but also of the external relations, of that which he unfolds; as the astronomer knows but little if, ignorant of the place and laws of moon and sun, he has examined only their mountains and their spots. The sense of proportion between the different parts and stages of a subject, the appreciation of every step at its true value, the foresight of the section that remains in its real magnitude and direction, are qualities so essential to the teacher, that without them all instruction is but an insult to the learner's understanding. And in virtue of these it is, that the most cultivated minds are usually the most patient, most clear, most rationally progressive; most studious of accuracy in details, because not impatiently shut up within them as absolutely limiting the view, but quietly contemplating them from without in their relation to the whole. Neglect and depreciation of intellectual minutiæ are characteristics of the ill-informed : and where the granular parts of study are thrown away or loosely held, there will be found no compact mass of knowledge solid and clear as crystal, but a sandy accumulation, bound together by no cohesion and transmitting no light. And above and beyond

all the advantages which a higher culture gives in the mere
system of communicating knowledge, must be placed that
indefinable and mysterious power which a superior mind
always puts forth upon an inferior; that living and life-
giving action, by which the mental forces are strengthened
and developed, and a spirit of intelligence is produced, far
transcending in excellence the acquisition of any special ideas.
In the task of instruction, so lightly assumed, so unworthily
esteemed, no amount of wisdom would be superfluous and
lost; and even the child's elementary teaching would be
best conducted, were it possible, by Omniscience itself.   The
more comprehensive the range of intellectual view, and the
more minute the perception of its parts, the greater will be
the simplicity of conception, the aptitude for exposition, and
the directness of access to the open and expectant mind.
This adaptation to the humblest wants is the peculiar triumph
of the highest spirit of knowledge.

In the same way it is observable that the trivial services
of social life are best performed, and the lesser particles
of domestic happiness are most skilfully organized, by the
deepest and the fairest heart.   It is an error to suppose that
homely minds are the best administrators of small duties.
Who does not know how wretched a contradiction such a
rule receives in the moral economy of many a home? — how
often the daily troubles, the swarm of blessed cares, the
innumerable minutiæ of arrangement in a family, prove quite
too much for the generalship of feeble minds, and even the
clever selfishness of strong ones? — how a petty and scrupulous
anxiety, in defending with infinite perseverance some small
and almost invisible point of frugality and comfort, sur-
renders the greater unobserved, and while saving money
ruins minds? — how, on the other hand, a rough and unmel-
lowed sagacity *rules* indeed and without defeat, but, while
maintaining in action the mechanism of government, creates
a constant and intolerable friction, a grating together of
reluctant wills, a groaning under the consciousness of force,

that make the movements of life fret and chafe incessantly? But where, in the presiding genius of a home, taste and sympathy unite (and in their genuine forms they cannot be separated), — the intelligent feeling for moral beauty and the deep heart of domestic love, — with what ease, what mastery, what graceful disposition, do the seeming triviali- ties of existence fall into order, and drop a blessing as they take their place! how do the hours steal away, unnoticed but by the precious fruits they leave! and by the self-re- nunciations of affection, there comes a spontaneous adjust- ment of various wills; and not an innocent pleasure is lost, nor a pure taste offended, nor a peculiar temper unconsid- ered; and every day has its silent achievements of wisdom, and every night its retrospect of piety and love; and the tranquil thoughts that, in the evening meditation, come down with the starlight, seem like the serenade of angels, bringing in melody the peace of God! Wherever this picture is realized, it is not by microscopic solicitude of spirit, but by comprehension of mind and enlargement of heart; by that breadth and nicety of moral view which discerns every thing in due proportion, and, in avoiding an intense elaboration of trifles, has energy to spare for what is great; in short, by a perception akin to that of God, whose providing frugality is on an infinite scale, vigilant alike in heaven and on earth; whose art colors a universe with beauty, and touches with its pencil the petals of a flower. A soul thus pure and large disowns the paltry rules of dignity, the silly notions of great and mean, by which fashion distorts God's real proportions; is utterly delivered from the spirit of contempt; and, in consulting for the benign administration of life, will learn many a task, and discharge many an office, from which lesser beings, esteeming them- selves greater, would shrink as ignoble. But, in truth, nothing is degrading which a high and graceful purpose ennobles; and offices the most menial cease to be menial, the moment they are wrought in love. What thousand

services are rendered, ay and by delicate hands, around
the bed of sickness, which, else considered mean, become
at once holy and quite inalienable rights! To smooth the
pillow, to proffer the draught, to soothe or to obey the
fancies of the delirious will, to sit for hours as a mere senti-
nel of the feverish sleep, — these things are suddenly erected,
by their relation to hope and life, into sacred privileges.
And experience is perpetually bringing occasions, similar in
kind though of less persuasive poignancy, when a true eye
and a lovely heart will quickly see the relations of things
thrown into a new position, and calling for a sacrifice of
conventional order to the higher laws of the affections ; and,
alike without condescension and without ostentation, will
noiselessly take the post of gentle service and do the kindly
deed. Thus is it that the lesser graces display themselves
most richly, like the leaves and flowers of life, where there
is the deepest and the widest root of love; not like the
staring and artificial blossoms of dry custom that, winter or
summer, cannot change ; but living petals woven in Nature's
workshop and folded by her tender skill, opening and shutting morning and night, glancing and trembling in the sunshine and the breeze. This easy capacity of great affections
for small duties is the peculiar triumph of the highest spirit
of love.

The same application of the loftiest principles to the most
minute details is still more perceptible when we rise a step
higher, and, from the operations of knowledge and of love,
turn to notice the agency of high religious faith. In the
management and conquest of the daily disappointments and
small vexations which befall every life, — the life of the idle
and luxurious no less than of the busy and struggling, —
only a devout mind attains to any real success, and evinces
a triumphant power. Who has not observed how wonderfully the mere insect-cares, that are ever on the wing in the
noon-day heat of life, have power to sting and to annoy even
the giant minds around which they sport, and to provoke

them into the most unseemly war? The finest sense, the profoundest knowledge, the most unquestionable taste, often prove an unequal match for insignificant irritations; and a man whose philosophy subdues nature, and whose force of thought and purpose gives him ascendency over men, may keep, in his own temper, an unvanquished enemy at home. Nor is this found only in cases of great self-ignorance, or impaired vigor in the moral sense. Even where the evil is self-confessed and felt as a perpetual shame, where the conscience sets up against it an honest and firm resistance, it is quite possible that very little progress may be made, and very little quietness attained. This is one of the many forms of duty in which mere moral conviction, however clear and strong, will continually fail. You may be per-suaded that it is wrong to be provoked; you may repeat to yourself that it is useless; you may command your lips to silence, and breathe no angry word : and yet withal the per-turbation is not gone, but only dumb; the conquest is not made, but the defeat concealed. There is nothing in the efforts of volition that has power to change the point of mental view; these self-strivings do not lift you out of the level of your trial; you remain imprisoned in the midst of it, wrestle with its miseries as you may ; wanting the uplift-ing faith, by which you escape from it, and look down upon it. It may be very absurd, nay very immoral, to be teased by trifles; but alas! while you remain in the dust, reason as you may, it *will* annoy you ; and there is no help for it, but to retire into a higher and grassier region, where the sultry road is visible from afar. We must go in contempla-tion *out of life*, ere we can see how its troubles subside and are lost, like evanescent waves, in the deeps of eternity and the immensity of God. A mind that can make this migra-tion from the scene by which it is surrounded, is removed from all vain strife of will, and gains its tranquillity without an effort; feels no difficulty in being gentle and serene, but rather wonders that it could ever be tempted from its pure

repose. How welcome would it often be to many a child
of anxiety and toil, to be suddenly transferred from the heat
and din of the city, the restlessness and worry of the mart,
to the midnight garden or the mountain top! And like
refreshment does a high faith, with its infinite prospects ever
open to the heart, afford to the worn and weary: no laborious travels are needed for the devout mind; for it carries
within it Alpine heights and starlit skies, which it may
reach with a moment's thought, and feel at once the loneliness of nature, and the magnificence of God.

Nor is it only in the government of ourselves that high
faith is found the most efficient aid for the less dignified
duties. In the services which benevolence must render to
others, the same truth is exemplified; and the humblest and
homeliest form of benevolence — attention to the grievances
and sufferings of the body — receives its most powerful
motive from the sublimest of all truths, the doctrine of
human immortality. A different result might perhaps have
been anticipated. It might have been thought that for the
truest sympathy with the pains of disease and the privations of infirmity, we must look to the disciples of materialism and annihilation; that they who take the body to be
our all, would most vehemently deplore its fragility, and
most affectionately tend its decline; that no love would be
so faithful as that which believed, at the death-bed of a
friend, that the real last look, the absolute farewell, was
drawing nigh. On the theory of extinction, oh, with what
close embrace would it seem natural to cling to each sinking life, — like kindred in shipwreck that cannot part! The
vivid expectation of futurity, which has so often led the
believer to ascetic contempt for his own physical wants,
would appear only consistent, if it passed by in equal scorn
the bodily miseries of others. But it has not been so. In
this, as in all the other instances, it appears that the sublimest instruments of the mind are the best fitted to the most
homely offices of duty; and that truths the most divine are

the gentlest servitors of wants the most humiliating. In the eye of one who looks on his fellow-man as a compound being, the immortal element imparts, not meanness, but a species of sanctity, to the mortal; just as the worshipper feels that of the temple whose space has been set apart for God the very stones are sacred, and the pavement claims a venerating tread. It is this constant penetration to the mind within, this recognition of something that is not seen, that overcomes the physical repulsiveness of corporeal want and pain, and gives a tranquil patience to the Christian who watches the ravages of disease and the approach of death. Nay, when he sees the soul, which is the heir of heaven, prostrated and tortured by a wretched frame, he thinks it almost an indignity that so kingly a habitant should pine in so poor a cell, and a native of the light itself cry thus aloud in dark captivity; and with touched and generous heart he flies to the sufferer, with such help and succor as he may.

Let us, then, cherish and revere the great sentiments which we assemble here to pour forth in worship, not as the occasional solace or the weekly dignities of our existence; but as truths that naturally penetrate to the very heart of life's activity, and best administer even the small frugalities of conscience. Nothing less than the majesty of God and the powers of the world to come can maintain the peace and sanctity of our homes, the order and serenity of our minds, the spirit of patience and tender mercy in our hearts. Then only shall we wisely economize moments when we anticipate for ourselves an eternity and lose no grain of wisdom, when we discern the glorious and immortal structure which its successive accumulations shall raise. Then will even the merest drudgery of duty cease to humble us, when we transfigure it by the glory of our own spirit. Seek ye then the things that are above, where your life is hid with Christ in God.

IV.

EDEN AND GETHSEMANE.

---◆---

1 Cor. xv. 46.

AND SO IT IS WRITTEN, THE FIRST MAN ADAM WAS MADE A LIVING SOUL, THE LAST ADAM WAS MADE A QUICKENING SPIRIT. HOWBEIT THAT WAS NOT FIRST WHICH IS SPIRITUAL, BUT THAT WHICH IS NATURAL; AND AFTERWARD THAT WHICH IS SPIRITUAL.

GREAT and sacred was the day of Adam's birth; if for no other reason yet for this, — that he was the first man and had a living soul. The impressions received by the original human being, dropped silently at dawn from infinite night upon this green earth, can never have been repeated. With maturity of powers, yet without a memory or a hope; with full-eyed perception, yet without interpreting experience; with all things new, yet without surprise, since also there was nothing old; he was thrown upon those primitive instincts by which God teaches the untaught: left to wander over his abode and note the ever-living attitudes of Nature, and from her bewildering mixture of the original with the repeated, from rest and weariness, from the confusion of waking and of dreams (both real alike to him), from the glow of noon and the fall of darkness and the night, from the summer shower and the winter snow, to disentangle some order at length, and recognize the elementary laws of the spot whereon he dwelt.

Fast as five senses and a receiving mind would permit, did he find *where* he was, and *when* he came, and by *what sort of scene* he was environed; how the fair show of creation came round, each part in its own section of space and time, persuading him to notice and obey. And when he is thus the pupil of the external world, he is in training to become its lord; by the discipline of submission learning the faculty of rule. Beneath the steady eye of human observation, nature becomes fascinated, and consents to be the menial and the drudge of man, doing the bidding of his wants and will, and apprenticing her illimitable power to his prescribing skill. And so was it given to the father of our race, for himself and for his children, to subdue the earth, to put forth the invisible force of his mind in conquest of its palpable energies, to give the savage elements their first lesson as the domestic slaves of human life, and make some rude advance towards that docility with which now they till and spin and weave and carry burdens, with the fleetness of the winds and the precision of the hours. To a living and understanding soul, what *was* the unexhausted world but in itself a Paradise? And was there aught else for its earliest inhabitant but to discover what fruits he might open his bosom to receive from the universe around? Worthily does the Bible open with the story of Eden,—the fresh dawn, the untrodden garden of our life. Truly, too, whatever geologists may find and say, is that day identified with the general act of creation; for in no intelligible human sense was there any universe, till there was a soul filled with the idea thereof. The system of things of which Moses proposed to himself to write the origin, was not a saurian's or a mammoth's world, not such a creation as was pictured in the perceptions of huge reptiles and extinct fishes; but such a universe as the spirit of a man discerns within and so spreads without him; and of this it is certain, that the instant of *his* birth was the date of *its* creation. For had he been different, it would not have been the same; had he been opposite, it would have been reversed; and had he not been at all, it would not have appeared. Whatever is solemn in the apparition of the fair and infinite universe, belongs to the day of Adam's birth.

Greater, however, and more sacred, was the day of
Christ's birth ; of that "second man," as Paul says with
glorious meaning, of that "last Adam," who was "a quickening spirit," and the first parent of a new race of souls.
He, too, was placed by the hand of God upon a fresh world,
and commissioned to explore its silent and trackless ways ;
to watch and rest in its darkness, and use and bless its
light ; to learn by instincts divine and true of its blossoms
and its fruits, its fountains and its floods.   But it was the
world within, the untrodden forests of the soul where the
consciousness of God hides itself in such dim light, and
whispers with such mystic sound, as befit a region so boundless and primeval, — it was this on which Jesus dwelt as the
first inspired interpreter.   To him it was given, not to cast
his eye around human life and observe by what scene it was
encompassed, but to retire *into* it, and reveal what it *con-
tained;* not to disclose how man is materially placed, but
what he spiritually is ; to comprehend and direct, not his
natural advantages of skill and physical power, but his
grief, his hope, his strife, his love, his sin, his worship.   He
was to find, not what 'comfort man may open his bosom to
receive, but what blessing he may open his heart to give;
nay, what transforming light may go forth from the conscience and the faith within, to make the common earth
divine, and exhibit around it the mountain heights of God's
protection : to show us the Father, not as the great mechanic of the universe, whose arrangements we obey that
we may use them, but as the Holy Spirit that moves us with
the sigh of infinite desires, and the prayer of ever-conscious
guilt, and the meek hope — that stays by us so long as we
are absolutely true — of help and pity from the Holiest.
And if the affections are as the colored window, — near and
small and of the earth, or far and vast and of the sky, —
through which we receive the images of all things, and find
them change with the glass of our perceptions, how justly
does the Apostle Paul deem the work of Christ "a new

creation "! If he that makes an eye, calls up the mighty
phantasm of the heavens and the earth; he that forms a
soul within us remodels our universe and reveals our God.
Eden, then, is less sacred than the streets of Bethlehem
and the fields of Nazareth ; though, as befits the cradle of
the natural man who needs such things, its atmosphere
might be purer and its slopes more verdant. Indeed in all
their adjuncts do we see the character of the two events,
and how " afterwards " alone came " that which was spiritual." When the first man heard the voice and step of the
Most High, it was outwardly among the trees, — as was
natural to one born of the mere physical and constructing
energy of God, without a mother and without a home:
when Jesus discerned the divine accents, the whispers of
the Father were *within* him, the solemn articulation of the
spirit infinitely affectionate and wise; — a distinction altogether suitable to one born of that mother who hid many
things in her heart, — granted to us by that gentlest form
of the divine love, whence alone great and noble natures
are ever nurtured. When Adam entered life, the *earth* was
glad and jubilant ; when Christ was born, the joy was testified by angels, and the anthem sounded from the *sky*.
The "first man " subdued the physical world ; the " last
man " won the immortal heaven.

Fellow-men and fellow-Christians, there is an Adam and
a Christ within us all ; a natural and a spiritual man,
whereof the father of our race and the author of our faith
are the respective emblems, both in the order of their succession and the nature of their mission. We are endowed
with powers of sense, of understanding, of action, by which
we communicate with the scene of our present existence,
and win triumphs over external and finite nature ; by which
we appropriate and multiply the fruits of Providence permitted to our happiness. And we are conscious, however
faintly, of aspirations and affections, of a faith and wonder,
of a hope and sadness, which bear us beyond the margin of

the earthly and finite, and afford some glimpse of the infinitude in which we live. By the one we go forth and discover our knowledge; by the other return within and learn
our ignorance: by the one we conquer nature, by the other
we serve God : by the one we shut ourselves up in life, by
the other we look with full gaze through death : by the one
we acquire happiness and sagacity and skill; by the other
wisdom and sanctity and truth : by the one we look on our
position and all that surrounds it with the eye of economy;
by the other with the eye of love. Our first and superficial aim is to be, like Adam, *lord below :* our last to be, like
Christ, *associate above.* In short, the individual mind is
conducted through a history like the sacred record of the
general race, and, if it be just to its capacities, passes
through a period of new creation ; and every noble life,
like the Bible (which is " the book of life "), begins with
Paradise and ends with heaven.

Ere Jesus became the Christ, he was led into the desert
to be tempted. And before the Messiah within us — the
messenger-spirit of God in the soul — can make his inspiration felt, and render his voice articulate and clear, we too
must have been called to severe and lonely struggles with
the power of sin. On no lighter terms can the natural man
pass into the spiritual, and Deity shape forth a dwelling
within the deeps of our humanity. In childhood, we live
in God's creation, as in the unanxious shelter of some Eden ;
the innocent in a garden of fruits, where the tillage demands
no toil, and, with smallest restraint, we have little else but
to gather and enjoy: and the utmost duty is to abstain,
rather than to do; to keep the lips from forbidden fruits,
not to spend the labor and sorrow of the brow or of the
soul, in order to raise and multiply the bread of nature or
of life. And many, alas! there are, who make their life
this sort of holiday thing unto the end, and retain its child-
ishness, only, from the nature of the case, losing all its
innocence ; strolling through it as a mere fruit-gathering

place, a garden of indulgence, a Paradise sacred no more because empty now of God, and unvisited by the murmurs of his voice. There comes a time to us all, when the sense of responsibility starts up and rebukes our anxiety for ease; tells us that we are living, fast and once for all, a life that enlarges to the scale of eternity, and is embosomed everywhere in God; bids us spring from our collapse of selfishness and sleep, take up the full dimensions of our strength, and go forth to do much, if it be possible, and at least to do worthily and well. And full often is the conflict terrible between the indolence of custom, the passiveness of self-will, and this inspiring impulse of the divine deliverer within us. Many a secret passage of our existence does it make bleak as the wilderness, and lonely as the Dead-Sea shore; in many an hour of meditation, seemingly the stillest, does it inwardly tear us, as in the mid-strife of heaven and hell, and leave us wasted as with fasting nigh to death: but oh! if we are only true to the spirit that declares " we shall not live by bread alone; " if we quietly descend from the pinnacle of our pride (though sin may pretend to make it sacred and call it a turret of the temple); if we keep close to the meek appointed ways of Him whom our presumption must not try: if we bend no knee to the majesty of splendid wrong, but, in single allegiance to the Holiest, drive away the most glorious spirit of guilt that honors our strength with his assault, — do we not find at length that angels come and minister unto us; that the waste appears to vanish suddenly away, and the desert to blossom as the rose; that we are restored as to a garden, not of the earth, but of the Lord, filled with the whispers of divinest peace? And so our energy is born from the moments of weakness and of fear; and, were there no hell to tempt us, there were no heaven to bless. From the crisis of trembling and of doubt, we issue forth to take up our mission gladly, with the unspeakable shelter of God without us, and the hidden life of his love within us.

Again : he who gave us the Gospel was "the Man of Sorrows;" and the glad tidings of great joy were pronounced by a voice mellowed by many a sadness. And not otherwise is it with the messenger-spirit of our private hearts ; which does not become the Christ, the consecrated revealer of what is holy, unless it be much acquainted with grief. Heaven and God are best discerned through tears ; scarcely perhaps discerned at all without them. I do not mean that a man must be outwardly afflicted, and lose his comforts or his friends, before he can become devout. Many a Christian maintains the truest heart of piety without such dispensations ; and more, alas! remain as hard and cold as ever in spite of them. That there is felt to be a general tendency, however, in the blow of calamity and the sense of loss, to awaken the latent thought of God and persuade us to seek his refuge, the current language of devotion in every age, the constant association of prayer with the hour of bereavement and the scenes of death, suffice to show. Yet is this effect of external distress only a particular instance of a general truth, viz., that religion springs up in the mind *whenever any of the infinite affections and desires press severely against the finite conditions of our existence.* In ill-disciplined and contracted souls, this sorrowful condition is never fulfilled, except when some much-loved blessing is forcibly snatched away, and their human attachment (which is infinite) is surprised (though knowing it well before) at the violence of death, knocks with vain cries at the cruel barriers of our humanity, and is answered by the voice of mystery from beyond. But such was not the sorrow with which Christ was stricken ; nor is such the only sorrow with which good and faithful minds are affected. There are many immeasurable affections of our nature, besides that which makes our kindred dear : the yearning for truth, the delight in beauty, the veneration for excellence, the high ambition of conscience ever pressing forward yet unable to attain, — these also live within us, and strive

unceasingly in noble hearts; and there is an inner and
viewless sorrow, a spontaneous weeping of these infinite
desires, whence the highest order of faith and devotion will
be found to spring; so much so, that no one can even think
of Christ, visibly social and cheerful as he was, without the
belief of a secret sadness, that might be overheard in his
solitary prayers. Those who make the end of existence to
consist of happiness may try to conceal so perplexing a
fact, and may draw pictures of the exceeding pleasantness
of religion: but human nature, trained in the school of
Christianity, throws away as false the delineation of piety
in the disguise of Hebe, and declares that there is something
higher far than happiness; that thought, which is ever full
of care and trouble, is better far; that all true and disinterested affection, which often is called to mourn, is better
still; that the devoted allegiance of conscience to duty and
to God — which ever has in it more of penitence than of
joy — is noblest of all. If happiness means the satisfaction
of desire (and I can conceive no other definition), then
there is necessarily something greater, viz., religion, which
implies constant yearning and aspiration, and therefore non-
satisfaction of desire. In truth, that which is deemed the
happiest period of life must pass away, before we can sink
into the deep secrets of faith and hope. The primitive
gladness of childhood is that of a bounded and limited
existence, which earnestly wishes for nothing that exceeds
the dimensions of possibility, — of a human Paradise, about
whose enclosure-line no inquiry is made; and through sorrow and the sense of sin we must issue from those peaceful
gates, and make pilgrimage amid the thistle and the thorn
instead of the blossom and the rose, and lie panting on the
dust, instead of sleeping on the green sward, of life, before
we learn through mortal weakness our immortal strength,
and feel in the exile of the earth the shelter of the skies.
Then, however, the spirit of Christ, the man of sorrows,
gives us a re-birth of joy through tears. Before, we were

simply unheeding of death; then, we enter into the consciousness of immortality. Before, our will was restrained
by a law which we could not keep; then, it is emancipated
by a fresh love that more than keeps it; whose free inclination goes before all precept and authoritative faith; and
hopeth all things, believeth all things, endureth all things;
nay, even can *do* all things, through the Christ that strength-
eneth it.

Children then of nature, we are also sons of God; born
of the genial earth, we are to climb the glorious heaven;
and to the human lot that makes us of one blood with
Adam, is added the divine liberty of being of one spirit
with Christ. That liberty we cannot decline, for we are
conscious of it now; and if we look not on it as on the face
of an angel, it will haunt us with its gaze like the eye of a
fiend. The severe prerogatives of an existence half-divine
are ours. To wear away life in unproductive harmlessness
is innocent no more : with the glory we take the cross; and,
instead of slumbering at noon in Eden, must keep the midnight watch within Gethsemane. We, too, like our great
leader, must be made perfect through suffering; but the
struggle by night will bring the calmness of the morning; the
hour of exceeding sorrow will prepare the day of godlike
strength ; the prayer for deliverance calls down the power
of endurance. And while to the reluctant their cross is too
heavy to be borne, it grows light to the heart of willing
trust. The faithful heirs of " the man of sorrows," transcending the trials they cannot decline, may quit the world
with the cry, " It is finished," and pass through the silence
of death to the peace of God.

V.

SORROW NO SIN.

Luke xxiii. 28.

BUT JESUS, TURNING UNTO THEM, SAID, DAUGHTERS OF JERUSALEM, WEEP NOT FOR ME, BUT WEEP FOR YOURSELVES AND FOR YOUR CHILDREN.

CHRIST then could invite to tears, — to tears over departing excellence, — to tears which men idly call selfish, — tears "for themselves and for their children." He whose mission it was to teach the paternity of Providence, and the serenity of the immortal hope; he who himself lived in the divinest peace which they can give, thought it no treason to these truths to weep. To the eye of the Man of Sorrows, sorrow was no sin : nor did he, who was emphatically the Son of God, see, in even the passionate utterance of grief, any of that spirit of filial distrust towards God and reluctant acceptance of his will, which have often been charged on it by the hard and cold temper of his followers. Religious professors have put their own congenial interpretation on the morality of Christ; and being themselves — but too frequently — unfeeling and unsocial mystics, they have multiplied the penances of natural emotion, and sublimed from the gospel its pure humanities. If we accept their representations, our religion aims to cancel our natural affections, and substitute others at variance with them ; the impulses of gladness and grief are alike to be condemned, as a rebel love of perishable things; the most agitating passages of our being, which convulse us to the centre, are to be met with a rigid and tearless piety; the future, though invisible and intangible, though approachable only by kin-

dled imagination, is to be acknowledged as the only region
of the fair and good, and to supersede all other claims upon
our desire and regard. The present, though the intensest
point of existence, is to be comparatively unfelt; and the
past, whereof the retrospect is sweet and solemn to the
travelled pilgrim, — the history of childhood and its unfor-
gotten friendships, of youth and its unchecked aspirations,
of maturity with its worn yet deeper love, its more crushing
yet worthier anxieties, its purer but more melancholy wisdom, — all this because it is human and not divine, of earth
and not of heaven, is to be refused the tribute of a sigh.
For my own part, regarding our human nature as the image
of its Divine Parent, and in nothing more truly that image
than in the impulses of its disinterested love, I bend in reverence before the emotions of every melted heart; believing
this present life to be the worthy childhood of futurity,
conceiving its interests, its happiness, to be substantially the
same, but framed upon a smaller scale and clouded with a
deeper shade, I see in its history nothing trivial, in its
events nothing contemptible, in its vicissitudes nothing
unworthy of a wise man's profoundest thought. And taking the gospel to afford a promise, not of the extinction of
human nature in heaven, but of its perpetuity, — an assurance not that we shall be converted into chill and pious
phantoms, but simply elevated into immortal men, — I
would gather from that hope a deeper veneration for all the
pure tastes and natural feelings of a good mind; I would
maintain the sanctity of human joy and human grief; I
would protest against all stern censure on the outbreaks of
true sorrow; and would plead that to mourn — ay, and
with broken spirit — the departure of virtue and of love,
is — not a resistance to a Father's will, not an oblivion of
his providence, not the expression of an ignoble selfishness,
not a mistrust of a restoring heaven; but only a fitting
homage to God's most benignant gifts, the grateful glance of
a loving eye on blessings, than which nothing more holy,

more peaceful, more exalting, is conferred by a guardian benevolence on man.

Those who blame as unchristian the deep grief which bereavement awakens, must extend their disapprobation much farther, and censure all strong human attachments. Sorrow is not an independent state of mind, standing unconnected with all others. It could not be cancelled singly, leaving all other qualities of our nature in their integrity. It is the effect, and under the present conditions of our being the inevitable effect, of strong affections. Nay, it is not so much their result as a certain attitude of those affections themselves. It not simply *flows from* the love of excellence, of wisdom, of sympathy, but it *is* that very love, when conscious that excellence, that wisdom, that sympathy have departed. The more intense the delight in their presence, the more poignant must be the impression of their absence ; and you cannot destroy the anguish unless you forbid the joy. Grief is only the *memory* of widowed affection ; and nothing but a draft of utter oblivion could lap it in insensibility. When the ties of strong and refined attachment have long bound us to a home ; when the sympathies of those who share with us that home have become as the needful light to our daily toil and the guardian spirits of our nightly rest; when years have passed on, and brought us many a sickness banished by their fidelity, many a danger averted by their counsels, many an anxiety rendered tolerable by their participation ; when often they too have gazed on us from the bed of pain, and threatened to depart, but we have been permitted to rescue them from the grave, and therein have doubled all our tenderness ; when, from this close inspection of pure hearts, we have learned to think nobly of human nature and hopefully of the providence of God; when their voices, common enough to other ears, but fraught to us with unnumbered memories of life, have become the natural music of the earth, — can this melody be silent, can these virtues depart, can these remembrances be deprived of their living centre, without leaving us trembling and desolate? Can all these fibres of our life be thus wrenched, and not bleed at every pore? And to forget, — it cannot be. We daily pass through places which are the shrine of a thousand recollections; we are startled by tones which pour on us a flood of conviction; we open a book, and there is the very name; we write a date, and it is an anniversary. These associations with the past I do not say *excite* sorrow, but to an affectionate mind *are* sorrow. The morality, then, which rebukes sorrow rebukes love. It is useless expatiating on the evils which strong grief inflicts on ourselves and others: you are bound to show that the affections, of which it is an inseparable form, contain no counteracting good; that it is more blessed, more holy, to freeze up the springs of emotion, than to suffer them perennially to fertilize our nature, though they sometimes deluge it; that it is better to keep loose from all that is human, and love nothing that we may lose. You cannot sever them: grief and love must stay or go together. And who can doubt that *that* is the truest duty to God, which permits to us the most disinterested heart for each other; *that* the purest devotion which sanctifies and not chills our affections; *that* the most genuine trust, which dares to cultivate to the utmost sympathies wounded here and serenely blest only hereafter; *that* the most filial hope, which, regarding the brotherhood of man as an inference from the paternity of God, looks to heaven as to another home?

There are doubtless cases not infrequent, in which the mind is unduly overpowered by affliction; in which the tranquillity of the reason is wholly overset, and the energy of the will utterly prostrated. Here, beyond controversy, is a state of mind morally wrong; for God never absolves us from our duties, however he may sadden them. But to rebuke the feelings of grief in such a case is to cast the censure in the wrong place: it is not that the sorrow is excessive, but that other emotions are defective in their strength. Nor is the distinction merely verbal and trivial. For the natural effect of such misplaced blame surely is, that the sufferer will endeavor simply to abate the intensity of his sorrow, to extrude from his mind the emotions which are charged with guilty excess: his aim will be purely negative, *not* to think so fixedly, *not* to feel so profoundly, respecting the bereavement which has fallen upon his life. And this aim is directed to an end both undesirable and impracticable. It is undesirable; for to touch the working of the affections with partial torpor, to benumb the tenderness without adding to the energy of the mind, to deaden the susceptibility of memory without quickening the vividness of hope, would surely be no improvement to the character; it would be a mere deduction from the amount of mind : and sorrow is at least better than dulness of soul. It is, moreover, impracticable; for our nature affords us no means of exerting a negative and destructive action upon our own characters. One class of feelings can be extinguished only by the creation of another; one sentiment banished only by inviting the antagonism of another; one interest supplanted only by the stronger occupancy of another. So long as this is unperceived, the over-grieving heart will seek in vain to discipline itself. Thinking of its sorrow as too much, instead of its sense of duty as too little, it fails to meet pointedly its own remedy. The will feebly casts about its efforts in the dark regions of the mind; wastes its vigor in trying to forget : sometimes fancies forgetfulness, then pretends it ; assumes a hollow tranquillity, and affects to itself and others an interest in topics and in duties which are not truly loved, for they have never been truly and distinctly sought. From all such aimless directions of the will there arises a far greater evil than simple failure : an unconscious insincerity grows up, a hazy perception of our real mental condition, a confusion of actual and fictitious feelings, of emotions which we merely

imagine with those which we truly experience, than which
few states of character can be more perilous to moral power
and progress. The wise interpreter of his own nature
will let his mourning affections alone. To interfere with
them would be wrestling with his own strength. But he
will draw forth, into prominent light, sentiments now
sleeping idly in the shaded recesses of his mind. He will
summon up the sense of responsibility, to rouse him with
the spectacle of his relations to God his father, and his
brother, man; to recount to him the deeds of .duty and the
toils of thought, which are yet to be achieved ere life is
done; to show him the circle of high faculties which the
Creator has given him to ennoble and refine and keep
ready for a world where thought and virtue are immor-
talized.   He will call forth his affections for the living
who surround him, and whom yet it is his happiness to
love, and his obligation to bless. And these sympathies
will be fruitful in work for his hands, and interests refreshing to his heart. To preserve in his home the graceful order of pure and peaceful affections; to omit in the
world no delicate attention of friendship; to forget not
the claims of poverty and ignorance and sin to the compassion of all who would be faithful to their kind, — here
are invitations enough to the aspirings of benevolence, to
bid the drooping soul look up. And the sufferer will
evoke the spirit of Christian trust and hope. For, as the
memory of bereaved affection is grief, so is its hope the
restorer of peace: from the past is forced on us the sense of
loss; from the future rises the expectation of recovery: in
traversing the past, our thoughts glide along a procession
of dear events arrested by a tomb; in conceiving of the
future, they behold the same events opening into renewed
being, and spreading themselves in all blessed varieties
along the vistas of interminable life: the sadnesses of each
successive point of remembrance are reversed, its losses
regathered; its tears, as it were, unwept before the smile

of God ; its plaints unsung amid the harmonies of heaven ; its sins untwined by the wounding yet healing hand of an angel penitence. Invoke the spirit of this trust ; and, though sorrow may not dry its tears, it rises to a dignity above despair.

It is not unusual to speak of sorrow for the dead as expressing a distrust of the providence of God, and a doubt of an eternal hereafter. In this, however, there is but little truth. True it is, wherever the reason actually dis-believes the great facts of a divine government and hu-man immortality, bereavement must indeed fall upon the heart with terrific weight. It is then a blow of tyrannic fate, a visible stroke of annihilation, a triumph of pure and final evil: and were it not that the mind of hopeless un-belief usually permits the susceptibility of its affections to grow dull, and seeks protection from the gloom of its thoughts by a spontaneous incasement of insensibility, its impressions from death would be appalling. But, though unbelief may be a natural cause of uncontrolled sorrow, it by no means follows that such sorrow implies unbelief. It is easy to say that if we acknowledged God to be good in all his dispensations, and trusted in some blessed spirit secreted in the present loss, we could not deeply mourn. I ask, is it reasonable to expect this abstract conviction to overpower a visible privation ? Assuage and sanctify the grief it unquestionably will ; but to heal entirely is beyond its power. The vacancy in home and heart is a thing felt ; its issue in good is a thing believed in and imag-ined ; that the blessings of the past are gone is a reality in the present ; that they will be restored is as yet but a vision in the future. The degree in which faith imparts consolation will somewhat depend on the natural vigor of the imaginative faculty : affliction is a pressure of actual experience ; faith is a series of mental creations ; its real-ities are invisible and intangible ; a mind bound down by the chain of experience, a mind whose memory is more

faithful than its conceptions are excursive, will catch but
faint and distant glimpses of the blessed idealities of hope.
And without one moment's murmuring against the benignity
of God, or doubt respecting his promised future, such a
mind may be ill able to reach the ever-flowing fountain of
his peace.

Nor is it less unjust to prefer against sorrow for the dead
the charge of *selfishness*. Selfish! What, that pure affection bowed and broken to the earth! yearning only to discharge again, were it possible, but the humblest service of
love! What would it not do, what sacrifice of self would it
not make, what toils, what watching, would it not hold
light, might it be permitted to perform one office for the
departed! unseen, unfelt, unheard, without the hope of a
requiting smile, to shed on that spirit one silent blessing!
Surely this insult to human grief must be the invention of
cold hearts, needing a justification for their own insensibility. True it is, there is no need to mourn for those who
are removed. True it is, we weep not for them, but for
ourselves and for our children. It is we only that suffer
and are sad. But emotions are not selfish, simply because
they are experienced *by* ourselves; were it so, every joy
and sorrow would be branded by that odious name. They
are selfish only when they are full of the idea of self, when
self is their object as well as their subject; when they tempt
us to prefer our own personal and exclusive happiness to
that of others, and to trample on a brother's feelings in the
chase after our own good. Of this there is nothing in the
tears of bereavement: they are the tribute, not of our self-
regarding but of our sympathetic nature. At last, indeed,
when the burst of grief has had its natural way, they lead
us to a generous joy. For, as we weep, we think how
blessed are the departed who " rest from their labors, while
their works do follow them:" their pure hearts jarred no
more by the harshnesses of this oft discordant life ; their
earnest minds drinking at the perennial fount of truth ;

their frailties cast away with the coil of mortality they have left behind ; their sainted love waiting to receive us, as we too may one by one pass the dark limits which sever us from their embrace, and seek with them the peace and progress of the skies.

VI.

CHRISTIAN PEACE.

JOHN XIV. 27.

PEACE I LEAVE WITH YOU: MY PEACE I GIVE UNTO YOU: NOT AS THE
WORLD GIVETH, GIVE I UNTO YOU.

THIS was a strange benediction to proceed from the Man of
Sorrows, at the dreariest moment of his life, — strange at
least to those who look only to his outward career, his
incessant contact with misery and sin, his absolute solitude
of purpose, his lot stricken with sadness ever new from the
temptation to the cross; but not strange perhaps to those
who heard the deep and quiet tones in which this oracle of
promise went forth, — the divinest music from the centre
of the darkest fate. He was on the bosom of the beloved
disciple, and in the midst of those who should have cheered
him in that hour with such comforts as fidelity can always
offer; but who, failing in their duty to his griefs, found the
sadness creep upon themselves; while he, seeking to give
peace to them, found it himself profusely in the gift. It was
not till he had finished this interview and effort of affection,
and from the warmth of that evening meal and the flush of
its deep converse they had issued into the chill and silent
midnight air; not till the sanctity of moonlight (never to
be seen by him again) had invested him, and coarse fatigue
had sunk his disciples into sleep upon the grass, that, having
none to comfort, he found the anguish fall upon himself.
Deprived of the embrace of John, he flew to the bosom of
the Father; and, after momentary strife, recovered in trust
the serenity he had found in toil: and while his followers

lie stretched in earthly slumber, he reaches a divine repose; while they, yielding to nature, gain neither strength nor courage for the morrow, he, through the vigils of agony, rises to that godlike power, on which mockery and insult beat in vain, and which has made the cross, — then the emblem of abjectness and guilt, — the everlasting symbol of whatever is holy and sublime.

The peace of Christ then was the fruit of combined *toil* and *trust;* in the one case diffusing itself from the centre of his active life, in the other from that of his passive emotions; enabling him in the one case to *do things* tranquilly, in the other to *see things* tranquilly. Two things only can make life go wrong and painfully with us; when we suffer or suspect misdirection and feebleness in the energies of love and duty within us, or in the providence of the world without us: bringing, in the one case, the lassitude of an unsatisfied and discordant nature; in the other, the melancholy of hopeless views. From these Christ delivers us by a summons to mingled toil and trust. And herein does his peace differ from that which " the world giveth," — that its prime essential is not ease, but strife; not self-indulgence, but self-sacrifice; not acquiescence in evil for the sake of quiet, but conflict with it for the sake of God; not, in short, a prudent accommodation of the mind to the world, but a resolute subjugation of the world to the best conceptions of the mind. Amply has the promise to leave behind him such a peace been since fulfilled. It was fulfilled to the apostles who first received it; and has been realized again by a succession of faithful men to whom they have delivered it.

The word " peace" denotes the absence of jar and conflict; a condition free from the restlessness of fruitless desire, the forebodings of anxiety, the stings of enmity. It may be destroyed by discordance between the lot without and the mind within, where the human being is in an obviously false position, — an evil rare and usually self-curative; or

4

by a discordance wholly internal, among the desires and
affections themselves. The first impulse of "the natural
man" is to seek peace by mending his external condition;
to quiet desire by increase of ease, to banish anxiety by
increase of wealth, to guard against hostility by making
himself too strong for it; to build up his life into a fortress
of security and a palace of comfort, where he may softly
lie, though tempests beat and rain descends. The spirit of
Christianity casts away at once this whole theory of peace;
declares it the most chimerical of dreams; and proclaims
it impossible ever to make this kind of reconciliation between
the soul and the life wherein it acts. As well might the
athlete demand a victory without a foe. To the noblest
faculties of soul, rest is disease and torture. The understanding is commissioned to grapple with ignorance, the
conscience to confront the powers of moral evil, the affections to labor for the wretched and oppressed: nor shall
any peace be found till these, which reproach and fret us
in our most elaborate ease, put forth an incessant and satis-
fying energy; till, instead of conciliating the world, we
vanquish it; and rather than sit still, in the sickness of
luxury, for it to amuse our perceptions, we precipitate ourselves upon it to mould it into a new creation. Attempt
to make all smooth and pleasant without, and you thereby
create the most corroding of anxieties, and stimulate the
most insatiable of appetites within. But let there be harmony within, let no clamors of self drown the voice which
is entitled to authority there, let us set forth on the mission
of duty, resolved to live for it alone, to close with every
resistance that obstructs it, and march through every peril
that awaits it : and in the consciousness of immortal power,
the sense of mortal ill will vanish, and the peace of God
wellnigh extinguish the sufferings of the man. "In the
world we may have tribulation; in Christ we shall have
peace."

This peace, so remote from torpor, — arising indeed from

the intense action of the greatest of all ideas, those of duty, of immortality, of God, — fell according to the promise on the first disciples. Not in vain did Jesus tell them in their sorrows that the Comforter would come : nor falsely did he define this blessed visitant, as "the spirit of truth," — the soul reverentially faithful to its convictions, and expressing clearly in action its highest aspirings. Such peace had Stephen : when before the Sanhedrim that was striving to hush up the recent story of the Cross, he proclaimed aloud the sequel of the Ascension; and priests and elders arose and stopped their ears and thrust him out to death ; — he had this peace : else how, — if a heaven of divinest tranquillity had not opened to him and revealed to him the proximity of Christ to God, — how, as the stones struck his uncovered and uplifted head, could he have so calmly said, "Lord, lay not this sin to their charge !" Such peace had Paul, — at least when he ceased to rebel against his noble nature, and became, instead of the emissary of persecution, the ambassador of God. Was there ever a life of less ease and security, yet of more buoyant and rejoicing spirit, than his? What weight did he not cast aside, to run the race that was set before him? What tie of home or nation did he not break, that he might join in one the whole family of God ? For forty years the scoff of synagogues and the outcast of his people, he forgot the privations of the exile in the labors of the missionary; flying from charges of sedition, he disseminated the principles of peace; persecuted from city to city, he yet created in each a centre of pure worship and Christian civilization, and along the coasts of Asia, and colonies of Macedonia, and citadels of Greece, dropped link after link of the great chain of truth that shall 'yet embrace the world. Amid the joy of making converts, he had also the affliction of making martyrs ; to witness the sufferings, perhaps to bear the reproaches, of survivors ; with weeping heart to rebuke the fears, and sustain the faith of many a doubter ; and in solitude and bonds to send forth the effu-

sions of his earnest spirit to quicken the life, and renovate
the gladness, of the confederate churches. Yet when did
speculation at its ease ever speak with vigor so noble, and
cheerfulness so fresh, as his glorious letters? — which recount his perils by land and sea, his sorrows from friend
and foe, and declare that " none of these things move " him ;
which show him projecting incessant work, yet ready for
instant rest ; conscious that already he has fought the good
fight, and willing to finish his course and resign the field ;
but prepared, if needs be, to grasp again the sword of the
spirit, and go forth in quest of wider victories. Does any
one suppose, that it would have been more peaceful to look
back on a life less exposed and adventurous? — on a lot sheltered and secured? on soft-bedded comfort, and unbroken
plenty, and conventional compliance? No! it is only *beforehand* that we mistake these things for peace ; in the retrospect we know them better, and would exchange them all
for one vanquished temptation in the desert, for one patient
bearing of the cross! What, — when all is over, and we lie
upon the last bed, — what is the worth to us of all our guilty
compromises, of all the moments stolen from duty to be
given to ease? If Paul had cowered before the tribunal
of Nero, and trembled at his comrades' blood, and, instead
of baring his neck to the imperial sword, had purchased by
poor evasions another year of life, — where would that year
have been now? — a lost drop in the deep waters of time, —
yet not lost, but rather mingled as a poison in the refreshing stream of good men's goodness by which Providence
fertilizes the ages.

The peace of Christ, thus inherited by his disciples, and
growing out of a living spirit of duty and of love, contrasts,
not merely with guilty ease, but with that mere mechanical
facility in blameless action which habit gives. There is
something faithless and ignoble in the very reasoning
sometimes employed to recommend virtuous habits. They
are urged upon us, because they smooth the way of right :

we are invited to them for the sake of ease. Adopted in such a temper, duty after all makes its bargain with indulgence, and is not yet pursued for its own sake and with the allegiance of a loving heart. Moreover, whoever has a true conscience sees that there is a fallacy in this persuasion : for, whenever habits become mechanical, they cease to satisfy the requirements of duty; the obligations of which enlarge indefinitely with our powers, demanding an undiminished tension of the will, and an ever-constant life of the affections. It can never be, that a soul which has a heaven open to its view, which is stationed here, not simply to accommodate itself to the arrangements of this world, but also to school itself for the spirit of another, is intended to rest in mere automatic regularities. When the mind is thrown into other scenes, and finds itself in the society of the world invisible, suddenly introduced to the heavenly wise and the sainted good, — what peace can it expect from mere dry tendencies to acts no longer practicable, and blameless things now left behind ? No; it must have that pure love which is nowhere a stranger, in earth or heaven ; that vital goodness of the affections, which adjusts itself at once to every scene where there is truth and holiness to venerate ; that conscience, wakeful and devout, which enters with instant joy on any career of duty and progress opened to its aspirations. And even in "the life that now is," the mere mechanist of virtue, who copies precepts with mimetic accuracy, is too frequently at fault, to have even the poor peace which custom promises. He is at home only on his own beat. An emergency perplexes him, and too often tempts him disgracefully to fly. He wants the inventiveness by which a living heart of duty seizes the resources of good, and uses them to the last ; and the courage by which love, like honor, starts to the post of noble danger, and maintains it till, by such fidelity, it becomes a place of danger no more. It is a vain attempt to comprise in rules and aphorisms all the various moral exigencies of life.

Hardly does such legality suffice to define the small portion of right and wrong contemplated in human jurisprudence. But the true instinct of a pure mind, like the creative genius of art, frames rules most perfect in the act of obeying them, and throws the materials of life into the fairest attitudes and the justest proportions. He whose allegiance is paid to a mere preceptive system shapes and carves his duty into the homeliest of wooden idols : he who has the spirit of Christ turns it into an image breathing and divine. Children of God in the noblest sense, we are not without something of his creative spirit in our hearts. The power is there, to separate the light from the darkness within us, and set in the firmament of the soul luminaries to guide and gladden us, for seasons and for years; power to make the herbage green beneath our feet, and beckon happy creatures into existence around our path; power to mould the clay of our earthly nature into the likeness of God most High; and thus only have we power to look back in peace upon our work, and find a sabbath-rest upon the thought, that, morning and evening, all is good.

But the peace which Christ felt and bequeathed was the result of *trust*, no less than of toil. However immersed in action, and engaged in enterprises of conscience, every life has its passive moments, when the operation is reversed; and power, instead of going from us, returns upon us, and the scenes of our existence present themselves to us as objects of speculation and emotion. Sometimes we are forced into quietude in pauses of exhaustion or of grief; stretched upon the bed of pain, to hear the great world murmuring and rolling by; or lifted into the watch-tower of solitude, to look over the vast plain of humanity, and from a height that covers it with silence, observe its groups shifting and traversing like spirits in a city of the dead. At such times, our peace must depend on the view under which our faith or our fears may exhibit this mighty "field of the world;" on the forces of evil, of fortuity, or of God, which we suppose to be secretly directing the changes on the scene, and calling up the brief apparition of generation after generation. And so great and terrible is the amount of evil, physical and moral, in the great community of men; so vast the numbers sunk in barbarism, compared with the few who more nobly represent our nature; so many and piercing (could we but hear them) the cries of unpitied wretchedness, which, with every beat of the pendulum, wander unnoticed into the air; so dense the crowds that are thrust together in the deepest recesses of want, and that crawl through the loathsome hives of sin; that only two men can look through the world without dismay: he, on the one hand, who, suffering himself to be bewildered with momentary horror, and in the confusion of his emotions, to mistake what he sees for a moral chaos, turns his back in the despair of fatalism, crying, "Let us eat and drink, for to-morrow we die;" and he, on the other, who, with the discernment of a deeper wisdom, penetrates through the shell of evil to the kernel and the seed of good; who perceives in suffering and temptation the *resistance* which alone can render virtue manifest, and conscience great, and existence venerable; who recognizes, even in the gigantic growth of guilt, the grasp of infinite desires, and the perversion of godlike capacities; who sees how soon, were God to take up his omnipotence, and snatch from his creature man the care of the world and the work of self-perfection, all that deforms might be swept away, and the meanest lifted through the interval that separates them from the noblest; and who therefore holds fast to the theory of hope, and the kindred duty of effort; takes shelter beneath the universal providence of God; and seeing time enough in *his* vast cycles for the growth and consummation of every blessing, can be patient as well as trust; can resign the selfish vanity of doing all things himself, and making a finish before he dies; and cheerfully *give* his life to build up the mighty temple of human improvement, though no inscription mark it for glory, and it be as one of the hidden stones of the sanctuary, visible only to the eye of God. Such was the spirit and the faith which Jesus left, and in which his first disciples found their rest. Within the infinitude of the divine mercy trouble did but fold them closer; the perversity of man did but provoke them to put forth a more conquering love; and though none were ever more the sport of the selfish interests and prejudices of mankind, or came into contact with a more desolate portion of the great wastes of humanity, *they* constructed no melancholy theories; but having planted many a rose of Sharon, and made their little portion of the desert smile, departed in the faith, that the green margin would spread as the seasons of God came round, till the mantle of heaven covered the earth, and it ended with Eden as it had begun.

Between these two sources of Christian peace, virtuous toil and holy trust, there is an intimate connection. The desponding are generally the indolent and useless; not the tried and struggling, but speculators at a distance from the scene of things, and far from destitute of comforts themselves. Barren of the most blessed of human sympathies, strangers to the light that best gladdens the heart of man, they are without the materials of a bright and hopeful faith. But he who consecrates himself sees at once how God may sanctify the world; he whose mind is rich in the memory of moral victories will not easily believe the world a scene of moral defeats; nor was it ever known that one who, like Paul, labored for the good of man, despaired of the benevolence of God.

Whoever then would have the peace of Christ, let him seek first the spirit of Christ. Let him not fret against the conditions which God assigns to his being, but reverently conform himself to them, and do and enjoy the good which they allow. Let him cast himself freely on the career to which the secret persuasion of duty points, without reservation of happiness or self; and in the exercise which its difficulties give to his understanding, its conflicts to his will, its humanities to his affections, he shall find that united action of his whole and best nature, that inward harmony, that moral order, which emancipates from the anxieties of self, and unconsciously yields the divinest repose. The shadows of darkest affliction cannot blot out the inner radiance of such a mind; the most tedious years move lightly and with briefest step across its history; for it is conscious of its immortality, and hastening to its heaven. And *there* shall its peace be consummated at length; its griefs transmuted into delicious retrospects; its affections fresh and ready for a new and nobler career; and its praise confessing that this final " peace of God " doth indeed " surpass its understanding."

scend to plead for it thus; and go ignominiously round, supplicating votes, in its behalf, for the vacant office of Master of Police! What sort of obedience is likely to be rendered to a creature of our own appointment, chosen from prudence, and removable at pleasure? Nothing can be more evident than that such advocates are thinking only of restraining *others*, and are by no means filled with the idea of submission *themselves*. A heart occupied and softened by the genuine spirit of allegiance will make a quite different appeal; will never dream that any suffrage can add authority to the faith that rules it rightly; will perhaps think it somewhat irreligious for even the most important persons to offer to the Almighty the weight of their great influence; and will feel that things divine are so much higher than things serviceable, that to recommend them for their use is to deny their essence and disown their obligation. Nay, does not a secret voice assure us all, that short of the sacrifice of self-will, and the cheerful movement within the limits of a supreme law, there is not even the faint beginning of religion; and that this concern for the common good, this idea of giving a sanction to the claims of piety, is an evasion of that *personal surrender*, which it is so easy to approve in others, so hard to achieve within ourselves? This temper feels as if it were *outside* the great and solemn conditions of humanity, and in concern for others' exposure to them lapses into forgetfulness itself; as if it had nothing to do with the strife of temptation, and the toil of duty, and the cry of grief. The complacent patron of religion, — will he not *die?* will he not go, all alone, into the silence of eternity, and personally look into the reality of those things of which he has always helped to keep up the show? Will he not stand face to face with the God whose service he has liberally encouraged? — empty, it is to be feared, of the only offering which he could tranquilly present, — the offer of *himself;* and thrown upon the Infinite, not as a child upon a parent's bosom, but as a

penitent in abasement before the Judge? — Nor does this
seem so distant, that there is much time to play at pretences
with it in the meanwhile. As sure as this world is swim-
ming fast through space and time, we are all afloat in the
same life-vessel, and have moreover a voyage before us, of
which even the stoutest heart may well think in earnest.

I do not, of course, mean that religious faith does not
conduce to the moral order of society; or that estimable
men may not innocently be aware of this and reckon on it.
But I do say, that it is not upon this that the obligatory
character of religion rests; that this social action is not the
source, but the effect, of its binding authority upon the
mind; and that to look first to its benefits, and then to its
sanctity, is to invert the true order of our moral life, and
set the pyramid of duty upon its point rather than its base.
If the great principles of religion were false, if it were all
a fiction that we lived under a God and in front of a heaven,
it is obvious that these beliefs would have no claim upon
us; that their relation to our conscience would even be
reversed; and that whatever support they might appear to
afford to the laws of rectitude and peace, our sole duty to
them, as delusions, would be to expose and expel them;
the looser dictates of expediency yielding at once to the
severer rule of veracity. And it is therefore not in their
usefulness, but in their truth, that their authority resides;
it is with that alone that our allegiance to them must stand
or fall; to that alone that our souls are permitted to bow;
nay, on that alone that all their moral excellence depends.
A devout man does his duty better than another, because he
sees his position more completely; gazes over the wide field
of his relations visible and invisible; exaggerates nothing
from its proximity, and overlooks nothing from its distance;
but, with the clear sense of moral proportion, receives from
all the true impression, and gives to all the fit affection.
He does not render his mental view false by ignoring the
whole region that lies beyond experience, and treating it as

if it had no existence; or fever his passions and fret away
his peace by imprisoning the whole energies of his nature
within some narrow object, — a section only of the life
which they are qualified to fill. It is because his *mind is*
right, that his *hand does* right.

The same insult which is committed against religion by
representing it as the tool of social order is repeated, when
it is prescribed as the only means of finding any semblance
of comfort in circumstances otherwise desperate. No one
can be ignorant that it is frequently exhibited in this light;
and that men are advised to lay by a prudent store of it, as
a resource of happiness during the dreary winter of distress.
Nothing can be more true to nature than the fact alleged :
nothing more false than the exhortation founded on it.
Certain it is, there is no real conquest of evil, except by the
devout mind, that can bleed beneath the thorny lot, yet
clasp it in closer love, like the piercing crucifix of self-morti-
fication upon the breast. Certain it is, that a pure trust,
defying nothing that is sent of God, but bending with self-
renunciation before his whirlwinds sweeping by, feels least
resistance of terrible necessity chafing against its peace.
But in mere cupidity for the comforts of faith there is no
religion, — on the contrary, the total privation of all religion : there is precisely that deliberate reservation of self,
that fencing of it round against the assaults of unhappiness,
that mere service for hire, in which is the very essence of
disloyalty to Heaven. Nor does God ever award the least
success to these insurance speculations on his service; and
only those who give themselves up to him without a question find their happiness returned. Vain every way are all
these attempts to make that which is divine subordinate to
our personal ends: we only bring down the awful rebuke,
" Ye have not chosen me, but I have chosen you."

Religion again is often represented, not exactly as the
instrument for producing good morals, but as in fact *the*
very same with good morals. We hear the sentiment con-

stantly repeated, that, after all, the service of man is the
truest service of God. Now if this maxim mean that so
long as human good is effected, it does not signify *on what
principles* it is done, no statement could well be more false.
Let us only see. Here is a man, who serves the common-
wealth from ambition, and merits the good-will of his neighbors, that he may mount by it. He selects some conspicuous
utility, labors at it visibly enough, and defends himself from
the aversion of the few by surrounding himself with the
plaudits of the many: and if you look at him, busy before
the face of his community, you will not fail to see the manner of his diligence; that in proportion as they raise the
shout, he prosecutes the work; that when they are tired, he
grows idle; and when they can lift their voices no higher,
and no more can be gained by laboring for their good, either
he begins to toil in the opposite direction, or, throwing
down all implements of work, gives himself up to strange
gambols, at which the spectators who have exhausted all
their praise may at least gratify him by being astonished.
Here is *another* man, smitten, we will say, with honest pity
for the degradation and misery of the great mass of every
civilized society; indignant, it may be (who can help it?),
that all citizens have not enough food and enough knowledge; studious of the economic causes which interfere with
such a result; but unhappily seeing no farther than the
mere sentient and intellectual man, and possibly dreaming
that their oppression and wretchedness have been aggra-
vated, instead of assuaged, by the restraints of the moral
and the aspirations of the spiritual nature. You see him,
accordingly, — a benignant thinking animal, — enthusiasti-
cally devoted to projects for making the life of man comfortable, intelligent, and clean; primarily impressed with
the necessity of increasing the productiveness of the earth,
and therefore secondarily with the importance of improv-
ing man as the producing instrument; trusting to a preternatural development of the physical and rational faculties to

supply some adequate counterfeit of moral order, that may
look the same from outside the heart; transferring to personal interest the venerated dress and badges of duty, but
really disowning any law higher than the collective forces
of self-will; loosening any particular ties with which the
feelings of mankind have connected a peculiar sacredness;
and suppressing, as an unmeaning weakness, any sentiment
above that of obtuse submission, in case of accident, to the
operation of crushing and fracture by the disordered mechanism of nature. And *once* at least there has been a CHRIST;
not seeking to thrust up human nature from below, but to
raise it from above; knowing that its earth could produce
nothing, except for its pure and spreading heaven; and so,
coming down upon it, as an angel soul from the highest
regions of the spirit; speaking seldom to it of its happiness,
constantly of its holiness; dwelling little on the arrangements, and much on the responsibilities of life; pitying its
woes, as it pities them itself in moments of truest aspiration,
not with mere nervous sympathy, but with godlike and
healing mercy; assuming its place in the midst of God, and
on the surface of eternity, and from this sublime position as
a base computing its obligations and uttering oracles of its
destiny.   Which now of these three, do you think, is truly
neighbor to our poor nature, wounded and bleeding by the
way?   Which of them has really tended and restored it
from being half dead?   It is impossible to deny to even the
least worthy of them the praise of rendering service to man
— but can we say of them all that there is a service of God?
Are all felt to be equally noble and venerable? or do we
measure our reverence for them by the scale and service of
their operation?   Is it not rather the different *principle*
which is at the root of each that determines the sentiment
we direct towards them?   No one, I believe, sincerely feels
that the simply humane and prosaic view of life and men,
such as a naturalist or statist might take, is as true and high
a source of benevolent action as the reverential and divine,

that commences with the spiritual relations, and thence descends to the economy of the outward lot. If then the maxim, that the service of men is the truest service of God, is adduced to excuse the indifference of many an amiable heart to the great truths of faith, and to palliate the defects of a merely ethical benevolence ; if it is the plea of social kindness to be let alone on the subject of diviner obligations, — it cannot be admitted. But as self-justification is seldom deficient in ingenuity, there is a sense in which this aphorism is unquestionably true ; in which indeed it does but contain the sentiment of the apostle : " He that loveth not his brother whom he hath seen, how can he love God whom he hath not seen ? " From the love of man we do not necessarily rise into the love of God ; but from any true love of God we inevitably descend into the love of man, — his child, his image, the object of his benediction, and the sharer of his immortality. Nor is this maxim without an important application to our moral estimates of *others*, whose acts alone are exposed to view, and of whose secret motives and affections we cannot take cognizance. Wherever we see in our fellow-men the outward life which *may possibly* be the fruit of religious principle, though perhaps explicable as some inferior growth, we have certainly no right to deny the existence of the nobler root; but must accept their service of man as presumption of their fidelity to God. I only protest against that self-flattery, which permits our good-nature towards earth to lull to sleep our aspirations to heaven.

Another spurious form of religion is discerned among those who regard it as an *indispensable ornament* of character; who speak much of the incompleteness of human nature without it; and plead the claims of piety on the ground that it is an offence against mental symmetry to be without it. The most palpable exhibition of this imitation of faith is found among those who, after craniological research, conceive that they have discovered a certain cere-

bral provision for a god; and who therefore conclude that
the culture of devotion is necessary to physiological consistency. They speak at large of man's need of a religion, of
his unsatisfied wants without it; of the grace which it adds
to his moral stature, the dignity it gives to his affections,
the power which it administers to his will : and then they
issue orders to their ingenuity to devise a religion suitable
to this discovered want, precisely adapted to the cravings
of this appetite. Alas! however, this is not the way in
which a religion can be found : it cannot by any skill be
thus carved and constructed according to measurements
taken on purpose from our nature. It is easy indeed to
imagine and invent a faith, seemingly just fitted to our
wants; but then comes the question, How are we to get it
believed? And here, it is to be feared, is the failure of this
school : they seem to have more faith in the religiousness of
man, than in the reality of God. The same danger attends
the idea, wherever found, of aiming constantly at our own
self-perfection, and, under the influence of this aim, striving
to put the last and saintly finish of a pure devotion to our
character. Surely there is something unsound and morbid
in thus resolving the whole idea of obligation and truth into
that of beauty. As long as we are but painting our own
ideal portrait, we can produce no living and substantial
goodness, but a mere canvas thing of surface dimension
only. Human character and life are something more than
mere matters of taste and propriety; and will attain to
nothing excellent till they are regarded in the spirit of an
earnest reality. Devotion can find no firm foundation in
the notion of its relative fitness to us, but must feel its foot
on the absolute truth of its glorious and sublime objects.
All else is abhorrent from the pure simplicity of faith, and
tends only to foster an indifference to truth, and an affectation of religion. God, refusing to be discerned through
the impure eye of expediency, reveals himself only to our
inward intuitions of conscience. The piety that loves him

will recognize no third thing between yea and no. To assume his reality, because the hypothesis seems to open the best training-school for our human nature; to treat the highest of all things as true, only because we want it to be true, and shall be the better for it if it is, — what is this but, under decent disguise, the French philosopher's characteristic exclamation, "If there were not a God, we should have to invent one." To an earnest mind this air of protection and appropriation towards things divine and holy is unspeakably offensive. It is for God to rule and guard our conscience, not for our conscience to take care of God. And to every pure submissive mind his voice within is heard rebuking this presumptuous spirit, and repeating the words of Christ: "Ye have not chosen me, but I have chosen you."

VIII.

MAMMON-WORSHIP.

———◆———

MATTHEW VI. 28.

CONSIDER THE LILIES OF THE FIELD, HOW THEY GROW; THEY TOIL NOT,
NEITHER DO THEY SPIN; AND YET I SAY UNTO YOU, THAT SOLOMON, IN
ALL HIS GLORY, WAS NOT ARRAYED LIKE ONE OF THESE.

IN no time or country has Christianity ever been exhibited
in its simple integrity. The soul of its author was the only
pure and perfect expression of its spirit: it was at once the
creature and the sole director of his mind; — born within
that palace to be its Lord. In every other instance Christianity has been only one out of many influences concerned
in forming the character of its professors; and they have
given it various shapes, according to the climate, the society,
the occupations in which they have lived. The prejudices
and passions of every community, — the inevitable growth
of its position, — have weakened its religion and morality
in some points, and strengthened them in others. So that
all particular Christianities are distortions of the great original: like paintings placed in a false light; or rather like
those grotesque images seen in the concave surfaces of
things, which, — lengthen or shorten as they may, — spoil
the beauty that depends upon proportion. The student will
find in his religion the nutriment of divinest speculation, —
the tenets of a sublime philosophy in which heaven resolves
the great problems of duty, fate, and futurity; and when
his genius soars to the highest heaven of invention, he feels
that he is borne upon his faith as on eagle's wings. The
patriot, cast on evil times, without a glimpse of these con-
templative subtleties, sees in it the law of liberty, — hears

in it a clear call, as from the trump of God, to vindicate the rights of the oppressed: he delights to read how Christ provoked bigots to gnash their teeth with rage, and Paul proclaimed that of one blood were all nations made. The peasant lays to heart its mercy to the poor, and its promise to the good. The merchant takes it as the root of upright-ness: the artist visits it as the source of moral beauty the most divine. The system is edited anew in the mind of every class.

We live in a country whose national character is very marked, and on whose people certain prevailing habits and employments are imposed by a peculiar soil, a northern climate, and an insular position. Various causes, both social and political, are filling England more and more with a manufacturing and mercantile population. The fact, taken in all its connections, is by no means to be deplored; and in various ways comprises in it auguries of vast good. But in the meanwhile it is attended with this particular result: that the *spirit of gain* is ascendant over every other passion and pursuit by which men can be occupied. Not pleasure, not art, not glory, can beguile our people from their profits. War was their madness once; but the temple of Moloch is deserted, and morning and evening the gates of Mammon are thronged now. *There* is the idol from whose seductions our Christianity has most to fear. Without indulging in any sentimental declamation against the pursuit and influ-ence of wealth, we may be permitted to feel that *this* is the quarter from which, specifically, our moral and religious affections are most in danger of being vitiated. The habits which produce the danger may be inevitable, forced upon us by a hard social necessity: still in bare self-knowledge there is self-protection. For, the danger of a vice is not like the danger of a pestilence, in which the most unconscious are the most safe: the fear of contagion, which, in the one case absorbs the poison into the veins of the body, repulses in the other the temptation from the mind.

The excess to which this master-passion is carried per-
verts our just and natural estimate of happiness. It cannot
be otherwise when that which is but a means is elevated
into the greatest of ends; when that which gives command
over some physical comforts becomes the object of intenser
desire than all blessings intellectual and moral, and we live
to get rich, instead of getting rich that we may live. The
mere lapse of years is not life: to eat and drink and sleep;
to be exposed to the darkness and the light; to pace round
in the mill of habit, and turn the wheel of wealth; to make
reason our book-keeper, and turn thought into an implement
of trade, — this is not life. In all this, but a poor fraction
of the consciousness of humanity is awakened: and the
sanctities still slumber which make it most worth while to
be. Knowledge, truth, love, beauty, goodness, faith, alone
give vitality to the mechanism of existence; the laugh of
mirth that vibrates through the heart, the tears that freshen
the dry wastes within, the music that brings childhood back,
the prayer that calls the future near, the doubt which makes
us meditate, the death which startles us with mystery, the
hardship which forces us to struggle, the anxiety that ends
in trust, — are the true nourishment of our natural being.
But these things, which penetrate to the very core and
marrow of existence, the votaries of riches are apt to fly;
they like not any thing that touches the central and immortal consciousness; they hurry away from occasions of sympathy into the snug retreat of self; escape from life into
the pretended cares for a livelihood; and die at length busy
as ever in preparing the means of living.

With a large and, I fear, a predominant class among us,
it is scarcely an exaggeration to say that money " measureth
all things," and is more an object of ambition than any of
the ends to which it affects to be subservient. It is the one
standard of value, which gives estimation to the vilest
things that have it, and leaves in contempt the best that are
without it. It is set up as the *measure of knowledge;* for

is it not notorious that no intellectual attainments receive a just appreciation, but those which may be converted into gold; that this is the rule by which, almost exclusively, parents compute the worth of their children's education, and determine its character and extent? It is not enough that the understanding burns with generous curiosity for the conquest of some new science, or the fancy for some new accomplishment; it is not enough that a study is needed to brace the faculties with health, or illumine the imagination with beauty, or agitate the heart with high sympathies; " but what is the use of it ? " is the question still asked, — as if it were not use enough, instead of a trader to make a man. Research and speculation which do not visibly tend to the production of wealth are regarded by all, except the classes engaged in their pursuit, as the dignified frivolities of whimsical men; and though they may bear the torch into the darkness of antiquity, or open some unexplored domain of nature, they must not expect more than a cold tolerance. Still worse; money with us is the *measure of morality ;* for those parts and attributes of virtue are in primary esteem which are conducive to worldly aggrandizement; and it is easy to perceive that no others are objects of earnest and hearty ambition. Industry and regularity, and a certain easy amount of pecuniary probity, being indispensable instruments of prosperity, the great moral forces of trade, are in no country held in higher worth; but the amenities which spread a grace over the harsher features of life, the clear veracity that knows truth and profit to be incommensurable things, and the generous affections whose coin is in sympathy as well as gold, are the objects of but slight care, and slighter culture. The current ideas of human nature and character are graduated by the same rule, and err on the side, not of generosity, but of prudence. The experienced are habitually anxious to give the young such an estimate of mankind as may prove, not the most true, but the most profitable, — an estimate so depressed into caution as

to be altogether below justice. To escape one or two possible rogues, we must suppose nobody true; for the sake of
pecuniary safety, we must submit to the moral wretchedness
of universal distrust, and blacken the great human heart for
our private ease: as if it were not better to run the risk of
ruin, than grow familiar with so vast a lie; happier to be
bankrupt in wealth than in the humanities. But alas! with
us, money is the *measure of all utility*; it is this which constitutes the real though disguised distinction between the
English notions of theory and practice. A truth may be in
the highest degree grand and important, may relieve many
a cold and heavy doubt, and open many a fair and brilliant
vision; but unless it has some reference to money, it is pronounced a mere theory. A social improvement may be
suggested, which promises to remove some absurd anomaly,
to assert some comprehensive principle, or annihilate some
sufferings of mere feeling; but because it has no direct
relation to the mechanism of property, it is set aside as not
practical. By an unnatural abuse of terms, "practical men"
are, with us, not those who study the bearing of things on
human life in its widest comprehension, but those who value
every thing by its effect upon the purse.

In obedience to the same dominant passion, vast numbers
spend their term of mortal service in restless and uneasy
competition, in childish struggles for a higher place in the
roll of opulence or fashion, in jealousies that gnaw to the
very heart of luxury, in ambition that spoils the present
splendor by the shadow of some new want. Happy they of
simpler feelings, who have taken counsel of a pure nature
about the economy of good; who know from what slight
elements the hand of taste can weave the colors into the
web of life, and from what familiar memories the heart
draws the song of cheerfulness as the work proceeds; who
find no true pleasure marred because it is plebeian, nor any
indulgence needful because decreed by custom; who discern
how little the palace can add to the sincere joy of a loving

and a Christian home, and feel that nature dwells at the centre after all; who have the firmness to retire to that inner region, and embrace the toils of reason, the labors of sympathy, the strife of conscience, the exhaustless ambition of duty, as Heaven's own way to combine the divinest activity with the profoundest repose.

The prevalent occupations of the community in which we live have a tendency to pervert our moral sentiments and social affections, no less than our estimates of happiness. In a society so engrossed by ideas connected with property, so eternally dwelling on the distinction of *meum* and *tuum*, men naturally learn to think and speak of all things in the language belonging to this relation; to use it as an illustration of matters less familiar to them, and apply its imagery and analogies to subjects of a totally different character. Over their property the authority of law gives them abso-- lute right and control; no man may touch it with his finger, or call them to account for its disposal. I need not stop to acknowledge, what is too plain for any one to doubt, that this sanctity of property from invasion is, to any society, the very cement of its civilization. Yet there is an unquestionable danger of giving this notion of irresponsible possession an application beyond its proper range ; of permitting the sense of legal right to creep insensibly into the domain of moral obligation, and spread there the feeling of personal self-will, and set up the caprices of inclination for the deliberations of duty. Men are exceedingly apt to imagine, that nothing can be seriously *wrong*, which they have *a right* to do; to forget that the license which is allowed by law may be sternly prohibited by morality. How little concern does any wise and conscientious principle appear to have with the expenditure of private revenue, especially where that revenue is the largest! How despotically there do mere whim and chance suggestion appear to reign ! How wastefully are the elements of human enjoyment squandered in ˙ pernicious luxuries, or dissipated in random experiments of

benevolence, of which a little knowledge beforehand might
have taught the result just as well as the failure afterwards!
And if ever a gentle remonstrance is insinuated, how instantly does the vulgar and ignorant feeling leap forth,
" And may I not do what I like with my own ?"   No, you
may not, unless your liking and your duty are in happy
accordance.   Morally you are as much bound to distribute
your own wealth wisely, as to abstain from touching another
man's; bound by the very same fundamental reasons, which
forbid the privation of human enjoyment no less than the
creation of human misery.   As large a portion of well-being
may be sacrificed by an act of wilful extravagance as by the
commission of a dishonesty : and were it of a nature to be
definable by law, would merit as severe a punishment.
Shall any thing then deter us from saying that such self-
indulgence is a thief?

But the feelings which are entertained towards property,
— the feelings of absolute and irresponsible control, — are
very apt to extend to whatever it can purchase and procure ;
and unhappily, to the services of those human beings who
yield us their labor for hire.   There is nothing over which
a man exercises such uncontrolled power as his purse ; and
(where no principle of justice and benevolence intervenes)
but one remove from this despotism are placed his depend-
ants.   In them the right of every human being to be appreciated according to his moral worth is forgotten ; and the
rule by which they are judged is, their mechanical use to
the master, not their excellence in themselves.   That they
are responsible agents (except to their employers), that they
have an intelligence receptive of truth, hearts that may
shelter gentle sympathies, and a work of duty to carry on
beneath the eye of God, that their bodies are of the same
clay and their life constructed of the same vicissitudes as ,
ours, — are thoughts that too seldom occur to lead us to
consult their feelings, to allow for their temptations, to
respect their conscience and improvement, as would become

a fraternal and a Christian heart. How hardly are they judged! By how much more rigid a rule than that which we apply to our friends or to ourselves! What order, what punctuality, what untiring industry, what equanimity of temper, what abstinent integrity, is imperiously and mercilessly demanded by many a master, lax, and lazy, and passionate himself! Oh with what biting indignation have I seen those most wretched of educated beings, the governess in a family and the usher in a school, worked to the bone without the help of a sympathy, moving in perpetual rotation, with no feeling but of the daily whirl, and of incessant friction upon all that is most tender in their nature ; expected to have all perfections, intellectual and moral, and to dispense with the respect which is their natural due ; copiously blamed for what is wrong, but scantily praised for what is right ; paid, but never cheered ; and when worn threadbare at last, put away as one of the cast-off shreds of society, that only deforms the house filled with purple and fine linen. This is the consequence of that state of things in which (to use the words of a Church Dignitary, who could find it in his heart to write them without a syllable of regret or rebuke) " poverty is infamous ; " and in which knowledge and virtue weigh nothing against gold. Let the children of labor remember, that they are of the class which he of Nazareth dignified ; that, peradventure, in his youthful days of mechanic toil, he too was looked on by the coarse eye of sheer power ; and yet nurtured, amid indignities and neglect, the spirit that made him divinely wise.

The despotic temper which is apt to be engendered by wealth in one direction, is naturally connected with servility in the opposite. For the very same reason that we regard those who are beneath us almost as if they were our property, we must regard ourselves almost as if we were the property of those above us. There is little, I fear, that is intellectual or moral in that sort of independence which is the proverbial characteristic of our countrymen ; it consists

either in mere churlishness of manner, or in overbearing
tyranny to those of equal or lower grade. It would be
inconsistent not to yield that respect to the purse in others,
which men are fond of claiming for it in themselves; and
accordingly it is to be feared that in few civilized countries
is there so much sycophancy as in this; so many creatures
ready to crawl round a heap of gold; so many insignificant
shoals gleaming around every great ship that rides over the
surface of society. It is a grievous evil arising hence, that
the judgments and moral feelings of society lose their clear-
sightedness and power; that the same rules are not applied
to the estimate of rich and poor; that there is a rank which
almost enjoys immunity from the verdict of a just public
sentiment, where the most ordinary qualities receive a mischievous adulation, and even grave sins are judged lightly
or not at all. But it is a more grievous ill that the witchery
thus strikes with a foul blight the true manhood of the children of God; — the manhood, not of limbs or life, but of a
spirit free and pure; — of an understanding open to all
truth, and venerating it too deeply to love it except for
itself, or barter it for honor or for gold; of a heart enthralled by no conventionalisms, bound by no frost of custom, but the perennial fountain of all pure humanities; of
a will at the mercy of no tyrant without and no passion
within; of a conscience erect under all the pressure of circumstances, and ruled by no power inferior to the everlasting law of duty; of affections gentle enough for the humblest
sorrows of earth, lofty enough for the aspirings of the skies.
In such manhood, full of devout strength and open love, let
every one that owns a soul see that he stands fast; in its
spirit, at once humane and heavenly, do the work, accept
the good, and bear the burdens of his life. Its healthful
power will reveal the sickness of our selfishness, and recall
us from the poisonous level of our luxuries and vanities to
the reviving breath and the mountain heights of God.
There could be no deliverer more true than he who should

thus emancipate himself and us. Oh blessed are they who, for the peace and ornament of life, dare to rely, not on the glories which Solomon affected, but on those which Jesus loved; — glories which even God may behold with compla-cency, — nay, in which he shines himself; glories of nature, richer than of man's device; genuine graces, resembling the inimitable beauties of the lilies of the field, painted with the hues of heaven, while bending over the soil of earth.

IX.

THE KINGDOM OF GOD WITHIN US.

PART I.

—•—

MATTHEW IV. 17.

FROM THAT TIME JESUS BEGAN TO PREACH, AND TO SAY, REPENT; FOR
THE KINGDOM OF HEAVEN IS AT HAND.

By the kingdom of Heaven was meant reformation upon
earth. Whatever difficulties there may be in filling up the
precise picture which the phrase would bring before the
mind of a Jewish audience, it was unquestionably the Hebrew formula for the expected golden age, and was the
popular symbol to denote perfected society; the final ascendancy of truth, justice, and peace; the expulsion of misery
and wrong; the eternal reign of all that is divine over the
world. This theocratic revolution was expected speedily,
when the words of the text were uttered. On the supposed eve of such a change, which would itself bring rem-
edies for every imaginable ill, physical and moral, all earnest
efforts at social amelioration might appear to be superseded;
the nearer the crisis of restoration, the shorter would be the
triumphs of oppression, and the feebler the mischiefs of
sin: nay, if corruption ripens for judgment, a more vehement outblaze of human crime might even be welcomed by
some, as likely to hasten the interposition which was to
quench and to regenerate. The appropriate lesson of the
hour might be thought to be one of passive watchfulness;
to lie in wait for the hoped-for redemption; to relax even
the accustomed energies of life and duty, as on a world

grown old ; and, in the words of one writing under the influence of this very expectation, to let " him that is unjust,
be unjust still ; him that is filthy, be filthy still ; him that is
righteous, be righteous still ; him that is holy, be holy still ;
for the time is at hand."

Instead of this, however, the great prophet of the hour
draws the opposite inference ; and utters the exhortation
short and sharp, " Repent ! " A life of worldly acquiescence, of selfish habit, of unloving and barren ease, will
not do, he conceives, for the kingdom of Heaven ; which, be
it what it may, is no system of mechanism for forcing men
to be wise and good without any trouble, but a social state
accruing from wisdom and excellence previously formed ;
not a scene from which souls acquire sanctity, but one to
which they give it. Personal repentance, the transference
of the life from conventionalism to conviction, the kindling
of pure and productive affections, must precede and usher
in the reign of God upon the earth ; men must truly venerate the Deity within them, and he will not be slow to
descend with his peace on society around them. The holy
and divine must first be recognized and enshrined in the individual and private heart; and then will follow its wider
conquests over humanity. *There* is the home and citadel
of its strength, from which it sallies forth to win its public
triumphs, and establish its general rule ; *there* the centre
whence its influence radiates, till it embraces and penetrates
even the outlying margin of barbarism and sin.

Christ, then, whose voice is Christianity, addresses himself first to the individual conscience ; indulges in no dreams
of a renovated world without, till he has flung his appeal to
the man within ; looks *there* for the creative and vital forces,
which are to make all things new. He speaks to his hearers, not as to passive creatures who might look about them
for some position in which it might befall them to be good,
but as to beings conscious of internal power to strive and
win the excellence they love ; to grapple athletically with

the oppositions of circumstance; and run the appointed race, though with panting breast and bleeding feet. Herein, I conceive, did Christ preach a gospel wholly at variance with the prevailing temper and philosophy of our times. It is their tendency not to excite men to become what they ought to be, but to manage them as they are. The age has been prolific (like many of its predecessors) in inventions and proposed social arrangements, by which we may sit still and be made into the right kind of men; which will render duty the smoothest thing on earth, by warning all interfering motives off the spot, and turn the Christian race into a stroll upon a mossy lawn. The trust and boast of our period is not in its individual energy and virtue, not in its great and good minds, but in its external civilization, in schemes of social and political improvement, in things to be done *for* us, rather than *by* us; in what we are to *get*, more than in what we are to *be*. We have had systems of education, which were to mould the minds of our children into a perfection that would make experience blush; systems of self-culture, to nurse our faculties into full maturity; systems of socialism, for mending the whole world, and presenting every one with a virtuous mind, without the least trouble on his part. Even those who escape this enthusiasm of system, are apt to place an extravagant trust in sets of outward circumstances; and, dazzled by the splendid forms which modern civilization assumes, to conceive of them as powers in themselves, independently of the minds that fill and use them. Commerce, mechanical art, and more reasonably, but still with some error, the school and the printing-press, are each in turn cited as in themselves securing the indefinite progress of nations and mankind. It would be absurd to doubt that these causes operate with constant and beneficent power on the mind of a people; but on this very account an exclusive and irrational reliance may be placed upon them. It is obvious that two methods exist, of aiming at human improvement, — by adjusting circumstances without

and by addressing the affections within ; by creating facilities of position, or by developing force of character; by
mechanism or by mind. The one is institutional and systematic, operating on a large scale ; reaching individuals cir-
cuitously and at last; the other is personal and moral, the
influence of soul on soul, life creating life, beginning in the
regeneration of the individual and spreading thence over
communities ; the one, in short, reforming from the circumference to the centre, the other from the centre to the circumference. And in comparing these it is not difficult to
show the superior triumphs of the latter, which was the
method of Christ and Christianity. Indeed the great peculiarity of the Christian view of life is to be found in its
preference of the inward element over the outward ; its reliance upon the least showy and most deep buried portions
of society for the evangelizing of the world ; and still more
upon the profoundest and most faintly whispered sentiments
of the soul for the regeneration of the individual. It forbids us to say, " Lo, here ! " or " Lo, there ! " and assures us
that "the kingdom of God is within" us.

In attributing the sanctification and moral growth of personal character to an agency *from within*, Christianity is
surely confirmed by experience. Rarely do these blessed
changes originate in any peculiarities of the individual's lot,
visibly favorable ; — else from a knowledge of his circumstances, we should be able to predict the history of his
mind. Most often they arise, without any marked revolution in his condition, from secret and untraceable workings
of the soul, from native forces of the inner man, merely
taking from external circumstances an excuse for breaking
into energy, — an excuse which a thousand different situa-
tions would have supplied as well. Feeble minds, in apology for their puny growth or premature decay in excellence,
complain of the climate in which God has planted them;
but where there is any vigor of life, the good seed will not
wait to burst, till it be removed to some sunny slope or lux-

6

uriant garden of the Lord : give it but a lodgment on the
rock, and feed it with the melting snow, and it will start a
forest on the hills, climbing with giant feet, fast as the
seasons can make steps. Whatever truth there may be in
the doctrine of circumstances, when applied on a large scale
to tribes of men, — however certain it may be that national
character is changed by the insensible influences of national
condition, — the application of the notion by individuals to
their own case is almost always fallacious ; and the very
fact of their throwing upon their fate the blame of their
own faithlessness and sin, is a sure symptom that *they* have
not the living conscience which would turn a better lot into
a better life. The souls that would really be richer in duty
in some new position, are precisely those who borrow no
excuses from the old one ; who even esteem it full of privileges, plenteous in occasions of good, frequent in divine
appeals, which they chide their graceless and unloving temper for not heeding more. Wretched and barren is the
discontent that quarrels with its tools instead of with its
skill ; and, by criticising Providence, manages to keep up
complacency with self. How gentle should we be, if we
were not provoked ; how pious, if we were not busy ; the
sick would be patient, only he is not in health ; the obscure
would do great things, only he is not conspicuous ! Nay,
the infatuation besets us more closely still, and tempts us
to expect wonders from some altered posture of our affairs
totally inadequate to their production. What we neglect in
summer is to be done in winter ; what present interruptions persuade us to forego is to be gloriously achieved at
some coming period of golden leisure, when confusion is to
cease, and life to be set into an order unattainable yet. As
if time and change, which should be our servants, and made
to do the bidding of our conscience, were to be waited on
by our servile will ; as if the pusillanimous submission, once
made, could be at once recalled. No ; as the captive of
old was carried off from the field of battle to the field of

slavery, the vanquished soul becomes temptation's serf, and, after tears and repinings, learns to be cheerful at the toil of sin. Once let a man insult the majesty of duty, by waiting till its commands shall become easy, and he must be disowned as an outlaw from her realm. If he calculates on this or that happy influence which is to shape him into something nobler; if he once regards his moral nature, not as an authoritative power invested within its sphere with a divine omnipotence that speaks and it is done, but as passive material to be worked by the ingenuity of circumstances into somewhat that is good, — it is all over with him ; the ascendancy of conscience is gone; collapse and ruin have begun. The mind has fallen into contentment with the mere conception, — the feeble and far-off imagination of excellence; confounds the look of duty, which indeed is a fair vision, with the strife and effort, the weary tension of resolve, the doubt, the prayers, the tears, which may bring our Christian manhood to exhaustion. Pleasant is it to entertain the picture of ourselves in some future scene, planning wisely, feeling nobly, and executing with holy triumph of the will; but 'tis a different thing, — not in the green avenues of the future, but in the hot dust of the present moment, — not in the dramatic positions of the fancy, but in the plain prosaic *now*, — to do the duty that waits and wants us, and put forth an instant and reverential hand to the noon-day or the evening task. It is a vain attempt, — that of the Epicurean moralist: to " *endure hardness* " is the needful condition of every service, and above all, for the good " soldier of Christ ;" and no man can try his utmost, with comfort to himself. Without great effort was nothing worthy ever achieved; and he who is never conscious of any strong, lift within the mind, may know that he is a cumberer of the ground.

This weak reliance then on outward occasions and influences for moral improvement is always ineffectual. And it is the constant experience of those who indulge in it, that to postpone the season is to perpetuate the sin. Instead of being lifted easily by the mechanism of new and more powerful motives into a higher life, the most overwhelming vicissitudes sweep over them, and after beating upon their defenceless affections, leave them where they were; not invigorated into effort, but simply wasted by passive anguish : just as danger, which may but reveal to the strong his strength, will sink the paralytic into death. But where, on the contrary, the soul rests, with implicit dependence, not on outward opportunities, but on inward convictions, on some venerated idea of right, there is the true germ of spiritual life, the element of a mighty power. This repose upon a supreme ideal as the only real is the true Christian faith; and he that has it, though it be little as a grain of mustard-seed, is able to cast the mountain into the sea. For, its force depends not on the greatness or rarity of the thoughts which enter into it; the simplest faith, be it only deep and trustful, the very smallest idea of a mission in life assigned by God, be it only lovingly and clearly seen, "lifteth the poor out of the dust," and " to them that have no might increaseth strength." As of old it banished disease, and couched the blind, and soothed the maniac, by miracles of power, so does it still heal and bless by its miracles of love. Who has not seen the frequent transformation it effects in the wayward, frivolous, self-indulgent child, when some living point has been touched within the heart; how it seems to create wisdom, experience, energy, and serenity at a stroke, and teaches her best to administer the daily and nightly medicine of an unspeakable affection to the sufferings of a sick brother, or the infirmities of an aged parent. It puts a divine fire into the dullest soul, and draws in Saul also among the prophets; it turns the peasant into the apostle, and the apostle's meanest follower into the martyr.

I have spoken of the *sudden* change of mind effected by a newly-opened faith. In the primitive Christian doctrine such change plainly seems to have been recognized as possible. And in spite of all that philosophers have written, with some truth but not the whole truth, respecting the power of habit, and the slow and severe pace of moral improvement and recovery, and the impossibility of abrupt conversion, I believe there is a profound reality in the opposite and popular belief; — as indeed there must be in all popular beliefs respecting matters of mental experience. It is quite true that instantaneous regeneration of the mind is not a phenomenon of the commoner sort, especially in the present day: but it is also true, that of all the remarkable moral recoveries that occur (alas! too few at best), almost the whole are of this kind. It is quite true that the upward efforts of the will, when it exchanges the madness of passion for the perceptions of reason, are toilsome, and, if successful, tardy; and if all transformations of conscience were of the deliberate and reasonable sort, philosophers could not say too much about their infrequency and slowness. But the process springs from a higher and more powerful source; the persuasion is conducted by some new and intense affection, some fresh and vivid reverence, followed, not led, by the conscience and reason. The weeds are not painfully plucked up by the cautious hand of tillage reckoning on its fruits, but burnt out by the blaze of a divine shame and love. It is quite true that such a change cannot be expected, — that to calculate on it is inexpressibly perilous; for the deeper movements of the soul shrink back from our computations, refuse to be made the tools of our prudence, and insist on coming unobserved or coming never ; and he that reckons on them sends them into banishment, and only shows that they are and must be strangers to his barren heart. It is quite true that self-cure is of all things the most arduous; but that which is impossible *to the man within us*, may be altogether possible *to the God*. In truth, the denial of such changes, under the affectation of great knowledge of man, shows an incredible ignorance of men. Why, the history of every great religious revolution, such as the spread of Methodism, is made up of nothing else; the instances occurring in such number and variety, as to transform the character of whole districts and vast populations, and to put all scepticism at utter defiance. And if some more philosophic authority is needed for the fact, we may be content with the sanction of Lord Bacon, who observed that a man reforms his habits either all together or not at all. Deterioration of mind is indeed always gradual; recovery usually sudden; for God, by a mystery of mercy, has established this distinction in our secret nature, — that while we cannot, by one dark plunge, sympathize with guilt far beneath us, but gaze at it with recoil till intermediate shades have rendered the degradation tolerable, — we are yet capable of sympathizing with moral excellence and beauty infinitely above us; so that while the debased may shudder and sicken at even the true picture of themselves, they can feel the silent majesty of self-denying and disinterested duty. With a demon can no man feel complacency, though the demon be himself; but God can all spirits reverence, though his holiness be an infinite deep. And thus the soul, privately uneasy at its insincere state, is prepared, when vividly presented with some sublime object veiled before, to be pierced as by a flash from heaven with an instant veneration, sometimes intense enough to fuse the fetters of habit and drop them to the earth whence they were forged. The mind is ready, like a liquid on the eve of crystallization, to yield up its state on the touch of the first sharp point, and dart, over its surface and in its depths, into brilliant and beautiful forms, and from being turbid and weak as water, to become clear as crystal, and solid as the rock.

Meanwhile, though acknowledging, for the sake of truth and the understanding of God's grace, the possibility and reality of such changes, we must remember that, like all vicissitudes of the affections, they neither come at the direct command of our will, nor descend on those who watch for external influences to produce them. There are those who go about in passive waiting for a call from heaven; who try this, and try that, and say, "Lo here!" and "Lo there!" And they find that "the kingdom of God cometh not of observation." Wanting to be holy, for the sake of being happy, they shall assuredly be neither; unless first the crust of their selfish nature is broken by affliction, and bending the head upon the shrine of sorrow, they cry with a contrition that forgets to be happy,—a cry that, it may be, the Divine Spirit will not despise. The kingdom of God *is* within us. In the latency of every soul there lurks, among the things it loves and venerates, some earnest and salient point, whence a divine life may be begun and radiate; some incipient idea of duty, it may be, some light mist of disinterested love, appearing vague and nebulous and infinitely distant within the mighty void,—a broken fringe of holy light, seen only in the spirit's deepest darkness: and therein may be the stirrings of a mystic energy, and the haze may be gathered together, and glow within the mind into a star, —a sun,—a piercing eye of God. But wherever the Deity dwelleth within us, he will be unfelt and a stranger to us till we abandon ourselves to the duties and aspirations which we feel to be his voice; till we renounce ourselves, and unhesitatingly precipitate our life on the persuasion of our disinterested affections. While his "Spirit bloweth where it listeth," yet certain it is that they only who do his will shall ever feel his power.

X.

THE KINGDOM OF GOD WITHIN US.

PART II.

----•----

MATTHEW IV. 17.

FROM THAT TIME JESUS BEGAN TO PREACH, AND TO SAY, REPENT; FOR THE KINGDOM OF HEAVEN IS AT HAND.

THAT the reformation and improvement of individual character proceeds from within, not from without; that it usually dates, not from any change in the condition and circumstances of life, but from the birth of some indigenous idea or affection in the mind, — is the doctrine which I endeavored to establish in the preceding discourse. However natural may be our reliance on external influences and marked transitions in our lot, as facilities for a change of mind, that reliance was shown to be delusive, and even to originate in a state of feeling, which itself forbids the change. A new and regenerative affection, wherever it finds root, springs up (like a kingdom of God within us), "not with observation," but silently and unconsciously; from suggestions seemingly slight or even untraceable; with power often sudden and triumphant; in a seat within the soul profound and central; whence a transforming force radiates over the whole character to its very form and visible expression.

From the case of an individual man, we will now pass to that of multitudes. In societies, the order of reformation will be found to be the same; — from the centre to the circumference; from a solitary point deep buried and unnoticed, first to the circumjacent region, and then over the whole service; from the native force and inspired insight of some individual mind, that kindles, first itself, and then, by its irresistible intensity, a wider and wider sphere of souls; spirit being born of spirit, life of life, thought of thought. A higher civilization, by which I understand neither superior clothes, nor better houses, nor richer wines, nor even more destructive gunpowder, but a nobler system of ideas and aspirations possessing a community, must commence, where alone ideas and aspirations can have a beginning, in somebody's mind. Hence, of all the more remarkable social revolutions, the seminal principle, the primitive type, may be traced to some one man, whose spiritual greatness had force enough to convert generations and constitute an era in the world's life; who preached with power some mighty repentance or transition of sentiment within the hearts of men, and thus rendered more near at hand that "kingdom of Heaven," for which all men sigh and good men toil. Private "repentance," individual moral energy, deep personal faith in some great conception of duty or religion, are the pre-requisites and causes of all social amelioration.

It might appear a waste of breath to make assertion of so plain a truth as this, were it not for the disposition of men to invert this order, to plan new systems of society in order to perfect the individual, instead of seeking in the individual conscience the germ of a nobler form of society. Every vice and grievance, every evil, physical and moral, which may afflict any class of a community, is apt to be charged exclusively upon faulty institutional arrangements; upon laws or the want of laws; on forms of government; on economical necessity; on some external causes which lift off the weight of responsibility from the individual will, and make men passive and querulous under wrong, instead of active and penitent. Their aspirations are turned outwards, rather than inwards; become complaints instead of efforts; and spoil their tempers instead of ennobling their energies. They must have the world mended, before they can be expected to be better than they are : they reverse the solemn exhortation of my text; and propose to make a stir to get the "kingdom of Heaven" established first; and then repentance and moral renovation will follow of course. The machinery of human motives being, we are sometimes assured, altogether out of order, the manufacture of characters is unavoidably far from satisfactory. And not unfrequently a truly surprising amount of faith is manifested in the skill of certain moral mechanists, who promise to rectify the disorder, and form for us the only true specimens of men. Self-interest is the one force by which all speculators of this class propose to animate their new framework of society; its application being ingeniously distributed so as to maintain an unerring equilibrium, and smoothly execute the work of duty. A hard-worked power is this self-interest; by which vulgar minds, in schools of philosophy or in councils of state, have from an early age thought to subdue and manage men ; but from which, time after time, they have broken loose in startling and remarkable ways. Against this reliance for human improvement on institutions and economical organization, apart from agencies internal and spiritual, Providence and history enter a perpetual protest. And it behooves all wise men to add their voices too : the more so, because it is the tendency of our times rather to criticise society, than to ennoble and sanctify individuals; to apply trading analogies to great questions of human improvement; to place as implicit a faith in the omnipotence of self-interest in morals as of steam in the arts; forgetting that between the grossest and the most refined form of this principle, there can only be the difference between the cannibal and the epicure. Let us not glorify the body of civilization, and overlook its soul; and while luxuriating in its fruits, neglect the waters at its secret root.

The systematic socialist, who is confident he "can explain the origin of evil," and no less sure that he can remove it by a kind of mental engineering or exact computation of human wants and desires, is the extreme exemplification of this spirit. In order to indicate the fallacy of his scheme, it is not necessary to travel beyond his own class of illustrations. He perpetually calls the arrangements into which he proposes to fit the world, a " machine." In every machine there is a power to move, and a resistance to be overcome: and in this particular project for curing the errors and perfecting the minds of men, it is clear that the social organization is relied upon as the *power* to repress the human passions and will, considered as *resistance*. Yet, as organization is nothing in itself, but merely a disposition of parts through which force may be transmitted from point to point, no effect can ensue till it is filled and animated with some energy not its own: nor in this case can the boasted engine of improvement be worked but by the very minds it is intended to control: and the power and the resistance being thus the same, the machine must stand still, as certainly as the inventions on which sciolists waste their ingenuity for producing perpetual motion and self-revolving wheels. Or, to take an illustration from morals rather than from physics, it is the same mistake, by which a disorderly mind expects to acquire faithfulness and punctuality of conscience from a neatly-arranged list of employments, and well-filled scheme for the disposal of the hours. While the force of good resolve which produced the list remains, the self-made law continues to be obeyed, and the programme looks up with a grave and venerable authority. But the occasion passes, the tension of the heart relaxes, temptations crowd and hurry back: and the slips of conscience recommence, and confusion triumphs again, though the paper plans of duty are symmetrical as ever; looking now with vain remonstrance at our rebellion, till discarded and trodden under foot for reminding us of our departed allegiance.

It is far from my desire to speak lightly of the importance of institutional and political change. But perhaps, at the present day, the true light in which to regard it is, that its function is to check evil rather than create positive good ; to prevent, by timely removal, an injurious variance between the mind of a people and its ways; and leave room for the unembarrassed operations of all active causes of improvement that may spread from the centres of private life. More than this is usually expected ; the intensity of political passion exaggerates the magnitude of the stake : and hence, measures, or the defeat of measures, of social innovation, usually disappoint by the smallness of the result; while the conceptions and acts of single minds, piercing the deeps of human sympathy, and touching the springs of the human will, often start from secrecy and neglect to a power transcendent and sublime. While the vastest and best-executed schemes of subversion and reconstruction are necessarily transient, the creation of deep individual faith is the mightiest and most permanent of human powers.

For an example we need only turn to the grandest of revolutions, the travels and triumphs of Christianity itself. We do injustice to the gospel, and gratuitously lessen the wonder of its spread, when we speak of it as a *system*, deliberately projecting the downfall of the existing order of things, and urged on mainly by the physical power or intellectual persuasion of miracle. No comprehensive scheme of policy, no continuous plan, no study of effect however benevolent, can be traced in our Lord's ministry. These ingenuities are the necessary resort of our feeble minds, which have to adapt themselves with nicety to foreign causes, to conciliate events instead of commanding them, to accumulate power by making each step contribute something to the next. But where there is an exuberance of strength, and every moment is in itself equal to the demand made upon it, the soul may retain its divine freedom, unchained by the successive links of preconceived arrangement. Art and strategy constitute the wisdom of those whose ends must be gained *against* the wills of others ;

but are misplaced in those who act *upon* and *by* their loving
and consenting mind. There is a wisdom of the understanding, arising from *foresight*, which demands policy;
there is a higher wisdom of the soul, derived from *insight*,
which dispenses with it. To discern "that which is before
and after," has been pronounced the great *human* prerogative: but to see clearly that which is *within*, is the *divine.*
And this was Christ's; the source of that majestic power
by which, as the hierophant and interpreter of the god-like
in the soul, he uttered everlasting oracles. He penetrated
through the film to the inner mystery and silence of our
nature: and when he spake, an instant music, — as of a
minster organ touched by spirits at midnight, — thrilled and
made a low chant within. Oh, when speech is given to a
soul holy and true as his, time, and its dome of ages, becomes as a mighty whispering gallery, round which the
imprisoned utterance runs and reverberates for ever! His
awful vows in the wilderness, the mournful breathings of
Olivet, the mellow voice that led the hymn at the Last Sup-
per, the faint cries of Calvary, the solemn assurance that
heaven and God dwell in us, — do they not ring and vibrate
in our hearts unto this day? It was not chiefly the force
of external miracle on the convictions, not the logical persuasion of his mere authority, not even the soundness and
reasonableness of his doctrine, that gave to his religion its
penetrative power; but the mind itself, of which his life and
discourse were but the symbol and expression; the clearness
and beauty with which he revealed that portion of the Deity
that may dwell in man, and by action as well as words
proved the reality of holiness, cast to the winds the doubts
that hung as foul mists around all that was divine, and
drew it forth from the world's background of night in
colors soft as the rainbow, yet intense as the sun. Had the
soul of Christ been different, in vain would all external endowments of verbal truth and physical omnipotence have
been accumulated on him. It was that spirit within, — the

impersonation of heavenly love and light, — that retained around him by unconscious attraction the little band of simple men, to whom it was " the Father's good pleasure to give " this " kingdom " — this transcendent dominion over the human heart. It was this that imparted to them their best inspiration, and made them missionaries and martyrs; that followed them like an unearthly vision through life, in persecution and peril giving them " that very hour what they ought to say; " in temptation and conflict coming as " an angel to strengthen " them; in prison and in bonds enabling them to say, " but none of these things move us." Here was one of God's great powers abroad among men, which it was impossible should die. True, the world's heart seemed old and withered : the more perhaps would the new element spread, like a fire bursting in the heart of a forest dry and dead. Soon, in the dark and unvisited recesses of many an ancient city, there lurked a living point of faith; perceptible at first only in the altered countenance of the Jew, whose lip no longer curled in scorn, and whose pride was turned to mercy; or in the opened brow of the slave, from whom abjectness seemed chased away; or in the murmurs of happy prayer, that strayed from some wretched cabin into the street, mingling there with the traffic, the revelry, the curse. This was the faith which was to tread the earth with royalty so great; precisely, be it observed, because it thus began its march, conquering each individual heart that came nearest to its reach, and leaving there a garrison of truth and love, before passing on to newer victories. Thus before the holiness of Christ, which was and is the supreme energy of the gospel, the craft of hierarchies, and the force of governments, and the inertia of a massive civilization, gave way. And while thousands of state-projects on the vastest scale have been conceived, executed, and forgotten; while on the field of history the repeated tramp of armies has been heard to approach, to pass by, to die away; while the noise of shifting nations, and the shriek of revolutions, have gone up from earth to heaven, and left silence once more behind, — this meek power triumphs over all; speaking with a persuasion which no vicissitudes of language can render obsolete, and throughout the ever-varying abodes of humanity singing its sweet songs to our heavy hearts.

The revival of Christianity from its corruptions illustrates the same truth ; that the greatest social changes begin in the creation of individual faith. I am aware that both the origin and the reformation of our religion are sometimes appealed to by sceptical and subversive minds, as justifying contentment with *their* method of procedure, which consists only in destroying something falsely esteemed venerable. No doubt, on a first view, both these revolutions seem to have overturned a great deal. But on nearer inspection this character will be found to have belonged to them as a mere accident, not as their essence ; as a symptom of something deeper, not as their ultimate spirit. Neither of them was a merely negative and disorganizing agency, simply annihilat-ing a sacred system of ideas : but each, on the contrary, was a positive and creative power, putting into the mind, not doubts, but faith ; not emptying and closing up the shrine of the secret heart, but consecrating and opening it afresh for worship. As new faiths however demand new forms, and a living religion cannot find a fitting church in the dead body of an old one, temples, rites, and priests, that once had greatness, ceased to be, replaced by other and sincerer ones. Thus, it is true, these revolutions over-whelmed ancient institutions, but only by creating new ideas : their internal spirit was organic ; their external effect, only, subversive. The Reformation can never be properly understood, so long as it is looked at either in the light of a change of doctrines, or a publication of the right of the intellect to free inquiry. It was, essentially, a substitution of individual faith for sacerdotal reliance, of personal religion for ecclesiastical obedience. The same spirit, in a less healthy form, reappeared, to reproduce the same phenomena, when Methodism arose, and diffused itself with gradual but triumphant power from the earnest souls of the Wesleys. In all these instances, the regenerative influence commences its action with the great mass of the people: for it is an apparent law of Providence, that while in society *knowledge descends, faiths ascend:* while science, doubt, opinion, all ideas of the understanding, gravitate from the few to the many; affections, convictions, truths of the conscience and the heart, rise from the many to the few.

Those who are unused to this mode of conceiving of human improvement, as spreading from secret centres to a wide circumference, and who are accustomed to the notion of civilization by external agencies, may perhaps adduce the printing-press as an instance of a vast engine of amelioration, mechanical rather than moral. It is obvious however that the press, with all its magic, is not a power in itself, but a mere instrument; — a *tool*, whose influence, in kind and degree, depends altogether on the spiritual forces that wield it; which might be given to the savage, without producing the smallest fruits of culture; and to a community of the vicious, without producing any culture that is good. It is simply an implement for the transmission of mental action; and it is the thought, not the machinery, that works the wonders of which we boast. Its function is, to bring into contact such minds as there are; and, as in private intercourse, it depends on the character of those minds, whether is circulated the vitality of health, or the contagion of disease. It is true indeed that, in the long run, the highest spirits are always the strongest too: but this is a law of nature, which human inventions did not make and cannot alter: and the press, giving equal voice to all, leaves the proportionate influence of different orders of minds precisely where it was; widening the empire, but not redisposing of the victory. And after all, it cannot serve as an equivalent to the living individual action of soul on soul. Who will compare a printed Testament with the voice and presence of an Apostle? The words may be the same, and what is called the meaning may be apprehended: but see how listlessly the poor laborer in his cottage turns over the dead page, missing the comment of imploring gesture, and kindling eye, and earnest tones, which doubtless pierced and fired the audience of Paul!

To individual faithfulness then, to the energy of the private conscience, has God committed the real history and progress of mankind. In the scenes wherein we daily move, from capacities common to us all, do drop the seeds from which, if ever, the Paradise of God must grow and blossom upon the earth. He that can be true to his best and secret nature, that can, by faith and patience, conquer the struggling world within, is most likely to send forth a blessed power to vanquish the world without. Mysteries of influence fall from every earnest volition, to return to us, in gladness or in weeping, after many days. No insult can we pass upon the divine but gentle dignity of duty, no quenching of God's spirit can we allow, that will not prepare a curse for others as well as for ourselves : nor any reverence, prompt and due, in act as in thought, can we pay to the God within, that will not yield abundant blessing. " See then that ye walk circumspectly, not as fools, but as wise."

XI.

THE CONTENTMENT OF SORROW.

ISAIAH LIII. 10.

YET IT PLEASED THE LORD TO BRUISE HIM; HE HATH PUT HIM TO GRIEF.

FROM age to age mankind have importunately sought for the reasons of sorrow; and from age to age have returned from the quest unsatisfied; for still is the question constantly renewed. How could it be otherwise? As sickness entered house after house, and waste made havoc on generation after generation, it was inevitable that our terrified hearts, ever clinging to that which must be wrenched away, and warmed by that which must be stricken by the frosts of death in our embrace, should cry, "Oh why these cruel messages of separation, these decrees of exile thrown amid groups of friends and kindred?" But the angel of destruction makes no reply: silently he executes his mission: only he relents not; and whether he be met by tears and prayers, or by frowns and the deplorable affectation of defiance, he does his sacred bidding, and passes on. It would seem that our passionate curiosity, which continues to urge its "*why?*" is never to be satisfied; but still to hand down its question as the eternal and unanswered cry of the human race. And however impatient some minds may feel at our helpless struggles with this difficulty, the thoughtful will acquiesce in them tranquilly. For they know that it is of such unsolved problems, of such mental strife with the mysterious, which uses up our knowledge, and lets us fall upon our conscious ignorance, that religion has its birth; and that the perpetual renewal of this great controversy maintains

the soul in that intermediate position between the known
and the incomprehensible, the finite and the infinite, which
excludes as well the dogmatism of certainty as the apathy of
nescience and chance, and calls up that wonder, reverence,
and trust, which are the fitting attributes of our nature.
There is a sense in which the maxim has a profound truth,
that " ignorance is the mother of devotion ; "— a sense however by no means justifying the continuance of any ignorance which can be removed, or can degrade one human
being below another ; but tending to reconcile us to such as
may be rendered inevitable by the limits assigned to our
faculties. If men knew every thing, they would venerate
nothing : reverence is not the affection with which objects
of knowledge, as such, are regarded ; and to place any object of thought under the eye of religious contemplation, it
must be stationed above the region of distinct perception, in
the shadows of that infinitude which sleeps so awfully
around the luminous boundaries of our knowledge. In this
position is the great question respecting the amount of evil
in human life ; near the highest summit of our knowledge,
and the deepest root of our religion.

To the demand of the human heart for less suffering and
a more liberal dispensation of happiness, no answer, *as from
God*, can be discovered in Scripture or in philosophy ; and
all attempts to assign *his* reasons for the present adjustments of the world in this respect have, I believe, signally
failed. But it is otherwise when we attempt an answer, *as
from ourselves ;* when, instead of taking for granted that
the demand is just, and waiting till it obtains its reply from
without, we look into the demand itself, and ask whether it
is wise and right ; whether it comes from a condition of
the understanding and the heart desirable and excellent,
or disordered and ignoble. Paradox as it may seem, it is,
I conceive, still true, that the state of mind which urges
the question is necessarily incapable of understanding the
answer.

At the foundation of all our difficulties and questionings respecting the evils of our lot, is a secretly-cherished notion, that we have *a right* to a more advantageous condition. We imagine ourselves in some way ill-treated, and think we might fairly have expected a happier life. We speak as beings who had formed anticipations more sanguine than have been realized. The feeling that asks for more happiness has evidently a private standard of its own, by which it tries the sufficiency of its own enjoyment; — an ideal measure which it applies in its judgment of the actual providence of God; and this is the rule by which alone the estimate of that providence is made. Now what is the origin of this criterion to which we submit the decision of the solemn question respecting the character of God? How do we make up our conceptions of the amount of happiness which we may fittingly expect? There is but one school in which all our expectations are trained, viz. experience ; but one source of belief respecting the future, viz. knowledge of the past ; that which actually *has been*, dictates all our ideas of what possibly *may be.* That image then of adequately happy life which we complain of not realizing, that picture which would perfect our content, is a repetition of what we have felt, a miniature of our habitual consciousness, painted in the colors of positive experience. Our present ideal is God's past reality ; nor could we ever have framed even the notion of such enjoyment, had not our own lot been one of peace : by blessing us, he gives us the power to entertain hard thoughts of him ; and we take occasion, from his claims upon our gratitude, to judge harshly of his government. Had he made us miserable (as we now count misery), inured us to severities so constant as even to shut out the conception of any thing better, we should have been ready with a song of thanksgiving for the mercies of a lot now raising only murmurs. Impious perversity, that thus renders to God evil for good, and, in answer to blessing, mutters forth a curse !

That the tacit claim which we make upon Providence has really its origin in a happy experience, is confirmed by a fact often noticed, that habitual sufferers are precisely those who least frequently doubt the divine benevolence, and whose faith and love rise to the serenest cheerfulness. Possessed by no idea of a prescriptive title to be happy, their blessings are not benumbed by anticipation, but come to them fresh and brilliant as the first day's morning and evening light to the dwellers in Paradise. Instead of the dulness of custom, they have the power of miracle. With the happy, it is their constant peace that seems to come by nature, and to be blunted by its commonness, — and their griefs to come from God, sharpened by their sacred origin : with the sufferer, it is his pain that appears to be a thing of course, and to require no explanation, while his relief is reverently welcomed as a divine interposition, and, as a breath of heaven, caresses the heart into melodies of praise. When the great Father, in his everlasting watch, paces his daily and nightly rounds, and through these lower mansions of his house gathers in the offered desires of his children, *where*, think you, does he hear the tones of deepest love, and see on the uplifted face the light of most heartfelt gratitude ? Not where his gifts are most profuse, but where they seem most meagre ; not where the suppliant's worship glides forth from the cushion of luxury, through lips satiated with plenty, and rounded by health ; not within the halls of successful ambition, or even the dwellings of unbroken domestic peace ; but where the outcast, flying from persecution, kneels in the evening upon the rock whereon he sleeps ; at the fresh grave, where, as the earth is opened, heaven in answer opens too ; by the pillow of the wasted sufferer, where the sunken eye, denied sleep, converses with a silent star, and the hollow voice enumerates in low prayer the scanty list of comforts, and shortened tale of hopes. Genial, almost to miracle, is the soil of sorrow ; wherein the smallest seed of love, timely falling, becometh a tree, in whose

foliage the birds of blessed song lodge and sing unceasingly. And the doubts of God's goodness, whence are
they? Rarely from the weary and overburdened, 'from
those broken in the practical service of grief and toil; but
from theoretic students at ease in their closets of meditation, treated themselves most gently by that legislation of
the universe which they criticise with a melancholy so
profound.

There are indeed those who discern nothing sanctifying
in sorrow; who say that they are best when they are happiest, — of prompter conscience, of nobler faith, of more
earnest aspirations; who seem sunk in apathy or stung into
irritability by affliction; and who pass through it, finding
therein no waters of life, but only a scorched desert, — where
the earth is as sand beneath, and the heavens as molten fire
above. Those whose sympathies thus dry up and wither in
grief, as if a hot wind had swept over them, are infected
with the fever of self. In the inner and subterranean chamber of their nature are no cool springs of affection, collected
from the treasured dews of heaven, but nether fires, glowing outwards to meet the heats that strike inwards from the
skies. They are given over to the insatiable idea of mere
happiness, in one form or other; and, this ungratified, find
refreshment in nothing more divine. Failing in the passive
half of life, they pride themselves on the energy with which,
in cheerful days, they execute their active duties. But it
is clear that these are not executed *as duties*, — as due, that
is, to the high and holy law by which God rules us with pure
affection. They have no deep root of love, but grow from
some shallower sentiment, — the sense of propriety, the
respect of opinion, the taste for order, the suggestions of
ambition : for were there the true affectionate heart of reverence, how could it thus stipulate in favor of its own self-
will; — how litigate with God for ampler wages; — how
refuse his willing service, unless the post of command and
action be given, and grow sullen to be appointed but a door-

keeper at the gate of his tent of dwelling, on the outside of its light and joy ?   Certain it is that no one possessed by this temper can be the true disciple of the man of sorrows, or look with the eye of Christ on nature and life.   No holy spirit fills and consecrates their scenes ; no silken cords of divine love weave together the whole tissue, dark or gay, of human existence, and make it all as a garment of God, more sacred than prophet's mantle.   What difference did it make to Christ, whether in the wilderness he did fierce battle with temptation ; or sat on the green slope to teach the people, and send them home as if God had dropped upon their hearts amid the shades of evening: whether he stood over the corpse, and looking on the dark eyes, said, " Let there be light," and the curtain of the shadow of death drew up ; or saw the angel of duty approach himself in the dress of the grave, and on the mournful whisper " Come away " tendered his hand and was meekly led: whether his walk was over strewn flowers, or beneath the cross too heavy to be borne ; — amid the cries of " Hosanna," or the murderous shout ?   The difference was all of pain ; — none was there of conscience, of trust, of power, of love.   Let there be a conscious affiliation with God ; and as he pervadeth all things, a unity is imparted to life, and a stability to the mind, which put not happiness indeed, but character and will, above the reach of circumstance: a current of pure and strong affections, fed by the fount of bliss, pours from hidden and sunlit heights, and winds through the open plains and dark ravines of life, till its murmurs fall into the everlasting deep.

Thus far our complaints against the evils of our lot would appear to indicate a wrong state of mind towards God. The disappointment in which they originate is the result of happy experience ; and had we never been blessed, we could never be querulous.   In the natural place of affectionate retrospect, we suffer the intrusion of murmurs ; and our quarrel with the present is a hostile substitute for gratitude towards the past. When the custom of God's mercies thus tempts us to forget that they are gratuities, and hardens us to make bold claims of prescriptive right; when we begin to reckon among his gifts only the extraordinary and un-expected benefits of our lot, and, measuring his goodness by the mere overflowings of the cup, become angry when happiness does not rise to the brim,—it is time for our pampered minds to learn, by discipline of grief, a less way-ward temper: the canker of too long a comfort is eating out the whole religion of our hearts. We are dressing up our life, as if it were the eternal palace of a god, instead of the brief halt and hospice of the pilgrim: and there were mercy in the stroke that should lay it in ruins, and send our unsheltered head into the storm, to seek our rest in a meeker and more suppliant spirit. It is no mere superstition that leads us sometimes to say, of a prosperity and outward peace, that it is "too great to last;" not indeed that any blessing is too great for God to give, but only too great for us to receive. Freely might he continue it, but innocently we should scarce enjoy it, in perpetuity; and it is the intuitive perception of this, the secret consciousness that the upward gush of gratitude is growing feebler, — that the incrustations of ease are creeping over the wells of spiritual life, — that causes us, amid our comforts, to tremble as in a day of wrath, and occasionally sheds over the brilliant colors of enjoyment a slight and mysterious tinge as from the shadow of guilt. 'Tis awful and prophetic as the handwriting on the wall; becoming a splendor, as of the heavens, to those who revere it, and a blackness, as of doom, to those that neglect it. Blessed are they that, turning an eye within, can discern and interpret it betimes!

And if our complaints of trial and suffering result from a wrong state of mind in relation to God, they no less imply mistake in relation to ourselves and erroneous ideas of our own welfare. At least our griefs of bereavement (which are the severest of all), our expostulations with death, treat

as utterly gone treasures whose best portion is with us still;
even proved to be present by the very tears that weep their
absence. For wherein consists the value of parent, child,
or friend ? Is it in the use we may make of him, or in the
love we feel for him ? Is it in his form, his voice, his features, — or in the dear memories and delightful affections
which these awaken in our minds ? As a foreign land differs
from our own, not in its soil, but in its recollections; as
another house differs from our own, not by its materials,
but by the spirit of its associated feelings, not as a substance,
but as a sign, — so does a friend differ from a stranger, not
in his person, but in his power over our hearts. He is
nothing to us, but for the impression he leaves upon our
souls, to present which is the mission whereto God has sent
him, and the office for which we love him. Of all the ingredients that enter into that infinitely complex thing, a
human life, of all the influences that radiate from it, and
proclaim it *there*, none surely are so essential as the affections
it kindles in others; and if beings around entertain of it a
blessed and noble conception, are filled by it with generous
aspirations, and feel the thought of it to be as a fire from
heaven, *in this* is its true and best existence; in this consists
its real identity, distinguishing it by strongest marks from
other minds. And all this does death leave behind, as our
indestructible possession : from our mere eyes he takes the
visible form of the objects of our love; for this is only borrowed : from our souls he cannot take the love itself to
which that is subservient; for it is given us for ever. The
very grief that wastes us testifies that, in his true worth,
the companion we lament as lost is with us still; for is it
not the idea of him that weeps in us, his image that supplies
the tears? His best offices he will continue to us yet, if
we are true to him; with serenest look, as through the
windows of the soul, rebuking our disquiet, bracing our
faith, quickening our conscience, and cooling the fever-heats
of life. Doubtless the thought of him is transmuted from

gladness into sorrow. But will any true heart say that an affection is an evil because it is sad, and wish to shake it off, the moment it brings pain? Call it what you will, *that* is not love which itself is anxious to grow cold: the emotions of a faithful soul never entertain a suicidal purpose, and plan their own extinction: rather do they reproach their own insensibility, and passionately pray for a greater vitality. Whether then in anxiety or in peace, in joy or in regrets, let the spirit of affection stay; and if the spirit stay, the objects, though vanished, leave their best presence with us still. No; that only is truly lost which we have ceased to love: if there be a friend whom in our childhood or our youth we venerated for the wisdom of virtue and beauty of holiness, and whom now we regard with the aversion of corrupted tastes, or the coldness of callous hearts, *he* indeed is lost: if there be a companion whose hand was once locked in ours with the vows, seemingly so firm, of our enthusiastic years, and on whom now we look with a mind frozen by the worldliness or poisoned by the jealousies and rivalries of life, such a one is surely lost: but not the departed who left our world with benediction, and fell close-locked in our embrace: such a one, though dead, yet speaketh; the others, though living, are silent to our hearts. Of the alienated the loss is absolute, an extinction of a part of our nature. But the sainted dead shall finish for us the blessed work which they began. They tarried with us, and nurtured a human love; they depart from us, and kindle a divine. Cease then, our complaining hearts, and wait in patience the great gathering of souls!

XII.

IMMORTALITY.

2 CORINTHIANS I. 9.

WE HAD THE SENTENCE OF DEATH IN OURSELVES, THAT WE SHOULD NOT
TRUST IN OURSELVES, BUT IN GOD WHO RAISETH THE DEAD.

PAUL, at his nearest view of death, obtained his firmest
"trust in God who raiseth the dead." Socrates, with the
cup of poison in his hand, declares it powerless : and, taking
it as the pledge of temporary parting from his weeping
friends, goes cheerfully forward to explore the future. We,
who are in no such extremity, but at ease and in command
of the strong posts of life, are seduced into sceptic misgivings of its perpetuity, and are conscious of at least transient
doubts, whether soul and body do not go out together.
And so indeed it ever is. Amid the so-called goods of
existence, we most shudder at the view of its privations;
while from active contact with its griefs, its grandeur
appears least doubtful, and, in the bold struggle with ills,
they prove a phantom and slip away. From the sunlit
heights of life, the deep vales and hollows of its necessities
look darkest : but to the faithful whose path lies there, there
is still light enough to show the way, and to no other eyes
do the everlasting hills and blue heavens seem so brilliant.
Our nobler faith is not dashed, as we suppose, by the severities, but rather enervated by the indulgences, of experience :
it is on the bed of luxury, not on the rock of nature, that
scepticism has its birth. Paul, the hardly-entreated apostle,
the homeless and ever-perilled missionary, — his back scarred
with stripes, his hands heavy with bonds, the outcast of

Jewish hate and Pagan scorn, — writes as he flies, to ask
the voluptuous Corinthians, "How say some among you
that there is no resurrection of the dead?" and to prove in
words that immortality of which his life was the demonstration in action. And while from the centre of comforts
many a sad fear goes forth, and the warmest lot becomes
often filled with the chillest doubts, hidden within it like a
heart of ice that cannot melt, you may find toiling misery
that trusts the more, the more it is stricken, and amid the
secret prayers of mourners hear the sweetest tones of hope.

This paradox is far from being inexplicable. All true
religion is a sense of want; and where wants go to sleep
upon possession, it becomes bewildered, and, when occasionally opening its eyes, sees nothing with the clearness
of reality. Religion implies a perception of the infinite and
invisible; and where the finite is illuminated too strongly,
nothing else can be discerned, and all beyond appears, not
dim twilight shadow, but blank darkness. The full-orbed
brilliancy of life brings out the colors of the earth, and
makes it seem as vast and solid as if there were nothing else :
in the midnight watch, it is felt only at the point beneath
our feet, and the sphere of stars in which it swims alone is
seen. Indeed the suspicion that this life is our all, appears
to be simply an example, upon a large scale, of a delusion
and disproportion of idea which we are continually experiencing in detail, and without which perhaps our discerning and our practical energies would be ill-harmonized. I
allude to that exaggeration of the present moment, that concentration of anxiety and effort on the present object, which
makes the point of pending action every thing, and for a time
kills the reality of all beside. Desire, else broken by dis-
persion, singles out project after project in succession, on
which to gather all its intensity : each in turn becomes the
vivid and sole point of life: as the eye applied to the
microscope may see the centre of the field without notice
of the margin of the very object beneath its view. This

optical exclusiveness of mind, this successive insulation of
effort, is the needful condition on which the will performs
its work with gladness: for who would not sink and faint
upon the dust, if the whole task of existence were spread
before him at once? Let us then in *practice*, as the *laborers*
of God, bless him for our blindness; but in *meditation*, as
the *believers* of God and explorers of his providence, not
on that account deny that there is light. Our delusion,
operating in detail, is corrected by experience, which shifts
us ever to a new point of view : and how often do we smile
in retrospect at the passionate self-precipitation, the silent
tension or stormy force of desire, with which we bent
towards some aim, that seemed for the instant the very goal
of life : the eagle-eyed precision with which we fell, as on a
prey, upon something that now seems one of the most trivial
creatures that stirs the grass ! Our eyes once opened thus,
we say that it "was a dream." And most truly : for those
who are awake always discover that they *have been dreaming ;*
but those who dream never suspect that they *shall wake.*
For the time, the images of sleep are the intensest of realities; they are the sleeper's universe; they agitate him with
hope and terror, with love and grief, with admiration and
transport, as genuine as human heart can feel; while they
continue to flit around him, they shut in and limit his belief,
and totally exclude the conceptions suitable to the world on
which he lies. And so is it with the long trance of human
life; we are ever dreaming to the present, and waking to
the past; clearly estimating each illusion when it is gone,
but too vividly occupied with new ones to expect any morning summons to a correcting world beyond. Not till we
are startled by that call, and stand outside our existing
sphere of thought, can we discover how much of phantasm
there is in life as a whole; but the wise will assuredly distrust their feeling of its exclusive reality; will know that
if it were a mere scenic image, a painted vacancy, environed
by immense and solemn realities, this same feeling would

have been no less strong; and they will rouse themselves
so far as at least to " dream that they dream."

The feeling of impossibility which, I believe, haunts many
persons in adverting to the immortality of the soul, the vague
apprehension of some insuperable obstacle to the realization
of any thing so great, appears to arise from mere indolence
of conception ; and vanishes in proportion as the affections
are deeply moved, and the intuitions of reason are trusted
rather than the importunities of sense. There is certainly
nothing in our idea of the mind, as there *is* in that of organization, contradictory of the belief of its perpetuity ; — nothing which involves the notion of dissolution, or of limited
duration. All the properties of the thinking principle, remembrance, imagination, love, conscience, volition, are irre-
spective of time; are characterized by nothing seasonal; are
incapable of disease, fracture, or decay. They have nothing
in their nature to prescribe their existence for an hour, a
century, a thousand years, or in any way to bring them to
termination. Were it the will of the Creator to change his
arrangements for mankind, and to determine that they should
henceforth live in this world ten or a hundred times as long
as they do at present, no one would feel that *new souls* would
be required for the execution of the design. And in the
mere conception of unlimited existence there is nothing
more amazing than in that of unlimited non-existence; there
is no more mystery in the mind living for ever in the future,
than in its having been kept out of life through an eternity
in the past. The former is a negative, the latter a positive
infinitude. And the real, the authentic wonder, is the actual
fact of the transition having been made from the one to the
other ; and it is far more incredible that from not having
been, *we are*, than that from actual being, we shall *continue
to be.*

And if there be no speculative impossibility in the immortality of the soul, it cannot be rendered inconceivable
by any physical considerations connected with death. We

are apt, indeed, to be misled by the appearances of the last hour; appearances so appalling, so humbling, so associated with the memories of happy affection and the approach of bleakest solitude, .that it would be surprising if we did not interpret them amiss, and see them falsely through our tears. As we turn away from that last agony, we are tempted to say in our despair, — there, there, is the visible return of all to darkness; the proof that all is gone; the fall of the lamp into the death-stream. Yet it is clear that neither the phenomena of death, nor any other sensible impression, can afford the least substantive evidence that the mind has ceased to be. Non-existence is a negation, which neither sight can see, nor ear can hear: and the fading eye, the motionless lips, the chill hand, establish nothing, and simply give us *no report:* refusing us the familiar expression of the soul within, they leave the great question open, to be determined by any positive probabilities which may be sought in other directions. In life, we never saw or heard the principle of thought and will and love, but only its corporeal effects in lineament and speech. If the bare absence of these signs were sufficient to prove the extinction of the spirit which they obey, the spectacle of sleep would justify us in pronouncing the mind dead; and if neither slumber nor silence have been found to afford reason for the denial of simultaneous thought, death affords no better ground for the dreary inference. It is to no purpose to say, that we have not experience of the separability of consciousness from bodily life; for originally there was no experience of the separability of consciousness from bodily waking; and with the same reason which would lead us to mourn the extinction of a friend's spirit in death, might Adam have bewailed the annihilation of Eve in the first sleep of Eden. Nay, if we are not to conceive of the existence of a friend, where there is no physical manifestation, it will follow that till there was a visible creation, there was no Infinite Spirit: and that if ever the Creator shall

cast aside the mantle of his works, if the order, the beauty,
the magnificence, of the universe, through which he appears
to us and hides his essence behind the symbol of his infinitude, are ever to have their period and vanish, if ancient
prediction shall be fulfilled, and "the heavens pass away
with a noise, and the elements melt with fervent heat," that
hour will be, by the same rule which declares human annihilation, not only the end of all things, but the death of God.

Indeed there is that in the very nature of the immaterial
mind, which appears to me to exempt it from the operation
of all material evidence of its destruction. It is impossible
to form a steady conception of *thought*, except as originating *behind* even the innermost bodily structures, and
intrinsically different from them. However much you refine
and attenuate the living organism, yet, after all, thought is
something quite unlike the whitest and the thinnest tissue ;
and the most delicate of fibres, woven if you please in fairy
loom, can never be spun into emotions. Nor is it at all easier
to imagine ideas and feelings to be the *results* of organization, and to constitute one of the physical *relations* of
atoms; and if any one affirms that the juxtaposition of
a number of particles makes a hope, and that an aggrega-
tion of curious textures forms veneration, he affirms a propo-
sition to which I can attach no idea. Agitate and affect
these structures as you will, pass them through every imaginable change, let them vibrate and glow, and take a
thousand hues ; still you can get nothing but motion, and
temperature, and color ; fit marks and curious signals of
thought behind themselves, but no more to be confounded
with it, than are written characters to be mistaken for the
genius and knowledge which may record themselves in language. The corporeal frame then is but the mechanism for
making thoughts and affections *apparent*, the signal-house
with which God has covered us, the electric telegraph by
which quickest intimation flies abroad of the spiritual force
within us. The instrument may be broken, the dial-plate ef-

faced : and though the hidden artist can make no more signs, he may be rich as ever in the things to be signified. Fever may fire the pulses of the body: but wisdom and sanctity cannot sicken, be inflamed and die. Neither consumption can waste, nor fracture mutilate, nor gunpowder scatter away, thought, and fidelity, and love, but only that organization which the spirit sequestered therein renders so fair and noble. To suppose such a thing would be to invert the order of rank which God has visibly established among the forces of our world, and to give a downright ascendancy to the brute energies of matter above the vitality of the mind, which, up to that point, discovers, subdues and rules them ; to proclaim the triumph of the sword, the casualty, the pestilence, over virtue, truth and faith ; to set the cross above the crucified ; to surrender the holy things of this world to corruption, and shroud its heaven with darkness, and turn its moon into blood. Think only of this earth as it floats beneath the eye of God, — a speck in the blue infinite, — a precious life-balloon freighted with the family of spirits he has willed to come up and travel in this portion of his universe. Remember that at this very moment, and at each tick of the clock, some fifty souls have departed hence, gone with their tempestuous passions, their strife, their truth, their hopes, into space and silence : not either with the appearance of forces spent and finished ; for there are children fallen away, with expectant look on life, nothing doubting the secure embrace that seemed to fold them round; there is youth, raised up to self-subsistence, not without difficulty and sorrow, with the clear deep light of thought and wonder shining from within, quenched in sudden night; there is many an heroic life, built on no delusion of sense and selfishness, but firm on the adamant of faith, and defying the seductions of falsehood and the threats of fear, — sunk from us absolutely away, and giving no answer to our recalling entreaties and our tears. And will you tell me that all this treasure, which is nothing less than infinite, is

8

cancelled and puffed away, like a worthless bubble, into emptiness? Does God stand ahead of this mighty car of being, as it traverses the skies, only to throw out the boundless wealth of lives it bears, and hurl them headlong into the abyss midway on their voyage through eternity? Put the question in conjunction with any overwhelming calamity, which perceptibly plunges into sudden silence a multitude of souls; like the dreadful destruction just announced from the Western world, of a ship* freighted with priceless lives, with the wealth of homes, the hopes of the oppressed, the lights of nations. Let any one think over the contents of that fated ship, when it quitted the port at even, amid the cheerful parting of friends, and consider well *where they were* when the morning broke. There were travellers from foreign lands, ready with pleased heart to tell at home the thousand marvels they had gathered on their way. There was a family of mourners, taking to their household graves their unburied dead. And there was *one* at least of rare truth and wisdom, of design than which philanthropy knows nothing greater; of faith that all must venerate, and love that all must trust; of persuasive lips, from which a thoughtful genius and the simplest heart poured forth the true music of humanity. And does any one believe that this freight of transcendent worth,—all this sorrow, and thought, and hope, and moral greatness, and pure affection, were *burnt,* and went out with flame and cotton-smoke? Sooner would I believe that the fire consumed the less everlasting stars! Such a galaxy of spiritual light and order and beauty is spread above the elements and their power, and neither heat can scorch it, nor cold water drown. The plaintive wind that swept in the morning over the black and heaving wreck would moan in the

---

* The steamboat *Lexington,* which left New York for Boston, 18th January, 1840, and was burned that night in Long Island Sound, with the loss of all on board except four. Dr. Follen was among the number that perished. The present discourse was suggested by that event.

ear of sympathy with the wail of a thousand survivors; but to the ear of wisdom and of faith, would sound as the returning whisper and requiem of hope.

There appears to be a caprice in the dispensation of death, quite at variance with the scrupulous regularity and economy of nature in less momentous affairs; and strongly indicative of a hidden sequel. The inferior departments of creation are marked by a frugality and seasonal order, that seems to gather up the very fragments of good, that nothing be lost. Scarcely does a moment elapse before the cast-off structure of plant or animal is put in requisition for some new purpose. Such value seems to be attached to the tree, that its seed is encased and protected with the nicest care, can retain its principle of vitality for thousands of years, and hold itself ready to germinate whenever the suitable conditions shall be presented. The wild animals have a certain term of life allotted to each species, which probably few individuals much exceed or fail to reach. Everything else seems to have its well-defined circuit and range of functions, its season of maturity and period of fall. But when we rise into the only community dignified by minds, all looks in comparison like confusion and fortuity. Infancy and age, strength and imbecility, the pure and the corrupt of heart, the full and empty souled, drop indiscriminately away; as if the spirits of men were the cruel sport of some high and invisible demon-game, — kindled and extinguished in remorseless and capricious jest. And if such a supposition is excluded by the harmony and exactitude which prevail in the other regions of creation, nothing is left but to believe that we see here only the partial operation of a higher law; that we witness no extinction, but simply migrations of the mind; which survives to fulfil its high offices elsewhere, and find perhaps in seeming death its true nativity.

Then, too, let us consider in what light we should see the character of God, if the fall of the body is really the fall of the soul; remembering that he has put into the hearts of

most men, by intuition or providential suggestion, a divine
hope of something future. Turn once more to the thought
of that burning ship, and think of the memorial sounds that
went up thence in the night to God. When the stars came
out the first shriek ascended; two hours past midnight the
last was drowned. And in the interval did a hundred and
seventy mortals shiver and cry to him from frost and flame,
with faith and prayers of various and unspeakable contents,
— the cold heavens looking serenely down, and gliding on
as if they enclosed nothing but peace. And what was the
answer of the hearer of prayer to that agony of despair?
Did he say, as no man or angel would have done, "Down,
begone for ever into darkness!" And did he so answer,
with the full knowledge of his omniscience, that many a
survivor would return this awful frown with the sweetest
and most unconscious smile of resignation, hiding her mourning head with him as in the bosom of a Father? Or, put
yourselves back into the presence of an earlier and sublimer
tragedy; remember the scene on Calvary, with the words
of assured hope and meek supplication that passed there from
holiest lips to God. When his own Christ gave the tranquil
assurance, "This day shalt thou be with me in Paradise,"
did He who inspired that promise, and alone could fulfil,
overhear it with secret rejection and denial? When the
fainting utterance exclaimed with most loving meaning, "It
is finished," did the ever-present Father put on that cry a
dreadful interpretation, "and make an end" of all things
to him — that Son of God? And when he breathed forth
those last words, "Father, into thy hands I commit my
spirit," did the All-merciful refuse the trust, and reply to
that pure faith, "Take away thy cry, for mine eye shall not
spare, neither will I hear with mine ear"? Did he do thus
to the Galilean, knowing that, night and morning, friends
and followers and disciples for ages would converse with
him about this departed one, with a trustful hope which he
had thus turned into a lie? Were this possible, God were

no "Father of Spirits," to waste and mock them thus; and
might no less fitly be termed the Destroyer than the Creator;
and every good man might feel an infinite pity for his kind,
diviner far than the very providence of heaven.

Thus, if the celestial hope be a delusion, we plainly see
who are the mistaken. Not the mean and grovelling souls,
who never reached to so great a thought; not the drowsy
and easy natures, who are content with the sleep of sense
through life, and the sleep of darkness ever after; not the
selfish and pinched of conscience, of small thought and
smaller love ; no, these in such case are right, and the universe *is* on their miserable scale. The deceived are the
great and holy, whom all men, aye, these very insignificants
themselves, revere ; the men who have lived for something
better than their happiness, and spent themselves in the race,
or fallen at the altar of human good ;—Paul, with his mighty
and conquering courage; yes, Christ himself, who vainly
sobbed his spirit to rest on his Father's imaginary love, and
without result commended his soul to the Being whom he
fancied himself to reveal. The self-sacrifice of Calvary was
but a, tragic and barren mistake; for Heaven disowns the
godlike prophet of Nazareth, and takes part with those who
scoffed at him and would have him die ; and is insensible
to the divine fitness which even men have felt, when they
either recorded the supposed fact, or invented the beautiful
fiction, of Christ's ascension. Whom are we to revere, and
what can we believe, if the inspirations of the highest of
created natures are but cunningly-devised fables ?

But it is not so : and no one who has found true guidance
of heart from these noblest sons of Heaven, will fear to stake
his futurity, and the immortal life of his departed friends,
on their vaticinations. *These*, of all things granted to our
ignorance, are assuredly most like the hidden realities of
God ; which may be greater, but will not be less, than
prophets and·seers have foretold, and even our own souls,
when gifted with highest and clearest vision, discern as truths

not doubtful or far off.   In this hope let us trust, and be true
to the toils of life which it ennobles and cheers.   Whoever
"fights the good fight" shall surely "keep the faith:" for
God reveals the secret of his future will to those who worthily
do it in the present.   This is our proper care.   Putting ourselves into his hands, and living in submissive harmony with
his everlasting laws, let us "finish our course;" and leave it
to him to take us, when he will, where our forerunners are,
and the unfoldings of his ways are seen with open eye.

XIII.

THE COMMUNION OF SAINTS.

EPHESIANS II. 19.

FELLOW-CITIZENS WITH THE SAINTS, AND OF THE HOUSEHOLD OF GOD.

SOCIETY becomes possible only through religion. Men might be gregarious without it, but not social. Instinct, which unites them in detail, prevents their wider combination. Intellect affords light to show the elements of union, but no heat to give them crystalline form. Self-will is prevailingly a repulsive power, and often disintegrates the most solid of human masses. Even the moral sentiment, so far as it recognizes man as supreme, and simply tries to make a prudent adjustment of his vehement forces, can produce among a multitude only an unstable equilibrium, liable every moment to be subverted by the ever-shifting gravitation of the passions. Some sense of a divine presence, some consciousness of a higher law, some pressure of a solemn necessity, will be found to have preceded the organization of every human community, and to have gone out and perished before its death. There is great significance in the tradition which, in every people of apparently aboriginal civilization, attributes an *inspired* character to their first lawgiver, and pronounces their subjection to moral order a task which only the force of Heaven could achieve. They only whose voice could reach the sleeping tones of worship in the hearts of men, and awaken some deep faith and allegiance, could so deal with their wild nature, as to chain the savage passions and set free the nobler will. And although, in old societies, the innumerable fibres of government, of

usage, of established ideas, supply a thousand secondary
bonds, which *seem* to make the mighty growth secure as the
forest oak, yet all this system of roots has, I believe, its
secret nutriment from the devout elements of a nation's
mind : and if these should dry up in any Arctic chill of
doubt, or be poisoned by any Epicurean rot of indulgence,
it would silently decay within the soil, and leave the fairest
tree of history, first with a sickening foliage, and soon with
a perished life. The most compact and gigantic machinery
of society, — as experience shows, — falls to pieces, wherever religious and moral scepticism, by paralyzing faith and
heroism and hope, has cut off the supply of spiritual power.
Rome, at the commencement of our era, had reached the
utmost point of material force and visible magnificence : her
organization held with an iron grasp the continents of
Europe and the East ; her military chain spread with unbroken links from Lebanon to Gaul, and from the Caspian
to the Æthiopic Nile ; her wealth and arts had called into
being ten thousand cities, — no mean imitations of her own
greatness ; her institutions had diffused a universal repose,
and the functions of government were exercised with a
rapidity and precision never surpassed. What brought a
power thus mighty, — a power that called itself " eternal,"
— to its dissolution ? Shall we be content with a figure of
speech, and say that it broke asunder from its excessive
mass ? Apart from spiritual decline and causes of moral
disunion, I know of nothing to prevent a uniform civilization
from reaching the most enormous bulk. Shall we refer
rather to external dangers ; and calling to mind the tempest
of barbarians that " roared around the gates of the empire,"
say that it perished like a mammoth, in a drift of northern
snows ? Yet with far less imposing resources, she had
stood up and lived through fiercer storms. No ; the stroke
was not of war, but of paralysis. The heart of religion had
ceased to beat : the high faith, the stern disinterestedness,
the sacred honor of the republic, had faded into tradition :

the sanctities of life were disbelieved even in the nursery:
no binding sentiment restrained the greediness of appetite
and the licentiousness of self-will : the very passions with
whose submission alone society can begin, broke loose again,—
attended by a brood of artificial and parasitic vices that spread
the dissolute confusion.   Yet it was not that the conditions
of social union had become impossible.   For observe ; in
the midst of this corruption, in the invisible recesses of
profligate cities, a small point of fresh young life is already
to be discerned, like the bud of some fair growth thrusting
up its head among the putrefying leaves.   A few poor
slaves and outcast Hebrews have heard the divinest whisper
borne to them from Palestine ; have discovered by it that inner region of love and hope and trust, in which all fraternity
of heart begins ; and are banded together with a spirit that
soon speaks out and prophesies in martyrdom.   While
Rome displayed its greatness even in death, and struggled
with the convulsions of a giant, the infant faith remained
unharmed ; healing as it could the wounds which the mad
world suffered ; and like a fair immortal child, winning a
blessed way by entrancing the souls of men with the forgotten vision of a divine simplicity and truth.   Christianity has
ever since been the bond of European civilization : and should
its spirit ever perish hence, this glorious family of nations
will be dissolved.

Let us look, with more detail, into some of the natural
groups which a genuine faith can form ; and we shall find
nothing incredible in its strong combining power.

Worship exhibits its uniting principle under the simplest
form, in the sympathies it diffuses among the members of
the same religious assembly.

It is universally felt that devotion must sometimes quit
the solitude of the cell, forget its mere individual wants, and
speak as from humanity's great heart to God.   The scruples
of the few who have objected to social piety have met with
no response ; they are justly regarded as the eccentricities

of a stiff and petty rationalism, that will not stir without a literal precept, and trusts any logical finger-post (possibly set the wrong way by the humor of some sophistry), rather than the cardinal guidance of those high affections which are in truth the imperishable lights of heaven. To this house we come, my friends, drawn not by arbitrary command which we fear to disobey; not by self-interest, temporal or spiritual, which we deem it prudent to consult; not, I trust, from dead conventionalism, that brings the body and leaves the soul; but by a common quest of some holy spirit to penetrate and purify our life; by a common desire to quit its hot and level dust, and from its upland slopes of contemplation inhale the serenity of God; by the secret sadness of sin, that can delay its confessions and bear its earthliness no more; by the deep though dim consciousness, that the passing weeks do not leave us where they find us, but plant us within nearer distance, and give us a more intimate view, of that fathomless eternity, wherein so many dear and mortal things have dropped from our imploring eyes. It is no wonder that in meditations solemn as these we love and seek each other's sympathy. It is easy, no doubt, to journey alone in the broad sunshine and on the beaten highways of our lot: but over the midnight plain, and beneath the still immensity of darkness, the traveller seeks some fellowship for his wanderings. And what is religion but the midnight hemisphere of life, whose vault is filled with the silence of God, and whose everlasting stars, if giving no clear light, yet fill the soul with dreams of immeasurable glory? It will be an awful thing to each of us to be alone, when he takes the passage from the mortal to the immortal, and is borne along, — with unknown time for expectant thought, — through the space that severs earth from heaven: and till then, at least, we will not part, but speak with the common voice of supplicating trust of that which awaits us all.

There is however no necessary fellowship, as of saints, in the mere assembling of ourselves together; but only in the true and simple spirit of worship. All these occasions of devotion assume that we have already some affections to express; that we have discernment of the divine relations of our existence; that we have souls seeking to cry out in prayer, and waiting to lie down before God in tears. The services of this place are quite mistaken by those who look on them as the means of obtaining a religion non-existent yet; who see in them only the instruments of self-discipline; who perform here no personal act of the mind, but passively wait such operation as may befall them; or who assume, in their mental offerings, not the desires and emotions which they really experience, but those instead which they only ought to feel and hope to realize at last by persevering false profession. The lips are to follow the heart and cannot lead it: and we are here, not to make use of God for the sake of our devotion, but to pour forth devotion for the sake of God. Were every one in a Christian assembly to be all the while intent on his own improvement, to be subordinating every thing to his own case, and with morbid scrupulosity to be prescribing throughout for his own temper, there would be simply no proper *worship* at all : there would be not the least union of hearts : each would sit insulated with his own separate self, and would be more naturally placed in a solitary cell, than amid an unsocial multitude : there would be none of that sublime ascent of soul, that common flight of love, in which all individuality is lost, all personal regards absorbed, and the vision of Heaven and God melts the many minds and many voices of the church in one. Oh how, within that Presence whose intimacy enfolds us here, can we ever stay outside the spirit of worship, and perform mere conscientious gestures of the mind, and act a .part even with ourselves alone as its spectator? Will nothing short of the death-plunge into eternity steep us in its mystery, and strip off the spirit-wrappings that cover us from the communion of God? We stand *here*, as in heaven's last resort for penetrating to the earnest centre of our nature : and if the fountain of the secret life is still encased and does not flow, no common shock can break the icy crust that binds it. Think only, in simplest and briefest review, of the considerations that pass before us at our meeting here. At this hour of prayer, when we stand within the reality of God, and face to face behold his awfulness, and tell how we are glad at all his graciousness; when we hear the sweet voice of Christ,—mellowed and deepened as it floats over eighteen centuries of meaning,—saying to us, as we bend beneath the weight of life, "Come unto me, ye heavy-laden;" when we own the shameful conquests of temptation, and repent of the abandoned strife, and rebuild the fallen purpose; when there is set before us the divine dignity of existence, and the majesty of our free-will, and the high trust of duty, and the tranquil power of faith; when we speak together of our dead, and memory beholds their solemn forms so silent in the shadows of the past; when we remember how, even while we think it, some souls are surely passing away, and soon we too shall lay the burthen down and go; when, as from the brink of being, we look into futurity, and the true voice of judgment falls upon the ear, startling as the trump of conscience or healing as the symphonies of the blest; when all periods of life assemble before the Everlasting that hath no age, and the light look of the child, and the steady features of manhood, and the shaken head of age, denote their several wants and prayers; when the tempted comes to seek new strength, and the mourner sees his sorrows from a higher point, and the anxious is beguiled into a loving reliance, and the contrite weeps his sin and distrusts his tears;—at such an hour, if the disguises fall not from our hearts, and leave us a disembodied fraternity of souls sending the chorus of common want to Heaven, then indeed are we slaves to the earthly life, without that enfranchisement of spirit, that makes possible a "fellowship of saints," and exalts us to " the household of God."

Where however a pure devotion really exists, the fellowship it produces spreads far beyond the separate circle of each Christian assembly. A single company of pious men, gathered together from among a race that could not worship, would indeed draw close their mutual sympathies at the expense of alienation from their kind. But it is not so. We are brought to stand side by side within this place by no exclusive propensity, no whimsical peculiarity of the few : the impulse is of nature, not of fancy ; and we know this at the moment we obey it. We meet, with the remembrance that we are in the midst of brethren who meet too : and every religious society, though physically shut in by its sanctuary walls, kneels in secret consciousness of the presence of kindred fraternities without number, subdued by the same sanctities, and pressing to the same end, not by human agreement, but a divine consent. As every individual in a place of prayer, overhearing the like spontaneous tones from many souls around him, cannot but deepen the fervor of his own ; so each assembly, feeling that its neighborhood is studded over with similar groups prostrate in adoration like itself, sends to Heaven a more genial and humaner cry ; and every neighborhood, mustering to prayer, thinks of the busy peals from clustered churches that cross and crowd one another in each distant town, or the single quiet chime in every village of the land, and finds in the thought a gladder and a kindlier praise ; and every land, aware that it is but one of a company of nations, federally bound of God by irrepressible aspirings to himself, chants its mighty note with deeper meaning, as part of a universal symphony heard in its unity in Heaven alone. Surely it is a glorious thing to call up, while we worship here, the wide image of Christendom this day. Turn your thoughts away from the noisy discord of sects ; believe nothing of their mutual slanders ; forgive the occasional weakness of superstition ; and be not angry with the narrow vision of earnest conviction that can see nothing but its own truth : and far beneath the superficial divisions created by the intellect,

see in the Sabbath spectacle of the world evidence of a
deep and wide-spread union of hearts. Could we be lifted
up above this sphere, and look down as it rolls beneath this
day's sun, and catch its murmurs as they rise, should we not
behold land after land turned into a Christian shrine? The
dawn, that summons mortals from their sleep, bears them
to-day a new and sacred message; the sunbeam touches the
gates of ten thousand temples, and they burst open to
receive the record of countless aspirations; the morning
shoots across the desert atmosphere of a weary world,
strikes on the stony form of giant humanity, and brings out
tones of celestial music. In how many tongues, by what
various voices, with what measureless intensity of love, is
the name of Christ breathed forth to-day! What cries of
penitence, what accents of trust, what plaints of earnest
desire, pass away to God! What an awful array of faces
that gaze forth into immortality with various looks of terror
or of love! The vows and prayers whose millions crowd
the gates of mercy no recording angel could tell, but only
the infinite memory of God. Of how glorious a church,
then, are we members when we kneel within this place! in
how solemn an act do we take our part! with how sublime
a brotherhood do we own our fellowship!

But our worship here brings us into yet nobler connections. It unites us by a chain of closest sympathy
with past generations. In our helps to faith and devotion
in this place, we avail ourselves of the thought and piety
of many extinct ages. We reverently read those ancient
scriptures, which have gathered around them the trust, and
procured the heart-felt repose, of so many tribes and periods, since prophets and apostles first gave them forth. We
sing the hymns which a goodly company of pious men have
left as the record of their communion with Heaven. And
it is impossible to look at the consecrated names of those
"sweet singers" of Christendom, without feeling ennobled
by their communion, and even astonished at our sympathy

with them. Do not we, the living, take up, in adoration
and prayer, the thoughts of the dead, and feel them divinely
true? Do they not come forth, as if fresh coined from our
own hearts? Indeed, could we ourselves so faithfully utter
the consciousness of our inner being, or shape so interpreting a voice for our secret life? What an impressive testimony this to the sameness of our nature through every age,
and the immortal perseverance of its holier affections! The
language of *their* confessions, their struggles, their desires,
speaks our own : the light that gladdened them, shines now
upon our hearts: and the mists they could not penetrate,
brood now upon our path. There is the choice minstrel of
Israel, true alike to the spirit of mourning or of joy; there
are the venerable fathers of the ancient church, whose ves-
pers, chanted centuries ago, will suit this night as well;
there is the adamantine yet genial Luther, telling, with the
severity of an eye-witness, the awfulness of judgment;
there is the noble Milton, breathing his sweet and rugged
music out of darkness; there is the afflicted Cowper, sending out the tenderest strains from his benighted spirit:
with an attendant multitude of the faithful, — the confessor,
the exile, the missionary, — a chorus of sublime voices, with
which it is a sacred privilege to be in harmony. And these
are not merely the accents of the past, but the anthem of
the sainted dead, — the strains of immortals that look back
upon their toils, and behold us singing their songs of sadness here, while they have already learned the melodies of
everlasting joy. Blessed communion of earth with Heaven!
making us truly one family, below, above ; and rendering us
fellow-citizens with the saints, and of the very household
of God!

And soon we too shall drop the note of earthly aspiration, and join that upper anthem of diviner love. The
hour cometh, when we shall cease the mournful cry with
which earth must ever pray to Heaven, and grief ask pity
to its tears, and the tempted call for help in the crisis of

danger, and the laboring will implore a freshened strength. Exiles as yet from the spirit of unanxious joy, we catch but the echoes of that heavenly peace, and yield response but faint and low.   Yet even now the free heart of the happy and triumphant shall be ours, in proportion as we are true to the condition of *faithful service*, which alone can make us one with them. The communion of saints brings to us their conflict first, their blessings afterwards; those who will not with much patience strive with the evil, can have no dear fellowship with the good; we must weep their tears, ere we can win their peace. This sorrowful condition once accepted, the sympathies of Heaven are not slow to arise within the soul : it is the tension of sacred toil, that on the touch of every breath of life brings music from the chords of love.   And then the tone that *here* sinks in the silence of death, shall *there* swell into an immortal's fuller praise. We shall leave it to others to take up the supplicating strain ; shall join the emancipated brotherhood of the departed ; and in our turn look down on the outstretched hands of our children, waiting our welcome and embrace.   Oh may the Great Father, in his own fit time, unite in one the parted family of Heaven and earth !

XIV.

CHRIST'S TREATMENT OF GUILT.

LUKE V. 8.

DEPART FROM ME; FOR I AM A SINFUL MAN, O LORD!

WHEN Simeon, on the verge of life, uttered his parting hymn within the temple, he told Mary, with the infant Jesus in his arms, that, by that child, "the thoughts of many hearts should be revealed." Never was prophecy more true; nor ever perhaps the mission of our religion more faithfully defined. For wherever it has spread, it has operated like a new and diviner conscience to the world; imparting to the human mind a profounder insight into itself; opening to its consciousness fresh powers and better aspirations; and penetrating it with a sense of imperfection, a concern for the moral frailties of the will, characteristic of no earlier age. The spirit of religious penitence, the solemn confession of unfaithfulness, the prayer for mercy, are the growth of our nature trained in the school of Christ. The pure image of his mind, as it has passed from land to land, has taught men more of their own hearts than all the ancient aphorisms of self-knowledge: has inspired more sadness at the evil, more noble hope for the good that is hidden there; and has placed within reach of even the ignorant, the neglected, and the young, severer principles of self-scrutiny than philosophy had ever attained. The radiance of so great a sanctity has deepened the shades of conscious sin. The savage convert, who before knew nothing more sacred than revenge and war, is brought to

9

Jesus, and, as he listens to that voice, feels the stain of blood growing distinct upon his soul. The voluptuary, never before disturbed from his self-indulgence, comes within the atmosphere of Christ's spirit; and it is as if a gale of heaven fanned his fevered brow, and convinced him that he is not in health. The ambitious priest, revolving plans for using men's passions as tools of his aggrandizement, starts to find himself the disciple of one who, when the people would have made him king, fled direct to solitude and prayer. The froward child blushes to think how little there is in him of the infant meekness which Jesus praised; and feels that, had he been there, he must have missed the benediction, or, more bitter still, have wept to know it misapplied. Nay, so deep and solemn did the sense of guilt become under the influence of Christian thoughts, that at length the overburdened heart of fervent times could endure the weight no longer : the Confessional arose, to relieve it and restore a periodic peace; and it became the chief object of the widest sacerdotal order which the world has ever seen, to soothe the sobs, and listen to the whispered record, of human penitence. Cities too, as if conscious of their corruption, bid the silent minster rise amid their streets, where, instead of the short daily or Sabbath service, unceasing, eternal orisons might be said for sin; where the door might open to the touch all day, and the lamp be seen beneath the vault by night, and the passer-by, caught by the low chant, might be tempted to interrupt the chase of vanity without, for the peace of prayer within. And so, in every ancient village church of Europe, there is a corner that has been moistened with the burning tears of many generations, and witness to the confessions and griefs that prove the children's conscience and affections to be such as their fathers' were : and the cathedral aisle, emblem of the mighty heart of Christendom, has for centuries been swelled with the plaint of a penitential music, shedding its sighs aloft into the spire, as if to reach and kiss the feet of God.

In private dwellings, too, from the hearts of parents and of children, every morning and evening for ages past has seen many sad and lowly prayers ascend. Everywhere the Christian mind proclaims its need of mercy, and bends beneath the oppression of its guilt; and since Jesus began to "reveal the thoughts of many hearts," Christendom, with clasped hands, has fallen at his feet and cried, " We are sinful men, O Lord!"

In nurturing this sentiment, in producing this solemn estimate of moral evil and quick perception of its existence, the religion of Christ does but perpetuate the influence of his personal ministry, and give prominence, on the theatre of the world, to the feature which singularly distinguished his life, viz. his *treatment of the guilty.* It is as if he dwelt among us still, and we saw him vexed and saddened by our evil passions, and travelled with him on the way, and felt his eye of gentleness and purity upon our homes, and he told us that "we know not what spirit we are of," and by these very words caused us to know it instantly. Nor can we obtain any juster and deeper impressions of the temptations of life, and the tendencies of all wrong desires, than by seizing that view of moral evil which dictated the mercies and the severities of his lips and life.

He lived amid dark passions and in evil days. Profligates and outcasts were near him : the ambitious and ignorant were his disciples : hypocrites conspired against him ; and treachery was ready to be their tool. He had to encounter malignant designs directed against himself, and selfish arts of delusion practised on the people ; to deal at one time with the despised but affectionate penitent ; at another, with recently-detected shame ; and again, with artifice and insincere pretension hardened into system, and administered by established authority. And in all is visible the same spirit of blended sanctity and humanity, adapting itself, with versatile power, to every emergency.

The guilty passions of his countrymen continually approached himself. They haunted his whole ministry, and hated him as soon as disciples began to love. They mixed with the multitudes whom he taught upon the hills; and he saw their evil eye peering on him and watching his words from amid the throngs that flocked round him in the temple. But they never embarrassed the flow of his dignified utterance, or fluttered his spirit with a moment's resentment. On occasion of the Feast of Tabernacles, — that annual jubilee of Jerusalem's heart, when the trees were robbed of their branches to turn the streets into an olive-ground, and make the city as verdant as the hills, — all was done that enmity could effect, to overcast his share of the national joy, to silence his teachings to the wondering people, and stop his efforts to extract from the picturesque and festive rites some lesson of gladder tidings and deeper wisdom. He saw amid the crowd the officers sent to take him, the wily steps and hesitating wills with which they tracked his wanderings over the temple courts, the exchange of whispers dropping into fixed attention with which they listened to him here and there. He stepped forward, and they recoiled, as he told them, with an air of divinest quietude, that he should be there yet longer, but no hand would touch him, and then he should be sequestered in a place which their violence could not reach. And there, day after day, they saw him still gladdening attentive hearts, and felt him subduing their own, so that again and again they ceased to be his enemies and became his followers: till on the last great day, they beheld him standing aloft on the precipitous edge of Moriah's rock, watching the procession that climbed with the water-bowl from Siloam's stream below, and as it entered with its pure libation, heard him pronounce that solemn invitation, "If any man thirst, let him come unto me and drink of living waters." They returned, and the attestation burst from their lips, "Never man spake like this man."

Nor was it merely that he regarded these men as the poor menials of others' designs, — hirelings of guiltier men. For the same impersonal tranquillity appears when he is in contact with the original agents, who endeavored to crush his cause, and actually compassed his death. Whatever the agony of Gethsemane may have been, it was no agony of resentment : the controversy of that bitter hour was with the Father whom he loved, not with enemies whom he feared. Indeed, the nearer these enemies came, the more did the serene power of his spirit rise. After those convulsive prayers which had pierced the midnight, it seemed as if angel-thoughts had stolen in to strengthen him. At the moment when the tramp of feet was first heard upon the bridge of Kedron, and the torches, as they passed, flashed upon its rapid waters, he was prostrate in a devotion from which tears and struggles had now passed away. When, later still, the hum of approaching voices became distinct, and the lights gleamed nearer and nearer through the trees, he was bending over his waking disciples, who overheard him breathing the wish, that they could indeed sleep on through the severities of that dreadful day, and be saved from the faithless desertion, the memory of which would be ever bitter. And when at length the armed band confronts them, and he startles them by stepping forth in answer to his name; when the kiss of betrayal has been given, and the momentary affray which Peter had challenged has been stopped by his healing power: when all are moving from the place with sullen haste, — the priests, doubtless, eager to be back within the city before it can be discovered by what nocturnal exploit they, the conservators of law and right, have sullied their dignity, — Jesus dives at once into their conscience, flurried already with fear and guilt, and asks, why such holy men, whom often he has seen listening to his daily teachings, should choose so ruffian a way, and so strange an hour, for a deed of public justice ? Throughout the scenes which followed, you well know how

Jesus maintained the same majestic and unruffled spirit; seeming nobler with every indignity, and of prompter self-forgetfulness with every added suffering; yet visibly agitating every person before whom he was brought, with the consciousness of crime and horror in the transactions of which he was the forgiving victim. Look where we may, it is clear that resentment had not the faintest share in Christ's feelings towards wrong: that the wrong was directed against himself, afforded no inducement for a severer or more excited estimate of its enormity. He put it at a distance from him: its relations to its authors and to others impressed him more than the suffering it brought upon himself; and every one must perceive that his eye is fixed, not on its cruelty, but on its awfulness, its blindness, its guilt.

Yet did Jesus give no sanction to the morbid doctrine of a sentimental fatalism, which forbids us ever to be angry with the wicked, talks whiningly of our common frailty, draws an immoral comfort from God's way of educing good from evil, and comprises all possible cases of duty to wrong-doers under one formula, " Pity and forgive." In nothing do we notice the depth and truth of his moral perception more clearly than in his different treatment of vice in its several forms and stages. When he comes before " Scribes and Pharisees, hypocrites," we do not hear the tones of forgiveness, the pleadings of the mild apologist for human infirmity, the effeminate offer of a futile pity. He pours forth an intense stream of natural indignation, and blights them with the flash of a terrible invective; he tears the veil from every foul purpose, and with severe justice brands every deed with its own black name. Here, exposure, not compassion, is the proper impulse and duty of a noble mind: for the people must no longer be deluded, their reason perplexed with wretched quibbles, and their too-trusting conscience corrupted by the sophistries of sin. It were poor generosity, from tenderness to a selfish faction, to let the good heart of a nation die. Nay, even for these deceivers themselves, this expression of moral anger was precisely the most salutary appeal. For it echoed the secret sentence of their own hearts, with which compassion would have been altogether discordant. The self-condemnation, only whispered before, it sent in thunder through their hollow souls; bringing many a hearer to tremble at the shock, who would have scoffed at pity as a weak and puling thing. This principle, of simply giving voice to the present sentiments of the conscience, and administering the feelings for which its natural justice was making a demand, Jesus appears intuitively to have followed in all his dealings with the vicious. When he reclined at the table of the Pharisee, and shocked him by allowing a woman who had been a sinner to find admission on the plea of discipleship, and the new reverential affections of her nature broke forth in passionate gratitude, he gave no check and no rebuke, nor simply a cautious sanction. The convictions which rebuke serves to awaken were already there: to reproach would be to crush the fallen: she had discovered the depth of her misery, and yearned for the profound compassion suited to so great a woe: Jesus knew that one who had been stricken by a love so pure and penitential as hers, needed only to have that love fostered and trained to act; and so, casting himself with a bold faith on the capacities of a truly melted soul, he declared her sins forgiven. But where again no such penitence appeared, and to resort to him was not spontaneous but compulsory, as in the case of the woman taken in adultery, he observed a striking neutrality of treatment. To a mind heated with so dreadful and public a shame, to administer reproach would be cruelty, to give consolation would be danger; and he simply wards off the savage penalties of the law, and turns all his direct dealings upon her foul and sanctimonious informers. Their conscience persuades them that he knows their secret history, and they skulk away, the accused instead of the accusers; while on the people that stand by is impressed the awful truth, that sinners are not fit to judge of sin. The blindness which is induced by all deliberate injury to our moral nature, and which thickens its film as the habit grows, is one of the most appalling expressions of the justice of God. Moral evil is the only thing in his creation of which it is decreed, that the more we are familiar with it, the less shall we know of it. The mind that is rich in holiness and the humanities, appreciates every temptation, computes the force of every passion, and discerns the degradation of every vice, with a precision and clearness unknown to the adept in wrong. When that wretched woman stood alone and confounded before Christ, how little did she know of her own abased and abject mind, how much less of the majestic being before her, whose steady eye, as it looked upon her, she could not meet! yet how vividly, and with what results of considerate yet cautious sympathy, did the disorder of her moral nature present itself to him who knew no defilement! Like the pure and silent stars that look down by night upon the foulness and the din of cities, his heavenly spirit gazed direct into the turbid hiding-places of sin. He saw it indeed, simply as it will see itself in retrospect; not perhaps any retrospect in this life; but such as may be inevitable, when the exchange of worlds takes place; when the urgency of pursuit and the distractions of amusement shall have ceased, and left us alone with our characters and our God; when, one order of employments being ended, and the other not yet commenced, there comes the appointed pause for thought and judgment; and having waved the last adieu, we flit away along that noiseless journey, on which we bear with us only the memory of the past, to knock at the awful gates of the unopened future.

What that retrospect may be, it is fearful, but not impossible, to think. To aid the thought, it has been remarked by one of the most distinguished physical philosophers of our own day, that no atmospheric vibration ever becomes extinct; that the pulses of speech, when they have done their work and become to our ears inaudible, pass in waves away, but wander still, reflected hither and thither, through the regions of the air eternally. He conceives that, as the atmosphere comprises still within itself the distinct trace of every sound impressed on any portion of it, as thus the record indestructibly exists, we have only to suffer a change of position, and receive the endowment of an acuter sense, to hear again every idle word that we have spoken, and every sigh that we have caused. The truth is, that already, and within the limits of our mental nature, there is a power that will effect all this; it is fully within the scope of our natural faculties of association and memory. It may be doubted whether any idea once in the mind is ever lost, and past recall: it may drop, indeed, into the gulf of forgotten things and the waves of successive thought roll over it; but there are in nature possible and even inevitable convulsions which may displace the waters, heave up the deep, and disentomb whatever may be fair or hideous there. There needs only that associated objects should be presented, and the whole past, its most trivial features even, — the remnant of a schoolboy task or the mere snatches of a dream, — will rise up to view. Make but a pilgrimage to the scenes of your early days, when more than half of life is gone; wander again over the peaceful fields, and stand on the brink of the yet gliding stream, that were the witnesses of youthful sports and cares; and are they not the records of them too? Does not remembrance seem inspired and commissioned to render back the dead? And do they not come crowding on your sense, — faces and voices, and moving shapes, and the tones of bells, and the very feelings too which these things awakened once? It is remarkable how slight a suggestion is occasionally sufficient to bring back vast trains of emotion. There are cases in which some particular function of the memory acquires an exquisite sensibility: and usually, as if God would warn us what must happen when our moral nature is divorced from the physi-

cal, it is the memory of conscience that maintains this preternatural watch. In many a hospital of mental disease
(as it is called) you have doubtless seen a melancholy being,
pacing to and fro with rapid strides, and lost to every thing
around; wringing his hands in incommunicable suffering,
and letting fall a low mutter rising quickly into the shrill
cry; his features cut with the graver of sharp anguish; his
eyelids drooping (for he never sleeps), and showering ever
scalding tears. It is the maniac of remorse; possibly indeed
made wretched by merely imaginary crimes; but just as
possibly maddened.by too true a recollection, and what the
world would esteem too scrupulous a conscience. Listen to
him, and you will often be surprised into fresh pity, to find
how seemingly slight are the offences, — injuries perhaps of
mere unripened thought, — which feed the fires, and whirl
the lash, of this incessant woe. He is the dread type of
hell. He is absolutely sequestered (as any mind may be
hereafter), incarcerated alone with his memories of sin; and
that is all. He is unconscious of objects and unaware of
time : and every guilty soul may find itself, likewise, standing alone in a theatre peopled with the collected images of
the ills that he has done; and turn where he may, the features he has made sad with grief, the eyes he has lighted
with passion, the infant faces he has suffused with needless
tears, stare upon him with insufferable fixedness. And if
thus the past be truly indestructible; if thus its fragments
may be regathered; if its details of evil thought and act
may be thus brought together and fused into one big agony,
— why, it may be left to " fools " to "make a mock at sin."

XV.

THE STRENGTH OF THE LONELY.

——◆——

JOHN XVI. 32.

BEHOLD, THE HOUR COMETH, YEA, IS NOW COME, THAT YE SHALL BE
SCATTERED, EVERY MAN TO HIS OWN, AND SHALL LEAVE ME ALONE:
AND YET I AM NOT ALONE, BECAUSE THE FATHER IS WITH ME.

THE different degrees of self-reliance felt by different minds
occasion some of the most marked diversities in the moral
characters of men. There is a species of dependence upon
others, altogether distinct from empty-minded imitation;
implying no incapacity of thought, no imbecility of judgment, but often connected with the best attributes of genius
and the choicest fruits of cultivation. It is a tendency
which has its root in the sensitive, not in the intellectual
part of our nature; and grows, not from the shallowness of
the reason, but from the depth of the affections. It arises
indeed from a disproportion between these two departments
of the mind; and would disappear, if force were either
added to the understanding, or deducted from the feelings.
It is the dependence of an affectionate mind, capable, it
may be, of manifesting great power, but trembling to feel
itself alone;— of a mind that has a natural affinity for sympathy, and cannot endure its loss or its postponement; but,
on whatever course of thought or action the faculties may
launch forth, finds them insensibly tending towards it for
shelter. This temper is not to be confounded with the vulgar and selfish craving after applause, that has no test of
truth and right but the voice of a multitude, and will sell
its conscience to buy off a frown. The feeling to which I

refer cares not for numbers or for praise; it deprecates nothing but perfect solitude. It has but one reservation in its pursuit of truth and reverence for duty; that they shall not drift it away from every human support. Place near it some one approving and fraternal heart, and its self-respect rises at once; it can listen unabashed to scorn; it can stand up against a menace with dignity; it can thrust aside resistance with energy. Lay to rest the trembling spirit of humanity within; and the diviner impulses of the soul will start to their supremacy.

This state of mind may be illustrated by reference to its extreme opposite; and the contrast may bring out in clearer light the strength and weaknesses of both. There are persons to be occasionally found whose minds appear to perform their operations as if they were in empty space; who reflect, and plan, and feel in secret; of whose processes of thought no one knows any thing more than happens to be indicated by the result; who look on men and events only as instruments for the execution of their designs; who are little damped by universal discouragement, or elated by universal approbation; and rarely modify an opinion or repent of a feeling, however singular may be their position in maintaining it. If others agree with their designs, it is so much force to be reckoned in their favor; if they disagree, it is so much resistance to be overcome. Human ties are formed, and their energies are not improved; are broken, and their energies are not weakened. In trouble, they apply themselves so promptly to the remedy, that, when you offer your sympathy, it is not wanted: they are fond of the maxim, " a good man is satisfied from himself;" and so truly act upon it, that the genial heart and helping hand instinctively shrink back from their hard complacent presence.

Each of these two forms of human character has a certain species of power of its own. He who is independent of sympathy is remarkable for power over himself. In speculation, his mind operates free from all disturbing forces: he

goes apart with his subject of contemplation, surveys it with
a serene eye, converses with it as an abstraction, having no
concern with any living interest. His faculties obey his
summons, and perform their task with vigor, paralyzed by
no anxiety, ruffled by no doubt, never lingering to plead
awhile for some dear old error before it go, nor pausing to
take the leap to truth entirely new. In action, his volitions
are executed at once; nothing intervenes (assuming him to
be a man of honest purpose) between his seeing a course of
wisdom and rectitude, and his taking it: he yields nothing
to his own habits; he waits for no man's support; if men
give it, it will show their good sense; if they withhold it,
it is the worse for themselves. He scorns concession either
to others or to himself; not in truth comprehending the
temptation to it. The past and the human have no power
over him; he needs no gathering of strength to tear himself
away; all his roots strike at once into his own present convictions; and whatever opposition may beat on him from
the elements around does but serve to harden them to rock,
and fix them there with immutable tenacity.

On the other hand, he who is dependent on human sympathy acquires far greater power over others. He reflects
and reciprocates the emotions of other minds; he understands their prejudices; he is no stranger to their weaknesses; he does not stare at their impulses, like a being too
sublime to comprehend them. He may not obtain that kind
of distant respect which is yielded to the man of cold but
acute and confident intellect; — a respect which is founded
in fear, — which suppresses opposition without winning trust,
— which silences objectors without relieving their objections;
— that unsatisfactory respect which we feel when conscious
that another is right, without perceiving *where* it is that
we are wrong. But he may earn that better power, which
arises from profound and affectionate knowledge of the
human heart. There is no human being to whom we look
with so true a faith, as to him who shows himself deep-read

in the mysteries within us; who seems to have dwelt where
Omniscience only had access, and traced momentary lines
of feeling whose rapid flash our own eye could scarcely follow; who puts into words weaknesses which we had hardly
dared to confess in thought; who appears to have trembled
with our own anxieties, and wept our very tears. This
initiation into the interior nature is the quality which, above
all others, gives one mind power over another. If it comes
upon us from the living tones of a friendly voice, we listen
as to the breathings of inspiration; if it act on us only from
the pages of a book, the enchantment is hardly less potent.
That a being, distant and unknown, perhaps departed,
should have so penetrated our subtlest emotions, and caught
our most transient attitudes of thought, should have so
detected our sophistries of conscience, and witnessed the
miseries of our temptations, and known the sacredness of
our affections, as to reveal us anew even to ourselves, truly
seems the greatest of the triumphs of genius. It is a triumph
peculiar to those who love the sympathies of their kind, and,
because they love them, instinctively appreciate and understand them. It is essentially the triumph which Christ won
when the minions of tyranny and hypocrisy shrunk back
from him in awe, saying, "Never man spake like this man."

With this quality, however, great feebleness of will, and
even total prostration of moral power, may sometimes be
found combined; and we may almost say, the greater the
intellectual endowments, the more likely is this to be the
case. If ordinary minds want sympathy before they can act
freely, they can easily obtain it; their ideas and feelings are
of the common staple of humanity, and some one who has
them too may be found across the street. But if those of finer
mould should have the same dependence of heart, it may
prove a sore affliction and temptation to them; for who will
respond to the desires, and aims, and emotions most dear to
them? They wed themselves to a benevolent scheme;—it is
thrust aside as a chimera. They demonstrate a truth of start-

ling magnitude ; — it is acknowledged and passed by. They describe some misery of the poor, the child, or the guilty ; — the world weeps, and the oppression is untouched. They pour forth their conceptions of perfect character, and seek to refresh in men's minds the bewildered sentiment of right ; every conscience approves, and not a volition stirs. And thus they are left alone, without the practical support of a single sympathy : what wonder that they think in one way, and act in another, when the world reverences their thoughts, and ridicules their actions? Compelled by their nature to desire what they are forbidden by men to execute ; unable to love any thing but that which is pronounced to be fit only for a dream ; secretly dwelling within a beauty of excellence which they would be held insane to realize, — what wonder is it, if their practical energies die of dearth, — if they begin to doubt their nobler nature, and, while cherishing it in private, dishonor it in the world, — if the pure sincerity of their mind is thus at length broken down, and they soil in act the spirit which they sanctify in thought ; and life wastes away in habits, on which the meditations of privacy pour a flood of ineffectual shame, and in impulses to better things, more and more passionate, as the springs of the will become broken, and prayers for peace of more mournful earnestness, as the vision sinks into melancholy distance ?

But the dangers of an excessive dependence upon sympathy are by no means confined to minds of this order. There are, within the range of every man's life, processes of mind which must be solitary ; passages of duty which throw him absolutely upon his individual moral forces, and admit of no aid whatever from another. Alone we must stand sometimes ; and if our better nature is not to shrink into weakness, we must take with us the thought which was the strength of Christ ; " Yet I am not alone, for the Father is with me." Jesus was evidently susceptible, in a singular degree, to the influence of human attachments ; he was the type of that form of character. Such indeed it behooved one to be who was to be regarded as the perfect model of humanity; for while the self-relying and solitary temper rarely, if ever, acquires the grace and bloom of human sympathies, the mind, originally affectionate, often, by efforts of moral principle, rises to independent strength; the sense of right can more readily indurate the tender, than melt the rocky soul. And that is the most finished character which begins in beauty, and ends in power; which wins its way to loftiness through a host of angelic humanities that would sometimes hold it back; that leans on the love of kindred while it may, and when it may not, can stand erect in the love of God; that shelters itself amid the domesticities of life, while duty wills, and when it forbids, can go forth under the expanse of immortality, and face any storm that beats, and traverse any wilderness that lies, beneath that canopy. The sentiment of Christ in my text, carried into the solitary portions of our existence, is the true power by which to acquire this perfection. What these solitary portions are will readily occur to every thoughtful mind. An example or two may be briefly noticed.

The vigils of sickness, — of those, I mean, who watch by the bed of sickness, — are solitary beyond expression. What loneliness like that, which is the more dreadful in proportion as the friend stretched at our right hand is more beloved? Those midnight hours, poised between life and death, that seem to belong neither to time nor to eternity, — claimed by time, when we listen to the tolling clock, — by eternity, when we hear that moaning breath; that silence, so solid that we cannot breathe into it, so awful that we dare not weep, and which yet we shudder to hear broken by the mutterings of delirium; that confused flitting of thoughts across our exhausted minds, strangely mingling the trivial and the solemn, — beginning perhaps from the grotesque shapes of a moonlit cloud, then sinking us deep into dreams of the past, till a rustling near calls us to give the cup of cold water, and that fevered eye that looks on us makes us think, where soon will be the perturbed spirit that lights it!—Oh, what relief can there be to this agony, what trust amid this despair, but in the remembrance, "I am not alone, for my Father is with me?" Serene as the star in the cool heavens without, gentle as the loving heart whose ebbing life we watch, his Infinite Mind has its vigils with us,—the vigils of eternal Providence, beneath whose eye, awake alike over both worlds, sorrow and death vanish away. Into what peace do the terrible aspects of things around subside under that thought! We are no longer broken upon the wheel of fatalism, given over to fruitless and unmeaning suffering: the feeling that life is going wrong, that all things are dropping into wreck, disappears. We rise to a loftier point of view, and perceive how all this may lie within the perfect order of benignity; how death in this world may be determined by the laws of birth into another; how our sensitive is connected with our moral nature, and from deep trial great strength may grow,—the capacious and enduring mind, the hardy and athletic will, the refined and gentle heart, the devoted spirit of duty. Enfolded within the Divine Paternity, we have one fixed and tranquil object of our thoughts. From that centre of repose we can look forth on the fitfulness of sickness without despair; the flying shadows of fear seem cast by an orb of everlasting light. He that in this spirit meets the trembling moments of life, will gather the sublimest power from events that seem to crush him, and come forth from the mourner's watch, not with wasted and haggard mind, not morose and selfish, not with passive and helpless air, as if waiting to be the sport of every blast that beats,—but with uplifted conscience, with distincter purpose, with will meeker towards others, and sterner towards self, and character tending towards the energy of the hero, and the calmness of the saint.

Again, we must be solitary when we are tempted. The management of the character, the correction of evil habits,

the suppression of wrong desires, the creation of new virtues, — this is a work strictly individual, with which no
" stranger intermeddleth," in which the sympathy of friends
may be deceptive, and our only safety is in a superhuman
reliance.   The relation of the human being to God is altogether personal: there can be no partnership in its responsibilities.   Our moral convictions must have an undivided
allegiance ; and to withhold our reverence till they are sup-
ported by the suffrages of others, is an insult which they
will not bear.   What can those even who read us best know
of our weaknesses and wants and capabilities?   They would
have to clothe themselves with our very consciousness,
before they could be fit advisers here.   How often does
their very affection become our temptation, cheat us out of
our contrition, and lead us to adopt some pleasant theory
about ourselves, in place of the stern and melancholy truth !
How often does their erring judgment lead us to indolence
and self-indulgence, to a dalliance with our infirmities, and
a fatal patience with our sins !   If indeed there were a more
prevalent conscientiousness in the distribution of praise and
blame, — if all men felt how serious a thing it is to dispense
such mighty powers, — friends might consult together with
greater security respecting their moral failures and obligations: penitence might pour itself forth into a species of
auricular confession no less safe than natural: the sense of
wrong would become more profound, when the violation
of duty had shaped itself into words; and the secret suggestions and resolves of conscience be doubly strong, when
echoed by the living voice of human tenderness.   Even
then, however, we must vigilantly guard our own moral
perceptions, clear the atmosphere between them and heaven,
and allow no sophistry to shade us from the eye of God.
At best, we must often have to forego all sympathy : none
can be with us in our multiform temptations.   Many a purpose fit only for ourselves, suited to the peculiarities of our
own character and condition, we must take up in private,

and in silence pile up effort after effort, till it be accomplished. And in these lonely struggles of duty, in this invisible repression of wrong impulses and maintenance of great aims, the inevitable loss of human aid must be replaced by our affinity with God. While He is with us we are not alone. He that invented human virtue, and breathed unto us our private veneration for its greatness, — He that loves the martyr spirit, scorning suffering for the sake of truth, — He that beholds in every faithful mind the reflection of himself, — He that hath built an everlasting world, at once the shelter of victorious goodness, and the theatre of its yet nobler triumphs, — enwraps us in his immensity, and sustains us by his love. The sooner we learn to lean on Him, and find comfort in the society of God, the better are we prepared for every solemn passage of our existence. It is well, ere we depart, to confide ourselves sometimes to the invisible : for *then* at least we must be thrust forth upon it in a solitude personal as well as moral. The dying make that pass alone : human voices fade away ; human forms retire ; familiar scenes sink from sight; and silent and lonely the spirit migrates to the great secret. Who would not feel himself then beneath the all-sheltering wing, and say amid the mystic space, " I am not alone, for the Father is with me ? "

XVI.

HAND AND HEART.

———◆———

John xiv. 23.

IF A MAN LOVE ME, HE WILL KEEP MY WORDS; AND MY FATHER WILL LOVE HIM, AND WE WILL COME UNTO HIM, AND MAKE OUR ABODE WITH HIM.

THERE is no point in theoretical morality more difficult to determine (if we may judge from the disputes of philosophers) than the comparative worth and mutual relation of good *affections* and good *actions*. Ought it to be the direct and primary aim of the teacher of duty to produce a harvest of beneficent deeds? or to impart clear perceptions and prompt sensibility of conscience in relation to right and wrong? If the former, his instructions will present an inventory and careful valuation of all possible "voluntary acts;" and his exhortations be addressed to the hopes and fears, to the prudential apprehensions of good and evil, which operate immediately upon the will. If the latter, he will meddle little with cases of casuistry, or problems which exhibit duty as an object of doubt; will define and illuminate the secret image of right that dwells within every mind; and present as incentives those models of high faith and disinterested virtue which kindle the reverence of the heart. In this country, especially among those who have been most anxious to "enlighten" its religion; the predominant attention has been given to external morality. The practical temper of the English, impatient of loud profession and sanctimonious inconsistency, reasonably enough cried

out for "*fruit.*" Philosophy caught this spirit, and embodied it in a system of no small pretensions. Seeing that
fine sentiments are worthless without good deeds, the masters of this school have decided, that the affections have *no*
excellence except as instruments for producing action; that,
intrinsically, they are all alike, without any distinction of
good or bad; that moral qualities *primarily* attach merely
to practice, *derivatively* only to the mental tendencies towards practice, and in any case are *constituted* by the *effects*
of conduct in producing enjoyment or pain; that the mor-
alist has no concern with the motives of an agent, provided
he does that which is useful; that the only measure of virtue, in short, is the amount of pleasure it creates.

This system has been embraced and is still held by many
Christians, chiefly among the churches within the sphere of
Dr. Priestley's influence. It is expounded, in a form full of
inconsistency and compromise, by Dr. Paley, in a work
whose popularity appears to me rather a discredit to England than an honor to him: and though it has been a general
favorite with irreligious moralists, and appears in natural
reaction from the enthusiasm of the most earnest pietists, it
has seldom been considered hostile to Christianity itself.
This is no fit occasion for discussing its philosophical pretensions: and were it not for the extent and nature of its
practical influence, it might be abandoned to the academic
lecture-room, where the rigorous methods of thought necessary for its examination would not be misplaced. But there
is one particular view of it which may naturally enough be
presented here. Its characteristic sentiment may be placed
side by side with those of the Christian morals, and the
relation between them ascertained. And no one, I imagine,
can perceive in it a trace of Christ's peculiar spirit: few
surely can be wholly unconscious of the wide variance
between its leading ideas and his: and all who have abandoned their minds to the impression of his teachings, must
feel that he assigned a very different rank to the affectionate

elements of character; that, not content with tasking the
hand, he makes high demands upon the heart; that public
benefit is subordinate with him to personal perfection; and
that, instead of merging the individual mind in the advantage of society, he is silent of the happiness of society,
except as involved in the holiness of the individual. Nothing surely can be further from the spirit of Jesus than to
measure excellence by the magnitude of its effects, rather
than the purity of its principle : else he would never have
ranked the widow's mite above the vast donatives of vanity ; or have praised the profuse affection of the penitent
that lavished on him costly offerings, esteeming them yet
less precious than the consecrating tribute of her tears.
Here, it was not the deed whose usefulness gave worth to
the disposition, but the disposition whose excellence gave
value to the deed. And this is everywhere the character of
Christianity. It plants us directly beneath an eye that look-
eth at the heart : it forgives, in that we "have loved much " :
it throws away without compunction the largest husk of cer-
emony, and treasures up the smallest seed of life : instead
of sharpening us for casuistry, it prostrates us in worship ;
reveals to us our inner nature, by bringing us in contact·
with God who is a spirit, and to whom we bear the likeness
of child to parent ; gives us an intermediate image of him
and of ourselves, Christ the meek and merciful, whose life
was a prolonged expression of disinterestedness and love ;
and imposes, as the sole condition of discipleship, " faith in
him," — implicit trust, that is, in the spirit of his mind ; —
self-precipitation upon a piety and fidelity like his, without
concession to expediency, without faltering in danger, without flight from suffering, without slackened step, though
duty should conduct us straight into the arms of ignominy
and death.

That Christianity does make high demands upon our
affections must then be admitted. Indeed this is virtually
confessed by the enthusiastic forms into which it has burst,

by the outbreak of fervor from which every new church is born, and the eager efforts made to sustain this vivid life. Nay, it is privately confessed by every cold and languid yet honest heart, that cannot lay open before it the story of Christ, without the secret consciousness of rebuke. It is confessed by the anxieties of many good minds, that are ashamed of the slow fires and faint light of their faith and love ; that can spur their will, more easily than kindle their affections ; and wish they were called upon only to *do*, and not also to *feel.* They cast about the vaguest and vainest efforts after deeper impressions of things holy and sublime : they wonder at the apathy with which they dwell amid the infinitude of God : they convince themselves how *untrue* is that state of mind which treats the " seen and temporal " as if there were no " unseen and eternal ; " they assure themselves how terrible must be the disorder of that soul, whose springs of pure emotion are thus locked in death. But with all this they cannot shame, or reason, or terrify themselves into any nobler glow : the avenues of intellect, and judgment, and fear, are not those by which a new feeling is permitted to visit and refresh the heart. The ice cannot thaw itself ; but must ask the warmer gales of heaven to blow, and the sun aloft to send more piercing beams. There is nothing vainer or more hopeless than the direct struggles of the mind to transform its own affections, to change by a fiat of volition the order of its tastes, and the intensity of its love. Self-inspiration is a contradiction : and to suspend, by upheavings of the will, the force of habitual desire, is no less impossible than, by writhings of the muscles, to annihilate our own weight.

This, you will say, is a hard doctrine ; that our religion demands that which our nature forbids, — invites a regeneration of the heart, after which the will may strive in vain. Yet, I think, you must be conscious of its truth, and acknowledge that no spasm of determination can make you regard with hate that which is now an object of your love.

But if Christianity presents the perplexity, its spirit affords the solution. It shows us, indeed, that to gain a pure and noble mind, great in its aims, resolute in its means, strong with the invincibility of conscience, yet mellowed with rev-erential love, is the end of all our discipline here. But it nowhere encourages a direct aim at this end, as if it could be reached by the struggles of a day or of a year : it nowhere invites a morbid gaze upon our own feelings, as if by self-vigilance we could look ourselves into perfection. In Christ it furnishes us with an image of divinest beauty that we may turn our eye on *that*, not upon ourselves : and perverse, even to disease, is the temper, which, instead of being engaged with that sublimest work of the great Sculptor of souls, whines rather over its own deformity, and seeks to cure it by unnatural contortions. Christianity sends each faculty of our nature to its proper office ; our veneration, to Christ ; our wills, to their duty. It precipitates us on action as the proper school of affection ; and, reversing the mor-alist's principle, values not the pure heart as the tool for producing serviceable deeds, but the good deeds as at once the expression and the nourishment of that greatest of pos-sessions, a good mind. It was not by retiring into himself, but by going out of himself, that Christ overcame the world ; not by spiritual pathology and self-torture, but by veritable " sufferings," that he " became perfect ; " not by measuring his own emotions, but by oblivion of them amid a crowd of toils, a succession of fulfilled resolves, a profuse expenditure of life and effort having others for their object, that he rose above the dignity of men, and ripened the divinest spirit for the skies.

Struck then by the word of Christ, the moral paralytic must "take up his bed and walk." It is surprising how practical duty enriches the fancy and the heart, and action clears and deepens the affections. Like the run into the green fields and morning air to the fevered limbs and tight-ened brow of the night-student, it circulates a stream of unspeakable refreshment, "and renews our strength as the eagle's." Indeed, no one can have a true idea of right, until he does it; any genuine reverence for it, till he has done it often and with cost; any peace ineffable in it, till he does it always and with alacrity. Does any one complain, that the best affections are transient visitors with him, and the heavenly spirit a stranger to his heart? Oh let him not go forth, on any strained wing of thought, in distant quest of them; but rather stay at home, and set his house in the true order of conscience; and of their own accord the divinest guests will enter; he hath "kept the words" of Christ, and the "Father himself will love him," and they "will come unto him, and make their abode with him." The man most gifted with genius and rich in intellectual wisdom, but withal barren of practice and self-indulgent, can call up before him no conception of moral excellence so authentic, so divine, as many an obscure disciple, who, through frequent tribulation, has done and borne the perfect will of God. Even the smallest discontent of conscience may render turbid the whole temper of the mind; but only produce the effort that restores its peace, and over the whole atmosphere a breath of unexpected purity is spread; doubt and irritability pass as clouds away; the withered sympathies of earth and home open their leaves and live: and through the clearest blue the deep is seen of the heaven where God resides. And here too we may observe the opposite effects which action and experience produce upon our *preconceptions* of wrong and of right. Do the right, and your ideal of it grows and perfects itself. Do the wrong, and your ideal of it breaks up and vanishes. The young and pure mind, stranger yet to the vehemence of appetite and revenge, looks on sin as a dreadful and demon image, and shrinks with awe from its approach; shudders at the laugh of guilty revelry, and gazes on the face of acknowledged crime, as if it were a phantom of the abyss. Guilt is then a thing unearthly and

preternatural, whose grasp is more terrible than death.
And truly, *if* this being, now innocent, should ever become
its prey, it will be through a struggle deep and deadly, as
with the tender mercies of a fiend. But once let that struggle
be over, and the fiend vanishes for ever; passes into plain
flesh and blood, that "is by no means so dreadful as was
imagined;" nay, even assumes the air of the jovial companion, and turns the dance of death into a comedy. The *true*
"superstition" of early years flies before the *false* "experience" of maturity. The ideal, so much juster than the
actual, is gone; and there falls upon the heart that folly
which "makes a mock at sin."

In saying that action is the school of affection, it is clear
that we cannot mean mere manual or physical labor, or
activity in business, or even the mechanical routine of any
practical life, however unexceptionable be its habits. The
regularities of constitutional goodness, the order of a simply
blameless existence, do not reach that pitch of energy which
sustains the noblest health of the soul: these may continue
their accustomed course, and yet the springs of inward life
and strength dry up. In the mere negative virtue which
abstains from gross outward wrong, which commits neither
theft, nor cruelty, nor excess, and paces the daily round of
usage, there is not necessarily any principle of immortal
growth. The force requisite to maintain it becomes continually less, as the obstructions are worn down by ceaseless
attrition; and the character may hence become simply automatic, performing a series of regularities with the smallest
expenditure of soul. To nourish high affections, worthy of
a nature that hath kindred with the Father of spirits, more
than this is needed : positive and creative power, spontaneous and original force, conquering energy of resolve, must
be put forth : from the inner soul some central strength
must pass upon the active life, to destroy that equilibrium
between within and without which makes our days mere
self-repetitions, and to give us a progressive history. There

is a connection profound and beautiful between the affectionate and the self-denying character of Christianity. The voluntary sacrifices feed the involuntary sympathies of virtue : and he that will daily *suffer* for his duty, nor lay his head to rest till he has renounced some ease, embraced some hardship, in the service of others and of God, shall replenish the fountains of his holiest life; and shall find his soul not settling into the flat and stagnant marsh, but flowing under the most delicious light of heaven above, over the gladdest fields of Providence below. I know that the moralists of whom I have before spoken, — they that turn the shrine of duty into a shop for weighing grains and scruples of enjoyment, — entertain a great horror of the notion of self-sacrifice, and ridicule the doctrine of denial as ascetic. Any interference with the luxury of virtue is to be deplored ; disturbance to its repose must be admitted to be disagreeable, and, " so far as it goes, an evil " : and though clashing pleasures will sometimes present themselves, we must take care never to let go the nearer, till we have in our hands the title-deeds of the remoter. It is surprising, we are told, how pleasant a thing true goodness is, if we will only believe it. It may be so ; or it may not be so : but at all events he who goes to it in this spirit has no true heart for it, and shall be refused the thing he seeks. God will have us surrender without terms ; and till then, we are fast prisoners, and not free children, in his universe. So needful is sacrifice to the health and hardihood of conscience, that if the occasions for it do not present themselves spontaneously in our lot, we must create them for ourselves : not reserving to ourselves those exercises of virtue which are constitutionally pleasant, but, on the contrary, esteeming the asperity of a duty as the reason why we should put our hand to it at once ; not acquiescing in the facility of wisely-adjusted habits, but accepting the ease of living well as the peremptory summons of God to live better. He, in short, is no true soldier of the Lord, nor worthy to bear the Christian

armor, who, in service so high, will not make an hour's
forced march of duty every day. So tasked and tested,
the inner power, the athletic vigor, of our moral nature,
will not waste and die. The perceptions of goodness,
beauty, truth, become, when we are thus faithful, singularly clear : there ripens within us the fullest faith in the
moral excellence of God; the ties that bind us to him and
to his children are drawn more closely round ; and in this
world we dwell as in the lower mansion of his house, where
also the " Father loveth us, and maketh his abode with us."

By such practical performance alone, can any genuine
love of man be matured in us. Beneficence is the true school
of benevolence. We are not to wait, till some descending
spirit, uninvoked and unearned, enters us, and makes the
labor of sympathy delightful ; but to go and do the deed
of mercy, though it be with reluctant step, with dry and
parched spirit, and without the grace of a free charity.
Perhaps we may return with more genial mind and liber-
ated affections : and, if *not*, we must the sooner and the
oftener do the act of blessing again, though it be amid self-
rebuke and shame, and recoil with no peace upon the soul.
He that with patience will become the almoner of God to
the poor and sad, and ask no portion of the blessing for himself, shall catch the spirit of the divine love at length : those
whom he steadfastly benefits he will rejoice in at the end.
Even with God this is the order too : we begin with being his
beneficiaries, and end with being his children. He created
us first (and that was blessing), placed us in the glory and
immensity of his universe, and conferred upon us the high
capacities and multiform nature that makes us his own
image : and then regarded us with his divine affectionateness, and embraced us in his everlasting Fatherhood.

By such practical performance alone, can we dismiss the
clouds of doubt and ignoble mistrust, which, really covering
our own disordered minds, seem to cast shadows around
the Most High, and to blot out the heavens from us. The

merely worldly man, interred amid mean cares, doubts the majestic truths of religion, simply from their sublimity and vastness, which render them incommensurable with his poor fraction of a mind : let him go and do a few noble deeds, and elevate the proportions of his nature, and it is wonderful what mighty things seem to become possible : Deity is near and even present at once, and immortality not improbable. And as for the self-inclosed and anxious student, his difficulties may be referred to the diseased and ascendant activity of a subtle understanding, without the materials of a deep moral experience on which to work. Let him remedy this fatal dearth ; rouse the slumbering strength of conscience ; and, quitting the theoretic problems, take up the practical responsibilities of life : and his work will clear his thought, rendering it not less acute, and more confiding and reverential. Seeing more into his own nature, he will penetrate further into all else, especially the source whence it proceeds, the scene in which it is, and the issue to which it tends. Of all depressing scepticism, of all painful solicitude, not the agility of thought, but the alacrity of duty, is the fit antagonist. At least, *until* we do the will of God, it becomes doubt to be humble : and *when* we do it, assuredly it will be yet humbler.

XVII.

SILENCE AND MEDITATION.

PSALM LXIII. 6.

I REMEMBER THEE UPON MY BED, AND MEDITATE ON THEE IN THE
NIGHT-WATCHES.

THE elder Protestant moralists laid great stress, in all their
teachings, on the duties of self-scrutiny and prayer. And
though their complaints show that there was a frequent
neglect of their injunctions, it cannot be doubted that, in
our forefathers' scheme of life, the exercise of lonely thought
filled a much larger space than it does in ours. It was
deemed shameful and atheistical to enter the closet for nothing but sleep, and quit it only for meals and trade: passing
the awfulness of life entirely by, and evading all earnest
contact with the deep and silent God. A sense of guilt
attached to those who cast themselves from their civil life
into their dreams, and back again. That the merchant or
the statesman should be upon his knees, that the general
should pass from his despatches to his devotions, and turn
his eye from the hosts of battle to the host of heaven, was
not felt to be incongruous or absurd. Milton's mind gave
itself at once to the discord of politics below, and the symphonies of seraphim above: Vane mingled with the administration of colonies, and accounts of the navy, hopes of a
theocracy, and meditations on the millennium; and it was
no more natural for Cromwell to call his officers to council
than to prayer. Nay, without going back so far, there are
few families of any standing, that do not inherit the pious

diaries of some nearer ancestry, betraying how real and large a concern to them were the exercises of the solitary soul.

It cannot be denied that there is a great difference now. Not that Christians may not be found in many sects, and copiously in some, with whom the old devout habit is maintained in all integrity; of whose existence it is a simple and sincere ingredient; who still find· an open door between heaven and earth, and pass in ·and out with free and earnest heart. But these represent the characteristic spirit of a former, rather than of the present age. The sentiments of our own times everywhere betray the growing encroachments of the outward upon the inward life. How different is our modern *"saying* our prayers" from those wrestlings of spirit, and groans and tears that convulsed the Covenanters of old: nay, how much is there in this, — that, unless there is a printed page before us, we know not what we want, and left to ourselves should scarcely find we had a want at all! Prayer by the printing-press is surely a very near approach to piety by machinery. The public changes in the faith of churches which are conspicuously taking place around us, indicate the same loss of depth and earnestness in personal religion: for what do the new doctrines say? "I cannot stand alone with God, and seek his pity to my solitary soul; I must put myself into the visible · church, and appropriate a share of his favor to that spiritual corporation; I can find no sanctification by direct contact of spirit with spirit, and must get it done for me through priests and sacraments." And what is this but an open proclamation that private audience with God has become impossible, and he can be approached only through ambassadors? Everywhere strength seems to have gone out from the devotional element of life. Those who display most of this element are no longer, like the Puritans, the *strongest* men of their day, most resolute, most simple, most powerful in debate, most direct in action ; but are felt to be feminine and subtle, without manly breadth of natural heart, and firm footing upon reality. The moments each man spends in it are seldom his *truest* and most unforced; it is not, as once, the clear, deep eye of his nature that he turns to Heaven, but the dead and glassy; and he who is without his sincerity in his closet, and with only half of it at church, flings it all into the work of civil life. In individual character, and in society at large, power seems to have gone over from the spiritual to the secular.

This change is no fit subject for unmixed complaint; much less must we desire to terrify men, like culprits, into an alarm at their impiety, and an affected resumption of the ancient discipline. Old ways of life are not thrown aside, until they become untrue: and when they have become untrue, their sanctity is gone; though the usage of churches may plead for them, the laws of God are against them. Who can recommend prayer to one who has lost the heart to pray?—confession to one who is stricken by no penitence?—the words of trust to one whose God has gone into the darkness of fate?—self-examination to one who, in too fine a knowledge of what passes within, finds no power to do the duty without? The *state of mind* which unfits men for the habits of our fathers, may be lower or may be higher; but be it what it may, there is no virtue in retaining what has grown false: let all, in their belief or unbelief, their clearness or perplexity, ground themselves . only upon reality, and live out the highest conviction not of yesterday but of to-day, and however the forms of our being may change, its spirit will remain unceasingly devout. If you ask, "What is it that has rendered the lonely piety of our forefathers less natural and possible to us?" I believe the reason to be this:—their lot was cast near the age of the Reformation; they breathed its spirit and lived its life; and as Protestantism was at first a simple insurrection against formalism and falsehood, and gave to the faith within the authority which it denied to the church without, so did it exclusively develop the inward religion of the soul, and put it in artificial contrast with outward interests and human duties. Installing the private conscience in the place of the anointed priest, it gave that conscience much of the priestly character, inquisitorial, casuistical, vigilant and stern; and sent a man to his self-examination, as before he would have gone to his confessional, to question himself as the church would have questioned him before, only with severity more searching as his consciousness knew better what to ask. Hence arose an anxious scrupulosity of mind; a loss of all dependence except on the divine offices of the solitary soul; a feeling of terrible necessity for the help and strength of God; a keen scrutiny into all the doublings of the heart, and an apprehension of every sophistry of sin; passing over at once from the gay laxity of the Catholic into a grim and solemn earnestness. The change was noble and healthy, only, like all reactions, capable of excess. Men may learn too much of what goes on within them; their spiritual analysis may be too fine; a morbid self-consciousness may be produced, which in giving sensitive knowledge, takes away practical power; and he who will microscopically look at the ultimate fibres of his life-roots, scrapes away the element in which they thrive, and withers them in the light by which he sees. We must ever grow from darkness and the earth; enough if the blossom and the fruit be worthy of the sunshine and the heaven. *Our* days witness a recoil from the extreme inwardness of our forefathers' religion: human affections warm us more; human duties are nobler in our view; social interests are of deeper moment; and the whole scene of man's visible life, no longer the mere vestibule of an invisible futurity, has a worth and dignity of its own, which philanthropy delights to honor, and only fanaticism can despise. For my own part, I think the change a sign of nature's restorative power, and see in it the stirrings of new health: even though partially brought about by temporary scepticism, I cannot deplore it, for it shows that the con-

science cannot go on living in a pretence, but, in retreating
from things of which it doubts, gets its foot upon duties
which it knows.   In this are the first beginnings of new
religion to replace the old : if the divine earnestness within
us only shifts and does not die, it matters little what becomes
of our mere theology; and deep-hearted practical faithfulness is not separable long from true-thoughted practical
faith.

Let us admit then that our revolt against the old spiritual-
ism has come about in quite a natural way; that the Puritan
sentiment was fast going down into mere moral hypochondria : and that, to work the cure, it was inevitable that
the *world* (as divines opprobriously term it), *i.e.* the opportunities of action with a view to temporal good, whether
personal or social, should re-assert its sway.   Like the sick
physician, who cannot let his pulse alone or cease to speculate on his sensations, Christendom, bewildered by its own
deep knowledge of the human heart, kept too inquiring a
finger on the throbs of its emotions, and fancied many an
action of healthy nature into a symptom of fatal disease :
and we are not to find fault with the remedy of Providence
— a turn-out into the open air and various industry of life;
a resort to the plough, the loom, the ship, and all the arts
by which it is given to man to make the earth at once his
subject and his friend.   But let us also admit that the outward life has for some time past tyrannized over us; ex-
travagantly invading our private habits; narrowing our
modes of thought and sentiment ; benumbing our consciousness of a spiritual nature ; and impairing to us the reality
of God.   Let us own that the Divine Spirit is gone into distance and strangeness from us, and is hard to reach ; that
solitude brings no unspeakable converse, no ready consecration; that things just next the senses and the understanding
seem nearer to us than those that touch the soul; that the
crowd and noise are too close and constant on us, confusing
our better perceptions, and leading us always to look round,

seldom to look up ; that the glare of the lamps has destroyed the midnight and put out the stars.

Now this despotism of the outward over the inward life, this suppression of every attribute not immediately wanted for business or society, is a misfortune which every noble mind will assuredly withstand. It is not right to live as if God were asleep, and heaven only a murmur from his dreams. It should make some difference to a man, whether his Creator be here in the present, or gone off into the past; whether he himself dwells in the hollow of a living hand, or, with nothing beyond him but necessity, struggles for his place in a dead, deserted world. And this difference will not be realized, nor any lofty truth of character attained, by those who disown the claims of lonely thought and silence in religion.

There is an act of the mind, natural to the earnest and the wise, impossible only to the sensual and the fool, healthful to all who are sincere, which has small place in modern usage, and which few can now distinguish from vacuity. Those who knew what it was, called it *meditation*. It is not *reading*, in which we apprehend the thoughts of others, and bring them to our critical tribunal. It is not *study*, in which we strive to master the known and prevail over it, till it lies in order beneath our feet. It is not *reasoning*, in which we seek to push forward the empire of our positive conceptions, and by combining what we have, reach others that we have not. It is not *deliberation*, which computes the particular problems of action, reckons up the forces that surround our individual lot, and projects accordingly the expedient of the right. It is not *self-scrutiny*, which by itself is only shrewdness or at most science turned within instead of without, and analyzing mental feelings instead of physical facts. Its view is not personal and particular, but universal and immense, — the sweep of the nocturnal telescope over the infinitely great, not the insight of the solar microscope into the infinitely small. It brings, not an intense self-consciousness and spiritual egotism, but almost a renunciation of individuality, a mingling with the universe, a lapse of our little drop of existence into the boundless ocean of being. It does not find for us our place in the known world, but loses it for us in the unknown. It puts nothing clearly beneath our feet, but a vault of awful beauty above our head. It gives us no matter for criticism and doubt, but everything for wonder and for love. It does not suggest indirect demonstration, but furnishes immediate perception of things divine, eye to eye with the saints, spirit to spirit with God, peace to peace with Heaven. In thus being alone with the truth of things, and passing from shows and shadows into communion with the everlasting One, there is nothing at all impossible and out of reach. He is not faded or slow to bring us light, any more than is that sunshine of his, which is bright and swift as ever. He was no nearer to Christ on Tabor or in Gethsemane, than to us this day and every day. Neither the nature he inspires, nor his perennial inspiration, grows any older with the lapse of time ; every human being that is born is a first man, fresh in this creation, and as open to Heaven as if Eden were spread round him ; and every blessed kindling of faith and new sanctity is a touch of his spirit as living, a gift as immediate from his exhaustless store of holy power, as the strength that befriended Christ in temptation, and the angel-calm that closed his agony. Is it not promised for ever to the pure in heart that they shall see God ? Let any true man go into silence ; strip himself of all pretence, and selfishness, and sensuality and sluggishness of soul ; lift off thought after thought, passion after passion, till he reaches the inmost depth of all ; remember how short a time, and he was not at all ; how short a time again, and he will not be here ; open his window and look upon the night, how still its breath, how solemn its march, how deep its perspective, how ancient its forms of light ; and think how little he knows except the perpetuity of God, and the mysteriousness of life : — and it will be strange if he does not feel the Eternal Presence as close upon his soul, as the breeze upon his brow ; if he does not say, " O Lord, art Thou ever near as this, and have I not known thee ? " — if the true proportions and the genuine spirit of life do not open on his heart with infinite clearness, and show him the littleness of his temptations, and the grandeur of his trust. He is ashamed to have found weariness in toil so light, and tears where there was no trial to the brave. He discovers with astonishment how small the dust that has blinded him, and from the height of a quiet and holy love looks down with incredulous sorrow on the jealousies and fears and irritations that have vexed his life. A mighty wind of resolution sets in strong upon him, and freshens the whole atmosphere of his soul ; sweeping down before it the light flakes of difficulty, till they vanish like snow upon the sea. He is imprisoned no more in a small compartment of time, but belongs to an eternity which is now and here. The isolation of his separate spirit passes away ; and with the countless multitude of souls akin to God, he is but as a wave of His unbounded deep. He is at one with Heaven, and hath found the secret place of the Almighty.

Silence is in truth the attribute of God ; and those who seek him from that side invariably learn that meditation is not the dream but the reality of life ; not its illusion but its truth ; not its weakness but its strength. Such act of the mind is quite needful, in order to rectify the estimates of the senses and the lower understanding, to shake off the drowsy order of perceptions, in which, with the eyes of the soul half closed, we are apt to doze away existence here. Neglecting it now, we shall wake into it hereafter, and find that we have been walking in our sleep. It is necessary even for preserving the truthfulness of our practical life. It is always the tendency of *action* to fall into routine and become mechanical ; to become less and less dependent on the living forces of the will, and to continue itself by mere

momentum in the direction it has once assumed. When
conscience and not passion presides over life, this tendency
is not abated but confirmed : for conscience is essentially
systematic, subdues every thing to a fixed order, and then is
troubled or content, according as this is violated or observed. But the inner spirit of the mind, which all outward
action should express, is not naturally thus inflexible : it
drifts away from its old anchorages, and gets afloat upon
new tides of thought; as experience deepens, existence
ceases to be the same, and the proportions in which things
lie within our affections are materially changed; as the
ascent of time is made, life is seen from a higher point,
and fresh fields of truth and duty spread before our view.
Habit being conservative, faith and feeling being progressive,
unless their mutual relation be constantly re-adjusted by
meditation, they will cease to correspond, and become miserably divergent; our action will not be *true,* our thought
will not be *real;* both will be weak and dead; both distrustful as a culprit; both relying on hollow credit, and empty
of solid wealth; and our whole life, begun perhaps in the
order of conscience, and moving on externally the same,
may become a semblance and a cheat. Bare moral principle, unless holding of something more divine, has but an
unsafe tenure of the wisdom and the strength of life.

    And even when the right is clearly *seen,* meditation is
needed to collect our powers to *do* it. It is the great store-
house of our spiritual dynamics, where divine energies lie
hid for any enterprise, and the hero is strengthened for his
field. All great things are born of silence. True, the fury
of destructive passion may start up in the hot conflict of
life, and go forth with tumultuous desolation. But all beneficent and creative power gathers itself together in silence,
ere it issues out in might. Force itself indeed is naturally
silent, and only makes itself heard, if at all, when it strikes
upon obstructions to bear them away as it returns to equilibrium again. The very hurricane that roars over land and

ocean, flits noiselessly through spaces where nothing meets it. The blessed sunshine says nothing, as it warms the vernal earth, tempts out the tender grass, and decks the field and forest in their glory. Silence came before creation, and the heavens were spread without a word. Christ was born at dead of night; and though there has been no power like his, " He did not strive nor cry, neither was his voice heard in the streets." Nowhere can you find any beautiful work, any noble design, any durable endeavor, that was not matured in long and patient silence, ere it spake out in its accomplishment. *There* it is that we accumulate the inward power which we distribute and spend in action; put the smallest duty before us in dignified and holy aspects; and reduce the severest hardships beneath the foot of our self-denial. There it is that the soul, enlarging all its dimensions at once, acquires a greater and more vigorous being, and gathers up its collective forces to bear down upon the piecemeal difficulties of life, and scatter them to dust. There alone can we enter into that spirit of self-abandonment, by which we take up the cross of duty, however heavy, and tread the dolorous way with feet however worn and bleeding. And thither shall we return again, only into higher peace and more triumphant power, when the labor is over and the victory won, and we are called by death into God's loftiest watch-tower of contemplation.

XVIII.

WINTER WORSHIP.

———◆———

JOHN V. 13.

AND HE THAT WAS HEALED WIST NOT WHO IT WAS.

IF the first power of Christianity was embodied in miracle, it was in miracle so distinctly expressive of its spirit, and so analogous to its natural agency in the world, as to invite rather than repel our imitation. Whatever be meant by the two great preternatural endowments entrusted to its earliest missionaries, — the gift of tongues and the gift of healing, — they represent clearly enough the two grand functions of our religion, — to bear *persuasion to the minds*, and bring *mercy to the physical ills*, of men. On that summer morning in Jerusalem, when the men of Galilee stood forth within the temple courts to preach the first glad tidings to the strangers of Parthia, and Greece, and Rome, and with their speech reached the minds of that multitude of many tongues, what better symbol could there be of that religion, whose spirit is intelligible to all, because it addresses itself to the universal human heart, and speaks, not the artificial jargon of sects and nations, but the natural language of the affections, which are immortal. And when the crowd of weary sufferers thronged around the Apostles' steps in the city, the blind supporting the lame, and the lame eyes to the blind; or when the solitary leper saw them in the field, and made his gesture of entreaty from afar, and all were healed, — how better could be represented the character of that faith, which has never set eyes on pain without yielding it a tear;—which, in proportion as it has been cordially embraced, has sickened the heart of scenes of suffering and blood, and lessened, age after age, the stripes wherewith humanity is stricken. We neither claim nor ask for the cloven tongues of a divine persuasion : we boast not of any arm of miracle which we can lay bare in conflict with disease and sorrow : but in the *spirit* of these acts of Providence we may participate. While fanatics vainly pretend to repeat their marvellousness, we may choose the better part, and copy their beneficence. The world needs the preachers of wonders, less than the apostles of charity.

And, whatever its accessories of miracle, nothing could be more unostentatious than the diffusion of Christ's mercy by its missionaries in the days of old. Beginning with the provinces of Palestine, it passed, from village to village of the interior, from city to city of the vast empire's various coast : along the shores of Asia, beneath the citadels of Greece, to the world's great palace on the Tiber, it stole along, fleet and silent as the wind that bloweth where it listeth, sweeping through many a foul recess, and leaving health where it found pestilence. Our imagination, corrupted by the pomp of history, dwells perhaps too much on the more brilliant positions and marked triumphs of the ancient gospel. We follow Paul through his vicissitudes, and feel an idle pride in his most conspicuous adventures : and when he stretches forth the hand and speaks before King Agrippa; when idolators mistake the bearer of a godlike message for a god, and bow before him, as to Mercury; when in Ephesus he becomes the rival of Diana, and ruins the craftsmen of the silver shrines; when philosophy listens to him on Areopagus, and the Furies still slumber within hearing in their grove, — we vainly think that he derives his greatest dignity from the scenes in the midst of which he stands, a contrast and a stranger. As we would deserve the Christian name, let us look more deeply into his mission, and adopt more fully the spirit of his mind. Watch him even in Rome, where he dwelt, though a prisoner, in his own hired house; and where shall we seek for him in that dazzling metropolis? He was not one to pass through its scenes of magnificence with stupid and fanatic indifference, to find himself surrounded by the monuments of ancient freedom, and listen for the first time to the very language of the world's conquerors, without catching the inspiration of history, and feeling the solemn shadow of the past fall upon him. I do not say that he never paused beneath the senate-house to think of the voices that had been heard within its walls; or climbed the capitol, once the palace of the republic, now its shrine; or started at the fasces, stern emblem of a justice now no more; or went without excitement into the imperial presence through the very gardens where his own blood should hereafter be shed in merriment. But his daily walks passed all these splendors by: they dived into the lanes and suburbs on which no glory of history is shed, and which made Rome the sink and curse, while it was the ruler, of the nations: they found the haunts of the scorned He-brew: they startled the degraded revels of the slave: they sought out the poor foreigner, attracted by the city's wealth, and perishing amid its desolation: they crept to the pallet on which fever and poverty were stretched, tendering the hand of restoration, and whispering the lessons of peace. This was his noblest dignity: not that he publicly pleaded before princes, but that he secretly solaced the outcast and the friendless; not that he paced the forum, but that he lingered in the dens of wretchedness, and refreshed the hardened heart with gentle sympathies, and linked the alien with the fraternity of men, and shed upon the darkest lot a repose on Providence and a light of hope. And what is true of this great apostle, is true of the religion which he spread, and which we profess. Its true dignity is, that un-seen it has ever gone about doing good. Link after link has it struck from the chain of every human thraldom: error after error has it banished: pain after pain has it driven from body or from mind : and so silently has the blessing come, that (like the lame whom Peter made to walk) " he that was healed wist not who it was."

It can *never* be unseasonable for those that bear the name of Christ to imitate his spirit, and to address themselves to the great mission which Providence has assigned to their religion (that is, to themselves), as the antagonist power to those human sufferings, which may be lightened at least, if not remedied. But this period of the year* brings with it a distinct and peculiar call to remember with a thought of mercy the several ills that flesh is heir to. Every season has its appropriate worship, and demands an appropriate recognition : for each presents in some peculiar form the physical activity of nature, which is, in fact, the immediate energy of God. If, in the picturesque spirit of ancient times, we had our annual festivals for remembering the several aspects of our lot, and bringing successively before the eye the many-colored phases of human existence, we should cast lots among the days of spring for an anniversary of life and health, when earth is unburdening her heart to God, and framing from a thousand new-born melodies an anthem of brilliant praise. For the celebration of disease and death we should resort to the days of the declining year : and instead of leaping on the green sod and pouring forth the hymn of joy, we should kneel upon the rotting leaves and pray. However constant the visitations of sickness and bereavement, the fall of the year is most thickly strewn with the fall of human life. Everywhere the spirit of some sad power seems to direct the time : it hides from us the blue heavens; it makes the green wave turbid; it walks through the fields, and lays the damp, ungathered harvest low; it cries out in the night wind and the shrill hail; it steals the summer bloom from the infant cheek; it makes old age shiver to the heart; it goes to the churchyard, and chooses many a grave; it flies to the bell, and

* This Discourse was preached at the end of November.

enjoins it when to toll. It is God that goes his yearly round; that gathers up the appointed lives; and, even where the hour is not come, engraves by pain and poverty many a sharp and solemn lesson on the heart.

How then shall we render the fitting worship of the season? We do so, when we think of these things in the *spirit of religion;* when we regard them in their relation to the great Will which produces them; when, instead of meeting them in the spirit of recklessness, or viewing in them the triumph of disorder, or shrinking from them in imbecile fear, we recognize their position in a system of universal Providence, various in its means, but paternal in its spirit and beneficent in its ends; when "none of these things move us," except to a more reverential sense of mystery, and a serener depth of trust. In a season of mortality, it is surely impossible to forget the relations of other scenes to this; that departure from this life is birth into another; that the immortal rises where the mortal falls; that the farewell in the vale below is followed by greetings on the hills above; so that, if sympathy with mourners here permit, the sorrows of the bereaved on earth are the festival of the redeemed in heaven.

We render the appropriate worship of the season, when we think of the painful passages of human life, not merely as proceeding from God, but as incident to our own lot; not merely in the spirit of religion, but in that of *self-application.* It is difficult for the living and the vigorous to realize the idea of sickness and of death: and though within a few paces of our daily walks there are beings that lie in the last struggle, and some sufferer's moan escapes with every breath that flies, yet whenever pain fairly seizes our persons in his grasp, or enters and usurps our homes, we start as if he were a stranger. And perhaps it will be asked, " Why should it be otherwise? Why forestall the inevitable day, and let the damp cloud of expectation fall on the illumined passages of life?" I grant that to remember the conditions of our existence with such result as this, to think of them in an abject and melancholy spirit, is no act of wisdom or of duty. I know of no obligation to live with an imagination ever haunted by mortality; to deem every enjoyment dangerous, lest it cheat the heart into a happy repose upon the present, and every pursuit a snare, which fairly embarks the affections upon this world; to consider all things here devoid of any good purpose except to tempt us. The theory which crowds this life with trials, and the other with rewards, which brightens the future only by blackening the present, which supposes that the only proper office of our residence here is to keep up one prolonged meditation on the hereafter, is a mere burlesque of nature and the gospel. Futurity is not to mar, but to mend, our activity; and earth is not given that we may win the reversion of heaven, so much as heaven revealed to ennoble our tenure of earth. I know of no peculiar preparation for immortality beyond the faithful performance of the best functions of mortal life; and if it were not that these will be more wisely discharged, and the attendant blessings more truly felt, by those who remember the sadder conditions of our lot than by those who forget them, there would be no reason why they should ever appear before the thoughts. But they are *facts*, solemn and inevitable facts, which come with least crushing power on those who see them from afar, and become reconciled to them, and even fill them by forethought with peaceful suggestion. The sense of their possibility breaks through the superficial crust of life, and stirs up the deeper affections of our nature. It refines the sacredness of every human tie: it dignifies the claims of duty: it freshens the emotions of conscience: it gives promptitude to the efforts of sympathy; and elevates the whole attitude of life.

But, above all, we pay the fitting worship of the season, when we greet its peculiar ills in the *spirit of humanity;* when we think of them, not simply as they come from God, and may come to ourselves, but as they actually do befall

our neighbors and fellow-men. It were selfish to gather
round our firesides, and circulate the laugh of cheerfulness
and health, without a thought or deed of pity for the poor
sufferers that struggle with the winter storms of nature or of
life. Who can help looking at this season with a more considerate and reverential eye upon the old man, to think
where he may be? Year after year he has been shaken by
the December winds, but not yet shaken to his fall: deeper
and deeper the returning frost has crept into his nature;
and will it reach the life-stream now? You watch him as
you would the last pendulous leaf of the forest, still held by
some capricious fibre, that refuses perhaps to part with it to
the storm, and then drops it slowly through the still air.
You gaze at him as he stands before you, and wonder that
you can ever do so without awe; for the visible margin of
existence crumbles beneath him, and he slips into the unfathomable. And as the tempest wakes us on our pillow, it is
but common justice to our human heart, to send out a
thought over the cold and vexed sea in search of the poor
mariner that buffets with the night, or perhaps sinks in that
most lonely of deaths, between the black heavens that pelt
him from above and the insatiable waste that swallows him
below. Nor will generous and faithful souls forget the
dingy cellar or the crowded hovel, where in a neighboring
street the fevered sufferer lies, and the ravings of delirium
and the sport of children are heard together, or life is ebbing
away in consumption, hurried to its close by the chill breath
of poverty and winter. Oh could we but see the dread gripe
of want and disease upon hundreds of this community at
this moment, and hear the cries of hungry children and the
moans of untended sickness, the only difficulty would be,
not to stimulate our generosity to do enough, but to persuade it to work out its good with patience and with
wisdom!

And here indeed *is* a difficulty, which every considerate
mind will feel to be grave, and even terrible. The multi-

tude of miseries spread around us make humanity easy, a
wise direction of its impulses, most difficult; the very spectacle which gives to benevolence its intensity, throws it also
into despair. The perplexity arises partly from the state of
society in which we live; from relations among its several
classes altogether new, and rendering the ancient and tra-
ditional methods of doing good in a great degree inappli-
cable. A slave-owning or feudal community, by killing out
from the great mass of men every thing above the rank of
hunger, reduces the office of compassion within a very
narrow compass: and the dish from the rich man's table, or
the garment from his wardrobe, sent as to the domestic animals of his estate, to stop their cries and soothe them to
sleep, are the only boons that are required, or possibly that
can be given without peril of social revolution. Happily,
— yet not without much unhappiness too, — such revolution
is now effected or in progress; greatly through the influence
of that Christianity, which pronounces all to be children of
One who is "no respecter of persons;" and assures us that
whenever we say, "Be thou warmed and filled," it is no
other than "*a brother or sister*" that comes before us
"naked and destitute of daily food." Our current notions
of benevolence have descended to us from the recent times
of feudalism: yet we are conscious that they do not come
up to the higher demands which have arisen, or adapt themselves to the new intellectual and moral wants comprised in
any Christian estimate of the poor of this world. The ease
of ancient condescension is gone: the graceful recognition
of human brotherhood is not attained. To aim at making
men like ourselves into creatures with enough to eat, —
though a thing unrealized as yet, — is felt to be insufficient;
and how to raise them into the likeness of the children of God
we cannot tell, — the very notion receiving at present but a
timid acknowledgment. This, however, if we are in earnest,
is but a temporary difficulty, attending on a state of hesitancy and transition. Let the mind fairly emancipate itself
from that debasing valuation of a human being which the

mere sentiments of property would dictate ; — trust itself, with high faith, to the equalizing spirit of Christian piety and hope ; and in paying, to all, the reverence due to an immortal, it will attain to the freedom and power of a divine love : it will speak to sorrow with the voice of another Christ, and restore his holiest miracles of mercy. Who can doubt that, were his spirit here, the work of good need not despair ?

But, for want of this spirit in perpetuity, another obstacle obstructs the course of bewildered charity. We form our good intentions too late : and while benevolence, to be successful, must work in the way of prevention and anticipation, — at the very least putting resolutely down each confused and hurtful thing as it appears, — men rarely bestir themselves till evils get ahead, and by no effort can well be overtaken. The physical, moral and religious condition of the poor, which in our days begins to excite so much attention, should have been studied thus half a century ago ; easy in comparison had it then been to prevent the ills which now we know not how to cure. We permit a generation to grow up neglected, with habits a grade below their fathers' ; and then consider how they may be reclaimed. We suffer a new manufacture to start into existence, and seize, with the hands of a needy giant, on infant labor ; and when it has appropriated a generation to itself, and boldly insists on its prescriptive right to be fed for ever from the same life-blood of our humanity, we look round on the degenerate bodies and stunted minds of an enormous population, and begin to cry out for an efficient public education, against which the immediate physical interests of poor as well as rich are now combined. The providence of God is retributory : and too often it happens that the sinful negligence of one age cannot be repaired by the penitent benevolence of many : the unpaid debt accumulates its interest, till discharge becomes impossible : misery grows impatient and clamorous ; and repays at length in fury the injuries inflicted by ancient wantonness and neglect. Neither in communities, nor in individuals, does God give encouragement to death-bed repentance: and societies that trust to it shall find themselves, after short delay, under the lash of demons and near the seat of hell. Let them be timely wise, and main-tain the vigils of benevolence, while the accepted hour remains.

Amid all controversies respecting the quarter from which the assault on the evils of indigence is best commenced, whether the physical wants should be remedied through the moral, or the moral through the physical, whether most is to be hoped for from legislative measures, or from individual efforts, one principle may be regarded as certain, and, con-sidering the tendencies of our age, not unseasonable. You cannot mechanize benevolence: you cannot put Christian love into an act of Parliament or a subscription list: and however necessary may be the remedial action of laws and institutions, on account of the comprehensive scale of their operation, the ties between man and man can be drawn closer only by personal agency. Not one new sympathy can arise but by the contact between mind and mind: in the spiritual world life is born only of life: nor is any abrogation possible of that law of God which requires that we *seek* whatever we would *save*. The good comfort which with willing soul we tender to each other is of all things most precious to the heart. As the blow of calamity falls with three-fold weight when it descends from the injustice of men, so the deliverance brought by their pity and af-fection is a blessing infinitely multiplied. The one poisons and prevents our submission, as to a will of God; the other sweetens and elevates our gratitude to him: the one cancels, the other creates, what is most divine in the dispensation. Only so far as there is a " charity " that " never faileth " from the souls of men, can they live in communion together on this earth: and from Christendom every "faith" shall be cast out as a dead heathenism, except such as " worketh by love."

12

XIX.

THE GREAT YEAR OF PROVIDENCE.

2 PETER III. 4.

WHERE IS THE PROMISE OF HIS COMING? FOR, SINCE THE FATHERS FELL
ASLEEP, ALL THINGS CONTINUE AS THEY WERE FROM THE BEGINNING
OF THE CREATION.

CHRIST quitted the world in benediction, and left upon it
a legacy of inextinguishable hope. The first manifestation
of the hopeful spirit of his religion was in the expectation,
confidently held by the Apostles and their followers, that
within "that generation" he would return from heaven in
triumph, gather together a faithful community, exterminate
the ills of human life, and become monarch over a renovated
and immortal world. Sufferers of every class (and the
church had mercy for them all) laid this hope to heart, and
stood silent beneath scorn and persecution, believing that
the lashes of oppression were numbered now. As the years
passed on, and the outer limits of the generation were approached, the flush of expectation became more intense.
One after another the Apostles dropped off, without wit-
nessing the desire of their eyes; till at last the protracted
life of John became the solitary and fragile thread on which
this splendid anticipation hung. He too died, and Jesus
had not returned: and the church, unwilling to confess its
disappointment, extended the term of hope by a liberal construction of the promise. Here and there among the communities of disciples there lingered a few aged men, whose
life reached back to the years of Christ's ministry: and till
they were gone, it was not too late for the Son of Man to

come. Expectation became more anxious and feverish every
year: passing events were perverted into auguries of its
impending realization: the rout of an army, the incursion
of a new invader, the rumor of an earthquake, the blaze of
a meteor by night, or a stroke of lightning upon a Pagan
shrine, was caught at with breathless eagerness, and watched
as a herald to the last act of human things. But as storm
after storm passed off and brought no change; as life after
life disappeared, and even rumor could find nowhere a surviving representative of Christ's generation, hope fainted
into doubt; and despair broke loose and cried, "Where is
the promise of his coming? for since the fathers fell asleep,
all things continue as they were from the beginning of the
creation." No brilliant exultation longer cheered the woes
of the church and of the world : they fell back again with
their dull weight upon the heart. The Christian mother
wept now for her martyred son, whom, in the thought of
instant restoration, she had forgot to mourn : the despised
teacher began to cower before the heathen's or the Hebrew's
scorn, which he knew no longer how to answer: and the
irons of the Christian field-slave, to which for years his faith
had given a farewell look each night before he slept, grew
heavy on his limbs again.

Almost eighteen hundred years separate us from the disappointment of this singular expectation; and the calmness
with which we can look back on a scene so distant, enables
us to draw from it a sacred lesson of Providence. Well
might God rebuke and disappoint this affectionate but erring
hope: for what, did it assume? — That a few years' preaching of a pure religion and the forcible enthronement upon
earth of one who had lived in heaven, were all that was
necessary for perfecting the world, for driving sin and sorrow from the hearts and homes of men, and giving life its
final sanctity. How imperfect was the estimate of this regenerative work, which could assign it to instruments so
inadequate, and a process so brief! God has taught us now,

that a moral change so various and stupendous, implying
the civilization of barbarism, the illumination of the ignorant,
the rescue of the oppressed, the pacification of nations, the
multiplication of Christ's own spirit of humanity over the
globe, is not to be wrought in an hour by Omnipotence itself; is beyond the reach of any mechanical scheme of rule,
though conducted by beings of another world; and must
wait on the silent operation of those spiritual laws of the
human mind which neither the individual nor the race can
be permitted to outstrip. We look back over the centuries
by which we have retired from the fountains of our faith,
and learn how solemn is the task of God's providence on
earth; for he labors at it still; and though its progress has
been visible to this hour, it seems but starting on its cycle
yet.

Who will not confess a strong sympathy with the early
Christians' delight, in anticipating certain great and divine
revolutions within their own generation? That human life
is too short to witness the fruits of its own efforts, that it
scatters in seed-time, but may not put the sickle to its own
harvest, that its whole career from infancy to age scarce
measures a solitary step in the march of humanity, has
always been felt to be an arrangement hard to bear. And
there is a peculiar fascination in the thought of personally
experiencing the realization of one's social dreams, of quickening a too tardy Providence to the pace of our fleeting
years, and finding the race of man give promise of perfection
during our mortal instead of our immortal lives. It is the
severest and sublimest duty of philanthropy to toil in faith
and die in tears; to grapple with ills that must survive it,
and may destroy; to remonstrate with oppression, and only
see its gripe tightened on its victim in revenge. The mistake of the early church is not theirs alone: it is a human,
rather than a theological, error. All men have the prime
element of such a superstition in themselves; an impatience
at the slow step of advancement, an eagerness for some visi-

ble and palpable progress in every thing which is thought
capable of indefinite improvement. Such "delusion" is the
only way in which the human soul can enter into God's
"everlasting NOW." Yet, while really springing from a
noble faith, it produces, in its reaction, many an ignoble
doubt. This disposition looks, for example, at the individual mind; and seeing it become stationary, the dull slave
of habit, declares that it cannot be immortal. Or it con-
templates the general community of men ; and imagining
its state little superior to some former condition of the world,
denies it the hope of unlimited amelioration. This spirit
of despondency is especially liable to visit us, when we stand
at one of the pauses of our time, — at the end of a season,
of a year, of a life, — of any unit that has had a predecessor,
and will have a successor, just like itself : still more perhaps,
when we review the progress (ever small compared with
our desires) of some benevolent work,* to which, from its
magnitude and character, we can see no definite termination.
The retrospect of a few years often seems to exhibit to us
a sameness the most depressing; to show us how little we
have done; to persuade us that, — as if in rebuke of our
hopes, — "all things continue as they were," and no advent
of a better life is heralded as yet. The same evils which
met our eye and our pity of old, encounter us this day : and
if in any instance they have been cancelled, others, not less
frightful, seem ever ready to rush up into their place : so that,
in turning to the future, no visible end appears to the sad-
dening task of Christian mercy. Under the influence of
this thought, the mind is haunted and harassed by the
image of all things circulating ; whirling in mysterious self-
repetition ; looking in upon us with the fixed full eye of an
ancient fatalism. And we are deluded into the fear that
nothing is ever to be better; that our faith in the progress
of our religion and our kind must be dragged into the vortex

* This Discourse was preached in behalf of the London Domestic
Mission, April, 1841.

of a wearisome periodicity, and expire in the exclamation, "Where is the promise of his coming? for since the fathers fell asleep, all things continue as they were from the beginning of the creation."

This distressing impression might be relieved, if we could only discriminate, by any rule, between those series of events which are periodical, and those which are eternal ; — between those changes in the moral world which visibly complete themselves, and those which at least *may* be interminable. Change of some kind is the law of the universe : every thing which God does is progressive : and the present question is, whether any of his progressions having reference to human beings appear to run on into infinitude?

Now in seeking for an answer to this question, we are encountered by an apparent law of the organized, or at all events of the sentient creation, of a truly remarkable character; — a law which, though discernible only in fragments and interrupted by seeming exceptions, holds with sufficient consistency to disclose the general method of nature; — viz., that in proportion to the excellence and dignity of any form of existence, is it long in coming to maturity; that the cycles of things are great, in proportion to their worth. It is needless to say that there is no other criterion of the worth of a being than the magnitude of its capacities, and the number of its functions.

In glancing our eye up the chain of animal races, however difficult it may be to arrange them symmetrically in an ascending series, the outlines of this law are surely sufficiently obvious. The creatures which, by universal consent, would be placed at the lower end of the scale, seem to come into life perfect at once, or, if they grow, to grow only in quantity : as if of an existence so inferior no part could be spared as preface to the rest. The perfect formation of creatures of a superior order divides itself into several distinguishable stages : and the greater the number of faculties and instincts, the longer is the period set apart for the process of development. The lion has a longer infancy than the sheep, and the sagacious elephant than either. The human being, lord of this lower world, is conducted to this supremacy through a yet more protracted ascent: none of the creatures that he rules have an infancy so helpless or so lasting: none furnish themselves so slowly with the knowledge needful for self-subsistence : — as if to him time were no object, and no elaboration of growth were too great for his futurity.

Compare also the different faculties and feelings of the individual human mind. You find them appear in the order of their excellence ; the noblest approaching their maturity the last. Sensation, which belongs to man in common with all other sentient beings, is the endowment of his earliest days. Memory, which simply prevents experience from perishing, which furnishes language to the lips, and preserves the materials of the past for future treatment by the mind, ripens next. The understanding, which makes incursions and wins trophies in the field of abstract truth, which devises measures for the dimensions of space and the successions of time and the great physical movements that circulate within them, is of later origin: while the great inventive power which distinguishes all genius, which seems to sympathize with the devising spirit of the Artificer of things, and apprehend by natural affinity the most subtle relations he has established, and anticipate by mysterious intimacy the future secrets of nature, and from old and gross ingredients create the useful, the beautiful, the true, is the last as it is the rarest and most glorious of intellectual gifts. And the moral powers, — so far as they can be regarded separately from these, — are seen and felt expanding later still. The true appreciation of action and character, the faithful and impartial love of whatever things are pure and good, the correct and profound estimate of life, the serenest spirit of duty and of faith, are scarcely found till most of the lessons of our mortal state have been read, and

the soul has caught some snatches of inspiration from the
"still sad music of humanity." We may even say, that
perhaps not all our faculties develop themselves here; and
whole classes of emotions and conceptions may wait to be
born beneath other influences. Certain at least it is, that
one who dies in infancy can have little idea of any thing
beyond sensation; that one who falls in childhood cannot know the toils and triumphs of the pure reason;
that one who dies in youth has not yet learned the sense
of power which belongs to the practised exercise of creative thought, and the sacred peace of disinterested duty
long tried in trembling and in tears. Certain too it is,
that to the open mind fresh gleams enter to the last;
strange stirrings of diviner sympathies; waves of thin transparent light flitting through the spaces of the aged mind,
like the aurora of the north across the wintry sky. Even
therefore when "maturity" has been passed, we may die,
peradventure, ignorant of the secret fountains of illumination that may be sequestered in the recesses of our nature:
and when we depart at three-score years and ten, our
experience may be as truly imperfect, — as much a mere
fragment, — as when we lapse in a mortality falsely called
" premature."

From the individual mind turn to the successive developments of society at large; and the same law is perceptible
still; that the superior attributes are of the longest growth.
The most rapid of social changes is found in the progress of
material civilization; and certainly it is the least dignified
element in the general advancement, though essential to the
rest. Of the rapidity with which a new art may be perfected, new channels of commerce filled, a new manufacture
start into gigantic existence, no age or country affords more
striking instances than our own. Let gain supply the adequate motive; and a few years suffice to reclaim the wilderness, and make the harvest wave where before the forest
rose; or to cover the soil with cities, busy with congregated

labor; or to enliven the sea with traffic, where none had disturbed its solitudes before. How much longer does it require to penetrate the mass of a community with knowledge; to fill a land with intelligence, than to throng it with life! Even in the long lives of nations, few have arrived at that season, when the demand for general instruction naturally appears, and the truth goes forth, that the people are not a herd of mere animals or instruments of mere wealth, but beings of rational nature, who have a right to their powers of thought: and even where this demand has arisen, scarce a people yet has lived long enough to answer it. The morality of a community cannot be matured till its intelligence is unfolded: in societies, as in individuals, character cannot set, till reason has blossomed. The pure tastes of virtue cannot be looked for in those who have never been led beyond their senses; nor even a wise self-interest be expected, where no habits of foresight have been acquired, and the intellect has not been taught to respect the future. I do not even suppose that the moral amelioration of a country immediately follows on the " diffusion of knowledge." On the spread of *education* it may : but it must be an education which comprises a principle of sympathy as well as of instruction; which has a discipline for the heart as well as for the understanding; which remembers the composite structure of our nature, and applies knowledge to no more than its proper office of enlightening the reason, and summons up *feelings* of right as the fit antagonists to passions that tend to wrong. But slower still than this is the religious civilization of a country: so that the history of a religion is usually a much longer and vaster one than the history of any people; a faith embracing many nations, but no nation many faiths. The most sacred ideas attach themselves with the greatest tenacity to the mind; entwine themselves with the principles of action and forms of the affections; and being most distrustful of change, are most tardy of improvement. The history of the past confirms these positions. Those countries whose progress has been the noblest and most durable, have attained their eminence by slow and imperceptible steps. And, on the other hand, the oriental tribes that have rushed into sudden splendor, have either stopped with the material or at best the intellectual form of greatness, without rising into the moral and spiritual: or else, their religion, resting on no adequate substrata of the lower ingredients of civilization, wanted an element of stability; manifesting the nomadic strength for conquest and weakness for repose; and becoming enervated by the arts and opulence and science which it first called into existence, and then could not command.

Wherever we look then, — to the chain of animal existence, to the faculties of the individual mind, or the stages of collective society, — we discover distinct traces of the same general law; that in proportion to the excellence of any form of being, is its progress tardy and its cycle vast. Contract the limits of any nature, and its changes become quick and visible: enlarge them, and its vibrations become slow and majestic. On the surface of a pool, the wind raises rapid billows that would agitate an insect; on the ocean, mighty oscillations that give a frigate time to think. "Like tide there is in the affairs of men:" and if we think nobly of the great element on which it rides, if we take humanity to be no foul and shallow marsh, but a boundless and unfathomable deep, we shall not marvel that our little life scarce feels its deliberate and solemn sweep. Why, even in physical nature, the more complex and extensive any system of bodies is, the longer is the period of its revolution, and the less perceptible its velocity as a whole. Our single earth, revolving round the sun, soon comes to the point from which it started: add the moon to it, and the three orbs demand a greatly increased duration to return to the same relative position: collect the planets into a group, and their cycle of return when every perturbation shall have had its revolution, and they shall look at each other as they did at first, becomes immense, and, in our poor conceptions, almost coincides with eternity itself: and the solar system, as a whole, is travelling on all the while, astronomers assure us, towards the constellation Hercules. Such are the natural periods of the moral world, in proportion to the grandeur of its parts and relations; such, the tendencies of man and society, considered as a complex whole : however insensible the parallax of their progression, they doubtless gravitate incessantly to some distant constellation in the universe of brilliant possibilities, — to some space in the future where dwell and move forms of power and of good which it is no fable to believe gigantic and godlike.

In proportion then as we think well of our nature and of our kind ; in proportion as we estimate worthily the task of Providence in ripening a world of souls, shall we be reconciled to the tardy and interrupted steps by which the work proceeds. We shall be content and trustful, though our personal portion of the work, and even the sum of our combined endeavors while we live, should be inconspicuously small. Have you resolved, as much as in you lies, to lessen the number of those who, in this metropolis of the charities, have none to help them, or lift them from the darkness wherein they exist and perish unseen ? It is good. Only remember, that if the ministry, which thus dives into the recesses of human wretchedness, and carries a healing pity to the body and the soul, which speaks to tempted, fallen, stricken men, from a heart that feels their struggle terrible, yet believes the conquest possible, be really right and Christian, then its slowness is but the attendant and symptom of its worth : and to despond because a few years' labor exhibits no large and deep impression made on the wickedness and miseries of this great city, would be to slight the work and forget its dignity. When London, mother of mighty things, after the travail of centuries, brings forth woes, how can they be other than giant woes,

which no faint hope, no puny courage, but only the enterprise of high faith, can manacle and lay low? Surely it is
an unworthy proposal which we sometimes hear respecting
this and other deputed ministries of good, " Well, it is a
doubtful experiment, but let us try it for a few years." If,
indeed, this means that, in case of too small a measure of
success, we are to do something more and greater; that we
must be content with no niggardly and unproductive operation, but recognize in scanty results a call to stronger efforts ;
that, failing a delegated ministry, we will go forth ourselves
into the places of want and sin, and make aggression on
them with a mercy that can wait no more ; in *this* sense,
let the mission pass for a temporary trial. But if it be
meant that, disappointed in our hopes, we are to give up
all and *do nothing ;* that, having once set plainly before our
face the beseeching looks of wounded and bleeding humanity stretched upon our path, we are to " pass by on the
other side," thinking it enough to have " come and seen
where it was," — then I must say that any work, under-
taken in this spirit, *has* failed already. For my own part,
I should say that were we even to make *no* visible progress,
were we able to beat back the ills with which we contend
by not one hair's breadth ; — nay, were they to be seen
actually advancing on us, still no retreat, but only the more
strenuous aggression, would be admissible. For what purpose can any Christian say that he is here in life, with his
divine intimation of what *ought to be,* and his sorrowing
perception of what *is,* if not to put forth a perpetual
endeavor against the downward gravitation of his own
and others' nature? And if in the conquest of evil God
can engage himself eternally, is it not a small thing for us
to yield up to the struggle our three-score years and ten ?
Whatever difficulties may baffle us, whatever defeat await
us, it is our business to live with resistance in our will, and
die with protest on our lips, and make our whole existence,
not only in desire and prayer, but in resolve, in speech, in

act, a remonstrance against whatever hurts and destroys in all the earth. Did we give heed to the counsels of passiveness and despondency, our Christendom, faithless to the trust consigned to it by Heaven, must perish by the forces to which it has succumbed. For, between the Christian faith, teaching the fatherhood of God and the immortality of men, — between this and the degradation of large portions of the human family, there is an irreconcilable variance, an internecine war, to be interrupted by no parley; and mitigated by no quarter: and if faith gives up its aggression upon the evil, the evil must destroy the faith. If the world were all a slave-market or a gin-palace, what possible place could such a thing as the Christian religion find therein? Who, amid a carnival of sin, could believe in any deathless sanctity? or, through the steams of a besotted earth, discern the pure light of an overarching heaven? or, through the moans and dumb anguish of a race, send up a hymn of praise to the All-merciful? And are there not thousands already, so environed and shut in, that *their* world *is* little else than this? In proportion as this number is permitted to increase, does Christianity lose its evidence and become impossible. Sensualism and sin cannot abide the clear angelic look of Christian faith; but if once that serene eye becomes confused and droops abashed, the foe starts up in demoniac triumph, and proclaims man to be a brute, and earth a grave.

As we love then the religion by which we live, let us give no heed to doubt and fear. In the spirit of hope and firm endeavor let us go forward with the work we have begun; undismayed by difficulties which God permits us to hold in check, but not to vanquish; and stipulating for no rewards of large success as the conditions of our constancy of service. Our reliance for good results, and our consolation under their postponement, is in the essentially religious elements of this ministry: were its methods purely economic, addressing themselves exclusively to the bodily wants of its

objects; or intellectual, working at their self-interest and
self-will, — I for one should despair of any return worthy
of much patience. But going forth as we do with that divine and penetrative religion, to whose subduing energy so
many centuries and nations have borne their testimony, and
continuing only that evangelizing process, before which so
much wretchedness and guilt have already yielded, we take
our appointed place in the long history of Christianity, and
attempt a work for which, like Providence, we can afford to
wait. It is human, indeed, to desire some rich success; and
each generation expects to gather and taste the produce of
its own toil: but the seasons of God are eternal; he "giveth
the increase," not for enjoyment only, but for reproduction;
and ripens secretly, beneath the thick foliage of events,
many a fruit of our moral tillage, for the sake of the little
unnoticed seed, which, dropped on the soil of his providence, shall spread over a future age the shelter of some
tree of life. Be it ours in word to proclaim, in deed to
make ready, the " acceptable year of the Lord."

XX.

CHRIST AND THE LITTLE CHILD. .

———◆———

LUKE XVIII. 17.

VERILY I SAY UNTO YOU, WHOSOEVER SHALL NOT RECEIVE THE KINGDOM
OF GOD AS A LITTLE CHILD, SHALL IN NO WISE ENTER THEREIN.

By the kingdom of God was meant neither the future state
of the righteous, nor the dominion of Christianity in the
world ; but the personal reign of Messiah over a favored
and faithful people, on a renovated earth. The prospect of
this period was, however, to the people of Palestine, nearly
what the hope of heaven is to the Christian : — it embodied
all their ideas of divine privilege and happiness, and, coinciding with their conception of religious existence, became
their great symbol, by which to express the most blessed
system of relations between the human mind and God.
Into this system they esteemed it their birth-right to enter :
the title and prerogative were in their blood, — the blood
of patriarchs whom they had ceased to resemble, and of
prophets of whose spirit they had none. At the gate of the
kingdom they looked with no meek and far-off desire ; they
knelt and knocked with no suppliant air, breathing such
confessions of unworthiness as give security for gratitude ;
but turned on it the greedy eye of property, and rushed to
it with intent to " do what they liked with their own," —
so that " the kingdom of heaven suffered violence, and the
violent would take it by force." Scarcely were they content
with the notion of admission as its subjects ; they must be
its lords and administrators too. For them, thought the

Pharisees, were its dignities and splendors created, for them its patronage reserved ; and the glorious sovereignty of God was to be not *over* them, but *by* them : so that, in every proffer of their services to Him, they contemplated, not the humility of submission, but the pride of command. Before such it was that Jesus held in his arms a child, gazing on his face, no doubt, in wonder, not without a pleased look of trust, and said, " Whosoever shall not receive the kingdom of God as a little child, shall in no wise enter therein."

The occasion was slight and transient; the sentiment is profound and universal. In no other way could our Lord have made the irreligion of the Pharisees' temper more obvious, because nowhere could he have found a more genuine emblem of the pure religious spirit, than in a child. Not, as will hereafter appear, because a child's heart is peculiarly devotional ; nor because the moral qualities of early life possess the romantic purity and perfection sometimes ascribed to them ; much less because maturity affords a less fitting scope for the exercise of a holy mind : but because the relations of infancy resemble the religious relations; the natural conditions of its existence are the same that are felt by the devout heart; and hence, without any singularity of merit, the spirit of childhood, acquired by simple accommodation to the law of its being, is a just representative of the temper which devotion imparts to the mature. Let us trace some of the analogies between the spirit of childhood and the spirit of religion.

Religion, it is obvious, can have place only in created and dependent minds. God cannot be devout: and though we have a term, viz. " *holy*," applicable, as an epithet of moral description, to him in common with good men, the word, singularly enough, expresses, in reference to the human mind, precisely the only quality which cannot possibly attach to the Divine ; — " *a holy man* " meaning one whose excellence has a religious root, — " a holy God " denoting the only being in the spiritual, universe, whose perfections are unsusceptible of the colors of religious emotion. He who has no higher than himself must be stranger to the unspeakable reverence that gazes upwards on a goodness not its own: he who is himself the measure of all that is divine is unconscious of the presence of a yet diviner: and though we cannot speak of his moral attributes, without implying that he respects and loves the right, yet his venerating regards must look for this great idea, not *forth*, as on some outward being who furnishes the conception, but *within*, where alone is the infinitude that befits the Infinite.

Yet it is not strictly Deity alone whose nature may exclude the possibilities of religion. This peculiarity may arise without our seeking it at that supreme height. A mind possessed, not of literal omniscience, but of power simply equal to its conceptions, a mind absolute within its own realm, and limited only by its desires, would be incapable of veneration, because unconscious of a superior: and though he might really live in a narrow ring environed by the immeasurable deep of things, — so long as he mistook its circle for the total universe, he would feel, not as dependent, but as God, — lord of his little island in the sea of things, and ignorant of all beyond. Not till we are embraced by some necessity, and see its limits closing us in, can the opportunity and spirit of religion begin. So long as self-will is the sole law, and sits upon its throne, surrounded by obedient servitors, and in unresisted practice of command, the relations from which piety springs do not subsist. The exercise of power will not induce the idea of obligation, or the temper of submission. It is when we are struck down by some blow that extorts the cry of dependence, when we feel the pressure of foreign forces like a weight of darkness on us, when within us moves the strife that ends sometimes in the triumphs of success, sometimes in the collapse of weakness, that the heart acknowledges a relation to that which is above, as well as to that which is beneath. And even then, though submission is clearly inevitable, not so are the sentiments of religion : for there is still a question, submit *with hate*, or submit *with love?* And it is the blessed peculiarity of devotion, that it abdicates self-will, not sullenly, but with joy, has no enmity to the power that restrains it, but a reverence deep and tender, so that to feel the controlling presence becomes the prime condition of its peace, and to be stricken of God and afflicted is better than to be left to itself, and be at peace. " Let me alone, and torment me not," is the cry of discontent : "break me in sorrow, but depart not from me," is the prayer of piety. Such a suppliant has found the force of compulsion turned into the law of duty ; and, inverting its direction, instead of crushing to the earth, it lifts him to the skies : if once he said with deep reluctance, " *I must*, therefore I will," he has now fused a divine element into that bitter word, and finds it a glad thing to say, " *I ought*, therefore I will." *Ought* is the heavenly reading for " *must.*" From the iron sceptre of necessity he has forged a weapon of ethereal temper ; wherewith may be won victories more sublime than all the achievements of physical omnipotence.

Self-will then, so far as it operates, excludes the sentiments of religion ; while it is of their very essence to live reverently and happily under a law not always coinciding with self-will. It is this which presents us with the first analogy between the spirit of childhood and the spirit of religion.

What indeed can be a truer picture of man in creation, than the position of a child in its own home? How silently, yet how surely, does the domestic rule control him, dating his rising and his rest, his going out and coming in, apportioning his duties and his mirth, ordering secretly the very current of his thoughts, whether it sparkle with gladness, or overflow with tears! Yet how rarely has he any painful sense of the constraining force which is every moment on him! Hemmed in on every side by a power more vigilant than the most jealous despotism, yet look at his open brow, and say, whether creature ever was more free? And why? Not certainly because childish minds are destitute of self-will that would seduce them into transgression; but because, where reverence and love make melody in the heart, the tempter is charmed and sleeps. Light therefore as the weight of the circumambient atmosphere upon the body, is the pressure of home duty upon the child; easy by the constancy and completeness with which it shuts him in; inseparable from the vital elements of his being. His life is an exchange of obedience for protection: he gives sub-mission, and is sheltered. Folded in the arms of an un-speakable affection, he is screened from the anxieties of self-care: not yet is he left alone upon the infinite plain of existence, to choose a path by the dim, sad lustre of his own wisdom, but is led gently on by the unextinguished lamp of a father's experience, and the meek starlight of a mother's love. In strangeness and danger, how close he keeps to the hand that leads him! In doubt, how he looks up to inter-pret the eye that speaks to him! In loss and loneliness, with what cries and tears he sits down to lament his free-dom! He asks, but claims nothing; his momentary froward-ness is stilled perhaps by a mere word; and, if not, yet his spontaneous return, after an interval, to his accustomed ways, confesses that in the order of obedience is the truest liberty.

In a like free and natural movement within the limits of a higher law, in like obedience refreshing because reveren-tial, in like consciousness of a wiser and holier presence, from whom we withhold nothing, not even ourselves, con-sists the spirit of true piety: nor can any dwell on earth or in heaven, finding it a kingdom of God, but as the loving child dwells within his home. Unhappily, this temper is apt to be worn away by the hard attrition of maturer life. Our human relations are then reversed; we succeed, in natural course, to habits of command; the pride of power spoils us; the mental attitudes of reverence become uneasy;

the eye bent unceasingly down on the petty realm of which
we are lords, omits to look up on the. infinite empire of
which we are subjects. And thus might we become shut
up in the dry crust of our self-will, if no embassage of suffering descended,. and loosed the fountain of grief. Then
the spirit of early years returns upon good hearts, and they
become ashamed, not of their new submission to the Great
Parent, but of their long estrangement from his abode. A
piety, like that of Christ, thus brings together the characteristic affections of different periods of life, and keeps fresh
the beauty of them all: it puts us back to whatever is blessed
in childhood, without abating one glory of our manhood;
upon the embers of age it kindles once more the early fires
of life, to send their genial glow through the evening chamber of the soul, and shine with playful and mellowed light
through its darkened windows, — brightest sign of a cheerful home to the passer-by in storm and rain. By this restoration, let me repeat it, the religious mind loses no one
glory of its manhood : it is not a substitution of passive
meekness for active energy, of a devout effeminacy for
natural vigor. For while the habit of successful rule, taking the lead, is apt to disqualify for submission, and render
the mind restive under necessity, there is nothing in a deep
reverence of soul which encroaches on the capacities for
command. What was it that armed the Maid of Orleans
for field and siege, and enabled her to erect again the prostrate courage of a nation? What was it that endowed a
Washington with a power, in arms and peace, which no
veterans could break, nor any rival supplant? It was this :
that with them the exercise of command was itself the
practice of obedience ; — obedience to a high faith within
the heart, — to a venerated idea of duty and of God ; and
authority, thus deprived of its imperiousness and its caprice,
thus moderated to an inflexible justice, and worn with a
divine simplicity, strikes into human observers an awe, a
delight, a trust, which are themselves the highest fruits of

power. When men perceive that their very rulers are susceptible of obedience, and are following the guidance of reverential thoughts, it establishes a point of sympathy, and softens the hardships of submission. What parent knows not that then only are his orders listened to as oracles, when they are sent forth, not with the harsh clangor of self-will, but in the quiet tones that issue from behind the shrine of duty?

In the construction which I have given to the sentiment of Christ, it is not necessary to assume that the infant mind is peculiarly susceptible of religious impressions; or that, because it is taken as the emblem of the kingdom of heaven, it must on that account be laboriously and prematurely crowded with theological ideas : the issue of which would be, an artificial assumption of states of sentiment, and an affectation of desires, wholly unnatural and unreal, and absolutely incapable as yet of any deep root of sincerity. Except in circumstances of sickness or grief, which prematurely ripen the mind and make its wants anticipate its years, childhood has little need of a religion, in our sense of the word; for God has given it, in its very lot, a religion of its own, the sufficiency of which it were impiety to doubt. The child's veneration can scarcely climb to any loftier height than the soul of a wise and good parent : — well even, if he can distantly, and with wistful contemplation, scan even that. How can there be for him diviner truth than his father's knowledge, a more wondrous world than his father's experience, a better providence than his mother's vigilance, a securer fidelity than in their united promise? Encompassed round by these, he rests as in the embrace of the only omniscience he can comprehend. Nor let this domestic faith suffer disturbance before its time. It is enough if he but sees the parents bend with silent awe, or hears them speak as if they were children too, before a holier still : this will carry on the ideal gradation of reverence, and show the filmy deep where the steps ascend the

skies. And then, when the time of free-will is come, and
youth is cast forth from its protection into the bewildering
forces, now fierce and now seductive, of mid-life, religion
comes in, as the just and natural successor to domestic influences; shaping forth, for the heart's shelter in the wild
immensity, the walls of an adamantine Providence, and
spreading over the uncovered head the dome of immortality.
Oh it is thus only that we mortals, in our maturity of energy
and passion, can dwell on earth in purity and peace. By a
polity of self-interest, and adjustments of promotion, and
agencies of fear, we might no doubt have the world gov-
erned as a camp or a prison; but by faith alone can we
dwell in it as a home, and nestle domestically in our allotted
portion of space and time. Taught by Christ, we glance
at the visible creation, once so awful, so full of forces rushing we knew not whither, and involving us in their indomitable speed, — and it becomes the mansion of God's house,
peaceful as a father's abode; the sun that warms us in our
domestic hearth; and the blue canopy roofs us in with unspeakable protection. And as for life and its struggles, its
stormiest conflicts are but the mimic battles, whereby the
spiritual athlete trains himself for a higher theatre; and if
perchance, among the restless multitude that hurry over the
scene, a neighbor should fall, shall I not help him, though
it be his own demon passion that rends him? O child of
my Father, wounded, bleeding, and worn by inward woes,
turn not thy face away! let me lift thee from thy bed of
rock, and stretch thee on the green sod of a pure affection;
for am I not thy brother, stricken in thy stripes, and healed
in thy rest?

This restoration to us of the filial feelings is the main
illustrative point in our Lord's analogy between the spirit
of piety and that of infancy. But there are other characteristics of childhood, which religion renders back to us,
freshened and ennobled. To the child, the time before him
seems to have no end. It is long before he essays to meas-

ure it at all; and when he does, it is only to prove it immeasurable. The next year is as a gigantic bridge that
·joins the two eternities; and as for all beyond, it is a
land boundless, safe; verdant as the spring meadow, and
flooded over with gladdest sunshine. The open graves lie
hid among the grass; and the horizon shows not the little
cloud, that shall bring up the overcasting of the heavens.
Let a few years pass, and how does the vast field contract
itself, and the stability of things seem shaken! The merry
playmates, whose laugh still rings in our memory, by what
storms have they been shattered; and now wander dis-
persed, like a shipwrecked crew, whose faithful hearts could
keep together no longer against necessities so sharp! Before the middle of our natural career the wastes of vicissi-
tude become deplorable: nor could any thoughtful man, if
abandoned to physical impressions, feel the great mountain
of life crumbling away beneath him, and see portion after
portion dropping into the abyss on which it seems built, till
but a film separates him too from the gulf, without the chill of
an awe most sad. But this impression of a mournful brevity
in our existence, the spirit of our faith corrects. To the
life which had begun to appear like a process of continual
loss, it adds another which is an everlasting gain; and we
look again upon the future with eyes of childlike joy, seeing
that, as our infant hearts had said, it *hath* no end, nor any
grief that can endure. From the cypress-tree beneath whose
shadow we had placed ourselves to weep, we pass on with
lightened step into the paradise of God, where is a rustling
as of whispers of divinest peace, and hills, truly called
eternal, close us round.

Oh blest beyond expression are they who, by this spirit of
Christ, call back the freshness of their early years, and shed
it over the wisdom of maturity; who, by attaching the
great and transforming idea of God to every thing, deprive
the humblest existence of its monotony! who hear in the
speech, and behold in the incidents, of every day, somewhat

that is sacred! For them life has no satiety, disappointment no sting. They bear within them a penetrative power,
which pierces beneath the earthy surface of things, and detects a meaning that is heavenly; enriching common sentiment with profound truth; lifting common duties from the
conventional and the respectable into the holy and divine;
and amid trials of the hour, giving dignity to that which
else were humiliating and mean.

XXI.

THE CHRISTIANITY OF OLD AGE.

PHILEMON 9.

FOR LOVE'S SAKE I RATHER BESEECH THEE, BEING SUCH A ONE AS PAUL
THE AGED.

THE reverence for age is a striking and refreshing feature
in the civilization of ancient and Pagan times. The frequent
traces of it in the literature of Greece and Rome, compared
with the silence of Christian precept on the subject, might
be thought to indicate, that this sentiment owes no obligation to Christianity, and has a better home in the humanities
of nature than in the suggestions of faith. The conclusion,
however, would be wholly unwarrantable ; and would never
occur except to those who do not look beyond the letter
into the spirit of a system, and who think to understand a
religion by arithmetical reckoning of its maxims. Every system naturally strengthens most its weakest points. That
Cicero wrote a treatise upon age, and expended on it all
the ingenuity of his philosophy, and the graces of his dialogue, proves that he regarded this department of morality
with anxiety and apprehension : nor would Christianity
have left the topic untouched, if its spirit and faith had
not lifted this class of duties beyond the danger of neglect.
A decline of tenderness towards the aged, — mean or even
melancholy sentiments with respect to their infirmities, —
can never arise without scepticism of human immortality,
and a total defection from the Christian mind.

The dignity of age, in the ancient world, was sustained
by many considerations, of mingled expediency and affection,

which retain with us but little force. Of how many honors has the printing-press alone deprived the hoary head! It has driven out the era, so genial to the old, of *spoken* wisdom, and threatens a reign of silence by putting all knowledge and experience into type. The patriarch of a community can never be restored to the kind of importance which he possessed in the elder societies of the world. He was his neighbor's *chronicler;* bearing within him the only extant image of many departed scenes and memorable deeds, and able to link the dim traditions of the past with the living incidents of the present. He was their most qualified *counsellor;* his memory serving as the archives of the state, and supplying many a passage of history illustrative of existing emergencies, and solving some civic perplexity. He was their *poet;* representative of an age already passed from the actual into the ideal; associate or contemporary of men whose names have become venerable; and in the oft-repeated tale of other days, from which time has expelled whatever was prosaic, weaving the retrospect of life into an epic. He was their *priest;* loving to nurture wonder and spread the sense of mystery, by recounting the authentic prodigies of his own or his fathers' years, when omen and prophecy were no dubious things, but sober verities which Providence had not yet begrudged the still pious earth. From all these prerogatives he is now deposed, supplanted in his authority by the journal and the library; whose speechless and impersonal lore coldly, but effectually, supplies the wants once served by the living voice of elders kindling with the inspiration of the past.

By far other and higher considerations does Christianity sustain reverential sentiments towards age. In the shape which they formerly assumed, they were the effects and marks of an imperfect intellectual civilization: surviving now, they are a part of the devout humanities diffused by the spirit of Christ. But for that spirit, every change which made the old less useful would have made them less revered.

But the merely social and utilitarian estimate of human beings can never become prevalent, so long as faith in the immortal soul is genuine and sincere, and Jesus is permitted to teach in his own way the honor that is due to all men. To him did God give it to be the great foe of all scorn and negligence of heart; nor are there any tenants of life on whose lot he has shed a greater sanctity, than on those who are visibly on the verge of their departure. Let us observe for a few moments how Christianity teaches the world to look upon the aged.

Not, certainly, as its worn-out tools, who have done their work, and are fit only to be flung aside to rust amid worthless things. Not with sordid discontent, as on unwelcome and tedious guests, that they linger still to consume a hospitality which they will never repay, and keep possession of sources of enjoyment, on which more vivid appetites are impatient to enter. For wherever the slightest vestige of such feelings exists, there can be no remembrance of that higher field of service, of that nobler and more finished work, for which time, to its last beat, continues to prepare. So Epicurean a thought harbors in the low grounds of selfishness and sense, and has never felt the pure breath of faith and reverence. Is there nothing which can drive us from this infatuation, and persuade us to look at a human being, not for what he *has*, but for what he *is?* Is he nothing then but a pensioner of Mammon, whose pittance is a pleasant sight for greedy eyes? Can we see him decline step by step to the brink of the dark abyss, till the ground crumbles beneath him and he slips in, and yet spend all our anxiety on the dropped cloak he has left behind?

Nor are the mere feelings of instinctive compassion towards weakness and helplessness those with which Christianity encourages us to look on age. For, these contemplate only its physical attributes; they virtually deny or overlook all its claims, except those of its animal infirmities; and show a mind forgetful of the capacities within, latent perhaps,

but yet imperishable, that have toiled in a great work, and
are on the threshold of a greater; that can know no eclipse
but that of shame, nor any decrepitude but that of sin.

It has been imagined that religious faith does not like to
draw, attention to the decline which precedes, often by years,
the approach of death; that the spectacle of a human being
in ruins terrifies the expectation of futurity, and humbles
the mind with mean suspicions of its destiny. Scepticism,
which delights in all the ill-bodings which can be drawn
from evil and decay, takes us to the corner where the old
man sits; shows us the bent frame, and fallen cheeks, and
closing avenues of sense; points to the palsied head, and
compels us to listen to the drivelling speech, or perhaps the
childish and pitiable cry; and then asks, whether *this* is the
being so divinely gifted and so solemnly placed, sharer of
the immortality of God, and waiting to embark into infinitude? I answer, — assuredly *not:* neither in the wrecked
frame, nor in the negation of mind, is there any thing immortal: it is not this frail and shattered bark, visible to the
eye, that is to be launched upon the shoreless sea. The mind
within, which you do *not* show me, whose indications are
for a time suppressed, — as they are in every fever that
brings stupor and delirium, in every night even that brings
sleep, — the mind, of whose high achievements, whose capacious thought, whose toils and triumphs of conscience and
affection, living friends will reverently tell you, — the mind,
which every moment of God's time for seventy years has
been sedulous to build, and from which the deforming scaf-
fold is about to fall away, — this alone is the principle for
which we claim immortality. Say not that, because we
cannot trace its operations, it is extinct: perhaps, while
you speak, it may burst into a flame, and contradict you.
For sometimes age is known to wake, and the soul to kindle,
ere it departs; to perforate the shut gates of sense with
sudden light, and gush with lustre to the eye, and love and
reason to the speech; as if to make it evident, that death

may be nativity; as if the traveller who had fallen asleep with the fatigues of the way, conscious that he drew near his journey's end, and warned by the happy note of arrival, looked out refreshed and eager through the morning air for the fields and streams of his new abode. And if any transient excitement near the close of life can, even occasionally, thus resuscitate the spirit ; if some vehement stroke upon a chord of ancient sympathy can sometimes restore it in its strength, it is there still; and only waits that permanent rejuvenescence which its escape into the infinite may effect at once.

It is not a little difficult to understand, in what way these objectors would desire to improve the adjustments of life, in order to get rid of the grounds of their scepticism. Would they totally abolish the infirmities of years, and maintain the energy of youth unto the end? *Then* would there remain no apparent reason for removal or change : death would have looked tenfold more like extinction than it does now : and we should assuredly have reasoned, " If the Divine Father, in his benignity, had intended us to persevere in life at all, he would have left us in peace in this dear old world." As it is, there appears, after the decrepitude of age, an obvious need of some such mighty revolution as death : the mortality of such a body becomes a clear essential to the immortality of the soul : and our departure assumes the probable aspect of a simple migration of the mind, — a journey of refreshment, — a passage to new scenes of that infinite universe, to a mere speck of which, since we can discover its immensity, it seems unlikely that we should be confined.

Or is the demand of a different kind; not for immunity from bodily decline, but for an exemption of the soul from its effects? for faculties unconscious of the sinking frame, — dwelling in a tenement of whose changes they shall be independent? And what is this, when you reflect upon it, but to ask for a total separation of the material from the

spiritual element of our nature, — for the very boon which
we suppose to be obtained in death, a disembodied mind?
For, a corporeal frame that did not affect the mental principle, would no more be any proper part of us, than the
limbs of another man or the substance of the sun : its mere
juxtaposition or coincidence in space with our sentient soul
(even could such a thing be truly affirmed) would not mix
it up with our identity. Unless it were the interposed
medium through which we communicated with the external
world, — the appointed pathway of sensation ; unless, that
is, we experienced vicissitudes of internal consciousness precisely corresponding to all its external changes, — we should
have no interest in it, and it would have as little concern
with our personality as the clothes or the elements in which
we live. A hand that should leave us affected in the same
way, whether it touched ice or fire ; a tongue that should
recognize no difference between food and poison ; an eye
that should convey to us the same impression through all
its altering states, — would be unfitted for all its functions,
and be a mere foreign encumbrance upon our life. That
our organization reports instantly, — with a speed that no
magnetic signal can surpass, — to the mind within ; that it
works changes in our conscious principle precisely proportionate to its own, and affording a true measure of them, —
is the very attribute which constitutes its exactitude and
perfection. If then it were absurd to wish for limbs that
could undergo exhaustion and laceration without our feeling
them, and nerves that would give no knowledge of fever
or inflammation, it would be no less irrational to desire a
release of the mind from those infirmities of age, which
are but a long fatigue, — life's final disease. All the lights
of perception and emotion flow in upon us through the
colored glass of our organic frame ; and however perfect
the power of mental vision may remain, if the windows be
darkened, the radiance will be obscure.

And in the two most marked characteristics of old age, —

the obtuseness of immediate perception, and the freshness
of remote memories, — may we not even discern an obvious
intimation of the great future, and a fitting preparative for
its approach? The senses become callous and decline, verg-
ing gently to the extinction which awaits them, and in their
darkness permitting the mild lustre of wisdom and of faith
— if it be there — to shine forth and glow; and if not, to
show in what a night the soul dwells without them. And
that the mind should betake itself, ere it departs, with such
exclusive attachment to the past, is surely suitable to its
position. True, the enthusiastic devotion of an awed spectator, standing near to say farewell, naturally takes the
opposite direction, and steals before the pilgrim to his home,
and wonders that the old man's talk can linger so around
things gone by. But is it not that already the thoughts
fall into the order of judgment, and practise the incipient
meditations of heaven? In that world of which we have
no experience, we can at first have no anticipation : and in
the place whither we go for retribution, we must begin with
retrospect. All things and thoughts, all passions and pursuits, must live again : stricken memory cannot withhold
them : there is a divination of conscience, at which their
ghosts must rise, to haunt or bless us. And when the old
man incessantly reverts to years that had receded into the
far distance, and finds scenes that had appeared to vanish
come back even from his boyhood and stand around ·him
with preternatural distinctness, when ancient snatches of
.ife's melodies thrill through his dreams, and the faces of
early friends look in upon him often, the preparation is sig-
nificant. He is gathering his witnesses together, making
ready the theatre of trial, and collecting the audience for
judgment. These are they that were with him in his manifold temptations, and can tell him of his victory or his fall ;
that exercised such spirit of duty as was in him ; whom his
selfishness injured, or his fidelity blessed. Remembrance
has broken the seals of its tombs ; its sainted dead come

forth at the trump of God within the soul, and declare the tribunal set.

With emotions then far different from the meanness of animal compassion, and the coldness of doubt, does the spirit of Christ teach the world to look on age. The veneration for it which our religion inspires, comes not from the past alone, but rather from the future. In *any* view indeed, the long-travelled and experienced mortal, in whose mind alone survive the pictures of many vanished scenes, and the land-scape of time sleeps in true perspective, must be regarded with strong interest. If life were but a brief reality, that fleetly passed into a shadow and nothingness, the point of vanishing would not be without its solemn grandeur. But with how profound a reverence must we look on its last stage, as entering the margin of God's eternity; as the land-mark of earth's boundary-ocean, fanned already by the winds, and feeling the spray, of the infinite!

Nor are the feelings less humanizing and holy with which Christianity teaches the aged disciple to regard the world and himself. He leaves it, — if he *be* a disciple, — not with censoriousness, but with faith; knowing that, with all its generations, the earth, as well as his own mind, is a thing young in the years of eternal Providence. He has too large a vision to be readily cast down about its prospects. If its social changes are not to his desire, if that for which he battled as for the true and good seems even to be retreating from his hopes, and questionable novelties to be deceiving the hearts of men, — yet he sinks without despair, and waves, as he retires, a cheerful and affectionate adieu. He has too vivid a sense of the brevity of a human life, to despond at any vicissitudes that may occur, any tendencies that may disclose themselves, within such space. He freely blesses God, that when, from its altered ways, the world has become no longer congenial to him, he is permitted to leave it; and he can rejoice that those who remain behind behold it with different eyes: for he recognizes and admires God's

law, that those who are to live in the world shall not be out
of love with it. From the mental station which he occupies
it certainly seems as if twilight were gathering fast and leading on the night: and so for two things he is thankful; that
the *vesper*-bell flings its note upon his ear, and calls him to
prayer and rest; and that on others of his race, who gaze
into the heavens from a different point, the morning seems
to be rising, and its fresh breeze to be up, and the *matin*
rings its summons:—for always there must be prayer; only
at dawn it leads to labor, and at eve to rest. Nor does he
leave the world which has been his locality so long, as a
scene in which he has no further interest. Possibly, even,
its future changes may not be hidden from his view: and at
all events his sympathies dwell and will dwell there still:
and all that most truly constitutes his being, the work he
has done, the wills he has moved, the loving thoughts he
has awakened, remain behind; enter the great structure of
human existence, and share its perpetuity.

The aged, ere they depart, are able to report to us something of the exactitude of the divine retribution. The justice of God does not always delay and postpone its sentence
till it is inaudible to the living. There are some of our
human works that "go before us to judgment;" and the
verdict may be apprehended by every attentive mind. Our
nature does not all die at the same moment; but the animal
elements begin to vanish, while the moral still remain. And
truly those in whom the lower self has been permitted to
gain a terrible ascendency, those whose life has been in obedience to the precept "eat and be filled," meet their dreary
recompense in age : one part of their moral probation is
visibly and awfully brought to its close ; and in the miseries
of a blank and chafing mind, a querulous imbecility of temper, a heart unrefreshed by a warm sympathy, every eye
may discern the issue. But when the soul has been faithful
to the higher purposes of existence; when there has been a
benign observance of the moral relations which give dignity

14

to life ; when the sympathies of kindred and neighborhood and society, the exercise of intelligent thought, the practice of unostentatious benevolence, the tranquil maintenance of faith and trust, have engaged and consecrated the years of best vigor, — there, even though the nobler fires of nature grow languid and decline, the mild light of a good heart shines to the last, cheerful to all observers, and casts no faint illumination on past and future. The peace of God full often survives the lapse of meaner comforts, and drives away every trace of fretfulness from age and terror from death ; leaving simply the rest incident to the completion of a good and worthy fight; and preparing all hearts to hope for a quiet migration to a better country, even a heavenly. Calm as this, after a fiery career, was the retirement of " such a one as Paul the aged," when " the time of his departure was at hand."

XXII.

NOTHING HUMAN EVER DIES.

ECCLESIASTES VII. 17.

WHY SHOULDST THOU DIE BEFORE THY TIME?

THE only resource for a man without faith is to be also
without love; which indeed, by the compassion of Heaven,
he will naturally be. For scarcely can any thing be more
serious, than the aspect which life assumes, when any considerable portion of it lies in retrospect, beneath an affectionate eye that can discern no more than its visible and
palpable relations. A few years of unconscious gain, followed by a long process of conscious loss, complete the
story of our being here. The best shelter that the world
affords us is the first, — the affections into which we are
born, and which are too natural for us to know their worth,
till they are disturbed; — for constant blessings, like constant pressures, are the last to be discovered. During the
whole period of childhood, when the most rapid and astonishing development of vitality and acquisition of power are
going on, the wonder and the bliss are hidden from our
eyes; gratitude is scarcely possible; and the delighted gaze
cf the contemplating spectator is unintelligible. We wake
up at our first grave affliction; our blindness is removed by
pain; the film is purified by tears, and alas! the moment
sorrow gives us sight, the good that we behold is gone.
And thenceforth we love knowingly, and lose constantly;
and after dreaming that all things were given to us, or were
even by nature our own, we find them only lent, and see in
our remaining years the undecyphered list of their recall.

Standing on the shóre which bounds the ocean of the past, we see treasure after treasure receding in the distance, or thrown into that insatiable waste, on whose surface they make a momentary smile of light, then leave the gulf in darkness. Into that deep, year after year has sunk, no less rich than this* in spoils from the human heart. Our fathers and our early homes, the dream of our first friendships, the surprise of new affections, and all the delicious marvels of life yet fresh, have vanished there. And soon, when we have been the losers long enough, we shall become the lost; and vainly struggle with the sweep of the unfathomable sea. Whether death, which treads closely on the steps of life upon our world, shall ever absolutely overtake it, and finally stop the race of beauty and of love, which now is perpetually begun afresh; — whether the chills of winter, transient now, will become eternal, and suppress for ever the flowers which can yet steal out again on the bosom of the earth ; — whether the frosts of mortality shall hereafter arrest the life-stream of our race, and dismiss us to that extinction which has fallen on other tribes before us ; — and the clouds fly, and the shrill hail fall over a naked world, — we know not. But to us, in succession, all things die. The past contains all that time has rendered dear and familiar; and *that* passes silently away: the future contains whatever is cold and strange: and its mysteries come swiftly on us.

Yet in this melancholy retrospect, natural as it is to our affections, there is a great deal of illusion, which is the occasion of half its sadness. When we go out of ourselves and our affairs, and seize a higher point of view, we see that this world is no such collection of perishable things, after all : that as God lives ever in it, he gathers around him all that is most like him, and suffers nothing that is excellent to die. There are things in his world which are not meant to perish ; — works which survive the workmen, and multiply blessings when they are gone, and which make

* This Discourse was preached on the last day of the year.

all who lend a faithful hand to them, part of the husbandry of God, laborers with him on that great field of time, whose culture and whose harvests are everlasting. The pains we spend upon our mortal selves, will perish with ourselves; but the care we give out of a good heart to others, the efforts of disinterested duty, the deeds and thoughts of pure affection, are never lost : they are liable to no waste; and are like a force that propagates itself for ever, changing its place but not losing its intensity. In short, there is a sense in which *nothing human ever perishes :* nothing, at least, which proceeds from the higher and characteristic part of a man's nature; nothing which comes of his mind and conscience ; nothing which he does as a subject of God's moral law. His good and ill live after him, an endless blessing or a lasting curse ; a consideration this which gives dignity to the humblest duty, and enormity to careless wrong. . I do not now refer to the consequences of conduct in a future life ; but to a certain perpetual and indestructible influence it must have upon this world. It is a mistake to suppose that any service rendered to mankind, any interesting relation of human life, any exhibition of moral greatness, even any peculiar condition of society, can ever be lost : their form only disappears; their value still remains, and their office is everlastingly performed. Material structures are dissolved, their identity and functions are gone. But mind partakes of the eternity of the great Parent Spirit ; and thoughts, truths, emotions, once given to the world, are never past : they exist as truly, and perform their duty as actively, a thousand years after their origin, as on their day of birth. I would endeavor to illustrate this in some separate instances.

(1.) The acts of our individual minds are never lost.

Every human deed of right or wrong fulfils two offices : it produces certain immediate *extrinsic* results; and it contributes to form some *internal* disposition or affection. Every act of wise benevolence goes *forth*, and alleviates a

suffering; it goes *within*, and gives intenser force to the
spirit of mercy. Every act of vindictiveness goes *forth* and
creates a woe; it goes *within*, and inflames the diseases of
the passions. In the one relation, it may be momentary
and transient; in the other, permanent and beyond arrest.
In the one, its dealings are with pain and physical ill; in
the other, with goodness or with guilt, and the solemn
determinations of the human will. And inasmuch as physical ill is temporary, while moral agencies are eternal
(for death is the end of pain, but where is the end of sin?)
inasmuch as a disinterested and holy mind is the sure
fountain of healing and of peace, — and a heart torn by
passions fierce or foul is at once the seat and source of a
thousand miseries, — no particular natural good or evil can
be compared in importance with the eternal distinctions
between right and wrong; nor any effect of an action be
ranked in magnitude with its influence on human affections
and character. The great office of virtue (we are told) is
to bless mankind: very well; but then the greatest blessing
is in the increase of virtue. The essential character therefore of every choice we make is to be found in its tendency
to promote or to impair the purity and good order, the
generosity and moral dignity, of the mind: and this element
of our actions can never die; but survives in our present
selves, more truly than the juices of the soil in the leaves
and blossoms of a tree. Such as we are, we are the offspring of the past; "the child is father to the man;" our
present characters are the result of all that we have desired
and done; every deed has contributed something to the
structure, and exists there as literally as the stone in the
pyramid on whose courses it was once laid. The action
of the moral agent does not consist in the contraction of a
muscle or the movement of a limb, — and this is all that
is really transitory, — but in the dispositions of the mind,
which are indelible. Our guilt as well as our goodness, once
contracted, is ineffaceable. No power within the circuit of

God's providence can blot out an idea from the pages of the secret heart, or.cancel a force of desire that has once gone forth. How vain then is the effort of thought to fly from the deed of sin, the moment it is finished, — the hurry of conscience to reach a place of greater peace, — the eager whisper of self-love that says, the lapse is over, and a firmer march of duty may be forthwith begun! If the foul thing were cemented to the hour that witnessed its commission, you might escape it; but being in the mind, you have it with you still, however fast you fly, and however little you look behind. Do you imagine that, the evil passion having spent its energy, you will be safer in its weakness now? It is the falsest of all the sophistries of sin! A moral impulse, unlike a physical force, is not exhausted, but augmented, by every effort it puts forth; not only does it part with no portion of its power, — but it receives a fresh intensity. There still does it abide, more ready than ever to come forth and assert itself with strength. Every one's present mind is, in truth, the standing memorial, distinct and legible to the eye of God, of all that he has willed in time past: the conduct and feelings of to-day are the resultant of ten thousand forces of previous volition; nor would any act remain the same if any one of its predecessors were withdrawn or changed. Even the silent and hidden currents of desire and thought leave their traces visible; as waves in the deeper sea are discovered, when the waters ebb, by the ripple-mark congealed upon the sand. Thus the acts of our will do not and cannot perish: they then truly begin to live, when they are past; for then only do they become deposits in our memory, and contributions to our affections; then only does their internal and mental history commence, and they put forth that viewless attraction by which, more than before, the heart gravitates towards good or ill. There is consolation as well as terror in this thought. No strife of a good heart, no performance of a kind hand, has been without effect. Not in vain have been the struggles, however trivial they seem, of our early conscience, the dreams of a departed enthusiasm, — the high ambition of our untried virtue : these things are with us always, even unto the end : in our colder maturity, even in the frosts of age, their central glow is with our nature secretly, and relaxes unobserved the binding crust of years. Perishable deeds and transient emotions are the materials wherewith God has given us to build up the eternal character ; and to raise the tower by which we escape the floods of death, and, with no impious intent, climb the mansions of the skies. Steadily must the structure rise, like the walls of the persecuted Jerusalem of old, at which some toiled while others watched. Unceasingly we must build ; parched, it may be, beneath the sultry sun, faint and sinking but for draughts from the " wells of salvation ; " on the side of the desert, it may be, where we should shudder at the tempest's moan, but for sweet songs of Zion that float to us from within ; — exposed, it may be, to treacherous and banded foes, whose surprises would terrify, but for the trusty weapon and the well-trained arm ; — at midnight and alone, it may be, cheerless but for the eyes of Heaven that look upon our toil, and the streaks of the east, which promise us a day-spring. Ye must build, over the valley and on the rock, till a wall of impregnable protection is thrown around the sanctuary within, and in securest peace ye can go in and out the temple of God's spirit ; — " which temple ye are."

(2.) The social and domestic relations whose loss we mourn do not really perish, when they seem to die.

Those relations, it is needless to say, do not consist in the mere juxtaposition of so many human beings. A certain number of animal lives, that are of prescribed ages, that eat and drink together, and that sleep under the same roof, by no means make a family. Almost as well might we say that it is the bricks of a house that make a home. There may be a home in the forest or the wilderness ; and there may be a family, with all its blessings, though half its members be in foreign lands, or in another world. It is the gentle memories, the mutual thought, the desire to bless, the sympathies that meet when duties are apart, the fervor of the parents' prayers, the persuasion of filial love, the sister's pride and the brother's benediction, that constitute the true elements of domestic life, and sanctify the dwellings of our birth. Abolish the sentiments which pervade and animate the machinery and movements of our social being, and their whole value obviously disappears. The objects of affection are nothing to us but for the affection which they excite; it is for this that they exist; this removed, their relation loses its identity; this preserved, it undergoes no essential change. Friends are assigned to us for the sake of friendship; and homes for the sake of love; and while they perform these offices in our hearts, in essence and in spirit they are with us still. The very tears we shed over their loss are proofs that they are not loss; for what is grief, but love itself restricted to acts of memory and longing for its other tasks, — imprisoned in the past, and striving vainly to be free? The cold hearts that never deeply mourn lose nothing, for they have no stake to lose : the genial souls that deem it no shame to weep, give evidence that they have, fresh and living still, the sympathies, to nurture which our human ties are closely drawn. God only lends us the objects of our affection ; the affection itself he gives us in perpetuity. In this best sense, instances are not rare in which the friend or the parent then first begins to live for us, when death has withdrawn him from our eyes, and given him over exclusively to our hearts : at least I have known a mother among the sainted blest, sway the will of a thoughtful child far more than her living voice ; brood with a kind of serene omnipresence over his affections and sanctify his passing thought by the mild vigilance of her pure and loving eye. And what better life for him could she have than this? Nay, standing as each man does in the centre of a wide circumference of social influences, recipient as he is of innumerable impressions from the mighty human heart, his inward being may be justly said to consist far more in others' lives than in his own; without them and alone, he would have missed the greater part of the thoughts and emotions which make up his existence; and when he dies, he carries away their life rather than his own. He dwells still below, within their minds: their image in his soul (which perhaps is the best element of their being) passes away to the world incorruptible above.

(3.) All that is noble in the world's past history, and especially the minds of the great and good, are, in like manner, never lost.

The true records of mankind, the human annals of the earth, are not to be found in the changes of geographical names, in the shifting boundaries of dominion, in the travels and adventures of the baubles of royalty, or even in the undulations of the greater and lesser waves of population. We have learned nothing, till we have penetrated far beyond these casual and external changes, which are of interest only as the effect and symptoms of the great mental vicissitudes of our race. History is an account of the past experience of humanity; and this, like the life of the individual, consists in the ideas and sentiments, the deeds and passions, the truths and toils, the virtues and the guilt, of the mind and heart within. We have a deep concern in preserving from destruction the *thoughts* of the past, the leading conceptions of all remarkable forms of civilization; the achievements of genius, of virtue, and of high faith. And in this, nothing can disappoint us: for though these things may be individually forgotten, collectively they survive, and are in action still. All the past ages of the world were necessary to the formation of the present; they are essential ingredients in the events that occur daily before our eyes. There is no period so ancient, no country so remote, that it could be cancelled without producing a present shock upon the earth. One layer of time has Providence piled up upon another for immemorial ages: we that live stand now upon this "great mountain of the Lord;" were the strata below removed, the fabric and ourselves would fall in ruins. Had Greece, or Rome, or Palestine, been other than they were, Christianity could not have been what it is: had Romanism been different, Protestantism could not have been the same, and we might not have been here this day. The separate civilizations of past centuries may be of colors singly indiscernible; but in truth, they are the prismatic rays which, united, form our present light. And do we look back on the great and good, lamenting that they are gone? Do we bend in commemorative reverence before them, and wish that our lot had been cast in their better days? What is the peculiar function which heaven assigns to such minds, when tenants of our earth? Have the great and the good any nobler office than to touch the human heart with deep veneration for greatness and goodness?—to kindle in the understanding the light of more glorious conceptions, and in the conscience the fires of a holier virtue? And that we grieve for their departure, and invoke their names, is proof that they are performing such blessed office still,—that this, their highest life for others, compared with which their personal agency is nothing, is not extinct. Indeed, God has so framed our memory that it is the infirmities of noble souls which chiefly fall into the shadows of the past; while whatever is fair and excellent in their lives, comes forth from the gloom in ideal beauty, and leads us on through the wilds and mazes of our mortal way. Nor does the retrospect, thus glorified, deceive us by any fallacy; for things present with us we comprehend far less completely, and appreciate less impartially, than things past. Nothing can become a clear object of our thought, while we ourselves are in it: we understand not our childhood, till we have left it; our youth, till it has departed; our life itself till it verges to its close; or the majesty of genius and holiness, till we look back on them as fled. Each portion of our human experience becomes in succession intelligible to us, as we quit it

for a new point of view. God has stationed us at the inter-
secting line between the known and the unknown: he has
planted us on a floating island of mystery, from which we
survey the expanse behind in the clear light of experience
and truth, and cleave the waves, invisible, yet ever breaking, of the unbounded future. Our very progress, which is
our peculiar glory, consists in at once losing and learning
the past; in gaining fresh stations from which to take a
wiser retrospect, and become more deeply aware of the
treasures we have used. We are never so conscious of the
succession of blessings which God's providence has heaped
on us, as when lamenting the lapse of years; and are then
richest in the fruits of time, when mourning that time steals
those fruits away.

XXIII.

WHERE IS THY GOD?

EZEKIEL VIII. 10-12.

SO I WENT IN AND SAW; AND BEHOLD EVERY FORM OF CREEPING THINGS
AND ABOMINABLE BEASTS, AND ALL THE IDOLS OF THE HOUSE OF
ISRAEL, PORTRAYED UPON THE WALLS ROUND ABOUT; AND THERE STOOD
BEFORE THEM SEVENTY MEN OF THE HOUSE OF ISRAEL, — WITH EVERY
MAN HIS CENSER IN HIS HAND; AND A THICK CLOUD OF INCENSE WENT
UP. THEN SAID HE UNTO ME, SON OF MAN, HAST THOU SEEN WHAT THE
ANCIENTS OF THE HOUSE OF ISRAEL DO IN THE DARK, EVERY MAN IN
THE CHAMBERS OF HIS IMAGERY?

To a wise man there is no surer mark of decline in the spirit
of a people, than the corruption of their language, and the
loss of meaning from their highest and most sacred words.
In the affairs of government, of morals, of divinity, we retain
the phrases used by our forefathers in Shakspeare's time:
but it is impossible to notice the dwindled thought which
they frequently contain, without feeling that the currency
struck for the commerce of giant souls has been clipped
to serve the traffic of dwarfs. Observe, for example, the
lowered meaning of the word RELIGION. If you ask, in
these days, what a man's *religion* is, you are told something
about the place he goes to on a Sunday, or the preacher he
objects to least; of his likings and dislikings, his habits and
opinions, his conventional professions. But who, from all
this, would draw any inference as to his *character?* You
know *where to find him*, and *how he looks;* but have obtained no insight *into what he is.* Yet, can it be doubted
that if we knew his *religion* in the true and ancient sense,
we should understand him perfectly? — should see him, as

God alone can see him now, stripped of the disguises that hide him even from himself, and with the vital pulse itself of thought and act laid bare to view? The divine Omniscience, in relation to our nature, may be said to consist in nothing else than a discernment of our several religions. Not indeed that in his infinite reason he knows any thing about Churchmen, and Methodists, and Quakers; or distinguishes the silent meeting from the organ's pomp; or takes account of vestments black or white. These things only denote what a man will *call himself when he is asked;* they refer, even when most sincere, to nothing that has necessarily any deep seat within the character; only to certain emblems, either in conception or in outward habit, adopted for the expression of affections the most various in direction and intensity. But whoever can so look into my heart as to tell *whether there is any thing which I revere:* and, if there be, *what thing* it is; he may read me through and through, and there is no darkness wherein I may hide myself. This is the master-key to the whole moral nature; what does a man secretly admire and worship? What haunts him with the deepest wonder? What fills him with most earnest aspiration? What should we overhear in the soliloquies of his unguarded mind? This it is which, in the truth of things, constitutes his *religion;* — this, which determines his precise place in the scale of spiritual ranks; — this, which allies him to hell or heaven; — this, which makes him the outcast or the accepted of the moral affections of the Holiest. Every man's *highest,* nameless though it be, is his " *living God:* " while, oftener than we can tell, the being on whom he seems to call, whose history he learned in the catechism, of whom he hears at church, — with open ear perhaps, but with thick, deaf soul, — is his *dead God.* It is the former of these that gives me his genuine characteristic: that uppermost term in his mind discloses all the rest. Lift me the veil that hides the penetralia of his worship, let me see the genuflexions of his spirit, and catch

the whiff of his incense, and look in the face the image at
whose feet he is prostrate; and thenceforth I know him well;
can tell where to find him in the world; and divine the temper
of his home. The classifications produced by this principle
are not what you will meet with in any "Sketch of all religions." Their lines run across the divisions of historical
sects, wholly regardless of their separations: but as they are
drawn by the hand of nature and of conscience, rather than
by that of pedants and of bigots, to study them is to gain
insight into divine truth, instead of wandering through the
catalogue of human errors. Let us endeavor then to distinguish between real and pretended religion, by adverting
to the several *chief aims* that manifestly preside over human
life.

Of many a man you would never hesitate to say, that his
chief aim was to obtain *ease*, or *wealth*, or *dignity*. These
are the objects manifestly in front of him, and, like some
huge magnetic mass, drawing his whole nature towards
them. The fact is apparent, not altogether from the amount
of time which he devotes to them; for often the thing dearest and most sacred to the heart may fill the fewest moments,
and, though providing the whole spirit, may scarcely touch
the matter, of our days; nor even from the topics of his
talk; for there are those who, in conversation, seek rather
to learn what is most foreign to them, than to speak what
is most native; but from certain slight though expressive
symptoms, hard to describe in detail, yet not easily missed
in their combination. The engagements to which he takes
with the heartiest relish, the sentiments that raise his quickest response, the occasions that visibly call him out and
shake him free, the moments of his brightening eye, and
genial laugh, and flowing voice, leave on us an irresistible
impression of his sincerest tastes and deepest desires. And
above all does he reveal these, when we discover the *persons*
who most occupy his thoughts; in whom he sees what he
would like to be or to appear, and whose lot or life he feels

it would be an *ascent* to gain. Judged by signs infallible
as these, how many are there, surrendered to a low epicurean life!—who know no higher end than to be comfortable or renowned!— whose care is for what they may *have*,
and not for what they might *be!* If they achieve any real
work, it is only that they may reach its end and take their
ease. If they do a deed of public justice, it is as much due
to the publicity as to the justice. If they are detected in
a charity, it is with the smallest possible mercy of heart,
and is performed as a slothful riddance of uneasiness, or a
creditable compliance with convention. If they pray not
to be led into temptation, it is only the temptation to im-
prudence and social mistake; if to be delivered from evil,
it is but the evil of trouble or derision. To make the largest
use of men, rendering back the smallest amount of service, to
reap the greatest crop from the present, and drop the scantiest
seeds for the future, is their true problem of existence. They
never rush on toil and struggle that bring no price; or
stretch their reason till it aches in search of truth; or cru-
cify their affections in redemption of human wrongs; or
spend their reputation and their strength in rousing the
public conscience from its sleep. Their whole faculties are
apprenticed to themselves. Unconscious of a heaven above
them and around, they live and die on principles purely
mercantile; and the book of life must be a common ledger,
if their names are written on its page.

It is needless at present to settle the comparative rank of
these three seducing aims; else we might decide, perhaps,
that, as a primary object of pursuit, ease is *more* ignoble,
and reputation *less*, than wealth, which excites the more
prevailing desire. The great thing to be observed is common to them all. They do not carry a man *out of himself*,
or show him any thing higher. He is the centre in which
they all terminate: he spins upon his own axis in the dark,
ineffectually shaping and rounding his particular world, but
wheeling round no glorious orb, feeling no celestial light,

flushed with no colors of morn and eve, and barren of seasonal foliage and fruit. What is his habitual day-dream? What the conception that moves before him in secret vision, and strives for realization? Is it the thought of the heroes and the saints of history? or of friends at his right hand, whose noble spirits shame his weakness? Is it not simply the image of *himself easy, himself rich, himself grand and famous?* This one corrupting picture is the substitute in him for the whole pantheon of great souls; for sages, prophets, martyrs, and whatever of beauty and sanctity has ever dwelt in earth or heaven. His whole system of desires is mere *personal greed:* he stands upon his own flat, without an aspiration. Nothing has a divine right to him, but he has a human appetite for all things. He worships nothing; he serves nothing : if God were away and heaven were not, it would make no difference to him ; he would never miss them : his life is Godless ! he is an atheist.

This, in fact, is the strict and proper meaning of the word atheism ; the absence from a man's mind of any object of worship; so that he is left with nothing above him, and lives wholly to himself. Hence this term, though often applied unjustly to very different states of mind, is properly one of odium : for it is impossible to contemplate such a condition of character without strong aversion ; or to conceive of its production without a large operation of moral and voluntary causes. We may observe too, that the effects of this irreligion are as disorganizing in society, as they are debasing to the individual. It wholly dissolves the great tie which binds men together, and is alone capable of forming them into a fraternity, — the sentiment of mutual reverence. Do you say, that among the servants of wealth or of fame also this sentiment has place, because he who has little is found to admire him who has more, and to wait upon him with vast humility ? He does no such thing. He admires *the lot*, but cares nothing for the man ; and this combination of positive and negative feelings, — aspiration

15

after another's state without any love for the person in it,
— is not honor, but simply envy. And as for the so-called
humility of the poor menial in this career, in the presence
of his worldly superior, the quality has no right to a moral,
much less to a Christian name. It is mere *unmanliness*
arising from the failure of self-respect as well as of mutual
reverence: human attributes are wholly emptied out of the
relation, and human possessions alone remain to look one
another in the face; and the men, losing all higher significance, are left in each other's presence, as two degrees of
comparison in the vocabulary of Mammon. Nay, in many
a one, this seeming subserviency is even worse; it is an
admiration of *himself as he is to be*, and no less full of pride
than it is of meanness. To mistake this servility for the
lowly dignity of worship, is to confound the slouch of
pauperism touching the hat, with the uplifted look of Mary
sitting at the feet. And what kind of community would
that be, whose moral composition was from these two elements, universal self-seeking, and general dearth of mutual
reverence? Go to the heart of the matter, and every man
would be a centre of repulsion, held to his particular sphere
of human atoms by an external frame-work of precarious
interests; instead of taking his place in a system of natural
attractions, which would endure though the world itself
were to sink away.

Beyond this stage of character, which I have described
by the word *atheism*, the smallest step introduces us to
some form of religion. There is no further condition of
mind, that is not marked by the consciousness of *something*
spiritually higher; something that has divine right over us;
something therefore which, to say the least, stands for us
in the place of God. Still, ere we reach the limit of pure
and perfect religion, which is that of Christ, there is an
ample range of error and imperfection, which may be desig-
nated by the general name of *idolatry*. This offence against
truth is far from being an obsolete historical affair, that is

gone out with the Old Testament, and of no concern except to missionaries now. It abounds (taking the strictest and most philosophic meaning of the term) in every Christian land, and every Christian sect; though it certainly constitutes a partial apostasy from the true faith of Christendom. To make this plain, let me ask you to reflect, what is the real essence of idolatry, and how we are to distinguish it from pure religion.

Some will affirm, that true worship addresses itself direct to the living God himself; appearing before him face to face, and discerning him as he is in his own nature; while idolatry interposes, before the eye of the body or the mind, some image, which is not God, but only represents him.

It is, however, impossible to rest the distinction thus, upon the absence of symbol in one case, and its presence in the other; for it is equally found in both, and is wholly indispensable to religion itself. On these terms, we should all (not men alone, but angels too) be idolaters alike. For God, being infinite, can never be fully comprehended by our minds: whatever thought of him be there his real nature must still transcend: there will yet be deep after deep beyond, within that light ineffable; and what we see, compared with what we do not see, will be as the rain-drop to the firmament. Our conception of him can never *correspond with the reality*, so as to be without omission, disproportion, or aberration; but can only *represent the reality*, and *stand for God* within our souls, till nobler thoughts arise and reveal themselves as his interpreters. And this is precisely what we mean by a symbolical idea. The devotee who prostrates himself before a black stone, — the Egyptian who in his prayers was haunted by the ideal form of the graceful ibis or the monstrous sphinx, — the theist who bends beneath the starry porch that midnight opens to the temple of the universe, — the Christian who sees in heaven a spirit akin to. that which divinely lived in Galilee, and with glorious pity died on Calvary; — all alike assume a representation of Him whose immeasurable nature they can neither compass nor escape. And the only question is, whether the conception they portray upon the wall of their ideal temple, is an abominable idol, or a true and sanctifying mediatorial thought.

Others, who admit the necessity of representative ideas in religion, will say that idolatry consists in making the symbol *visible*, while true religion leaves it *mental and invisible*.

Yet it could hardly be deemed impossible for a *blind man to be an idolater :* superstition and sin are not to be escaped through mere physical privation. And if an image, present to the mind's eye alone, suffices to constitute an idol, then nothing remains for true religion, but to think in mere abstractions; to worship, not a thinking, ruling, loving, holy *Being*, but thought, and power, and love, and holiness themselves ; to adore, not a divine Architect of creation, but the bare skill itself of the architecture; to avoid all approach to *impersonation* of divine attributes, and to fly, as from a sin, before the uprising of a concrete and a living God. Yet, I need not say, this is an impossible and untenable state of mind : the aim at it is that which constitutes a lifeless pantheism ; and the mere poetical contemplation of nature does not deepen into the adoring service of God, till we feel creation and life to be at the disposal of a present Mind, a personal and moral Will, with absolute love of good and perfect abhorrence of evil, with distinct and self-directing activity, to which the laws, the order, the beauty, the scale, the progression, the issues of all things, are devoutly referred. And wherever such a faith exists, there is a conception in the mind, as truly representative and as little restrained within the limits of abstract thought, as the notion we may entertain of a character in history whom we have never seen, or of an angel in heaven whom we cannot see. There is no one even, through whose prayers and meditations transient lights of beauty and floating fringes of imágery will not be found to pass ; nor is it in mortal thought otherwise to realize the majesty, the purity, the constancy, the tenderness of God.

The genuine characteristic of all idolatry, then, can only be found in this: that the symbol it adopts in worship is *a false and needlessly partial* representation of the divine nature ; while pure religion holds to one which is *true and perfect*, wanting of the reality, not in the quality of its spirit, but only in the scale of its dimensions. Our minds are so ill-proportioned, and through ignorance and evil violate so much the proper symmetry of a spiritual nature, that, left to their own wilful ways, they misrepresent to us the true essence of perfection ; and many an image does our adoring fancy grave, and then obey, which cannot innocently stand in the place of God, and supplants a worship of diviner right. Thus, there is the *philosopher's* idol, shaped and set up by intellect unsanctified of conscience. To this is attracted an exclusive reverence for wisdom, thought and skill : the votary has learned how little is all he knows, and stands with serene aspiration before the presence of Infinite Reason ; unconscious meanwhile of his children neglected at his feet, and the cries of humanity bleeding near him in the dust. There is the *artist's* idol, portrayed upon the wall of nature with the pencil of beauty, and reflecting a flush of loveliness over heaven and earth : many a glorious soul has bowed down before this, and been inspired by it to do great and wondrous things ; yet how often betrayed at the same time into passionate license, and mean peevishness ! There is the *stoic's* idol, chiselled by austere conscience, from the granitic masses of spiritual strength, and worshipped as the image of divine justice, majesty and holiness. This has won and held captive the noblest spirits that are not wholly Christian, and glorified them to a manliness approaching something divine ; yet wanting still the mellowing of pity, and the grace of sweet and glad affections. And there is the *woman's* idol, with Madonna look,

captivating to gentler minds; embodying and awakening
the reverence for mercy and disinterested love; and, by
omission, enfeebling the severe healthfulness of duty, and
merging the struggling heroism of this life in the glorified
saintship of another.   All these are but delusive impersonations of separated attributes of God; of his intellect; his
creative thought; his will; his affectionateness.   They
are mutilated representations of his nature; idols of the
worshipper's heart, the serving of which will rather confirm
and exaggerate, than remedy, the defective proportions of
his soul; elevating him indeed above himself, but still leaving him below his powers.   Nor is there any security against
this devotion to idols of the mind, except that which Heaven
itself has furnished to all Christendom; the reverential
acceptance of Christ as the highest image of the invisible
God, the complete and finished representation of his moral
perfections.   Here, nothing is exuberant, nothing deficient;
here prevails a harmony of spirit absolute and divine.   In
the Eternal Providence that rules us, reason can conceive,
conscience can demand, affection can discern, nothing which
has not its expression in the author and perfecter of faith.
In worshipping the combination of attributes, through which
he has shown us the Father, there can be no fear that any
duty will be forgotten, any taste corrupted, any aspiration
laid asleep.   Drawn upward by such an object, nothing in
us can remain low and weak: the simplicity of the child,
the strength of the man, the love of the woman, the thought
of the sage, the courage of the martyr, the elevation of the
saint, the purity of the angel, press and strive to unite and
realize themselves within our souls.   Standing before a God,
of whose *mind* the universe, of whose *spirit* the Man of
Nazareth, is the accepted symbol, we must become, in proportion to the sincerity and depth of our devotion, transfigured with the divinest glory of reason and affection, that
can rest upon a nature like ours; and raised to a comprehension of that "love of Christ which passeth knowledge,"

our souls must not only attain a fairer proportion, but ex-
pand also to nobler dimensions, as they become "filled with
the fulness of God."

Thus, "to as many as receive him," does Christ "give
power to become sons of God." By such worship is the
nature of the individual disciple glorified. And what is
true of a single mind, is no less true of communities of men.
They also have their atheisms, and their several idolatries;
from which they too can be recalled and preserved only in
proportion as they find their principle of combination, and
their mode of action, in the deep love and reverence of the
perfectness of Christ. No age, since the Reformation, has
been so marked by idol-worship as our own; — so prolific
of favorite and one-sided schemes of social improvement,
founded on the sense of some solitary want of human nature,
but barren of good from neglect of all the rest. Our Christianity is no longer *catholic*, rich in provisions for the whole
faculties and being of man. With the expansion and com-
plication of our life, religion has lost its comprehensive grasp
of all the elements of our well-being, and permitted them
to escape and break up in mischievous analysis, and consign
themselves to separate trusts. In answer to the earnest cry
of society, " What shall we do to be saved from all our miseries and sins?" there are countless fragmentary answers,
in place of the deep full harmony of response, from the soul
of Christian inspiration. "Give us more bread," says one;
"more money," says a second; "more churches, more belief,
more priests," say others in their turn; and not the least
intelligent and worthy will exclaim for the diminution of
distilleries, or the multiplication of schools. For my own
part, I believe that human nature is not like a house, which
you may build up piecemeal, — first the stone, then the
wood, — to its true finish and proportion; but, rather, like
the lily or the tree, which grow in all parts, — the stem, the
root, the leaf, — *at once*, and keep a constant symmetry. It
must be nourished and unfolded simultaneously in all its

dimensions, or its enlargement is mere distortion and disease. There is truth with those who idolize the *physical* means of augmenting the comforts of the people; but it is only the truth which lurked in the foul Egyptian adoration of the prolific powers of nature. There is truth with those who trust in the ameliorating energy of knowledge and of art; but it is the truth which filled Athens with the worship of the wise Minerva, and which left it still, in the estimate of the Christian apostle, " in all things too superstitious." There is truth with those who say we want more faith and devout obedience; but if the temple of our life be denied the light of thought, then, though every man stands, saint-like, with his censer in his hand, he will just repeat "what the elders of Israel did in the dark," — send up his foolish cloud of incense before "creeping things and abominable beasts." Society, to avoid corruption in any of these agencies, must concurrently avail itself of all. And there is no power, which embraces them all, and assigns to each its proper rank, except that divine religion which makes Christ the model and the end of life. Trusting to inferior forces, we shall find that each is blind to all that lies above it, and provides for the world only up to its own level. But Christian faith, in aiming at once at the highest elements of good, necessarily includes the lowest; it contains within itself an epitome of all the parts of human perfection; and in the heart of a nation, as of a man, it is the grand source of moral salubrity and inextinguishable hope. In proportion as they have receded from this, have states and generations slipped into thraldom to partial theories and unworthy aims; and in the devouring haste of gain, or the mad passion for war, or the blindness of mutual distrust, have brought down the weighty penalties by which Heaven recalls society from its unfaithfulness. But while the image of Christ remains as the central and holy light of every home, the moral delusions that waste a people's strength can find no place of entrance; and moderate desires in private life, with a paramount sense of justice in the state; — guardianship over the weak, with vigilance against the strong; care of neglected childhood, reverence for lingering age, and a share of willing honor for all men; with a hearty homage to all truth as the reflected light, and duty as the express law of God, must characterize and consolidate that happy people, from whom no cloud of idol-incense yet hides the beauty of the Son of Man.

XXIV.

THE SORROW WITH DOWNWARD LOOK.

MARK x. 20–22.

AND HE ANSWERED AND SAID UNTO HIM, "MASTER, ALL THESE THINGS
HAVE I OBSERVED FROM MY YOUTH." THEN JESUS, BEHOLDING HIM,
LOVED HIM, AND SAID UNTO HIM, "ONE THING THOU LACKEST; GO THY
WAY, SELL WHATSOEVER THOU HAST, AND GIVE TO THE POOR, AND
THOU SHALT HAVE TREASURE IN HEAVEN; AND COME, TAKE UP THE
CROSS, AND FOLLOW ME." AND HE WAS SAD AT THAT SAYING, AND
WENT AWAY GRIEVED; FOR HE HAD GREAT POSSESSIONS.

WHAT made this young man retire in sorrow from before
the face of Christ? That the demand made upon him was
quite irrational, all political economists would confidently
assure him. That he had every reason to be satisfied with
a life so pure and orderly, would be declared by every
worthy neighbor and all judicious divines. And if he
carried home with him any traces of the sadness with which
he turned from the eye of Jesus, no doubt he was cheered
up, as far as might be, by the loving rebukes of wife or
friends, chiding his misgivings, and laughing his thoughtfulness away. If a man who keeps all the commandments may
not be happy, who may! With a memory clear of reproach
from the youth up, whence can he have drawn the cloud to
shade so innocent a soul? All the sources of inward care
and conflict seem to be excluded here; and we appear to
have the perfect representative of a life at peace. To say
nothing of the ruler's property, which was ample for external comfort, he had fulfilled the one grand requisite of moral
contentment and repose; he had established a harmony
between his perceptions and his actions, and framed his

modes of conduct by his sentiments of right. Now there is, apparently, no other condition of inward peace than this. All men feel the *worth* of the spiritual affections that solicit them, and revere the obligation of the better to exclude the worse. All men feel also the comparative *strength* of these same affections, and find in some a power which others ineffectually dispute. Wherever the order of strength agrees exactly with the order of worth; wherever the desire known to be the highest is also the most intense, and no brute passion usurps the throne instead of serving as the footstool; wherever the habits are shaped and proportioned by the scale of excellence and beauty within; there, strife and sorrow cannot be; there, is the glad consent between hand and heart, the concord between our worship and our will, which charms away the approach of care. This harmony may be attained in either of two ways: by tuning up the life to the key-note of thought; or by letting down the thought to the pitch of the actual life. He who will persistently follow his highest impulses and convictions, who will trust only these amid noisier claims, and constrain himself to go with them alike in their faintness and their might, shall not find his struggle everlasting: his wrestlings shall become fewer and less terrible: the hand of God, so dim to him and doubtful at the first, shall in the end be the only thing that is clear and sure: his best shall be his strongest too. But this, which is a holy peace, is not the only rest open to the contradictions of our nature. There is also an escape from discord by an inverse and descending path. And if a man will steadily follow his strongest impulses, without regard to their vileness or their worth, will give no heed to any whispering compunction, will do only and always what he likes; from him too the jarring and conflict of nature shall pass away: God's spirit will not always strive with him, to turn his wilful steps: the angels that beset his path with entreaty, with protest, with defiance, will thin off till they are seen no more: he will enjoy a cheerful and

comfortable exemption from any thing divine; and, by
withdrawal of all else, his strongest affections will become
his best. So far as mere ease and pleasure are concerned,
there is not perhaps much to choose between these two
opposite modes of self-reconciliation. If a man resolves to
disown the upper region of his nature, he may find entertainment, if that be all, in the lower; and care may be made
to fly before the gas-lamps and merriment of the vault, as
well as beneath the star-light of the observatory and the
silence of the skies. The difference is not sentient, but
moral; between the harmonies of the world above, and the
enchantments of Circe's isle; the one, a music straying from
the gate of heaven, and waking the soul to share the vigils
of immortals; the other, composing it to sleep upon the
verge of hell. It was, however, in the nobler way that the
young man in the text had established his right to an unanxious life, and attracted the love of Christ: he had con-
formed his habits to his moral sense, not sunk his moral
sense to the level of his habits. What then had happened
to disturb the rest arising from their concord?

The truth is, this young ruler had *had* all the content
that noble minds can derive from the order of a well-regu-
lated life. He had come to the end of all such satisfactions,
and found them fairly spent. They had become to him
mere negative conditions of repose, without which indeed
he would sink into self-contempt; but with which he rose
into no self-reverence, and scarce escaped the hauntings of
a perpetual penitence. He felt that if this were all — this,
which was but the native path and beaten track of his soul,
— the field of duty was no such glorious thing; and some
diviner terms might have been asked, ere this flat earth
should win eternal life. A store of unexhausted power, a
pressure towards loftier aspiration, led him to fix an eager
eye on Christ, and be ready for intenser work; and to be
referred only to the old commands, and sent back to the
familiar task, spread the dull shade over his heart again.

He had reached the stage of character, which all men, as
they are more faithful, the sooner reach, when the conscience breaks out beyond the life, and demands a sphere
of enterprise larger than the home domain with all its settled'
ways.   There is, there can be, no list of actions, no scheme
of habits, that will permanently represent your duty, and
stand as a perpetual diagram of right.   Only while it is yet
unrealized, while it rises ideally above you, and reproaches
your slurred and broken lines of order, is it truly the
emblem of your obligations : the moment you overtake it,
and fall into coincidence with it, its function is gone, and it
guides and teaches you no more ; it becomes simply what
you are, which is always parted by an interval from what
you *ought to be*.   Moral excellence is a state of the affections, and must be measured by their purity and depth; and
in doing merely what is habitual the affections cannot keep
awake : they live upon fresh thoughts and demand ever
new toils : their eye is intent upon the future, drawn thither
by a holy light ; and if once it retires upon the present, it
droops into a fatal sleep.   Obedience to a perfect God can
be nothing less than a *service* constantly rendered by the
will ; a voluntary effort, given largely and ungrudgingly in
proportion to the gratefulness and magnanimity of the soul,
and not therefore stinted in the angel, while it is lavished
in the man.   But from all that is customary the living forces
of the will retire ; achieving ease, it loses sanctity : it is a
slain victim, acceptable to-day, unclean to-morrow ; for God
will have at his altar the very breath and blood of life, and
not alone its shape and shell.   And so it is, that there is
something truly infinite in duty : it is a region that can
never be enclosed ; we pitch our tent upon its boundary
field, and as we survey it, we detect an ampler realm beyond.
As the body could, by no far travelling, find a station where
the arm might not yet be stretched forth ; so the soul can
be borne by no progress to a point where the freewill shall
not take another step.   Hence it is evident that, in the mind

of all responsible beings, there must be a perpetual alternation between two opposite states, of rest and unrest, suc-
ceeding and reproducing each other. While the moral
conceptions are in clear advance of the actions, there is a
secret shame which forbids repose : a sense of sorrowful
aspiration impels the will to earnest effort, and sends it
panting after the divine form that invites it on. At length
faith and resolution overtake the image ; the interval is
conquered, and that which was a·vision in the past is a
reality of the present : the outer and the inner life concur ;
and for awhile the healthy joy of a good conscience touches
the features with its light. But in this absence of moral
confusion, and under the shelter of a sacred peace, the
energies of a pure mind, released from severer action, push
forward to the seizure of higher thoughts. The conscience,
wounded and bleeding no more, and cherished by the
healthful air of God's approval, is sure to open into nobler
dimensions. In truth it is the chief good of a well-ordered
structure of habits that it protects the living soul within,
frees it from mean dangers, and gives it leave to grow.
And so the sentiments of duty burst from their confinement,
and leave the life again behind ; restoring the spirit to its
strife, till the intolerable chasm be traversed as before.
This *systole* and *diastole* of the moral nature is as truly
needful to its vital action, as the pulsations of the heart to
our physical existence. Only, their *period* is indefinitely
various, from a moment to a life. Some men you may find,
whose habits and whose conscience settle down in fixed
partnership for this world, and are never seen diverging;
not, alas! from the agility of their habits, but from the
sluggishness of their conscience. Their moral perceptions
are absolutely stationary, or show them even less of heaven
in their manhood than in their youth. Doing what they .
think right, and thinking nothing right but what they do,
they approve themselves and look up to nothing. They are
not, however, exempt from the great law of alternation ;

only, its oscillation is dull and slow; and its sweep of rest
having occupied this life, its sorrowful return must begin
another.   In nobler men, the period of the soul is quicker:
for awhile, they fulfil their moral aims, and after conquest
enjoy the victory; they pitch their tent upon the field, and,
not without a glad thanksgiving, accept a brief repose. But
high hearts are never long without hearing some new call,
some distant clarion of God, even in their dreams : and soon
they are observed to break up the camp of ease, and start
on some fresh march of faithful service.   And to such productive wills the era of rest, like the Creator's Sabbath, is but
as a sixth — and that all filled with hallowed hours, — to the
working days whose morning and evening enclose and reclaim some realm of beauty out of chaos.   And finally, looking higher still, we find those who never wait till their
moral work accumulates, and who reward resolution with
no rest ; with whom therefore the alternation is instantaneous and constant; who do the good only to see the better,
and see the better only to achieve it; who are too meek
for transport, too faithful for remorse, too earnest for repose; whose worship is action, and whose action ceaseless
aspiration.

   This last case, in which the law of alternation has its
period reduced to a vanishing interval, fulfils our conception
of an angel-mind.   To higher natures it belongs to have
nothing discordant, nothing intermittent : their thought
ever advancing, their will never lingering, the disturbance
between them is annihilated as fast as it is created ; and
with activity more glorious than ours, they substitute for
our human periodicity a diviner constancy.   If, as the
prophet's dream proclaims, there is "no night" in the
better world, the scene, unshaded by the darkness, un-
kindled by the blaze of day, is the fitting residence for
beings exempt from the ebb and flow of energy and repose ;
who have no morning and evening sacrifice, but from whose
fragrant and fervid mind the cloud of incense eternally

ascends; whose affections send forth no interrupted anthem, but in ever-living harmony *continually* cry, " Holy, Holy, Holy Lord God Almighty, who art, and wast, and art to come." This characteristic in our conception of more heavenly natures presents them to us under an aspect of intent, yet passionless, serenity. We attribute to them a perfect moral beauty, — a godlike symmetry of goodness, — which fills us with reverence, trust, affection, which draws from us the sigh of hope, and refreshes us in the weariness of our harsher life. But we ascribe to them no *merit ;* we desire for them no *reward ;* no plaudits burst from our hearts as we meditate their high career. As soon almost should we think of applauding the perfectness of God. A spirit that undergoes no struggle is out of the sphere of recompense; being either below the point of noble strife, so as not to *deserve* reward; or above, so as not to *need* it. The perfect proportion between power and perception which we recognize in diviner natures excludes all idea of *resistance:* there is no hesitation for volition to encounter; whatever is felt to be best is also loved as dearest, and simply pursued without a rival in the thoughts. This entire coalescence of the order of goodness and the order of desire, this instant and spontaneous adaptation of the will to the conscience through every stage of moral progression, distinguishes our notion of *saintly* excellence, and furnishes our clearest image of a higher world.

The conditions of this world, however, are of a lower and less glorious kind. We must rise by successive stages, not by perennial flight. We have always something to overtake; and there is a distance, but too appreciable, between what we are and what we ought to be, — between what we wish and what we reverence. This distance can be recovered only by successive paroxysms of effort, prolonged into patient perseverance. We cannot hope to be released from this demand upon our half-reluctant powers, and must hold ourselves ready, with resolute alacrity, now to lash and now to cheer them on. When we have fairly won a point, and brought up our habit to our conscience, the penitential interval, destroyed for the moment, instantly begins to grow again. For, while action, breathless with successful toil, sits down to rest, affection, which has long been there, is moving on. While our moral love is ever in the future, our will becomes entangled in the past; detained by clinging habits and lulled by old contentments, it sleeps upon its triumphs till it is surprised by sudden foes. Every new perception of good, every dawning upon us of higher obligations, finds our active forces pledged and pre-engaged to some poorer work, from which we have to tear ourselves away. This it is that makes all human faithfulness not holy but strenuous, and constitutes the difference between the saint and the hero. In proportion to the resistance which is felt, and the effort set up against it, in proportion to the *strength* of natural desire which is put aside for its inferior worth, — is the virtue admitted to be noble and heroic : we praise it with a glad and glorious heart: we celebrate it as a triumph ; and cry — what we could never say to angel or to God, — " Well done ! " The sentiment seems to imply that the achievement is something more than could be expected. · But if such crisis of conflict comes to ourselves, we know well that it is not in our option to shrink from it with innocence ; that to discern a moral good as possible, is to come under the obligation to make it real. And if the effort is faithlessly declined, there inevitably creeps upon us, first, an ignominious sorrow ; and next, a sadder and more fatal *loss* of the sorrow, and of all true worship of the heart.

This first grief it was that took the young ruler with mournful steps away : and an anticipation of the second that led Jesus to look on him with a boundless pity. Christ saw in him the soul, which, if it could but be the hero, would become the angel ; if not, would sink, with many an ineffectual horror, into infinite depths. The man's early life had enabled him to see, what was hidden from consciences

16

more confused, the divine perfectness of Christ. The chief
value of his good ways, of his steady heed to the commandments, was that it just brought him favorably to this
very moment, and set him with open-eyed perception before
Messiah's face. By the vision of so holy a spirit, as it
passed near him, he had caught the feeling of a higher
life than that of well-ordered habit ; had been irresistibly drawn to put the question so fatal to his peace ; had
heard his own consciousness repeated, and sent like a bell-
stroke to his heart, in the deep words, " Yet lackest thou
one thing ; " yet withal he had not strength to follow, and
went away with the cloud settled on his spirit. And once
having seen and refused a better life, he finds that the
merely good life, adequate before, has lost all its sacredness. Henceforth it is without a charm, and empty of
every inspiration ; and lies before him with dead and
leaden aspect, tinged with no glory, and promising no heaven.
And every mind of imperfect earnestness has to bear a like
burden of sorrow ; — not the Christ-like sorrow of infinite
aspiration, chasing a good it cannot fully overtake ; for that
is a sorrow with upward look, piercing the heavens with a
gaze of prayer : — but the shameful sorrow of penitent infirmity, retreating from the good it has refused to follow ;
a sorrow with ever downcast look, to which the heavens are
hid, and the earth bereft of beauty and soiled with common
dust.

All men are liable to this grievous experience ; for all are
visited by gleams of something fairer and more faithful than
their own lives. But those are most fearfully exposed to it,
who have the dangerous yet glorious gift of high powers
and opportunities. Had Christ never crossed the path of
that youth of great possessions, his imagination would have
remained without its divinest picture, and his conscience
without its deadliest reproach. Or had he been rich only,
and not thoughtful too, he might have passed that consecrated figure by, and felt no shadow fall on his content.

The privilege and the sadness came together. And those who are haunted by no visions of higher good, who see only what the sun or moon may shine upon; — on whom no lifted veil lets in the splendors so kindling to the nobler reason, so fatal to the feeble will, — escape the sighs of bitterest regret. Whoso is placed of God upon the loftiest heights, is on the verge of the most enshadowed chasms. The revelations of thought and conscience are awful privileges, vainly coveted by profane ambition, and, even to the devout and wise, safe only when received with pure self-renunciation. The richest lights that fall upon the soul lie next to the deepest tones of shade. Messiah's first gaze of divine affection on the half-earnest youth would doubtless send through his heart a hopeful joy : but afterwards, when he had lapsed into the old and common self, that very glance would become a terrible remembrance. And so is it with us all : every light of moral beauty, permitted to enter, but not allowed to guide us, becomes, like the after-image of the sun when idly stared at, a dark speck upon the soul, which follows us at all our work, adheres to every object, approaches and recedes in dreams, and is neither evaded by movement, nor washed out by tears. If the fairest gifts are not to be turned into haunting griefs, it can only be by following in the ways of duty and denial along which they manifestly lead ; and, while yet they look upon us, like the eye of Christ, with a sacred love, resolving on that quiet self-surrender, which shall meet their solemn claim, and prevent our ever hearing again the words, " Yet lackest thou one thing."

XXV.

THE SHADOW OF DEATH.

PHILIPPIANS I. 21.

FOR TO ME, TO LIVE IS CHRIST, AND TO DIE IS GAIN.

IT is natural to conclude that one who could feel death to be a gain, must have had few treasures in life to lose. The sentiment evidently belongs to a heart that had either out-lived the objects of affection and favorite pursuit; or else had loved little, while capable of loving much, and was unattached to the scene of human existence except at its points of duty. It is perfectly conceivable that a mind dis-engaged from external realities, keeping together and entire in its own feelings, interested most profoundly in the ab-stractions of its own faith and hope, may welcome the tran-sition to another form of being, in which it will retain its individuality complete, and be surrounded by new objects tempting it at length to open forth. He that has no deep root in this world, may suffer transplantation without pain. And thus it was with Paul. His ardent and generous soul had fastened itself on no one living object, but on an abstrac-tion, a thing of his own mind, *the truth.* For half his life a wanderer over the earth, no place looked up at him with a domestic eye. Called as he was into ever new society, and passing rapidly through all orders of men; accustomed to study in quick succession the feelings of slave and philoso-pher, of Jew, of Asiatic, of Athenian and Roman, his per-sonal sympathies were disciplined to promptitude rather than to profundity. He rested nowhere long enough to feel his nature silently yet irrevocably depositing itself there; but was at all times ready to gather up his feelings and pass on. Christ and God, the objects of his most earnest love, were viewless and ideal here, and would become realities only when death had transferred him to the future. It is true that a noble attachment bound him to his disciples; but he loved them, less in their individual persons and for their own sakes, than as depositaries of the truth, — as links of a living chain of minds by which that truth would complete its circuit, and find a passage for its renovating power. Nor was there any thing in his outward condition to which his desires could eagerly cling. The world, as a place of shelter, had been spoiled for him by the gospel: his pure tastes were revolted, his sympathies stung at every turn: at Jerusalem, the impending fate of friends and country brooded on his spirit like a cloud: in Rome, the springs of social enjoyment were poisoned by the penetrating taint of a voluptuous polytheism; at every table was the altar, on every tongue the light oath, of idolatry. In every aspect society presented a scene, not for rest, but for toil: not to be enjoyed, but to be reformed: it offered no place where the Christian might innocently retreat within the sanctity of a home; but summoned him forth, in the spirit of an earnest and almost impatient benevolence, to purchase, by his own good fight of persuasion and of faith, a fuller purity and peace for coming times. In this noble conflict, life afforded to Paul the satisfactions of moral victory; but death offered the persecuted Apostle the only prospect of personal release: from the prison it would transfer him to the skies; and the fetters would fall from his hand in the freedom of immortality.

That Paul, thus insulated from earthly attachments, should feel a deeper interest in the future than in the present, is perfectly natural. But when Christians take up this feeling as essential to every disciple; — when they proclaim it a solemn duty to postpone every human feeling to the attrac-

tions of the eternal state; — when they say, " it is not enough
to take the promises to your heart as true comfort in your
sorrow, but even in glad scenes of life, in youth, amid the
ties of nature, in the very jubilee of the affections, you must
yearn towards heaven more than to the world, and feel
that to go is far better than to stay;"—they are guilty of
an insincere and mischievous parody on the sentiments of
the Apostle. If we are to believe the rhapsodies of a prevalent fanaticism, no one has any vital religion, who does not
think the world a waste, and life a burden, and all human
affections snares of sin: whose impressions of God, and
emotions towards Christ, do not far transcend in their intensity the love of kindred and of men; and who do not, in all
earnest moments of reflection, sigh for the hour which shall
rescue them from their mortality. If a shade creeps upon
the countenance at the consciousness that youth departs,
and that the foot has already entered the declining path;
if we cannot think of the wreck of vigor without regret, or
look into a grave without a sigh; if we manifest in any way
that the mystery of mortality presses upon our hearts to
sadden them;—the only comfort that is offered us is, that
we can have no real Christianity within us; and, since we
shrink from the thought of death so much, and yearn for
heaven so little, we must expect the retribution that never
ends. Even those who hold a creed more merciful than this,
regard such feelings with grave disapprobation, and suppose
them to have their root in distrust of Providence, and doubts
of immortality. Yet the human heart quietly vindicates its
own right, and still weeps for death: the last hour is still
felt to be a trial, not a joy, — a fitting time for resignation
and meek trust, not for transport; and *to bear it well* is
held sufficient proof of a good and faithful hope. In spite
of the imagined eagerness to depart and be with Christ,
even the elect preserve their mortal life with no less care
than the unbeliever; and religious suicides, in impatience
for an assured salvation, are crimes unheard of yet: nor is

the funeral converted yet from a scene of grief into an ova-
tion. It is obvious then that in this assumption of the
apostolic sentiment there is a latent insincerity, — an unconscious self-delusion, — as indeed there always is, where
states of feeling rarely attainable are insisted on as essential
duties. Unhappily, this hollow and inflated religion is far
from being a harmless self-deception. Sarcastic sagacity
sees its emptiness and scoffs. Minds affectionate and refined are revolted by a faith, calling for the excision of
human affections which are an integral portion of their life,
and scowling on that lofty melancholy which has been often
declared inseparable from superior natures. And thus the
profession of religion, in its more earnest form, is apt to
be found in association with the cold heart that, caring but
slightly for any thing here, gains an easy credit for sublimer
aspirations; that reviles a scene of existence to whose beauty
it is insensible, and plumes itself on freedom from human
attachments, which it is not noble enough to feel; that has
no better way of clothing the heaven above with glory,
than by making the earth below look hideous. In order to
present some counteraction of conceptions so injurious, it
may be useful to define the actual place which the immortal
hope should occupy in our regards.

The true and natural state of mind is found, I apprehend,
when the futurity offered to our hopes is less loved than
happy and virtuous existence on earth, but more loved than
life here upon unfaithful or forbidden terms; — when, leaving unimpaired our content with permitted happiness, it
brings the needful solace to affliction. It matters not that
the realities of that higher world will doubtless transcend
our happiest life, and the successive stages of our being be
ever progressive in excellence. The reality can affect us
only through our ideas of it; and these ideas present us
with so faint an image of the truth, that its vividness must
be surpassed by the warmer and nearer light of our actual
and happy experience.

The future cannot reasonably be expected to compete with the present in our desires, because our conceptions of it are necessarily nothing more than a selection from the present. The scenery of our immortal hope is constructed from the scattered elements of our mortal life. We borrow from memory its peaceful retrospect, from conscience its emotions of satisfied duty, from reason its delighted perceptions of truth, from affection and faith the repose of human sympathy, and the glow of diviner aspiration: and, combining all into one full thought glorified by the element of eternity, we see before us the future of our hopes. Whatever other resources the great reality may contain, whatever impenetrable mysteries lie within the ample folds of its duration, must be inoperative on us, because not present to our minds. We look therefore at earth as comprising *all* the good which we have ever experienced: we look at heaven as repeating *some.* And though *in words* we may be assured of the superior intensity of the latter, *in thought* we can but dwell on it as it has been felt; — he who has felt profoundly, anticipating vividly; — he whose emotions are obtuse, looking on nothing but a blank. Nor does the conception of immense duration practically impart much brilliancy to the impressions of faith; for time is nothing to us, except as it is replete with events, compounded of successive points of consciousness; and we have no adequate stock of conceptions of the future wherewith to fill so mighty an expectancy, and people with various interest the vacuity of infinite ages. The actual effect of the eternal hope is derived from the imagination of single passages of experience, — from the instantaneous glance of some moment of blessedness or awe, — the smiting of a reproachful thought, — the solution of a sad perplexity, — the vision of a recovered friend. It is not in ordinary human nature to prefer the fragmentary happiness of heaven, as alone it can appear before our thoughts, to the complete and well-known satisfactions of this life in its peaceful attitudes.

Again, the future is to us an abstraction, a phantom, a floating vision, which cannot reasonably be expected to rival in interest the positive recollections of the actual scene in which we are placed. Sensible impressions, ideas of visible and audible objects, would seem indispensable to the existence of distinct and vivid conception: and when they depart, and we are called to think of events without any scenery; of emotions without utterance; of love without a hand to grasp; of knowledge without the converse with men and books, without the real study of light and air and water, and the solid rocks, and the living things of the forest and the ocean; of moral growth without a known theatre of action; — the vision is apt to flit away in impalpable and spectral forms. It is not that we derive our chief enjoyment from the senses: but material impressions are needful as the centres, the fixed points, round which feelings and recollections and imaginations cluster, and without which they are speedily dissipated. We love them, not on their own account, but as the shelter and the shrine of sentiments ineffably dear. The memories of childhood, — how do they rush upon the heart when we revisit the very scenes in which they had their birth! One tone of a bell whose summons we were accustomed to obey, — the sight of a field where we met the companions of some favorite sport, — the re-entrance beneath a roof under which we gathered with brothers and sisters around the Christmas fire, — how do they do blessed violence to time, and snatch us into the past! How do they make the atmosphere of our thoughts ring with the merry shout of playmates, or paint on the very space before us the smile of some dear absent face, or whisper the meek counsel of some departed voice! So dependent are we on such outward things, that even slight changes in the parts of such a scene disturb us; and the disappearance of a building or a tree seems to bereave us of a thousand sympathies. Long habit endears even the most homely familiarities of our existence, and we cannot

part with them without a pang : we hang our thoughts upon
the surfaces of all things round us, — on the walls of our
home, the hours of the day, the faces of neighbors, the quiet
of country, or the stir of town. And then, too, the domesticities of life! O God! they would be too much for
our religion, were they not themselves in pure hearts a very
form of that religion. If we could all go together, there
would be nothing in it : but that separate dropping off, —
that departing one by one, — that drift from our anchorage
alone, — that thrust into a widowed heaven, — who can
deny it to be a lonesome thing? It is mere ignorance of
the human mind to expect the love of God to overpower all
this. Why, the more we have thought of him, the more we
have venerated and trusted him, so much the more closely
has he too become associated with the familiar scenery and
companions of our life ; they have grown into his image
and interpreters; they have established themselves as the
shrine of our piety, the sanctuary of his spirit, the expression of his love : and when we are torn from *them*, we seem
to retire to a distance from *his* shelter. If Christ felt the
cup to be bitter, and turned for a moment from the draught;
if he trembled that he should see no more the towers of
Jerusalem, though to see them had drawn forth prophetic
tears; if he sorrowed in spirit to bid adieu to the family of
Bethany, though the tie was that of friendship and not of
home ; if he hid his head at parting in the bosom of the
beloved disciple, though to Mary the mother that disciple
was needful still ; if he had rather that the immortal spirits
of the elder time should come to commune with him under
the familiar oaks of Tabor, than himself be borne to them
he knew not whither ; if the Mount of Olives, his favorite
retreat of midnight prayer, and the shore of the Galilean
Lake, witness to the musings and enterprises of his opening
ministry, and the verdant slopes of Nazareth, sacred with
the memories of early years, seemed to gaze in upon his
melted soul with a beseeching look that he would not go ;

— may not we, without the reproach of impiety or the suspicion of unacknowledged doubts, feel that to depart is no
light struggle, and cast a lingering glance at the friendly
scene we quit? It is not the animal conflict of death, the
corporeal pain of an organization ceasing to be : to be much
concerned about that were an unmanly fear. It is not any
torturing apprehension about the mysterious future, any
dread of the great secret, any questioning whether all will
be well there : for a good man to be disturbed with such
feelings, shows a morbid timidity of faith, a feeble distrust
of the benignity of Providence, with which an affectionate
piety will have no sympathy. It is simply and solely the
adieu to things loved and left, the exchange of the familiar
for the new, from which our hearts may be justified if they
recoil. Doubtless, the time will come, when successive
strokes of bereavement have fallen upon our homes, for that
recoil to cease. When in the sanctuary of the affections
the lights are almost extinguished, and those that remain
only enable us to read the inscriptions on the multitude of
surrounding tombs; when, in fact, the solitude would be,
not to depart, but to remain, — we may well and naturally
feel that it is time to go, and our prayer may be to be
speedily withdrawn to the place of rest. For now, whatever may be the indistinctness of the future, the groups of
friendship are there ; they make the best part of its scenery ;
and wherever they are is a shelter and a home. However
strange to us the colony may be in which they dwell, if, as
we cross the deeps of death, their visionary forms shall
crowd the shore, and people the hills of that unvisited abode,
it will be to us " a better country, even a heavenly."

There is then a glow in this world more genial and less
faint than the orb of everlasting hope ; and yet a darkness,
too, most thankful for its mild and holy beams. Pale at
our mid-day, it attains its glory at our noon of night; and
if it does not light us at our work, lifts us when we watch
and pray. The proper entrance for faith and hope lies

between the ripeness of blessing and the deepening of sadness; between the crown and the cross of life. Do you
think that so modest a place for so great an expectation is
injurious to the dignity of religion? Perhaps it is in the
better harmony with its humility: at least it seems not
unsuitable to a mind which is so grateful for the present,
as to shrink from pressing anxious claims upon the future:
which loves so well the *given* world of God, as not often
to remind him of the *promised* one. Were this the only
eclipse which the immortal prospect is liable to suffer, there
would be little need to lament the languor of its light.
That causes less excusable also intercept its influence, is not
indeed to be denied: but when are we to seek the remedy?
Shall we endeavor to loosen the affections from this life,
and forbid all heart-allegiance towards a scene to which we
are tempted so strongly to cling? Alas! we shall not love
heaven more for loving earth less: this would be a mere
destruction of one set of sympathies, in no way tending to
the creation of another. The love of God may even find its
root in the love of kindred; and admiration of his works
and ways is the germ of adoration of himself. If it is from
the blessings of the present that we construct our conception
of the future; to enfeeble our sense of these blessings, is to
take away the very materials of faith. No; the needful
thing is not that we abate, but that we consecrate, the interests and affections of our life; entertain them with a
thoughtful heart; serve them with the will of duty; and
revere them as the benediction of our God. The same spirit
which takes the veil of Deity from the present will drive
away the clouds that overhang the future: and he that
makes his moments devout, shall not feel his eternity to
be cheerless. And as it is the fascinations of affectionate
memory that hold us back, they may be not a little counteracted by the creations of sacred hope. We shall be less
servilely detained among things seen, when we are less
indolent in our conceptions of things unseen; when we

freely cast into them every blessed remembrance, every high pursuit, every unanswered aspiration, every image pure and dear; and invest them with the forms of a divine and holy beauty. If the particular good which we imagine should · not arrive, it can only be because God will present us with far better. Without this free license for the creations of faith, I see not how, while we are mortals yet, immortality can exercise its due attraction upon our minds. To *die*, can never, without an enthusiasm which does violence to reason and little credit to the heart, be an act of *transport:* so low as an act of *submission* it need not sink; for that would imply a belief that the change from the present to the future is for evil. It is most fitly met in the spirit of *trust*, — an unbroken belief that it is for the better, but a feeling of reluctance, which we distrust and check, as though it were for the worse; a consciousness that if we chose for ourselves, we should remain where we are, yet not a doubt of the greater wisdom and goodness of God's choice, that we should go. If this spirit of humble faith be not high-wrought enough, may God forgive the loving hearts that can attain no better!

XXVI.

GREAT HOPES FOR GREAT SOULS.

1 CORINTHIANS XV. 48.

AS IS THE HEAVENLY, SUCH ARE THEY ALSO THAT ARE HEAVENLY.

THE contempt with which it is the frequent practice of divines to treat the grounds of natural religion, betrays an ignorance both of the true office of revelation, and of the true wants of the human heart. It cannot be justified, except on the supposition that there is some contradiction between the teachings of creation and those of Christ, with some decided preponderance of proof in favor of the latter. Even if the gospel furnished a series of perfectly new truths, of which nature had been profoundly silent, it would be neither reasonable nor safe to fix exclusive attention on these recent and historical acquisitions, and prohibit all reference to those elder oracles of God, by which his Spirit, enshrined in the glories of his universe, taught the fathers of our race. And if it be the function of Christianity, not to administer truth entirely new, but to corroborate by fresh evidence, and invest with new beauty, and publish to the millions with a voice of power, a faith latent already in the hearts of many, and scattered through the speculations of the wise and noble few, — to erect into realities the dreams which had visited a half-inspired philosophy, interpreting the life and lot of man ; — then there is a relation between the religion of nature and that of Christ, — a relation of original and supplement, — which renders the one essential to the apprehension of the other. Revelation, you say, has

given us the clew by which to thread the labyrinth of creation, and extricate ourselves from its passages of mystery
and gloom. Be it so; still, *there*, in the scene thus cleared
of its perplexity, must our worship be paid, and the manifestation of Deity be sought. If the use of revelation be to
explain the perplexities of providence and life, it would be
a strange use to make of the explanation, were we to turn
away from the thing explained. We hold the key of heaven
in our hands; what folly to be for ever extolling and venerating it, whilst we prohibit all approach to the temple,
whose gates it is destined to unlock!

The great doctrine of human immortality has received
from Christianity its widest and noblest efficacy; has been
lifted for many a generation from a low point of probability to the confines of certainty; and has found in the
glorified "Finisher of faith" an answer to the difficulties
which most embarrass the divine hope of the human mind.
But the influence which is most effectual in diffusing a
truth in the first instance, is not always the best for creating
the later and calmer faith of the reflecting heart : and when
the historical illustration has parted with something of its
power, it may be useful to the feelings and imagination to
dwell on considerations, of feebler force perhaps, but of
nearer and deeper interest. Thus it is with the natural
indications of human immortality. Nature and life, our
sins and sorrows, our virtues and our peace, have on them
the traces of a great futurity; and to neglect these is to pay
a dubious and even a fatal honor to revelation. The Christian history is a matter long past; the resurrection of our
great Prophet is viewed by us at the remoter end of a series
of centuries ; and the vibration with which it should thrill
our affections is almost lost in traversing so vast a gulf.
But if in the actual phenomena of human life and its distribution of good and ill, — if in the very constitution of our own
minds, there are evidences of a cycle of existence beyond
the present, we have here a voice, not of history, but of

experience, bidding us look up; a warning from the living present, not from the tomb of the past: and though it may be less clear in its announcements, yet may the gentlest whisper at our right hand startle us more than the loudest echo from afar. It is a solemn thing, when we gaze intently at the dial of our fate, and listen to the beats that number our vicissitudes, to see its index distinctly pointing to eternity. The exclusive appeal to the historical evidence of futurity is one great cause, I believe, of the feeble effect of this mighty expectation. Till it is felt that heaven is needed to complete the history of earth, till men become conscious of capacities for which their present sphere of action is too contracted, till the wants of the intellect and the affections cry aloud within them for the boundless and eternal, the distant words of Christian promise will die away, ere they reach their hearts; there will be no visible infinitude of hope; and amid the incessant verbal recognition of the great hereafter, practical doubts will brood over the feelings, which will blight all true sincerity of faith. The character of some of these doubts I proceed to indicate, — doubts, not of direct speculation, not arising from any perception of fallacy in the evidence, not therefore leading to any denial of the doctrine of futurity, — but doubts that lurk obscurely in the feelings, cold, silent, undefined; that come and go like spectres, — come when we abhor, and vanish when we seek them; that shun the steady gaze of the intellect, and haunt with fiend-like stare the uplifted eye of broken hope and trembling love. It will appear that these doubts are peculiar to our inferior states of character; that when the higher parts of our nature are developed, and the adaptation of immortality to our true wants is felt, they disappear.

There are doubts obtruded on us by our *animal* nature. It is not at all surprising that in proportion as we attend to the perishable part of our nature, our nature should appear perishable; and that in proportion as we neglect the mind,

which alone has any heritage in the future, the future should
become obscure. True though it is that we are fearfully and
wonderfully made, there is something humiliating in the
protracted and exclusive study of man's physical organization ; and whatever indications it affords of the designing
benevolence of God, it rather troubles than assists the conception of the immortality of man: for that benevolence,
being equally manifested in the structures and laws of the
brute creation, cannot direct us to the hopes of higher
natures. When the thoughts have been intently fixed on
the physiology of the human body, when the frame has
been analyzed into its several organs, and the functions of
our corporeal life described ; or when, in studying the natural history of man, we are led to compare him with the
other tribes that people the earth, the imagination rises
from such studies with secret uneasiness : it has been, for
the sake of knowledge, to the meaner haunts of our being,
just as the philanthropist, for the sake of benevolence, fre-
quents the dingy recesses of sin and misery: it finds itself
surrounded with clinging impressions of materialism, from
which it must shake itself free, before it can again realize
the holier relations and loftier prospects of human existence. Nor is it unusual for death to be presented to us in
an aspect which unreasonably, but irresistibly, troubles the
heart's diviner trust. Sometimes indeed the last hour of a
human life comes on so gentle a wing, that it seems a fit
passage of a soul to God : the feeble pulse which flutters
into death, the fading eye whose light seems not to be
blotted out but only to retire within, the fleeting breath
that seems to stop, that the spirit may depart in reverent
silence, — are like the signs of a contented exchange of
worlds, of a mind that has nothing for which to struggle,
because it passes to the peace of God. But when the strife
is strong, — when, at the solemn point of existence which
seems most to demand an intent serenity of soul, the animal
nature starts to its supremacy and fiercely claims the mas-

17

tery, and clings with convulsive grasp to the margin of mortality, our imaginations are visited with a deeper trouble than would arise merely from sympathy with the departing sufferer. " Is this," we think, " the transition to the skies, — this, more like the end of hope than the beginning of peace, more like a thrust into the blackest night, than an ushering into the beautiful dawn of the eternal land?" And why is this? It is the tyranny of our animal sympathies; which may well be sceptical of immortality, for it is not for them. The corporeality of our nature is for the time so vehemently forced upon the attention, that we forget what else there is: the half of the being is taken to represent the whole; and that half is really coming to a close. When we retire from the dread impression of this scene, and remember the bright mind eclipsed only during the last hour; when we recognize in its history many a noble toil for truth, many a holy effort of duty, many an exhibition of moral and mental capability too great and gentle to find their gratification here, we gradually return from the shock of nature to the quietude of faith. But this return depends on regarding the body as the instrument of the mind; and there are people who never do this, — men who take their limbs to be their life, and confound their senses with their soul, — who say wise things about the blessings of health and ease, and hear only empty words when there is mention of a full mind, and pure and resolute sentiments of conscience, and earnest affections human and divine. To such, — the sensual, — there is nothing else in man but body; take that from their conceptions, and nothing remains. What then but an absolute blank before their mind can be an existence in which the material interests of our present being utterly vanish, and a spirituality unknown to them even in idea assumes the place? To say that they must look forwards to it with the same kind of feeling as the musician to becoming deaf, and the artist to becoming blind, fails to convey an adequate idea of the emptiness, the

absolute nothingness, of their anticipation. If we could
conceive a being created with no inlet of consciousness but
the sense of sight, — without thought, without emotion,
without other sensation, — a being in fact *all eye*, we perceive that it would be the same thing to him, whether his
vision be paralyzed, or he himself be planted in the midst of
deep and rayless night. To such a one, both conditions
would be a total annihilation : as life was nothing more than
visual perception, so the privation of such perception would
be death : the preservation of the organ would be attended by
no consciousness : in eternal darkness, its function, its pleasures and its pains, are for ever gone ; and had it never been,
its non-existence could not be more perfect. Precisely similar is the view of futurity, — the futurity of the intellectual
and social and moral powers of our nature, — to the sensual
in whom these powers sleep. All the functions of existence
with which he is familiar vanish from him; and as well
might he himself be blotted out, as be placed where all the
offices and elements of his life disappear. He is an eye
dipped in darkness, — an ear left alone in an infinitude of
silence; immortality is to him but prolonged paralysis; it
has nothing to distinguish it from death. What wonder
then that, in proportion as we resemble such a being, our
feelings are harassed by a thousand doubts of renovated
life! The doubts are indeed perfectly well founded : for
this nature there *is* no further life; its mechanism wears
out, and death casts it aside for ever : and, till that higher
nature, of which it is the organic instrument, is born to full
life within us, we have no kindred or affinity with the
eternal state. But when, by nobler culture, by purer experience, by breathing the air of a higher duty, vitality at
length creeps into the soul, the instincts of immortality will
wake within us. The word of hope will speak to us a language no longer strange. We shall feel like the captive bird
carried accidentally to its own land, when, hearing for the
first time the burst of kindred song from its native woods,

it beats instinctively the bars of its cage in yearning for the
free air that is thrilled with so sweet a strain.

There are doubts forced on us by our *selfish* nature. A
hard and self-enclosed mind is destitute of the feelings that
look most intently on the future, and make it most credible,
because most urgently needed, by us. It is rather our sympathetic than our personal happiness that is wounded by the
conditions of our mortal being. For ourselves alone, if we
love not deeply our own kind, it is usually possible to preserve a decent and sober life, a small order of happiness,
respectably ensured from ruin, which will never feel impelled
to look up and cry aloud to God. It is when we suffer ourselves to seek a profounder but a frailer bliss; when the
heart possesses a terrible stake in existence ; when we yield
ourselves to the strongest love, and yet can love nothing
that we may not lose; that we feel capacities which are
mocked by the brevity of life, and totally incapable of exhaustion here. It is our affections chiefly that are disproportioned to our condition : they are an over-match for us
in this world. God would never launch so frail a vessel on
so stormy a sea, where the roll of every wave may wreck
us, were it not designed to float at length on serener waters,
and beneath gentler skies. O God! it is terrible to think
what may be lost in one human life; what hope, what joy,
what goodness, may drop with one creature into the grave!
how all things, now so full of the energies of a cheerful
being, so copious in motive and in peace, so kindled by the
smile of Providence, and ringing with the happy voices of
nature and our kind, may droop and gloom before us by one
little change! It is not from without, but from within, —
from the sacred but changing orb of our own love, — that
the light and colors come, in which we see the scenery of
existence clad ; and if there be an eclipse within, creation
mourns beneath a film of darkness. It is, however, in such
moments of sorrow, and in the perpetual consciousness that
they may come, that we find the strongest call of thought

to a more peaceful and stable being; and that we are urged
to fly to the distant regions in which the intercepted light
still shines. But all this the heart of the selfish can never
know : his sympathies are well proportioned to the dimensions and the securities of this state : for all that he yet
feels, an eternal life would be an enormous over-provision :
he has no passionate tenacity of love that clings imploringly
to any blessing; but is able to shrink into his shell of personal ease, and sleep. Nor does the wider benevolence, the
spirit of Christian philanthropy to which the selfish man is
equally insensible, stimulate less urgently the demand for
immortality. How is it possible to study deeply the lot
of the great majority of men; — to see them ground down
by toil; spending their years in bare self-continuation,
and ending life without tasting of its fruits; filled to satiety
with labor and starved to death within the mind; — how
is it possible to see so much noble capability wasted, so
much true blessedness lost, so many, first created a little
lower than the angels, and then forced nearly to a level
with the brutes, — without providing in our thoughts a
future vindication of the Creator, — a life in which the
fearful inequality will be compensated, and the suspended
good at length born? But the cold and self-regarding
mind cannot understand a sentiment like this. It has no
such sympathy with the well-being of others as to feel that
their habitual privations constitute a moral claim upon the
benevolence of God. It has no generous faith in the possibilities of human improvement; but, thinking meanly of
its kind, is not disconcerted by the meanness of its destiny.
Ignorant of the immeasurable contents of our nature, of
the resources of our human affections, of the heroic energies of duty, and the sublime peace of God, he sees nothing worth immortalizing; and because he himself would
be an anomaly in heaven, he fancies heaven too good for
man. Thus selfishness, like sensuality, secretly conscious of
its ignobility, and interpreting by its own experience the

whole race of human kind, stifles within us the eternal hope.

Causes, not moral, like the foregoing, but merely intellectual, tend also to disturb the feelings with doubts on this subject. Very contracted knowledge and feeble imagination will usually possess but a fluctuating faith in all truths remote from experience. Though our faith may go far beyond our experience, it must always be chained down by it at a distance : our conceptions of probability are limited by the analogies within our reach : the magnitude of each one's possible must bear some proportion to his actual: the invisible scenes which he imagines will be graduated by the visible which he beholds. In proportion, therefore, as our ideas are few, and the circle of our intellectual perceptions more narrowly bounded, will it be difficult for us to feel the possibility of a state so totally new, so little familiarized to us by any known resemblances to our present condition, as the futurity to which we tend. This incompetency of religious imagination is far from being exclusively attendant on what the world calls ignorance. It may be found often beneath the polished speech, the practised address, the agile faculties of men conspicuous in affairs; being as much the creation of voluntary habit, as the consequence of helpless incapacity. Aptitude for business is not power of reason ; and a grandee on the exchange may be a pauper in God's universe. To calculate shrewdly is different from meditating wisely ; and, where turned into an exclusive engagement, is even more hostile to it than the torpor of the entire mind. The pointed, distinct, and microscopic attention which we direct upon the details of human existence here, is unfavorable to the comprehensive vision of a boundless sphere : the glass through which we best look at the minutiæ near us, serves but to confuse our gaze upon the stars. Growing knowledge, enlarging thought, the reverent estimate of truth and beauty, furnish us with a thousand facilities for illustrating and realizing the unseen, and replenishing its blank abyss with bright creations. Nay, the mental horizon spreads by mere extension of the physical; and as our station rises above the world, our range of possibilities and our willingness of faith appear to grow. For who can deny the effect of wide space alone in aiding the conception of vast time? The spectator who in the dingy cellar of the city, under the oppression of a narrow dwelling, watching the last moments of some poor mendicant, finds incongruity and perplexity in the thought of the eternal state, would feel the difficulty vanish in an instant, were he transplanted to the mountain-top, where the plains and streams are beneath him, and the clouds are near him, and the untainted breeze of heaven sweeps by, and he stands alone with nature and with God. And when, in addition to the mere spectacle and love of nature, there is a knowledge of it too; when the laws and processes are understood which surround us with wonder and beauty every day; when the great cycles are known through which the material creation passes without decay; then, in the immensity of human hopes, there appears nothing which need stagger faith : it seems 'no longer strange, that the mind which interprets the material creation should survive its longest period, and be admitted to its remoter realms.

Thus, in proportion as our nature rises in its nobleness, does it realize its immortality. As it retires from animal grossness, from selfish meanness, from pitiable ignorance or sordid neglect, — as it opens forth into its true intellectual and moral glory, — do its doubts disperse, its affections aspire : the veil is uplifted from the future, the darkness breaks away, and the spirit walks in dignity within the paradise of God's eternity. What a testimony this to the great truth from which our hope and consolations flow! What an incitement to seek its bright and steady light by the culture of every holy faculty within us! The more we do the will of our Father, the more do we feel that this doctrine is indeed of him. Its affinities are with the loftiest parts of our nature; and in our trust in it, we ally ourselves with the choicest spirits of our race. And while we sympathize with them in their past faith, we prepare to meet them where we may assume their nearer likeness. Ever seek we therefore the things which are above.

XXVII.

LO! GOD IS HERE!

——◆——

ACTS XVII. 30.

AND THE TIMES OF THIS IGNORANCE GOD WINKED AT; BUT NOW
COMMANDETH ALL MEN EVERYWHERE TO REPENT.

PAUL, it would appear, looked with a very different feeling
on times past, and times present. Behind him, he saw the
age of ignorance and irreligion, so dark and wild, that life
appeared to lie quite outside the realm of Providence, and
earth to be covered by no heaven. Around him, he beheld
the very era of God, in which the third heaven seemed
almost within reach,· and life was so filled with voices of
duty and hope, that it appeared like some vast whispering
gallery, to render what else had been a divine silence and
mystery, audible and articulate. Behind, he saw a world
abandoned; from which the great Ruler seemed to have
retired, or at least averted the light of his countenance; to
which he spake no word, and gave no intelligible sign;
about whose doings it were painful to say much; for so little
were they in the likeness of his government, so abhorrent
from the spirit of his sway, that they must have been en-
acted during the slumber of his power. But *now*, the hour
of awakening had arrived: the foul dream of the world's
profaneness must be broken; and Heaven would forbear no
more. The divine light was abroad again: divine tones
were floating through this lower atmosphere, and came, like
a solemn music, across the carnival shouts of sensualism and
sin. Out of hearing of these tones the far-travelled Apostle

never passed : they reached him through the rush of waters, as he sailed by night over the Ægean : the voluble voices of Athens could not drown them : they vibrated through the traffic and the cries of Roman streets, and even pierced the brutal acclamations of the amphitheatre ; they were ubiquitous as God, who was *everywhere* commanding *all* men to repent. Whether in his own life, or in the world, Paul found *the past to be profane, the present, divine.*

With us this order is reversed. Our faith delights to expound, not what God is doing *now*, but what he did *once ;* to prove that *formerly* he was much concerned with the affairs of this earth and the spirits of men, though he has abstained from personal intervention for many ages, and become a spectator of the scene. The point of time at which our thoughts search for his agency, and feel after him to find him, lies not at hand, but far ; belongs not to to-day, but to distant centuries ; and must be reached by an historical memory, not by individual consciousness. To our feelings, the period of Divine absenteeism is the present ; wherein we live on the impression, half worn out, of his ancient visitations ; obey as we can the precepts he is understood to have given of old ; and, like children opening again and again the last tattered letter from a parent mysteriously silent in a foreign land, cheer ourselves with such assurance of his love as he may have put on record in languages anterior to our own. " O happy age," — we think, — " that really heard his voice ! O glorious souls, that felt his living inspiration ! O blessed lot, though it passed through the desert and the fire, that lay beneath the shelter of his peace ! " In short, our experience is the opposite of Paul's. That voice which commanded all men to repent, resounds no more ; its date has gone clear away into antiquity ; and it can faintly reach us only through the dead report of a hundred witnesses. Once it was the very spirit of God quivering over the soul of man, — a mountain-air stirring on the face of the waters. The frosts of time may have fixed the

surface, and caught the form ; but how different this from
the trembling movement of our humanity beneath the sweep
of that living breath ! No such holy murmur reaches us, to
whom the *present is earthly,* and *the past, divine.*

Perhaps some one may deny that there is any real variance between Paul's estimate and ours ; on the ground that,
in his view, the time sacred above all others was *his own ;*
and in our retrospect *that* time remains so still. Yet it may
be conjectured, that if we could be put back into his age,
we should hardly see it with his eyes. Possibly enough,
we might look about to no purpose for that presence of the
Holiest which followed him through life ; and listen with
disappointed ear for that whisper that "everywhere" came
to him from the Infinite ; and though at his side when he
was in the third heaven, might see nothing but the walls of
his apartment, in coldest exile from the transports of the
skies. If you go into the tent-maker's warehouse, where he
worked at Corinth, you find the canvas and the tools, and
even the men that ply them, such as you may pass without
notice every day. The lane in which he lived in Rome
seems too dingy for any thing divine, and the noisy neighbors too ordinary to kindle any elevated zeal. The city's
heat and din, the common crush of life, the hurry from task
to task, seem far enough from the cool atmosphere of prayer,
and the glad silence of immortal hopes. And if you converse with the men and women for whom the Apostle gave
his toils and tears, who received the whole affluence of his
sympathies, you may be amazed, perchance, that he could
find them so interesting; and lament to discover, in such
an age of golden days, the vulgar speech, the narrow mind,
the selfish will, the envious passions, of these later times.
And, taking the converse supposition, — think you, if he
had been transplanted from Mars Hill to Westminster, he
would have been beyond the hearing of that voice of God
which he proclaimed and obeyed ? — that the celestial light
which rested upon life would have passed away ? — that his

hope would have been as faint, his worship as unreal, his
whole being as mechanical, as ours? Ah, no! let there be
a soul of power like his within; and it matters not what
weight of world may be cast on it from without.. Be we in
this century or that, — nay, in heaven or on earth, — it is
not that we find, but that we must make, the present holy
and divine.

In vain then do we plead, that our view of time coincides
with that of Paul. With such temper as we have, we
should have listened to him on Areopagus in the spirit of
the Epicureans that heard him; not refusing perhaps to
join the light laugh at his enthusiasm; and wondering how
a man, with his foot on the solid ground of life and nature,
can cast himself madly into the abyss of a fancied futurity,
and an absent God. And as, in yielding to the suggestions
of such temper, we should have felt falsely, and have looked
on Paul's age with a deluded eye, so would *his* be the true
vision of our times; and his earnest proclamation of the
continued sanctity of existence would show his discerning
intuition of realities concealed from us. For God has not
faded into a remembrance : he has not retired from this
scene with the generations known only to tradition. His
energies have no era; his sentiments cannot be obsolete;
"his compassions fail not." Why, even sense and material
nature, his poorest and faintest interpreters, rebuke this
foolish dream, — that he *was*, rather than *is*. They forbid
us to think of him thus, were it only in the mere character
of Creator. They show us, in the very structure of our
globe, — in the rocks beneath our feet, — in the vast cem-
eteries and monuments they disclose of departed races
of creatures, — that creation is not single, but successive;
not an act, but a process; not the work of a week or of a
century, but of immeasurable ages; not moreover past, but
continuous and everlasting; as busy, as mysterious, as vast,
now, as in the darkest antiquity : so that Genesis tells the
story of last week, as truly as of the six days that ushered

in the world's first Sabbath. The universe indeed is not so much a definite machine which once he made, and beyond which he dwells to see it move, as his own infinite abode and ever-changing manifestation ; — living, because the dwelling of his power; boundless, because the chamber of his presence ; ever fresh, because the receptacle of his designs ; fair, because the expression of his love. Now, as of old, he that will listen with the open ear of meditation, may surely hear the Lord God walking in his garden of creation in the cool of every day.

The same temper which leads us to search for Deity only in distant times, causes us to banish him also into distant space ; and persuades us that he is not *here*, but *there*. He is thought to dwell above, beneath, around the earth ; but who ever thinks of meeting him on its very dust? Awfully he shrouds the abyss ; and benignly he gazes on us from the stars : but, in the field and the street, no trace of him is felt to be. Under the ocean, and in the desert, and on the mountain-top, he is believed to rest ; but, into the nearer haunts of town and village, we rarely conceive him to penetrate. Yet where better could wisdom desire his presence, than in the common homes of men, — in the thick cares, and heavy toils, and grievous sorrows, of humanity? For, surely, if nature needs him much in her solitudes, life requires him more in the places of passion and of sin. And in truth, if we cannot feel him near us in this world, we could approach him, it is greatly to be feared, in no other. Could a wish remove us bodily to any distant sphere supposed to be divine, the heavenly presence would flit away as we arrived ; would occupy rather the very earth we had been eager to quit ; and would leave us still amid the same material elements, that seem to hide the infinite vision from our eyes. Go where we may, we seem mysteriously to carry our own circumference of darkness with us : for who can quit his own centre, or escape the point of view, — or of blindness, — which belongs to his own identity? He

who is not with God already, can by no path of space
find the least approach : in vain would you lend him the
wing of angel, or the speed of light ; in vain plant him
here or there, — on this side of death or that : he is in the
outer darkness still ; having that inner blindness which
would leave him in pitchy night, though, like the angel of
the Apocalypse, he were standing in the sun. But ceasing
all vain travels, and remaining with his foot upon this
weary earth, let him subside into the depths of his own
wonder and love ; let the touch of sorrow, or the tears of
conscience, or the toils of duty, open the hidden places of
his affections ; — and the distance, infinite before, wholly
disappears : and he finds, like the Patriarch, that though
the stone is his pillow, and the earth his bed, he is yet in
the very house of God, and at the gate of heaven. O my
friends, if there be nothing celestial without us, it is only
because all is earthly within ; if no divine colors upon our
lot, it is because the holy light is faded on the soul : if our
Father seems distant, it is because we have taken our portion of goods and travelled into a far country, to set up *for
ourselves*, that we may foolishly *enjoy*, rather than reverently *serve*. Whenever he is imagined to be remote and
almost slumbering, be assured it is human faith that is really
heavy and on the verge of sleep ; drowsy with too much
ease, or tired with too much sense : that it has lapsed from
the severe and manly strivings of duty and affection, and
given itself over to indulgence, and become the lazy hire-
ling of prudence. An Epicurean world inevitably makes
an Epicurean God : and when we cease to do any thing
from spontaneous loyalty to the great Ruler, we necessarily
doubt whether he can have occasion to do any thing for
us. Such doubts are vainly attacked by speculative proof,
and evidence skilfully arranged : the clearest and the cloud-
iest intellect are liable to them alike : for they arise from
the practical feebleness of the inner man ; from a dwindled
force in the earnest, self-forgetful affections ; and can be

dissipated only by trustful abandonment once more to some object of duty and devotion. The times and people that have vividly felt the proximity of God have always been characterized by hearty and productive affections; by vast enterprises and great sacrifices; by the seeds 'of mighty thought dropped upon the world, and the fruits of great achievements contributed to human history. In contact with every grand era in the experience of mankind will be found *the birth of a religion;* — a fresh discovery of the preternatural and mysterious; a plenary sense of God; the descent of the Holy Spirit on waiting hearts; a day of Pentecost to strong and faithful souls, giving them the utterance of a divine persuasion, and dispersing a new gospel over the world. We, alas! are far enough, — far at least as the days of Wesley, — from any such period of inspiration in the past; — perhaps, however, the nearer to it in the future, as there is no night unfollowed by the dawn. It is not permitted us too curiously to search the hidden providences of our humanity; but one thing we cannot fail to notice: that a return to simple, undisguised affections, — to natural and veracious speech, — to earnest and inartificial life, — has characterized every great and noble period, and all morally powerful and venerable men. To such taste and affections, and to the secret rule of conscience which presides among them, we must learn to trust, whatever be the seductions of opinion, and the sophistries of expediency, and even the pleadings of the speculative intellect. When thus we fear to quench his spirit, God will not suffer our time to be a dreary and unconsecrated thing. Swept by the very borders of his garment, we shall not look far for his glorifying presence. The poorest outward condition will have no power to obliterate the solemnity from life. Nay, of nothing may we be more sure than this; that, if we cannot sanctify our present lot, we could sanctify no other. Our heaven and our Almighty Father are there or nowhere. The obstructions of that lot are given for us to heave away by the concurrent touch of a holy spirit, and labor of a strenuous will; its gloom, for us to tint with some celestial light: its mysteries are for our worship; its sorrows for our trust; its perils for our courage; its temptations for our faith. Soldiers of the cross, it is not for us, but for our Leader and our Lord, to choose the field : it is ours, taking the station which he assigns, to make it the field of truth and honor, though it be the field of death.

It is part of the illusion which contrasts us with Paul, that we esteem God to be *without* us, rather than *within* us; a mode of conception which I believe to be ultimately fatal to that religious life, from the incipient feebleness of which it originally springs. What has been really meant by those devout men who have freely spoken of God's communion with them, and of the thoughts which he has put into the heart? That these thoughts did actually arise and must be accepted as facts, will hardly be denied. Nor will it be doubted that, in the thinker's view, they appeared most high and solemn; and that in no other way could their beauty and authority be expressed, than by calling them emanations from the supreme Source of the binding and the beautiful. To affirm the purest and deepest movements of our nature to be from God, is the natural utterance of full reverence for them; to deny their origin from him, is a distinct profession that that reverence has declined : they are sought for at a lower source, because they have descended to a meaner place. And while this denial indicates a fainter piety, it is no sign of stronger reason. What emboldens you to contradict the universal testimony of souls aloft in worship, — the natural language of poet, saint and prophet? How do you know that in the affections that most glorify their hearts, there is no immediate light of Heaven? You say, perhaps, they are experienced by the worshipper's own mind, and must be parts of the nature that feels them. But it does not follow that, because they are included in the consciousness of men, they indicate no presence and living touch of God. Or you say, there is no miracle in them, and they come and go by laws not quite untraceable. But this only shows that the divine agency, if there, is free from disorder and caprice, and loves to be constant in behalf of those who are faithful to its conditions. Or do you complain of the idle fanaticisms, which often have preferred this tempting claim? Idle they may be to you, to whose mind they stand in quite different relation; but not perhaps to those whom assuredly they raised to higher life. We are not all alike; and God does not exist for any miserable egotist alone. We are all indeed set in one infinite sphere of universal reason and conscience; but scattered over it to follow separate circles, and attain every variety of altitude in faith. Like stars upon the same meridian, whose culminating points cannot be alike, we touch our supreme heights at different elevations; and the measure which is far down on the course of one mind, may be the acme of religion in another. And it is as worthy of God to lift every soul to the ethereal summit proper to it, as to roll the heavens, and call forth their lights by interval and number, and see that "not one faileth." And as there is no ground in experience for rejecting the old language of devotion, neither is there any in the claim of consistent philosophy. We find men ready enough to allow that there is no place where God is not, perhaps no time when his external power is not active in some realm or other. And why then withhold from him that internal and spiritual sphere of which all else is but the theatre and the temple? What can dead space *want* with the divine presence, compared with the ever-perilled soul of man, perpetually trembling on the verge of grief or sin? Shall we coldly speculate on the physical omnipresence of the Infinite, and question the ubiquity of his moral power? — diffuse him as an atmosphere, and forget that he is a Mind? — plead for his mechanical action on matter, and doubt the contact of spirit with spirit? — admit the agency of the artist on his work, and deny the embrace of the Father and the child?

18

It were indeed strange if this anomaly were true. Where
is this blessed object of our worship, if not within our souls ?
What possible ground is there for affirming him to be elsewhere and *not* here ?   Far more plausible would the limita-
tion be, if we were to declare him manifestly existent here
alone.   All external things are apprehensible by sense, and
it is to discover the outward creation that the senses are
given.   All internal things are apprehended by thought,
and it is to seize this far higher order of realities, that
thought is given.   Never was eye or ear made perceptive
of Deity: "no man hath heard his voice at any time or
seen his form : " he is the object of simply spiritual discernment, the holy image, mysteriously shaped forth from the
quarries of our purest thought, and glowing with life, beauty
and power, in the inmost sanctuary of the mind.   And his
reality there is a certainty of the same rank as the existence
of the universe without.   There is truth then, and only a
wise enthusiasm, in the established strains of Christian piety ;
invoking the presence of the Holiest to the soul as his loved
retreat, and humbly referring to him the purest thoughts
and best desires.   I pretend not to draw the untraceable
line that separates his being from ours.   The decisions of
the will, doubtless, are our own, and constitute the proper
sphere of our personal agency.   But in a region higher than
the will, — the realm of spontaneous thought and emotion,
— there is scope enough for his "abode with us."   Whatever is most deep within us is the reflection of himself.   All
our better love, and higher aspirations, are the answering
movements of our nature in harmonious obedience to his
spirit.   Whatever dawn of blessed sanctity, and wakening
of purer perceptions, opens on our consciousness, are the
sweet touch of his morning light within us.   His inspiration
is perennial; and he never ceases to work within us, if we
consent to will and to do his good pleasure.   He befriends
our moral efforts; encourages us to maintain our resolute
fidelity and truth; accepts our co-operation with his designs

against all evil; and reveals to us many things far too fair and deep for language to express. But, while he is thus prompt to come with his Spirit to the help of seeking hearts, he is expelled by the least unfaithfulness; and when the "spirit of truth" is driven away, this holy "Comforter" no more remains. To receive the promise, we must deserve the prayer, of Christ, — that we "may be kept from the evil," and "sanctified through the truth." Finding a holy of holies within us, we need not curiously ask whether its secret voices are of ourselves or of the Father. Christ felt how, within the deeps of our spiritual nature, the personalities of heaven and earth might become entwined together and indissolubly blended: "Thou, Father, art in me, and I in Thee, and they also one in us." And so, the holy spirit within us, the spirit of Christ, and the spirit of God, are after all but one; — a blessed Trinity, our part in which gives to our souls a dignity most humbling yet august.

XXVIII.

CHRISTIAN SELF-CONSCIOUSNESS.

———◆———

GENESIS III. 22.

AND THE LORD GOD SAID, BEHOLD, THE MAN IS BECOME AS ONE OF US, TO KNOW GOOD AND EVIL.

IT is a favorite doctrine of one of the wisest thinkers of our day, that "if Adam had remained in Paradise, there had been no anatomy, and no metaphysics." In other words, it is only on the lapse from the state of health, that we find we have a body; and on the loss of innocence, that we become conscious of a soul. Disease and wrong are the awakeners of our reflection: they bring our outward pursuits to a pause, and force us to look within: and the extent of our self-study and self-knowledge may be taken as a measure of the depth to which the poison of evil has penetrated into our frame. The man who, instead of being surrendered to spontaneous action, voluntarily retires to think, has fallen sick, and can effect no more. The art which has recovered from its trance of inspiration and found out that it has rules, begins to manufacture and ceases to create. The literature which directs itself to an end, and critically seeks the means, may yield the produce of ingenuity, but not the fruit of genius. The society which understands its own structure, talks of its grievances, plumes itself on its achievements, and prescribes for its own case, is already in a state of inevitable decadence. And the religion which has begun to *inquire*, to sift out its errors, and treasure up its truths, has lost its breath of healthy faith, and only gasps in death. With sighs and irresistible longings, does this noble writer look back upon imaginary ages of involuntary heroism, when the great and good knew not their greatness and goodness, and genius was found which was a secret to itself, and men lived for God's sake, instead of for their own. Could he realize his dream of perfection, he would stock the world with unconscious activity, and fill it with men who know not what they do.

This celebrated paradox could never occupy a mind like Mr. Carlyle's, did it not envelop an important and season-able truth. But before we give ourselves up to the despond-ency it must inspire, it is as well to see whether there is no illusion in its sadness; and whether its pathetic com-plaints may not even be turned, by an altered modulation, into a hymn of thanksgiving.

To sigh after an unconscious life, — what is it but to pro-test against the very *power of thought?* To *think* is not merely to have ideas, — to be the theatre across which images and emotions are marched ; — but to sit in the midst as master of one's conceptions ; to detain them for audience, or dismiss them at a glance ; to organize them into coher-ence and direct them to an end. It implies at every step the memory and deliberate review of past states of mind, the voluntary estimate of them, and control over them. It is a royal act, in which we *possess* the objects which engage us, and are not possessed by them. It is an act of intense self-consciousness, whose whole energy consists in this, that the mind is kindled by seeing itself: as if the light were to become sensitive, and turn also to vision.

Again, to sigh for an unconscious life, is to protest against *conscience.* For what is this faculty but, as its name denotes, *a knowledge with one's-self* of the worth and excel-lence of-the several principles of action by which we are impelled? Shall we desire to be impelled by them still, only remaining in the dark as to their value and our obliga-tions? — to be the creature of each, as its turn may come,

without choice between the baser and the nobler, or perception of difference between appetite and inspiration? Duty
implies, in every form, that a man is entrusted with himself;
that he is expected to overlook and direct himself; to maintain therefore an open eye on the spiritual world within,
and preserve throughout a sacred order.

And once more, to pray for an unconscious life, is to
desire an incapacity for *faith*. For what is faith, but trust
in an Infinite and Holy One, of whom we could have no
conception, if our aspirations did not transcend our realities; if the ideal faculty did not survey the actual and find
it wanting? Our own spirit is the vestibule which we must
enter, as threshold to the temple of the Eternal, and wherein
alone we can catch any whisper from the Holy of Holies.
A man who had never found his soul, could assuredly never
see his God.

Scarcely can we admit a theory to be true, which implies
that thought, duty, will, and faith are so many diseases
in our constitution, over which it becomes us to weep the
tears of protestation. These, and the self-consciousness
which renders us capable of them, are the supreme glory of
our nature; raising it above the mere instinctive life of the
brute creation, making it agent as well as instrument, and
giving it two worlds to live in instead of one.

If, however, this power of self-consciousness be assigned
to us as our special dignity and strength, it may be turned
to our weakness and our shame. The peculiar faculty in
man, of *overlooking* himself, is but the needful condition and
natural preparation for another, — that of *directing* himself.
Why show him his place, but that he may choose his way?
Why wake him up, — alone of all creatures, — if the night-
mare of necessity is to sit upon him still? If his course be
determined *for* him, and not *by* him, why not lock him fast,
like all similar natures, in the interior of his perceptions and
impulses, as in the scenery of a dream, instead of carrying
him outside to survey them? A thing that is entirely at

the disposal of foreign forces, that is moved hither and thither by laws imposed upon it, would plainly be none the better for the gift of self-knowledge. If the planet, urged through an inflexible orbit by determinate mechanism, were made aware of its own history, no hair's-breadth of guidance would the revelation give. If the tree could study its own physiology, its growth would be no nobler, and its fruit no fairer. If the animal could scrutinize its instincts, they would perform no new function, and afford no happier guid-ance. And if man can superintend his own 'mind, it is because he is *not*, like the planet, the tree, the brute, the mere theatre on which forces display themselves, but a fresh power in himself, able to originate action in the same sense in which God originates the universe. Every sentient being perceives enough for its own direction : if you look round the circle of its perceptions, you ascertain the sources of its guidance. Animals, that are at the exclusive disposal of the external objects related to them, are alive to the external world alone. Man, capable of withstanding extrinsic agencies, and having a creative centre within him, is alive to his own soul as well. Shut us fast up in the line of nature, and nature is all that we want to know. Set us free to stand above nature, and live with an upper region of the spirit stretching beyond her realm, not subject only but also lord, and we need for the first time that self-consciousness which is the condition of liberty, and the first element of wisdom. It is because we have a *work of choice* assigned us, because we are entrusted with the power to control our instincts, and subject the spontaneous natural life to the voluntary and the spiritual, that we alone have the faculty of reflection. It is the superior light awarded to our special obligations. Self-consciousness, thus superadded to our mere sentient nature, becomes, by this association, not less our temptation than our dignity. If pain and pleasure constituted the ultimate interests of life, we could dispense with the attribute of self-inspection as well as the brutes : in short, we should be in that case but a nobler sort of brute, differing from other species only in having more numerous resources for our sensitive nature,—a richer table spread for more varied appetites, of the palate or of the mind. Senses, however multiplied; taste, however exquisite; capacities for enjoyment, never so fine,—*want* no faculty of reflection, and must know that it is not for them. But while it is not for their sakes, it is of necessity in their presence, and within their hearing, that the *arcana* of life are revealed to us. Appetite and conscience, like two spirits of the lower and the upper world, live together in the same house, so that the revelation made for one is little likely to remain secret from the other; and it is in the power of the fiend to steal the privity of the angel, and break the seals of the divinest message. Hence there comes about an impious abuse of the godlike gift of self-conscious life ; and instead of serving as the handmaid of duty, it is degraded into the pander of appetite. Nothing can be baser than this sweet poisoning of moral truth for the relish of sin. Thus to use our human secret as a cunning way of getting an advantage over the brutes, is a downright betrayal of the confidence of God,—a bartering in hell of that which we have overheard in heaven.

This faculty, then, of reflection upon himself, his life, his nature, his relations, is the peculiarity which, in proportion as it becomes marked, places man at a distance from the brutes. When applied to its true purpose, of surveying his responsibilities, judging his modes of activity and affection, and enforcing a Christian order throughout his soul, it becomes a godlike prerogative, and lifts him to an angel-life. When perverted to a false purpose, of prying into his passive sensations, and discovering the means of getting drunk with instinctive pleasures, and turning the healthy hunger of nature into the feverish greed of Epicurism, it becomes a fallen spirit, and allies its possessor with the fiends. Man, the self-conscious animal, is the saddest spectacle in creation : man, the self-conscious Christian, one of the noblest. Reflecting vitality is hypochondria and disease : reflecting spirituality is clearness and strength.

This general doctrine has a direct bearing upon a question which is often raised, and which presses upon the attention of the present age with an anxious earnestness : — What is the effect on human character of a high and complicated civilization ? Are its vast accumulation of commodities, its rapid circulation of activity and thought, its minute division of employments, its close interlacing of interests, its facilities for class-organization, to be looked upon with joy and gratulation, as so many triumphs of intelligence and refinement over ignorance and barbarism ; or with grief and consternation, as the gathering of an uncontrollable and aimless power, destined, like the mad Hercules, to destroy the offspring of its strength ? The exulting and jubilant feeling on this matter which prevailed some years ago, is now generally replaced, I believe, in thoughtful minds, by a more sober and even melancholy order of expectations. The change may be justified, if it be made a step, not to passive despair, but to the faithful and energetic performance of a new class of social duties. Let us search for some principle which may aid in the solution of this great problem.

The specific effect on human character produced by a high state of civilization may be expressed in a single phrase : it develops the self-consciousness of men to an intense degree, or, to borrow the venerable language of Scripture, immeasurably increases their "knowledge of good and evil." This indeed arises necessarily from our living so closely in the presence of each other. A perfectly solitary being, who had a whole planet to himself, would remain, I suppose, for ever incapable of knowing himself and reflecting upon his thoughts and actions. He would continue, like other creatures, to *have* feelings and ideas, but would not make them his *objects* and bring them under his will. This human

peculiarity would remain latent in him, till he was introduced before the face of some kindred being, and he saw
his nature reflected in another mind. Looking into the
eyes of a living companion, changing with laughter and with
tears, flashing with anger, drooping with sleep, he finds the
mirror of himself; the passions of his inner life are revealed
to him ; and he becomes a *person*, instead of a *living thing*.
In proportion as society collects more thickly around a man,
this primitive change deepens and extends: the unconscious,
instinctive life, which remains predominant in savage tribes,
and visible enough in sparse populations everywhere, gradually retires. He knows all about his appetites, and how to
serve them; can name his feelings, feign them, stifle them;
can manage his thoughts, fly from them, conceal them; can
meditate his actions, link them into a system, protect them
from interrupting impulse, and direct them to an end; can
go through the length and breadth of life with mind grossly
familiar with its wonders, or reverently studious of its wisdom ; and look on death, with the eye of an undertaker, or
through the tears of a saint. In an old and artificial community, all the common products of experience appear stale
and exhausted, and ingenuity is plied for the means of
awakening some new emotion. The inmost recesses of our
nature are curiously explored, and its most sacred feelings
submitted to the coolest criticism, and brought under the
canons of art. The self-consciousness of individuals is shared
by society at large: it studies itself, talks of its past, is anxious about its future ; becomes aware of its own mechanism,
and tries to estimate its strength. And with a universal
discussion of wide social problems, an unparalleled egotism
and isolation are apt to seize upon every sect, class, and
nation.

If this be true, then we must admit that a high civilization unfolds the characteristic endowment of our nature ;
and so far, may be said to raise and dignify it, and leave
far behind the mere animal and instinctive life which be-

longs to beings of lower grade. The most ignorant man in England possesses a knowledge of good and evil, and a various skill in commanding them, which the hoariest patriarch in a barbarian village would look upon with awe. It is only however in the naturalist's scale, not in the Christian, that man is elevated by the influences of artificial society. He becomes a well-marked specimen of his kind, broadly separated from other races upon earth : but how he ranks among spiritual beings, — whether he approaches the confines of heaven, or touches the verge of hell, — is wholly undecided still. Superior *knowledge of good and evil* involves no change in the *proportionate love of them ;* self-consciousness being a neutral faculty, the condition alike of whatever is pure and noble, and of all that is most foul and mean ; the ground at once of the fidelity of Abdiel and the guilt of Lucifer. Hence it is that the mere progress of civilization involves no spiritual advance, and miserably disappoints those who trusted that it was to deliver men from the yoke of their follies and their sins. Vast as is the spectacle of our material magnificence, and intense as may be the traces of mental vitality, there is no certain decline of selfishness and corruption in any class : or if on the right hand you can point to some evil extinguished, on the left there springs some new enormity to balance the success. How many are there who basely avail themselves of all the ease and luxury of our complicated civilization, compared with the few who feel its obligations, and take up its work! How little security do the most practised thought and refined scholarship seem to afford against shameful jesuitry and abject superstition! And how often is the nimble intelligence of the artisan wholly unproductive of any self-restraint or reverence ! The mere *cleverness* indeed of the modern townsman, derived from thé heated and sensitive atmosphere around him, implies no hardy spiritual life within him, and ensures no moral thoughtfulness or wisdom. It is a mere aptitude for the germination of ideas of any sort; whereby flowers of Paradise may come sprouting up without ripening their proper fruits, or the deadly nightshade drop its poison unperceived. Intellectual irritability may leave the conscience wholly dead. And assuredly only that knowledge which a man wins for himself by the spontaneous efforts of his own mind has the proper and purifying effect of *truth* on him, and renders his nature *clearer* than it was before.

And unhappily this self-acquired knowledge and faculty are, in one respect, less likely to be found among us in these days than of old. The direct influence of occupation is less and less favorable to their production. Nothing that has ever been advanced by economists can convince me, that the extreme division of employments which characterizes modern industrial operations, is any thing but deadening and unhealthy to the mental nature of those engaged in them. To spend every working day of half or the whole of life, not in a craft of various nicety and skill, but in a solitary process of a single manufacture, in tying threads or pointing pins, can assuredly give no discipline to any faculty, unless those of muscular alacrity or mental patience : and compared with the work of an earlier world, I should as little call this *skill*, as I should class among literary men a scribe who should devote his life to crossing *t*s and dotting *i*s. With long habit the monotony of such a lot may cease to be positively felt. But it taxes no worthy power : it enlists no natural interest : it presents only vacancy and listlessness to the thought : and the more so, as the work is another's, and not the laborer's own. The occupation does not educate the man. It may be true, in point of fact, that workers of this class are as intelligent as others. But if so, this is owing to influences extrinsic to the cause on which I dwell, and in spite of it; especially to their residence in the stimulant atmosphere of great cities, and the habit of association with large bodies of men. And this intellectual counteraction itself, there is reason to fear, is purchased at the cost of vast moral dangers. For, in proportion as men cease to have an intelligent interest in their work, and go through it with the weariness of a necessary task, do they quit it with a susceptibility to foreign excitements, and a more open avidity for the temptations of the passions : and losing the even glow of a constant activity, they fall under fearful inducement to alternate the stagnant blood of dulness with the throbbing pulse of revelry.

Who then can be so blind as to deny the dangers amid which we live? We have created around us a scale of opportunity, and temptation, and risk, frightfully vast. We are wholly out of reach of the narrow safety of simple and instinctive life. We stand in the presence of a gigantic amount of good and evil. Yet we have not stronger spirits to bear the mightier strain. So far as our condition forms us, we are less *complete* men, and therefore of less massive stability, than were our forefathers. The moral structure of society partakes of the character of those huge machines which have done so much to make at once its wealth and weakness : each man being but as a screw or pinion of the whole, locked into a system that holds him fast or whirls him on, and having no longer a separate symmetry and worth. The results indeed which are turned out from this involuntary co-operation of parts, are of overwhelming magnitude and wonderful variety. Our country is a vast congeries of exaggerations. Enormous wealth and saddest poverty, sumptuous idleness and saddest toil, princely provision for learning and the most degrading ignorance, a large amount of laborious philanthropy, but a larger of unconquered misery and sin, subsist side by side, and terrify us by the preternatural contrast of brilliant coloring with blackest shade. It is appalling to think of the moral cost (a cost most needless too) at which England has become materially great. Do you found that greatness on the culture of the soil ? Alas ! where is the laborer by whose hand it has

been tilled? In a cabin with his children, where the domestic decencies cannot be, and where Christ, did he enter,
might give his pity, but could hardly ask obedience. Or do
you point rather to our mineral wealth? See the picture,
which has scarcely ceased to be true, of crawling women,
and harnessed children, of whose toil this glory comes! I
know not which is most heathenish, the guilty negligence
of our lofty men, or the fearful degradation of the low.
But this I do believe, that unless some holier spirit dart
quickly down for the conversion of our rich and great,
put into them a wise and Christian heart, and dispose them
to sacrifices never dreamt of yet, our social repentance will
come too late, and we shall die with our Jerusalem, seeing
only the image of a tearful Christ, and hearing the words,
" Oh that thou hadst known, at least in this thy day, the
things that belong to thy peace! "

Moreover, we live, as we have seen, in an age of excited
and self-conscious men. And in all minds awakened and
reflective to even a very moderate degree, there arises and
accumulates a secret fund of dissatisfaction; a dark, mysterious speck of care upon the heart, which turns to a point
of explosive ruin in bad men, to a seed of fruitful sorrow
with the good. The natural mind, untouched by religious
wisdom, always refers its wants and miseries to outward
things, which alone it strives to mend and change. So
this hidden discontent leads men to love themselves the
more, and quarrel with their neighbors, *until* they become
Christians in soul: and *then* it shows them a far higher
truth, and leads them to love their neighbors and reproach
themselves. The strife and struggle which are inseparable
from our self-conscious life, are directed to mutual hate,
while under the guidance of self; to common aspiration,
under the discipline of Christ. Who can doubt that under
our present spiritual condition, it is the anarchy, and not
the love, to which this feeling tends? And who would not
pray for an infusion of the light of God to paint the bow of

peace and promise on the cloud where the muffled thunder growls? Oh that to us, otherwise than to Elijah in the cave, it may be given to hear the still small voice, not after, but before, the strong wind, the earthquake, and the fire!

To avert the dangers, and remedy the peculiar evils of our social condition, many conjoint agencies are doubtless required. But there is not one whose neglect offers more certain peril, whose right and timely application presents more reasonable hope, than a Christian training for the new generation of our people. Could this, indeed, be universally given, could all good men set to work with one heart and hand, and see to it that no desert spot be unreclaimed, all would yet be well. But, alas! we are so afraid of each other's doctrines, that we cannot cure each other's sins; and while the most appalling evils threaten us, and more than once the symptomatic smoke has puffed up from the social volcano, we stand round the crater and discuss theology! Ah! how much more is there in our Christendom of the contentious mind, than of the disciple's pure and unperverted heart! Which, I would know, is the worse evil, an actual gin-shop, or a possible heresy? Yet in dread of the latter, we cannot unite together in the only means of putting down the former. However, by such means as our infirmities still leave open, we must *go and teach this people.* In proportion as their occupations educate them less, and their circumstances tempt them more, a *direct and proposed culture* must be provided; — a culture which keeps in view the great primary end of responsible existence; which looks not at their trade, but at their souls, and brings them not as apt servants to the mill, but as holy children to their God. Education, in the Christian sense, is truly everlasting: childhood preparing for maturity, maturity for age, and the whole of life for death and heaven. The early training of the young is but that portion of this series, which prepares for self-government and the exercise of free-will within the limits of Christ's law. Doubtless the responsibility of this task rests, by the decree of Nature and Providence, with the parents to whom the young life is committed as a trust; nor will it ever have settled on its genuine basis, till there shall exist, in every class, an effective domestic sentiment, sufficient to sustain it. But amid the grievous decay of the old and healthful parental conscience, it becomes needful to awaken a wider interest in the work, and to call upon neighborhood and country to take up the neglected office of the home. Nor should any individual, or any family, exempt from the constant cares of subsistence, be held to have discharged the obligations of the Christian life, till they freely give some steady help to this essential work; and provide some fitting care for the neglected child, as still an infant disciple claimed by the arms, and consecrated by the benediction, of the heavenly Christ.

XXIX.

THE UNCLOUDED HEART.

JOHN v. 30.

MY JUDGMENT IS JUST, BECAUSE I SEEK NOT MINE OWN WILL, BUT THE
WILL OF THE FATHER WHICH HATH SENT ME.

For the training of goodness, the ancient reliance was on
the right discipline of habit and affection : the modern is
rather on illumination of the understanding. The notion
extensively prevails that vice, being only the mistaken pursuit of that personal happiness for which virtue is an equal
but more sagacious aspirant, is a blunder of the intellect ; a
defective or erroneous view of things ; and, like the optical
delusions incident to weak eyes, to be cured by use of the
most approved instruments for seeing clearly. The guilty
and degraded will, it is said, differs from the pure and
noble, not by aiming at a less innocent end, but by being
less happy in its choice of means : point out the miscalcula-
tion, instruct it to weigh causes with greater nicety in
future, and you cannot fail to promote the needful reformation. The sinner is but the most deplorable of fools ; and
if you banish folly, you extinguish sin.

This prescription for the advancement of human excellence possesses an apparent simplicity, which gives it a
great attraction to some minds. All the varieties of character among men it reduces to an arrangement easily understood ; distributing them along a single line, in the order of
their intelligence. It seems to take away all mystery from
the moral emotions, whose rapidity and intensity had awed
and startled us ; and by converting them into plain judg-

19

ments of the intellect, makes them the voice of man instead of God. Unhappily, however, the value of this tempting theory disappears the moment we seek to use it. Let its most ingenious advocate try it upon the miser, the cheat, the insane candidate for glory; let him reason with them on their ignorance and imbecility of judgment, expose every fallacy of self-justification, and establish against them an unanswerable case of mistake; and then let him come and tell us whether he has made them generous, just, and meek. Perhaps he will confess his failure, but persevere in ascribing it to the unhappy state of his pupils' understanding, rather than any distinct affection of their passions. " I could not convince them," he will say, " of their error; or, if my arguments impressed them at the moment, the persuasion passed away; and habit proved the more successful advocate, because it was, though not the truer, yet the more importunate." But were not your appeals just and forcible, and your instructions indisputably true? Then there must be something in the heart where evil passions dwell that baffles the chance of reason, that takes from evidence its natural force, and gives to error an unmerited triumph. And what advantage do we gain by representing men as the subjects, and their morality as truths, of the pure intellect, if it be an intellect that may lose its distinguishing function, and become inaccessible to just persuasion? What comfort is it to know that guilt is only error, if it be error so peculiar as to be insensible to the merits of the most unquestionable proof? Why tell us that right and wrong are but the love of happiness making its computations, when it is admitted that passion was never computed out of the heart, and that self-interest itself is whiffed away by the tempest of its rage? It is true that you have *only* to give the slave of guilty passions a different view of the objects of desire, and he is set free from his miserable thraldom. It is equally true that you have *only* to make the collapsed paralytic start up and run, — and he will be well.

No doubt, the weakest reason and the most ungovernable desires are constantly found together. But there are at least two ways of reading connected appearances like these. The attempt to resolve all the phenomena of character into a condition of the understanding is a futile exaggeration. The great author of Christianity, reversing the order of the explanation, placed the truth in a juster point of view. He well knew that if, sometimes, because the reason is darkened, the passions are awake, it more often happens that because the passions are awake, the reason is eclipsed. To him it could not but be clear, from consciousness itself, that pure sympathies make a clear intellect, and, with their sweet breath, wonderfully open to the mind new perceptions of things heavenly. While auditors, feeling "that never man spake like this man," asked "how knoweth he letters, having never learned?" Jesus led them to a different explanation of his wisdom, "My judgment is just, *because* I seek not mine own will, but the will of the Father who hath sent me." And he instructed others how to gain a like discernment of things divine, when he said, "If any will do *his* will, he shall know of the doctrine, whether it be of God, or whether I speak of myself." The words express a universal truth. Whatever be the work on which the judgment may be engaged, it will be invariably aided by the natural sympathies of a just, disinterested, and holy mind.

Even in his abstruser toils, these are often the wise man's mightiest power. The most turbid clouds that darken the vision of reason are those which interest, and fear, and ambition spread : and these the pure affections sweep away. They give to the soul the unspeakable freedom of just intents and elevated trusts : and where there exist no complicated aims, no retarding anxieties, but the whole absolute energy of a mind is gathered upon the search of truth, it is amazing what vast achievements may be made. How often will a child, by mere force of unconsciousness and simplicity, penetrate to the centre of some great truth with a startling ease and directness! And in this the greatness of genius is like the power of a child : it is as much moral as intellectual; it arises from emotions so distinct and earnest as to secure singleness of purpose and vivacity of expression; from some absorbing reverence which disenthrals the mind from lower passions, and gives it courage to be true. There is always a presumption that a pure-hearted will be a right-minded man ; and it is delightful to see such a one stand up before the ambitious sophist, and dart on his ingenuities a clear ray of conscience that scatters them like mist. The divine light of a good mind is too much for the mystifications of guilt. "The foolishness of God is wiser than the wisdom of men."

All the great hindrances to impartiality in the quest of truth have obviously their seat in some class of selfish feelings. Interest, promising to one set of opinions emolument and honor, and to their opposite poverty and disgrace; or passing over to the future world, and there displaying to us the alternative of absolute blessedness or ruin, — crushes the natural justice of the understanding, and offers stupendous temptations to palter with evidence, and shuffle inconvenient doubts away. No inquirer can fix a direct and clear-sighted gaze towards truth, who is casting side glances all the while on the prospects of his soul. Again, the excessive eagerness about reputation produces a thousand pitiable distortions of understanding. In one it takes the shape of a determination to be original (which, I suppose, never befell any man by deliberate resolve), and so extinguishes his perception of all ancient excellence, and confines his appreciation to his own obscurities and affectations. In another it passes into an opposite folly, — the pride of being peculiarly moderate and sound; and so he dreads eccentricities far more than falsehoods, and weighs proprieties, instead of investigating truths. And what is the partisanship that wearies every good man's heart, but a collection of selfish feelings, fatal to all the equities of reason ; a gross association of the idea of self with abstract questions? It is said to be of service in keeping alive the mental activity of the community; but how poor a service, when the activity consists so largely in the ferment of bad passions, and conducts the tranquil tasks of reason in the spirit of a gamester. Argument, in such case, loses its natural power of persuasion, and operates like a weapon of vengeance; only raising higher the note of triumph in those who wield it, and irritating instead of convincing the minds that it assails. Indeed, it is humiliating to think how poor a pittance of reasoning conducts the gigantic mutations of human sentiment; how arguments, at which a quiet understanding would smile, rise to grave importance in the confusion of polemic rage; how light the sophistries which sway the tide of success when the hosts of party wrestle in the fight; how foolish the sounds that seem to award possession of that great capitol of opinion which overlooks the empire of the world.

Though, however, narrow feelings and selfish desires, intruding on the province of the understanding, prevent its judgments from being just, it is not true that their simple absence constitutes the best state for speculative research. It is sometimes said, that, were it possible, the inquirer's mind should be absolutely emptied of every desire, and be exposed, in entire passiveness, to the action of evidence brought before its tribunal; that a being incapable of emotion, a mere machine for performing logical operations, would be the most efficient discoverer. But surely his impartiality, however perfect, would accomplish nothing without an impulse : intensity of intellectual action is needed, as well as clearness of intellectual view. And this will be most certainly found, not in one who follows the light without deep love of it; not in one who simply finds it a personal convenience, and desires it for its use; not even in one who has simply a relish for mental occupations, and prolongs them from pure taste; but in him who traverses the realm of thought, as if "seeking the will of One that sent him;"

who reverently looks on the features of truth as on the face
of God, and listens to its accents as to its whispered oracle ;
who trusts it with a "love that casteth out fear," and feels
on him the blessed light of heaven, when bigots pronounce
him in a dreadful gloom.

On questions of practical morals, yet more emphatically
than on subjects of speculative research, is it true that pure
sympathies produce a clear intellect, and that *his* judgments
are most likely to be just, who most habitually seeks the
will of the eternal Father.   The moral habits and tastes of
men form their opinions, much more frequently than their
opinions form their habits : — so that often their theoretical
sentiments are little more than a systematic self-defence
after the act, and afford an approximate index to the character of themselves and the society in which they live.
The positions they assume having been taken up first, the
reasons for maintaining them are discovered afterwards :
and it is surprising to observe the confidence with which
questions of morals are discussed, as if on grounds of absolute philosophy, when every quiet observer perceives that
the alleged premises would appear ridiculous except to
persons already possessed of the conclusion.   There is a
test, — imperfect I admit, — by which to judge whether
this is so or not, and to disenchant the imagination of the
mere effect of usage.   Any moral practice which admits of
genuine defence, and has a permanent foundation in nature
as well as in custom, might surely be recommended to an
intelligent community hitherto ignorant of it, and success-
fully urged upon their deliberate adoption.   Yet how many
things are we accustomed to palliate or uphold, which we
should be ashamed to submit to this criterion, and which
the very act of expounding to child or stranger would sufficiently condemn !   In how many societies are the mis-
named laws of honor, for example, still justified, as if they
satisfactorily met the conditions of a problem else insoluble !
But if they be so sound and useful, it would be safe to try

the argument in their behalf on those to whom the whole
system of ideas is entirely new; to preach the admirable
wisdom of the duel to some tribe having only such civilization as may be attained without it; and proselytize to it as
if it were an *à priori* invention of philosophy. If the apostles of the world's law feel that in a mental clime so new,
they would plead in vain, should they not suspect that they
may be talking absurdities at home, which have no force
but in the social prepossessions in their behalf? It is fearful
to reflect indeed to what an extent our native moral sentiments are modified by the atmosphere of social influence
perpetually spread around us; how the indications of the
unperverted conscience may become obscured and lost, and
a fatal blindness and sleep disqualify it for its waking office.
It is the natural mistake of just minds to believe it vigilant
and incorruptible as God. When we fix our gaze on some
dread crime; when we see, it may be, the outrages of a tyrant's profligacy and vengeance, crushing the life of resolute
purity, or consigning to the dungeon the virtue which it
fears; — under the impulse of poetic justice, we imagine
the perpetrator secretly agonized by the consciousness of
guilt; writhing at midnight beneath the lash of a fiery remorse, while his chained victim sleeps the light slumbers
of innocence, and wakes with a brow cooled by the peace
within. But we impose upon ourselves by a natural illusion:
we conceive a wretch to judge himself by a good man's conscience, and to view his own deeds in a light which, had it
been accessible to him, must at least have induced a hesitation about their commission. No, remorse is the attribute,
not of the simply guilty, but of the *fallen*: it is the bitter
memory which sin, yet fresh, retains of departed goodness;
the mind's convulsive grasp on the retreating purities of
the past : and, however vehemently it protests against
moral *deterioration*, the consolidated guilt of habit it lets
alone. Shall any one then assure himself that all is right,
because he is clear of compunction ? Shall he suffer his in-

dulgent years to ebb idly away, because they are placid as
the summer wave? Shall he thrust aside the pleadings of
those who would kindle in him higher thoughts and brace
him to nobler deeds, — by saying that he is comfortable and
does not need them? If so, he satisfies himself by the
same argument which sophists use in defence of slavery;
— the creatures are easy, have been seen to laugh merrily
by day, and are known to sleep well at night! As if it
were the whole life of man to have a sleek skin and a
drowsy brain! As if any existence upon ideas were not
better than any without them; and to perceive one's
misery were not the best consolation for its infliction;
and to aspire to a nobler existence, though with faintest hope, to chafe against the chain that binds us, though
it gnaws our flesh, were not preferable to that most abject condition of humanity in which conscious degradation becomes impossible. We should beware then how
we rely on this unconsciousness as a security. Of every
low state of character this apathy towards all that is above
it is the worst symptom. This torpor should not lull,
but rather terrify. When this motionless repose reigns
within, — this breathless atmosphere of the heart, — the
freshness of health is no longer there: it is the pestilent
dreariness of the waste; the awful silence of moral death.

In its judgment of *human character*, more even than in
matters of personal morals, a mind under the governance of
pure and disinterested affections will evince the clearest
insight. He would be the most impartial spectator of the
great theatre of human life, who should be raised into a
sphere of pure contemplation above its scenes; to a position
beyond its competitions, its disappointments, its rewards;
where the voice of its restless multitudes floated but in
whispers, articulate enough to report its passions with precision, but not thrilling enough to agitate the spirit by their
power. Such an observer, himself acted on by no sympathies but those of conscience, — perfectly perceptive, but

entirely passionless, — would behold us in true relations and proportions. The pure affections create a mental position somewhat similar to this. They still the confusion of the senses. They remove all motive for not seeing men and life exactly as they are. One who looks on the world as his appointed post of strenuous duty, and feels on him the divine charge to leave it better than he found it, must close neither eye nor heart against any of its ills. And as for its good, — for the charities that bless, the virtues that ennoble, the genius that illuminates our human lot, — delighting in them all, he discerns them all: bringing to him as they do the refreshment of a generous veneration, what temptation has he to doubt, decry, and disbelieve them? In a mind where any selfish end habitually prevails, men are regarded as tools: their services are wanted, and their complacency must be secured: they are looked upon as objects of management, on whom the arts of influence must be tried. Hence the mental eye is insensibly trained to a sly and circumventing gaze upon our fellows: the hand of cautious power steals forth, and makes a lever of their weaknesses: the tongue, encouraged by its first experiments of delicate insincerity, grows rash and voluble in flattery. And those whom a man is conscious of praising too much, he is sure to value too little. Accustomed to speak of good qualities which they do *not* possess, to invent merits of which they are empty, his mind is always dwelling on the negation of excellence, and growing familiar with it exclusively as an object of fiction; till at length he ceases to believe in its reality, and attributes to every thing human the hollowness which he practises himself. By the interposition of his own selfishness, the nobler half of human nature undergoes total and permanent eclipse. How should it be otherwise? For who would spread the tender colors of the soul before an eye like his, where they can bask in no light of love? Who would lay the head to rest on a bosom cold as marble? Will any make confession of an unworldly aspiration to one, who

keeps always ready some vile interpretation of whatever
seems most excellent; who sees in the pious only traders in
hypocrisy, in the patriot a speculator in power, in the martyr
a candidate for praise? All that is beautiful shrinks from
the presence of one who delights to soil it with instant dust.
Oh how unblest are they who have fallen into an incapacity
to admire, and bid adieu to the solace of a deep reverence;
who can take up without awe the leaves scattered on the
earth by departed genius, or read of the struggles of liberty
without enthusiasm, or follow the good in their pilgrimage
of mercy without the heavings of a mighty joy! No grief
deserves such pity as the hopeless privations of a scornful
heart.

Those who seek only their "own will" lose, then, by
natural process, the faculty of judging justly respecting
human character. They are liable to fall into no less mistake in their anticipations of those *changes in society* which
are brought about by the nobler forces of the human will.
It is happy for the world, that over the vision of its greatest
enemies their own selfishness spreads a film, concealing from
them, as in judicial blindness, the generous powers which
will effect their overthrow. Tyrants and self-seeking rulers
are, by nature, Machiavelian moralists: they have no faith
but in the most vulgar incentives to action, and are familiar
with no engines of influence but force and corruption. Accustomed to rely on these, they know not that there are
emergencies, in which even a herd of slaves may be inspired
with an enthusiasm that makes such implements of no avail;
— when high sentiments of social justice, or aspirations
towards an invisible God, vibrate through the dull clay of
ordinary men. Thus, often has the pampered despot been
blinded to his fate, and led unconscious on, like a decorated
and sportive victim, to the sacrificial altar of a people's
indignation. In spite of all his vigilance, conspiracy, conducted by lean and praying patriots, has gone on unnoticed
beneath his very eyes. While the sunshine smiles upon his

palace, and glances from the swords of faithful troops, he despises the gathering clouds of a nation's frown : till suddenly the tempest bursts upon the hills, and the heavy tramp, as of the men of toil, thunders on the ground ; and, after a flash of vented wrath, the veterans and their leader lie low upon the field, and the thanksgiving of the free goes up into a sky serene. Thus it is of the very nature of guilty power to be surprised by the apparition of high-minded virtue in a people. And though the resistance it offers to the demands of conscience may, on this very account, be the more exasperated, and the vindication of an abstract right, like that of free worship, may cost a country the life of her best sons, we may yet be permitted to rejoice at the infatuation of selfish rule : for even the sanguinary triumph of a great and righteous principle is often better than the sly and bloodless ascendancy of a bad one. War, with all its horrors, may be half forgotten in two generations : but the rights which it may establish may prove the causes of perennial peace. Men, at the best, must die as the grass; but the principles of justice are blessings for evermore.

The selfish, then, in perpetually seeking their own will, and contemplating mankind chiefly as possible instruments for its accomplishment, necessarily overlook the best elements of our nature, and form judgments that are not just of human character, and its collective effects on the condition of the world. Moreover, while selfishness makes some men tools, it finds in others rivals ; and, under the form of jealousy, draws another cloud over the judgment, and hides from it all that is fairest in kindred minds. He that cannot enjoy, with genuine exultation, the reputation of another, and admire with tranquil spirit the excellence that borders on his own, loses the best joy of a good heart. To the very merits which, from being most akin to his own, he is most fitted to appreciate, he becomes insensible : and a bitter poison drops into the fountains of his most generous peace.

There is no more melancholy sight than that of a mind, otherwise great, succumbing beneath a mean and fretful passion like this; indulging in petty cavils at worth, before which he should lead on the multitude to bend the knee; so visibly greedy of others' praise, that the most vulgar observer laughs to think that the great man is just like himself. It was a grief, like an absolute bereavement, to find that our own Newton, who should have lifted a brow as pure and smooth as the heavens he interpreted, and have greeted all that was good beneath them with a smile of godlike benediction, could tease a brother laborer, like Flamstead, and shrivel up his temper into peevishness, and be driven hither and thither by trivial suspicions, like a blind giant led about by a little child. Let us hope, what indeed there is some reason to believe, that all this was rather the tremulousness of shattered nerves, than the per-. turbations of the native mind. Yet is it sad to have even to make excuse for such as he.

Our judgments of human character and relations will not be right, unless our sympathies be not disinterested only but pure. The moral feelings must transcend the social; the sense of duty be stronger than the instincts of affection. In addition to the negative qualification of *not* seeking our own will, we must have the positive one of seeking the will of the Father who is in heaven. The partialities of the affections are nobler every way than those of self-love: but they are partialities still; and while they make our judgments merciful, may prevent their being just. They may bewilder our moral perceptions, and, in pure tenderness for the guilty, seduce us to think lightly of the guilt. There are in life few temptations so severe as those which our human love may thus offer to our conscience. If, for example, children around a mother's knee betray their first unanswerable suspicion of their father's vices, and urge her with wondering questions, which she has long dreaded to hear, that press hard upon his guilt; what is she to do?

Is she to hide the anguish that trembles on her features, and, in fidelity to him, be, for the first time, untrue to them? Is she to say the evil thing of him for whom she lives, and make him as a byword and a warning on his children's lips? And yet, is she to take it on herself to soil the purity and simplicity of their moral perceptions, and blow, with the foul breath of falsehood, on the lamp of God within their hearts? Her first duty is, doubtless, to the sanctities of their young minds; but so hard a lot forces us to think how dreadful is the guilt that makes a contradiction between the sympathies of virtue and of home, and turns into a sin the natural mercy of disinterested love.

Whatever then be the office required of the judgment; whether to seek truth along difficult ways, or, amid the sophistries of custom, to interpret our own responsibilities; whether it is invited to the generous appreciation of excellence, or summoned to the stern duties of disapprobation and rebuke; *he* only who can abandon his own will, and seek that of the Father in heaven, will either discern his position clearly, or discharge its obligations with simplicity and courage. Nor will this clearness of view and directness of aim be likely to desert him in the greater emergencies of life. Then it is that meaner principles of action, all mere personal desires, collapse in weakness and bewilderment. In times of danger, where it is needful to risk something or lose every thing, men, possessed of no higher inspiration, lose their presence of mind : and while they stand in timid calculation, the one only moment of faithful duty slips away. They will profess perhaps to have been overpowered by the sense of their responsibility ; — an unconscious acknowledgment of the confusion into which all self-regarding feelings throw the mind ; — for no man, truly earnest about an object, critically pauses or turns aside to examine how he is acquitting himself. No! great as are the achievements of inferior principles of action, — the love of power, the pursuit of glory,—the only heroism, fitted for the last extremity of circumstance, is that of disinterested duty. Others may skilfully and firmly use up their outward resources to the last: but the Christian hero, when all these are gone, has yet to spend *himself.*

XXX.

"HELP THOU MINE UNBELIEF."

—◆—

MARK IX. 24.

LORD, I BELIEVE; HELP THOU MINE UNBELIEF.

THAT this is an age most sensitive as to its belief, is evident on the slightest inspection of its moral physiognomy. A profound curiosity is awakened respecting the foundations of faith, and the proper treatment of those high problems which religion undertakes to solve. An unexampled proportion of our new literature is theological; of our new buildings, ecclesiastical; of our current conversation, on the condition and prospects of sects. The social movements which are watched with the most anxiety on the one hand, and hope on the other, are recent organizations of religious sympathy and opinion. Even the interests of industry and commerce find, for the moment, rival attractions to dispute their omnipotence; and the church is almost a balance for the exchange. A converted clergyman is as interesting as an apostate statesman; a visit to Rome, as a mission to Washington; a heresy from Germany, as a protocol from Paris; and a new baptism is no less the theme of talk than a new tariff. If theological gossip were the measure of religious faith, we should be the devoutest of all human generations.

Yet with all this currency of holy *words*, rarely, I believe, has there been a scantier exchange of holy *thought*. We do not meet, eye to eye and heart to heart, and say, with bosomed breath, "Lo, God is here!" But, rather, with

quick observant glance, and loud harsh voice, we notice the
postures of others, and discuss the things they say; and go
round like a patrol to look in upon the world at prayers.
The talk is all *critical*, about the length or shortness of some
one's creed, the warmth or coldness of a people's worship.
It tells you what each church thinks of all of its neighbors,
and repeats to you the image of Christendom in every phase.
But, flitting from image to image, we nowhere alight upon
the reality. We stand in one another's presence, like so
many mirrors ranged round empty space: turning to each,
you see only a distorted grouping of all the rest; which
being gone, it would be evident at once, that that polished
face could show merely vacancy without a trace of God.
Of old, when the saints and prophets lived whose names
we take in vain, the language of religion was itself the very
incense that rose from burning, fragrant souls to heaven:
now, it does but analyze the smoke, and explain of what
chemistry it comes.   Christ " came to bring fire upon earth ; "
and his disciples, after eighteen centuries, are discussing the
best patent match to get it kindled !

There is one feature in the professions of the present
times, as compared with past, on which it is impossible to
reflect without astonishment.   There is everywhere the
sharpest discernment of unbelief in others, with an entire
freedom from it in one's self.   The critic, if you will only
go round with him, can show you how it is lurking here and
there.   He keeps a list of all that his neighbors do *not*
believe.   Through the powerful glass of his suspicions he
can make you aware of the nicest shades of heresy: and
from writers who open new veins of thought, can pick out
passages so dreadful as to constitute a kind of infidel an-
thology.   From whatever class you choose your guide, this
is what he will point out to you.   Yet if you turn round
and say, " And now, good friend, what of thine own faith ? "
you will be delighted to find that it has altogether escaped
the universal malady: it has never had a shake ; or, if ever

ailing, has long got up its good looks, and remains quite
sound and firm. Trust, in short, the churches' report of
one another, and godlessness is universal ; trust their account of themselves, and scepticism is extinct. Nobody
hesitates about any thing which it is respectable to hold ;
and the clearest atmosphere of certainty overarches every
life, and opens a heaven undarkened by a doubt. And who
are these men, before whom the universe is so transparent;
for whom the veil of mystery is all withdrawn, or at least
hides no awful possibilities ? who are always ready to say
the proud words, " Lord, I believe ! " but would look askance
at the brother who should meekly respond, " Help thou mine
unbelief ! " — Smooth, easy men, with broad acres in the
country, or heavy tonnage on the sea ; with good standing
in their profession, or good custom at their shop ; living a
life so rounded with comfort, and showing a mind so content
to repose on it, that, while rents and freights keep up, you
cannot fancy they would much feel the loss of God : and
to part with the reversion of heaven would hardly affect
them like the news of a large bad debt. They believe
soundly, in the same way that they dress neatly : it no more
occurs to them to question their habitual creed, than to think
in the morning whether they shall put on a toga or a coat :
it is a matter of course, that the proprieties be observed,
and things that are settled for us be left untouched. Besides, what could be done with the " common people," if it
were not for God ?

Now from this easy faith, sitting so light upon our modern men, I turn to the old Puritan, and am startled by the
contrast. However much you may dislike his uncouth looks,
and be offended with his whining voice, he is not a man
without religion ; — a pity, it may be, that he has taken the
holiness and left the beauty of it. Missing it, however, in
his person and his speech, you find it penetrating his life,
and shaping it to high ends of truth and right. He can act
and suffer for God's sake ; can stand loose from the delu-

20

sions of property, — say that nothing is his own, — and occupy his place as a fiduciary fief from the Lord Paramount of all; can despise gaudy iniquity and see to the heart of every gilded flattery; — can insist on veracity in the council, and simplicity in the church; — feel the Omniscient eye on his State-paper as he writes; and the Eternal Spirit directing the course his persecuted step shall take. Yet look into this man's diary, and stand by and overhear his prayers. He loudly bewails his *unbelief;* — confesses a heart chilled with the very shadow of death; — complains that the Most High has hid his face from him; and with tears and protestations calls on the spirit of Christ to exorcise the demons of doubt that are grappling with his soul. Surely this is a strange thing. Here is a man plainly living for sublime ends, beyond the baubles of this world; a man, who has got fear and pain beneath his feet; — who welcomes self-denial as an angel of the way, and watches every indulgence as a traitor offering the kiss; — to whom the purest human love appears a snare tempting him to linger here; — who walks the earth, as in the outer fringe of the beatific vision : and his cry is, " Help thou mine unbelief!" And here are we, strangers to wrestlings such as his; who sleep soundly by nights, and manage prosperously by day; whose grand care is to get a living, rather than to live, and to cure by rule the health impaired by luxury : — we, to whom the earth answers well enough as a kitchen, a parlor, an office, or a theatre, but hardly as a watch-tower of contemplation, or a holy of holies for the oracles of God : — we can stand up, and have the assurance to say, " Lord! we believe!"

The difference between these two states of mind does not require that we should charge either of them with hypocrisy. There is truth in the professions of them both; truth enough to vindicate their veracity, though not to equalize their worth. The unbeliever in the one case and the believer in the other are measured off from a different scale;

our fathers looking up to the faith they ought to gain, their children looking down to the faith they have yet to lose. The former had so lofty a standard, that every thought beneath the summit-level was reckoned to their shame: the latter have so low a standard, that all above the dead level at the base of life is counted to their praise. Nor is this at all inconceivable, even though we were to reduce all religion to a single article of faith. To me, I confess, it seems a very considerable thing, just to believe in God; — difficult indeed to avoid honestly, but not easy to accomplish worthily, and impossible to compass perfectly: — a thing, not lightly to be professed, but rather humbly to be sought; not to be found at the end of any syllogism, but in the inmost fountains of purity and affection; — not the sudden gift of intellect, but to be earned by a loving and brave life. It is indeed the greatest thing allowed to mankind, — the germ of every lesser greatness : and he who can say, " I have faith in the Almighty," makes a higher boast than if he could declare, "The Mediterranean is in my garden, and mine is every branch that waves upon its shores, from the cedars of Lebanon to the pine upon the Alps." How often, in the stifling heat and press of life, when trivial cares rise with dry and dusty cloud to shut us in, do we wholly lose our place in the great calm of God, and fret as if there were no Infinite Reason embracing the vortex of the world ! In loneliness and exhaustion, when the spirits are weak, and the crush of circumstance is strong; — when comrades rest and sleep, and we must toil and watch ; — when the love of friends grows cold, and the warm light of youth is quenched, and the promises of years seem broken, and hope has but one chapter more ; — how little do we think, as the boughs drip sadly with all this night-rain, that we lodge in Eden still, where the voice of the Lord God rustles in the trees, and bespeaks the blossom and the fruit that can only spring from tears ! Fear too, in every form except the fear of sin, is a genuine atheism. The very child knows that : for if a terror comes on him because he is in the field alone by night, he chides himself for his false heart; stops and looks tranquilly round; relaxes the rigid limbs, and lets go the stifled breath; putting forth a thought into the Great Presence, and drawing a holy quiet from the stars. And through all manhood's fears, no one loses his presence of mind, who has not lost the presence of his God. In the battle-field, where justice sometimes makes appeal to the Lord of Hosts: in the shipwreck, where death seizes the storm as his trumpet, and, with the lightning as his banner, comes streaming down the sky: in courts of sacerdotal inquisition, where the branding-iron is hot, and instruments of torture tempt the lie: in the careless world, where prosperity is worshipped, and nice scruples are laughed down: in the sleepy church, which can wink at oppression, and give comfort to unrighteous Mammon, and cover with obloquy the heroes of God's truth: — no man could sink into an unworthy thing, did he keep within his everlasting fortress, instead of rushing unsheltered into the wild.

There is then every gradation even of this simple faith, spreading over a range quite indefinite. Only by a reference to its two extremes can we describe the position of each mind and of each age. *Complete belief* is attained, when God is realized as much in the present as in the past. *Complete unbelief*, when God is excluded from the past as much as from the present. Measuring from this lowest limit, we are certainly in a state of *imperfect atheism*. We do not negative as yet the sanctities of old: we only deny the inspirations of to-day. We recognize certain ages of the bygone world, as the real centres of divine activity, — the sole witnesses of creation and of miracle, the happy points where heaven vouchsafed to commune with the earth. They lie in our imagination, like brilliant islands rising distant in the seas of time; vainly dashed by the dark waters of human history; and lighted by a glory-column from above, piercing the leaden heavens that elsewhere overhang the waste. There, in old Palestine, we think, the august voice broke for a moment its eternal silence. There, upon the mountains, was a murmur more than of the wind ; and in the air a thunder grown articulate ; and on the grass a dew of fresher beauty ; and in the lakes a docile listening look, as if conscious of a Presence higher than the night's. In this retrospect, it will not be denied, lies the ground of our prevalent religion : it contains the strength of our case : our assurance of divine things refers pre-eminently thither, and scarcely at all to any more recent age. "The men in those days" (we virtually say) "had the best reasons for believing and recognizing God. Had we too been there, we should have known for ourselves, and have shared the great fear and faith that fell on all. But as we are placed afar off and have the sacredness at second hand, we must take their reasons upon trust, having none that are worth much of our own." Our faith, therefore, is not personal, but testimonial : it is an hypothesis, a tradition. It thinks within itself, " If we had stood where Moses was, and travelled at the right hand of Paul, we should have felt as they." And this justification of their ancient state of mind makes the substance of our belief to-day. And with like view do we turn our gaze upon the *future*. That also spreads before us radiant with a light divine. There we shall find better reasons for our faith than meet us here; an audience-hall of the Most High where his spirit may be felt ; a clear touch of his living presence, glowing through our thought with conscious truth, and spreading through our hearts a saintly love, denied us in this court of exile. And so it happens, that ages gone, and ages coming, absorb from us the whole reality of God, and leave the life on which we stand an atheistic death. The heaven that spans us touches the earth on the right hand and the left, at an horizon we cannot reach, but keeps its infinite zenith-distance overhead. We believe in One who looks at us, but not in One who lives with us. We are in

the house he built; but we work in it alone, for he is gone
up among the hills, and will only come to fetch us by-and-
by. And it is no wonder that, in a banishment like this,
our worship loses its immediate reality, and prays no more
with a fresh strong heart. It is not bathed in the flowing
tides of Deity, but keeps dry upon the strand from which
he has ebbed away. If ever it says, " Lo, God is here ! " it
instantly belies itself, by drawing out the telescope of history to look for him. It is not a communion face to face,
wherein he is near to us as the light upon our eye or the
sorrow on our hearts. It has become a *commemoration*,
telling what once he was to happier spirits of our race,
and how grateful we are for the dear old messages that
faintly reach our ear, how we will cherish the last remnant
of that precious and only sure memorial, — the fragile and
consecrated link between his sphere and ours. Thus our
worship is a monument of absent realities, and serves at
best but to keep alive, like an anniversary, the remembrance of things else fading in the distance. Or, if we
direct our face the other way, and look towards the future, we throw our prayers still farther from the actual duties at our feet. We plainly say that there can be no true
worship here, — it is too poor and dull a state : — we
only expect it hereafter, and would bear that greater prospect in our mind. And so we fall into the insincerity of
coming before God by way of keeping ourselves in practice,
and turning our religion into a *rehearsal*. What wonder
that, amid these histrionic affectations, the healthy heart of
faith gets sicklier till it dies ?

To approach again to the theocratic faith of our fathers,
we must leave the atmosphere of sacredness upon the past
and the future ; only spread its margin either way, till it
envelops and glorifies the present. For my own part, I
venerate not less than others the birth-hour of Christianity,
and the creative origin of worlds. But I do not believe that
God lived then and there alone ; or that if we could be

transplanted to those times, we should find any such difference as would melt down the coldness of our hearts, or
leave us more without excuse than we are now. There is
no chronology in the evidence, any more than in the presence, of Deity. Since the fathers fell asleep, all things
continue as they were from the beginning, — or rather the
*un*beginning, — of creation. The universe, open to the eye
to-day, looks as it did a thousand years ago : and the morning hymn of Milton does but tell the beauty with which our
own familiar sun dressed ˏthe earliest fields and gardens of
the world. We see what all our fathers saw. And if we
cannot find God in your house and mine, upon the roadside
or the margin of the sea ; in the bursting seed or opening
flower ; in the day-duty and the night-musing ; in the genial
laugh and the secret grief ; in the procession of life, ever
entering afresh, and solemnly passing by and dropping off ;
I do not think we should discern him any more on the grass
of Eden, or beneath the moonlight of Gethsemane. Depend upon it, it is not the want of greater miracles, but of
the soul to perceive such as are allowed us still, that makes
us push all the sanctities into the far spaces we cannot
reach. The devout feel that wherever God's hand is, *there*
is miracle : and it is simply an indevoutness which imagines
that only where miracle is, can there be the real hand of
God. The customs of heaven ought surely to be more sacred
in our eyes than its anomalies ; the dear old ways, of which
the Most High is never tired, than the strange things which
he does not love well enough ever to repeat. And he who
will but discern beneath the sun, as he rises any morning,
the supporting finger of the Almighty, may recover the
sweet and reverent surprise with which Adam gazed on
the first dawn in Paradise. It is no outward change, no
shifting in time or place, but only the loving meditation
of the pure in heart, that can re-awaken the Eternal from the
sleep within our souls ; that can render him a reality again,
and vindicate for him once more his ancient Name of "THE
LIVING GOD."

XXXI.

HAVING, DOING, AND BEING.

—◆—

1 John ii. 17.

THE WORLD PASSETH AWAY, AND THE LUST THEREOF; BUT HE THAT
DOETH THE WILL OF GOD ABIDETH FOR EVER.

Few things can strike a thoughtful man with greater wonder,
than the different estimate he makes, in different moods, of
the same portion of time. To-day, he is engaged with some
speculation, in which a millennium is not worth reckoning:
to-morrow, he is brought to some experience, in which a
minute bears the burden of an eternal weight. With the
geologist, we may go out beyond the limits of human events,
and grow familiar with those vast periods during which the
earth's crust was deposited in the oceans, or smelted in the
furnaces, or upheaved from the gas-caverns, of nature : and,
accustomed to call the Alps and Andes recent elevations,
and to treat all living species as only the newest fashion of
creative skill, we may well feel as though the hasty sands
of our particular generation were lost, and God could have
no index small enough to count our individual life. With
the astronomer, we may take a station external to this earth
itself, recede to an era when possibly the solar system was
but one of creation's morning mists, and trace its history
as it first spun itself into orbital rings, and then rolled itself
up into planetary globes : and with an imagination occupied
by cycles so capacious, for which the old granite pillars of
the world can scarce, with utmost stretch of age, afford a
unit-measure, it is not strange if we deem ourselves trivial

as the insect, and transient as the flake of summer snow.
Whoever approaches the human lot from this side of thought,
descending upon it from the *maxima*, instead of ascending
from the *minima* of calculable things, will be apt to think
it a poor affair, and to regard it as a dream, really com-
pressed into a moment, but with a delusive consciousness
of years. Seeing at night how calm and silent are the stars
far greater than ours, sending down the same cold sharp
light as they did on the first traveller lost upon the mountains
or sinking in the sea, he may naturally look with a smile or
a sigh at the ferment of human passion and pursuit, and
gaze on it as on the dust-cloud of a distant army marching
to immediate death. "What," he might say, "are the
achievements of your mightiest force, and the last triumphs
of your boasted civilization? What do you effect by the
vaunted efforts of your locomotive skill? Only certain
glidings, which, a short way off, are but invisible changes
of place on the surface of a bead. And what is the end of
all your successive systems of health and disease? — what
the utmost hope of the skill of all physicians, and the cries
and prayers from the whole infirmary of human ills? Only
this, — that a little respite may be given, till the rising
pendulum shall have reached its fall. Nay, what is the aim
even of your nobler institutions, devoted to the mind? On
what do your ancient schools and universities, with generation after generation of students, spend themselves amid
the murmurs of polite applause? On the attempt to recover
a few snatches from the sayings and doings of spirits that,
like yourselves, had to vanish at cock-crowing. And all the
while, as you pant and strive and hope, the great immovable
God is with you close at hand, and could tell you all by a
whisper, if he would!"

It is quite possible, in this way, by bringing the human
career into comparison with the stupendous cycles that lie
around it, to dwarf its magnitude, and throw contempt upon
its purposes. The prevailing tendency, however, is all in

the opposite direction. The thoughts which *science* presents
may operate as a telescope to show us what else there is
besides ourselves, and persuade us that we are but as the
trembling leaf in the boundless forests of existence. But
those which are offered by *affection* and natural experience
are rather apt to interpose a microscopic medium ; and,
instead of diminishing by comparison the whole of life, to
magnify every part by concentration. If that life, as you
affirm, be but a short visit to this sphere, it is yet our only
visit; and the moments of our stay acquire an intenser
worth. If it has just begun, and is also on the verge of
close, then we must revere it doubly, as a fresh thing, and
as a thing about to perish : two sanctities comprise it all, —
a first day and a last ; and there is no time for custom to
dull the space between the welcome and the adieu. Nor,
after all, is any conscious life proper to be compared with
the huge periods of the inanimate world. Their giant
strides may roughly step from century to century, and have
less in them than its quivering undulations over the smallest
surface of time. The two things are absolutely incommensurable; and there is no chronometer that can reckon
both. In moments of deep sorrow, or high faith; when we
either fear the last extremity, or hope for the dawn of new
deliverance ; when we are sinking to the point of lowest
depression, or struggling on the wing of highest resolution ;
in startling agonies of duty that goad our jaded strength;
in helpless vigils, when we must sit with folded hands and
wait ; in all crises of duty, of misery, of joy, of aspiration ;
— how little can the beat of any clock count the elements
of our existence then! The moments are stretched into
an awful fulness; and while the midnight star strikes the
meridian wire, we pass through more than common years.
Hence it is, that no familiarity with physical periods can
induce us to think lightly of the contents of life. If God,
affluent in eternities, is lavish of time upon his universe,
he is economic of it with us : filling it with unutterable

experiences, and charging it with irrevocable opportunities. With so small an allowance of it here, every part of it may well appear a priceless treasure. And though too often we grow careless of the portion which we have, we complain if there is any that we seem to lose. 'We throw away whole handfuls of time in heedless waste, and suffer no compunction; but if God, with heavenly will, take from us any expected hours, we burst into faithless tears. The term assured to us, we think, has been cut short; and the promised value cruelly withheld.

The truth is, that neither of these views, — that which looks with philosophic slight on the whole of mortal life, and that which clings with human fondness to every part, especially if it be denied, — can stand the light of devout and Christian thought. On the one hand, *that* cannot be insignificant which God has deemed it worth while to call out of eternity, and to set upon a theatre like this, fresh with duty ever new, and old with memories ever sacred; rich as Paradise with wonder and beauty, only covered now through sorrow with a conscious heaven. And that which God himself has brought hither to look for awhile through real living eyes of thought and love, transparent to the answering gaze, can scarce, if we reflect on the difference between its presence and its absence, be of less than infinite value. Yet, on the other hand, it were wrong to measure its worth to us by the mere duration of its stay. It would be a far inferior treasure, were it calculable thus: and we can say nothing so depreciatory of a human life, as that we have lost half its value, because it was not twice as long. If this be so, the function it performs for us must be of the lowest order; not to our love, and faith, and aspiration, which, once awakened, can be doubled by no addition and consumed by no subtraction of moments; but to our pleasures or our gains, to which alone this arithmetic of quantity can be applied. To treat a life as incomplete, is to say that its proper end is unfulfilled; is to assume that a certain amount of time was needful to realize that end; and that, for want of such amount, the existence granted becomes an aimless fragment. Some lives do, no doubt, present so poor an aspect, that only by an effort of strong faith can we refrain from thinking thus: but else, it is of the mere meanness and penury of our own spirits, that we lapse into so unworthy a complaint. If we look for a few moments into the different ends to which men live, we shall soon see, *which* of them are measurable by quantity, and proportioned to the time spent in their attainment.

Some men are eminent for what they *possess:* some, for what they *achieve:* others, for what they *are.* *Having, Doing, and Being,* constitute the three great distinctions of mankind, and the three great functions of their life. And though they are necessarily all blended, more or less, in each individual, it is seldom difficult to say, which of them is prominent in the impression left upon us by our fellow-man.

In every society, and especially in a country like our own, there are those who derive their chief characteristic from what they *have;* who are always spoken of in terms of revenue; and of whom you would not be likely to think much, but for the large account that stands on the world's ledger in their name. In themselves, detached from their favorite sphere, you would notice nothing wise or winning. At home, possibly, a dry and withered heart; among associates, a selfish and mistrustful talk; in the council, a style of low ignoble sentiment; at church, a formal, perhaps an irreverent, dulness; betray a barren nature, and offer you only points of repulsion, so far as the humanities are concerned: and you are amazed to think that you are looking on the idols of the exchange. Their greatness comes out in the affairs of bargain and sale, to which their faculties seem fairly apprenticed for life. If they speak of the past, it is in memory of its losses and its gains: if of the future, it is to anticipate its incomings and investments. The whole chronology of their life is divided according to the stages of their fortunes, and the progress of their dignities. Their children are interesting to them principally as their heirs : and the making of their will fulfils their main conception of being ready for their death. And so completely do they paint the grand idea of their life on the imagination of all who know them, that when they die, the Mammon-image cannot be removed, and it is the fate of the money, not of the man, of which we are most apt to think. Having put vast prizes in the funds, but only unprofitable blanks in the admiration and the hearts of us, they leave behind nothing but their *property ;* or, as it is expressively termed, their " *effects,*" — the thing which they caused, the main result of their having been alive. How plain is it that we regard them merely as *instruments of acquisition ;* centres of attraction for the drifting of capital ; that they are important only as indications of commodities ; and that their human personality hangs as a mere label upon a mass of treasure! Every one must have met with a few instances in which this character is realized, and with many in which, notwithstanding the relief of some redeeming and delightful features, it is at least approached. In proportion as this aim, of possession, is taken to be paramount in life, length of days must no doubt be deemed indispensable to the human destination. The longer a man lies out at interest, the greater must be the accumulation. If he is unexpectedly recalled, every end which he suggested is disappointed : the only thing he seemed fit for cannot go on ; he is a power lost from this sphere, an incapacity thrust upon the other; missed from the markets here, thrown away among sainted spirits there. For himself, and for both worlds, the event seems deplorable enough : and it is difficult to make any thing but confusion out of it. An imagination tacitly filled with this conception of life, as a stage prepared for enjoyment and possession, must look on a term that is unfulfilled as on a broken tool, dropping in failure to the earth.

Of those who have thus lived to accumulate and enjoy, *history* is for the most part silent; having in truth nothing to say. Not doing the work, or joining in the worship of life, but only feasting at its table, they break up and drive off into oblivion as soon as the lights are out and the wine is spilt. Belonging entirely to the present, they never appear in the past; but sink with weight of wealth in the dark gulf:—unless perchance some Crœsus the rich is fortunate enough to fall into association with a Solon the wise. There are no historical materials in simple animal existence, nor in the mere sentient being of a man, considered as the successful study of comfort and receptacle of happiness. History is constructed by a second and nobler class, — those who prove themselves to be here, not that they may *have*, but that they may *do ;* to whom life is a glorious labor; and who are seen not to work that they may rest, but only to rest that they may work. No sooner do they look around them, with the open eye of reason and faith, upon the great field of the world, than they perceive that it must be for them a battle-field : and they break up the tents of ease, and advance to the dangers of lonely enterprise and the conflict with splendid wrong. Strong in the persuasion that this is a God's world, and that his will must rule it by royal right, they serve in the severe campaign of justice; asking only for the wages of life, and scorning the prizes of spoil and praise. Wherever you find such, whether in the field, in the senate, or in private life, you see the genuine type of the heroic character, — the clear mind, the noble heart, the indomitable will, pledged all to some arduous and unselfish task : and whether it be the achievement, with Cobden, of freedom of pacific commerce between land and land ; or, with Clarkson, of freedom of person between man and man ; or, with Cromwell, of freedom of worship between earth and heaven ; the essential feature is in all instances the same : the man holds himself as the mere instrument of some social work ; commits himself in full allegiance to it ;

and spends himself wholly in it. These " have a baptism to
be baptized with; and how are they straitened, till it be
accomplished !" During the glorious conflict of such lives
it is impossible not to look on with breathless interest.
Once possessed of their great design, we watch its development with eager eye and beating heart. And if, early in
the day, they are struck down, we clasp our hands in sudden anguish, and a cry goes up that the field is lost. And
though this despair is a momentary lapse from true faith;
though God never fails to rally the forces of every good
cause that has mustered for battle on his earth ; yet, no
doubt, the victory in such a case is deferred : the plan is
broken off : the painful sense of a suspended work, that
might have been finished, remains upon survivors' hearts.
On behalf of the noble actors themselves, indeed, we have
no embarrassment of faith : there is that within them which
may well find a home in more worlds than one, and meet a
welcome wherever Almighty Justice reigns. We are not
ashamed, as with the man of mere possession, to follow them
into the higher transitions of their being, and knock for
them at the gate of better spheres. But there appears
something untimely and deplorable in the providence of the
world they quit. The fruit has not been permitted to ripen
ere it dropped. The great function of their life required
time for its fulfilment; and time has been denied. Their
beneficent action was wholly through the energies of their
living will : and these energies are laid for us in unseasonable sleep. And thus, while we are ashamed at the grave
of the Epicurean, we weep over the departure of the hero.

But there is a life higher than either of these. The
saintly is beyond the heroic mind. To get good, is animal :
to do good, is human : to be good, is divine. The true use
of a man's possessions is to help his work: and the best
end of all his work, is to show us what he is. The noblest
workers of our world bequeath us nothing so great as the
image of themselves. Their *task*, be it ever so glorious, is

historical and transient: the majesty of their *spirit* is essential and eternal. When the external conditions which
supplied the matter of their work have wholly decayed
from the surface of the earth, and become absorbed into its
substance, the perennial root of their life remains, bearing
a blossom ever fair, and a foliage ever green. And while
to some God gives it to show themselves *through* their
work, to others he assigns it to show themselves without
even the opportunity of work. He sends them transparent
into this world; and leaves us nothing to gather and infer.
Goodness, beauty, truth, acquired by others, are original to
them; hiding behind the eye, thinking on the brow, and
making music in the voice. The angels appointed to guard
the issues of the pure life, seem rather to have taken their
station at its fountains, and to pour into it a sanctity at first.
Such beings live simply *to express themselves:* to stand
between heaven and earth, and mediate for our dull hearts.
With fewer outward objects than others, or at least with
a less limited practical mission devoting them to a fixed
task, their life is a soliloquy of love and aspiration; the soul
not being, with them, the servant of action, but action
rather the needful'articulation of the soul. Not, of course,
that they are, in the slightest degree, exempt from the
stern and positive obligations of duty, or licensed, any
more than others, to dream existence away. If once they
fall into this snare, and cease to work, the lineaments of
beauty and goodness are exchanged for those of shame and
grief. Usually they do not *less,* but rather *more,* than
others; only under somewhat sorrowful conditions, having
spirits prepared for what is more than human, and being
obliged to move within limits that are only human. The
worth of such a life depends little on its *quantity:* it is an
affair of *quality* alone. These highest ends of existence
have but slight relation to time. Years cannot mellow the
love already ripe, or purify the perceptions already clear,
or lift the aspiration that already enters heaven. It is with

Christ-like minds, as it was with Christ himself. His divine work was not in the task that he did, but in the image which he left. You cannot say that there was any great business of existence, estimable by time, which he set him-self to achieve, and which you can even imagine to be broken off by his departure. He lived enough to manifest the heavenly spirit and solemn dignity of life. At thirty years he passed away: and no one, I suppose, was ever heard to lament that he did not stay till sixty. He thought indeed, as the faithful must ever think, that there was a " work given him to do ; " unaware that, by his very manner of devotion to it, it was already done. So eager was he worthily to finish it, that, of all his sorrows, to be cut short in it was the bitterest cup that might not pass from him except he drank it ; unconscious that the spirit and the con-quest of that agony did actually bring it to the sublimest close. His life stood in different relations to himself and to the world. To himself it was a solemn trust ; to the world, the truth and grace of God : to him, it was given as the subject of achievement ; to the world, as the object of new faith and love. And so, the early cross, so dark to him, becomes the holiest vision of our hearts. It broke nothing abruptly off for us ; and enabled him to leave a presence upon the earth, sufficient to soothe the sorrows, inspire the conscience, and deepen the earnestness, of suc-ceeding ages. And so is it with the least of his disciples, whose mind is truly tinged with the hues of the same heavenly spirit. The very child, of too transient stay, may paint on the darkness of our sorrow, so fair a vision of loving wonder, of reverent trust, of deep and thoughtful patience, that a divine presence abides with us for ever, as the mild and constant light of faith and hope. What we had deemed a glory of the earth may prove but the image of a star upon the stream of life, effaceable by the first night-wind that sweeps over the waters. But that we have seen it, and looked into the pure depths given for its light, is enough to assure us that, though visionary below, it is a reality above, and has a place among the imperishable lustres of God's universe. Thus, with attributes of being that have little concern with time, the reckoning of moments is of less account. The transitory reflection points to an eternal beauty. And while human things are learned by the lessons of a slow experience, a momentary flash of blessing may give us what is most divine; and like the lightning that strikes us blind, leave a glory on the soul, when our very sight is gone.

XXXII.

. THE FREE-MAN OF CHRIST. .

———◆———

1 CORINTHIANS VII. 22.

HE THAT IS CALLED IN THE LORD, BEING A SERVANT, IS THE LORD'S
FREE-MAN: LIKEWISE ALSO, HE THAT IS CALLED, BEING FREE, IS
CHRIST'S SERVANT.

FREEDOM, in the most comprehensive sense of the word, can evidently belong to Omnipotence alone. To be exempt from all controlling force without, is the exclusive prerogative of a Being, within whose nature are folded all the active powers of the universe, and to whom there is no external cause but the acts projected from his own will. To be at rest from all conflict within, can be the lot of no mind, susceptible of progressive attainment in excellence: for moral growth is but a prolonged controversy in which conscience achieves victory after victory: and He only whose holiness is eternal, original, incapable of increase or decline, can have a mind absolutely serene and unclouded; of power immense, but rapid and unreluctant as the lightning; of designs, however majestic, bursting without appreciable transition from the conception to the reality. Descend to created natures; and whatever force they comprise, is a force imprisoned and controlled; if by nothing else, at least by the laws of that body which gives them a locality, and affords them the only tools wherewith to work their will. The life of beings that are born and ripen and die, or pass through any stages of transition, floats upon a current silent but irresistible. In other spheres there may possibly exist rational beings un-

conscious of the restraining force of God exercised upon
them; whose desires do not beat against their destiny;
whose powers of conceiving and of executing, whether
absolutely small or great, are adjusted to perfect correspondence. And since we measure all things by our own
ideas, he whose conception never overlaps his execution,
can never detect the poorness of his achievements, how
trivial soever they may be in the eye of a spectator. But
man, at all events, palpably *feels* his limits; receives a
thousand checks, that remind him of the foreign agencies to
which he is subject; glides like a steersman in the night
over waters neither boundless nor noiseless, but broken by
the roar of the rapid, and dizzy with the dim shapes of rocky
perils. Our whole existence, all its energy of virtue and of
passion, is, in truth, but the struggle of free-will against the
chains that bind us : — happy he, that by implicit submission
to the law of duty escapes the severity of every other ! Our
nature is but a casket of impatient necessities; urgencies
of instinct, of affection, of reason, of faith ; the pressure of
which against the inertia of the present determines the living
movements, and sustains the permanent unrest, of life. To
take the prescribed steps is difficult; to decline them and
stand still, impossible. We can no more preserve a stationary attitude in the moral world, than we can refuse to
accompany the physical earth in its rotation. The will may
be reluctant to stir; but it is speedily overtaken by pro-
vocatives that scorn the terms of ease, and take no heed of
its expostulations. Driven by the recurring claims of the
bodily nature, or drawn by the permanent objects of the
spiritual, all men are impelled to effort by the energy of
some want, that cannot have spontaneous satisfaction. The
laborer that earns his bread by the sweat of his brow, is
chased by the hindmost of all necessities, — animal hunger.
The prophet and the saint, moved by the supreme of human
aspirations, — the hunger and thirst after righteousness, —
embrace a life of no less privation and of severer conflict.

And between these extremes are other ends of various kinds,
— renown for the ambitious, art for the perceptive, knowledge for the sage, — given to us to graduate and allow in
fair proportion. All these are conscious powers, but all
imply a conscious resistance. Each separately precipitates
the will upon a thousand obstacles ; and all together demand
the ceaseless vigilance of conscience to preserve their order,
and prevent the encroachments of usurpation. Thus, all
action implies the presence of some necessity. And if
other and more liberal conditions are requisite to perfect
freedom, then can no man be ever free.

Exemption then from the sense of want and the need of
work is not that which constitutes freedom to the human
being. Another form of expression is sometimes resorted
to, in order to discriminate the free from the servile mind,
and contrast the nobleness of the one with the abjectness
of the other. It is said that the free-man acts from within,
on the suggestion of ideas ; while the slave is the creature
of outward coercion, and obeys some kind of physical force.
But this language still conceals from us the real distinction.
Even the man whose person, as well as mind, is in a condition of slavery, is not necessarily, or usually, under any external and material constraint. Hour by hour, and day by
day, he enjoys immunity from bodily compulsion ; and
habitually lives at one remove or more from the application of direct sensation to his will. He too, like other men,
is worked by an ideal influence, — a fear that haunts, an
image that disturbs him. When the field-serf plies his
spade with new energy at the approaching voice of the
steward, it is not that any muscular grasp seizes on his
limbs and enforces a quicker movement; but that a mental
terror is awakened, and the phantom of the lash flies
through his startled fancy. And, in higher cases of obedience, it is proportionally more evident, that the physical
objects which are the implements for procuring submission
fulfil their end by the mere power of suggestion. The

eagle of the Roman legion, the cross in the battles of the crusades, reared its head above the hosts upon the field; and wherever this instrument, made by the chisel and the saw, was moved about hither and thither, it drew to it the wave of fight, and swayed the living mass, content to be mowed down themselves, if it alone were saved. It was an emblem of things most powerful with their hearts; and illustrates, by another example, the truth, that the force which persuades the submissive will is, in all instances, from the highest to the lowest, internal and ideal. The difference between the free and the servile must be sought, not in the distinction between a physical and a mental impulse, but in the different order of ideas in which the action of the two has its source.

There are two governing ideas that, without material error, may be said to rule the actions of mankind, and share between them the dominion of all human souls; the idea of *pleasure and pain ;* and the idea of the *noble and ignoble.* Every one, in every deed, follows either what he enjoys, or what he reveres. Now he and he only is *free* who implicitly submits to that which he deeply venerates; who takes part, offensive and defensive, with the just and holy against the encroachments of evil; who feels his self-denials to be his privilege, not his loss ; a victory that he has won, not a spoil that he has been obliged to forego. Such a one is free, because he is ruled by no power which he feels to be unrightful and usurping, but maintains in ascendency the Divine Spirit that has an eternal title to the monarchy of all souls; because he is never driven to do that which he knows to be beneath him; because he is conscious no longer of severe internal conflict, or it issues in secure enfranchisement ; because self-contempt and fear and restlessness, and all the feelings peculiar to a state of thraldom, are entirely unknown. And *they* all are slaves,— liable to the peculiar sins and miseries of the servile state,— to its meanness, its cowardice, its treachery ; — who either have

nothing which they revere, or, having it, insult its authority, and trample it under the Bacchanalian feet of pleasure.
It is the worst and last curse of actual personal slavery, that
it extinguishes the notion of rights, and with it the sense
of duties; that it quenches the desire and conscious capacity
for better things ; that degradation becomes impossible ;
that blows may be inflicted, and the pain go no farther
than the flesh ; and that by feeding the eyes with the
prospect of pleasure, or brandishing the threat of infliction,
you may move the creature as you will. And whenever, by
men at large, nothing is esteemed holy and excellent, and
enjoyment or suffering are the only measures of good, the
essence of the same debasement exists. The slave flies the
idea of pain ; the voluptuary pursues the idea of pleasure :
a menace or a bribe is the force that makes a tool of both ;
and they must be referred to the same class. Nor does the
analogy between them fail in cases of mixed character and
imperfect degradation. If the serf has not sunk to the level
which it is the tendency of his condition to reach, if he has
still his dreams of justice, his half-formed sense of human
dignity, it is then his privilege to be wretched ; to feel an
agonizing variance between his nature and his lot, and
writhe as the iron enters his soul. And a like miserable
shame does every one suffer, who offers indignity to his
own higher capacities ; who suppresses in silence and in-
action the impulses of his devout affections, and is seduced
or terrified into conscious vileness. It is not without suf-'
ficient reason that all those whose wills are of self-indulgent make, are charged with being enthralled. Their minds
have the very stamp of slavery.

The essential root then of all dependence and servility of
soul lies in this, that the mind loves pleasure more than God.
The essence of true spiritual liberty is in this ; that the
mind has high objects which it loves better than its own
indulgence ; in the service of which hardship and death are
honorable and welcome ; which must be subordinated to

nothing; which men are not simply to pursue in order to live; but which they live in order to pursue. In acknowledging the pleasurable as supreme, consists the real degradation and disloyalty of the one: in vowing undivided allegiance to what is worthy, true, and right, consists the power and freedom of the other.

Let the Christian beware, as he loves the birth-right of a child of God, how he takes up any other and more superficial idea of moral liberty than this. Especially let him not yield to the prevalent and growing feeling of these days, that there is something disgraceful in obedience altogether; — that it is an unmanly attitude of mind; and that if occasions do occur in human life when self-will must succumb, it is best to slur over so annoying a crisis, and at all events avoid the appearance of capitulation. The heart that secretly feels thus has never felt the contact of Christ's divine wisdom: the slightest touch of but the hem of his garment in the press and crowd of life, would have cured the burning of this inward fever. For, is not this insubordinate will fighting with its lot, instead of loving it, — trying bolts and bars against it, and standing hostile siege, instead of throwing open its gates, and with reverent hospitality entertaining it as an angel visitant? Great and sacred is obedience, my friends: he who is not able, in the highest majesty of manhood, to obey, with clear and open brow, a Law higher than himself, is barren of all faith and love; and tightens his chains, moreover, in struggling to be free. A childlike trust of heart, that can take a hand, and wondering walk in paths unknown and strange, is the prime requisite of all religion. Let the Great Shepherd lead; and by winding ways, not without green pastures and still waters, we shall climb insensibly, and reach the .tops of the everlasting hills, where the winds are cool and the sight is glorious. But, in the noon of life, to leap and struggle against the adamantine precipice will only bruise our strength, and cover us with sultry dust. Among the thousand indications

how far men have wandered from this temper, and poisoned
their minds with the sophistries of self-will, this is enough:
— that there are some who, instead of self-abandonment to
God, appear to think that they can put him and his truth
under obligation to themselves, and that they confer a great
favor in encouraging the public regard to his will and worship; who, having made up their minds that Christianity is
useful in many ways, and of excellent service in managing
the weaker portion of mankind, resolve to patronize it.
Well;— it is an ancient arrogance, lasting as the vanities of
the human heart. The Pharisee, it would appear, belongs
to a sect never extinct: he lives immortal upon the earth;
and in our day, like Simon of old, graciously condescends to
ask the Lord Jesus to dine!

Nor is there any truth in the notion that it must be disgraceful to serve and obey the will of our fellow-men; of
our equals; of those even who are weaker and not wiser
than ourselves. It depends altogether on the feeling that
prompts the submission; whether it be self-interest or reverence. To be controlled by others against our idea of the
pleasant, is by no means necessarily debasing: to be controlled by them against our idea of the right, is. The gross
conception of liberty, which takes it to consist in *doing
whatever we like,* tends only to a restless personal indulgence,
— to a burning, insatiable thirst for selfish happiness, the
importunity of which renders this fancied freedom bitter
as the vilest slavery. Does any one doubt, whether subjection the most absolute can ever be noble? Go into a
home where a child lies sick, — one of a joyous family where
often merry voices ring from morn to night. Silence, the
unconscious forerunner of death, flits through the house,
touching with her seal the lips even of the gayest prattler;
and when the faint cry of feverish waking frets forth from
the pillow, how fleet the answer to the call! how soft the
mother's cheerful words from out the anguished heart! how
prompt the father's hand with the cup of cold water to cool

the parched tongue! Every wayward wish, perhaps discarded soon as formed, swift messengers glide to and fro to gratify: every burst of impatience falls softly and without recoil on playmates never wounded so before. No despot was ever so obeyed as this little child, whose will is for awhile the sole domestic law : for despots acquire no such title to command. But this title, recorded in God's hand-writing of love on the tablets of our humanity, we must recognize and obey. The terms of it proclaim, in defiance of the pretensions of self-will, that the service of others is our divinest freedom ; and that the law which rules us becomes the charter that disenthrals us. Nay, to work patiently in faith and love, to do not what we like, but what we revere, confers not liberty only but power. He at least who, of all our race was the most indubitably free, and the great emancipator too, had in him this attribute, that " he pleased not himself," and esteemed it his mission " not to be ministered unto, but to minister." And therefore did he obtain a name above every name, and put the world beneath his feet. Having claimed nothing, not even himself, it is given him to inherit all things. His power indeed over men was slow in gathering, and they that loved him in his mortal life, and lived and suffered for his sake, were few. Had he needed *then* a rescue and a retinue, he must have looked to the "legions of angels" who alone were qualified for a reverence and fidelity so true. But *now* let him come; and would not the legions of our world throng forth to meet him ; casting the will of pride beneath his feet, strewing his path with flowers of joy which he has caused to bloom, and flinging their glad hosannas to the sky !

By the meekest ministrations did the Lord acquire his blessed sway. How different is the method usually resorted to in order to obtain the services of others ! Instead of thinking, speaking, acting freely, and in the divine spirit of duty, and leaving it to God to append what influence and

authority he may see fit, men begin by coveting the services
of others, and resolving to have them: and, being sure that
they can at least be purchased by money, they "make haste
to get rich;" often hurrying over every species of mean
compliance for this purpose, in the wretched hope of earning
their enfranchisement in the end. This process of making
their moral liberty contingent upon the purse, is character-
istically termed "*gaining an independence.*" This very
phrase is a satire upon the morals of the class that invented
it, and the nation that adopts it. We then are a people
who express by the same word the freedom of the mind,
· the high rule of conscience and conviction, and a thing of
gold, that can be kept at a bank, or invested in the funds.
With us, broad acres must go before bold deeds: one must
· possess an estate before he can be a man. And so, to "win
an independence," many an aspirant becomes a sycophant:
to "win an independence," he licks the feet of every disgrace that can add a shilling to his fortune: to "win an
independence," he courts the men whom he despises, and
stoops to the pretences that he hates: to "win an independence," he solemnly professes that which he secretly
derides, and grows glib in uttering falsehoods that should
scald his lips. Truly, this modern idol *is* a god, who compels his votaries to crawl up the steps of his throne. And
when the homage has been paid, and the prize is gained,
how noble a creature must the worshipper issue forth,
who by such discipline, has achieved his "independence"
at last!

   This miserable heathenism is simply reversed in the
Christian method and estimate of liberty. The road to
genuine spiritual freedom, taking, it may seem, a strange
direction, lies through what the older moralists term "Self-
annihilation." Renounce we our wishes, and the oppositions that bear against us inevitably vanish. As force is
made evident only by resistance, necessity is perceptible only
by the pressure it offers to our claims and desires. He who

resists not at all, feels no hostile power; is chafed by no irritation; mortified by no disappointment. He bends to the storm as it sweeps by, and lifts a head serene when it is gone. Nor is his liberty merely negative: self-will is displaced only to make way for God's will: and weakness is surrendered that almightiness may be enthroned. The positive empire of the right takes the place of a feeble and contested sway. The efficacy of the change is sure to be seen in achievement no less than in endurance. Over him that shall undergo it, the world and men lose all their deterring power. Do what they may with their instruments of persecution and derision, none of these things move him. They cannot sting him into scorn. His ends lie far beyond their reach. Who can hinder him from following that which he reveres; from embracing in his love the world · that crushes him; and remaining true to the God that tries him as by fire? It is the Son that has made him free, and he is free indeed!

XXXIII.

THE GOOD SOLDIER OF JESUS CHRIST.

——◆——

2 Timothy ii. 3.

THOU THEREFORE ENDURE HARDNESS, AS A GOOD SOLDIER OF JESUS CHRIST.

There would seem to be an incurable variance between the life which men covet for themselves and that which they admire in others; nay, between the lot which they would choose beforehand, and that in which they glory afterwards. In prospect, nothing appears so attractive as ease and licensed comfort; in retrospect, nothing so delightful as toil and strenuous service. Half the actions of mankind are for the diminution of labor; yet labor is the thing they most universally respect. We should think it the greatest gain to get rid of effort; yet if we could cancel from the past those memorable men in whom it reached its utmost intensity, and whose whole existence was a struggle, we should leave human nature without a lustre, and empty history of its glory. The aim which God assigns to us as our highest is indeed the direct reverse of that which we propose to ourselves. He would have us in perpetual con-flict;—we crave an unbroken peace. He keeps us ever on the march;—we pace the green sod by the way with many a sigh for rest. He throws us on a rugged universe;—and our first care is to make it smooth. His resolve is to demand from us, without ceasing, a living power, a force fresh from the spirit he has given; ours, to get into such settled ways, that life may almost go of itself, with scarce

the trouble of winding up. So that time, administered by
him, is always breaking up the old : by us, is riveting and
confirming it. With him, it is the source of new growths
and fresh combinations; which we proceed, as long as we
can, to cut down and accommodate to the order which they
interrupt. He employs it in rolling the forest into the river,
and turning the stream from our abodes; in burying our
fields and villages beneath the shifting sand-hills, which we
strive to bind with grassy roots; in bringing back the marsh
on our neglected lands, and setting us again the problem
of pestilence and want. Every way he urges our reluctant
will. He grows the thistle and the sedge : but expects us
to raise the olive and the corn; having given us a portion
of strength and skill for such end. He directs over the earth
the restless wave of human population, and brings about
those new conditions from which spring the rivalries and
heats of nations : and expects us to evolve peace and justice;
having inspired us with reason and affection for this end.
He leaves in each man's lot a thicket of sharp temptations :
and expects him, though with bleeding feet, to pass firmly
through; having given him courage, conscience, and a guide
divine, to sustain him lest he faint.

And, after all, in spite of the inertia of their will, men are,
in their inmost hearts, on the side of God, rather than their
own, in this matter. They know it would be a bad thing
for them to have nothing to resist. They would like it, but
they could not honor it; and in proportion as it was comfortable, it would be contemptible. They have always paid
their most willing homage to those who have refused to sit
down and break bread with evil things, and have made a
battle-field of life. Even out of the primitive conflict with
brute *Nature*, in which rocks were split, and monsters tamed,
they evoked a God; and, under the name of *Hercules*, invented an excuse for their first and simplest worship. No
sooner is this physical contest closed, and the earth compelled to yield a roadway and a shelter to men, than the

scene of struggle is changed, and they come into conflict
with *each other*. Instead of dead resistance they encounter
living force : from obstructive matter their competitor rises
to aggressive mind : and whoever shows himself master of
the higher qualities demanded in the collision, for justice'
sake, of man with man, — the fixed resolve, the dauntless
courage, the subjection of appetite, the sympathy with the
weak and the oppressed, — is honored by all as a hero, and
remembered by his nation as its pride. But when the game
of war is done, it is found that in struggling to a firm and
established order of society, men have not got rid of all
their foes and driven evil from off their world. Inward
corruption may waste what outward assault could not destroy. Amid the luxuries and repose of peace, the springs
of moral hardihood become enfeebled; guilty negligence,
indulgent laxity, plausible selfishness, and even greedy
hypocrisy, eat into the world's heart. A secret spirit of
temptation, too powerful for its degeneracy, hovers over it
and threatens to darken it into a hell: when lo ! at the
crisis of its fate, there comes forth one to meet and to defy
even this invisible fiend of *moral evil*, and by the wonders
of prayer and toil and sorrow, make Lucifer as lightning fall
from heaven ; one, far different from the strong arm that
subdues creation, and the brave heart that conquers men;
being the Divine Soul that puts to flight the hosts of Satan,
and, as the leader and perfecter of faith, pushes the victories of men into the only unconquered realm, — the shadowy
domain of sin and its dread prisons of remorse. Thus the
primitive conflict with nature, which makes a Hercules,
rises into the conflict with man, which makes the hero, and
culminates in that infinitely higher conflict with the spirit
of evil, which is impersonated in Christ. We instinctively
do homage in some sort to them all; only admiring the
former as manly ; and reverencing the last as godlike. And
it may be remarked that, as the world has passed through
these several stages of strife to produce a Christendom ; so,

by relaxing in the enterprises it has learnt, does it tend downwards, through inverted steps, to wildness and the waste again. Let a people give up their contest with moral evil; disregard the injustice, the ignorance, the greediness, that may prevail among them, and part more and more with the *Christian* element of their civilization; and, in declining this battle with sin, they will inevitably get embroiled with men. Threats of war and revolution punish their unfaithfulness : and if then, instead of retracing their steps, they yield again and are driven before the storm ; — the very arts they had created, the structures they had raised, the usages they had established, are swept away: " in that very day their thoughts perish." The portion they had reclaimed from the young earth's ruggedness is lost; and failing to stand fast against man, they finally get embroiled with Nature, and are thrust down beneath her ever-living hand.

The law of conflict which God thus terribly proclaims in the history of nations, is no less distinctly legible in the moral life of individuals. In an old and complicated structure of society, the number is multiplied of those who exist in a state of benumbed habit; who walk through their years methodically, not finding it needful to be more than half awake; who take their passage through human life in an easy chair, and no more think of any self-mortifying work than of the ancient pilgrimage on foot ; and are so pleased with the finish and varnish of the world around them, as to fancy demons and dangers all cleaned out. And thus the perfected customs, the smooth, macadamized ways of life, which are all excellent as facilities for swifter activity, have the effect of putting activity to sleep ; the means of helping us to our proper ends become the means of our wholly forgetting them; and looking out of the windows, we leave behind the commission on which we are sent, and set up as travellers for pleasure. This kind of peril is the peculiar temptation which besets all, and makes imbeciles of many, in an artificial community like ours. The battle of life is not now, so often as of old, thrust upon us from without; it does not give us the first blow, which it were poltroonery to fly; but it is internal and invisible; it has to be sought and found by voluntary enterprise; it is not with palpable flesh and blood beneath the sun, but with viewless spirits, that cling to us in the dark. To capture the appetites and make them content with their proper servitude; to change the heart of ambition, and turn its aspiring eye from the lamp of heathen glory to the starlight of a Christian sanctity; to seize anger and yoke it under curb of reason to the service of justice and of right; to lash the sluggish will to quicker and more earnest toil; to charm the dull affections into sweeter and more lively moods, and tempt their timid shyness to break into song and mingle voices with the melody of life; to rouse pity from its sleep and compel it to choose a task and begin its plans; — all this implies a vigilance, a devotion, an endurance, which, though only natural , to the " good soldier of Jesus Christ," are beyond the mark of the sceptics and triflers of the present age.

I have said, *sceptics and triflers.* And be assured that the conjunction is true and natural. The shrinking from difficulty, the dread of ridicule, the love of ease, which drain off the sap of a man's moral earnestness, soon dry up the sources of all moral faith from the very roots of him. Though in one sense it is true that he must believe before he acts, yet assuredly he will not long go on believing, when he has ceased to act. The coward who skulks from the fight mutters, as he retires, that " there is really nothing worth fighting for." And those who decline the high battle of the Christian life persuade themselves, that there is no worthy field, no peremptory call, no dreadful foe ; and the clarion of God, which pierces and inspires faithful souls is no more to them than the pipe of hypocrites. The plain of prophet's warfare, where every step should be circumspect, becomes in their eyes a soft and fruitful stroll; and

22

the sins which good men have spent themselves in driving
back, turn out to be the pleasantest companions, of whom it
was quite a bigotry to think harm.   Instances of this kind
of self-sophistication must have presented themselves to the
observation of all.   They plainly show, that any truth a
man ceases to live by necessarily becomes to him, if he only
persevere, an entire falsehood.   God insists on having a con-
currence between our practice and our thought.   If we
proceed to make a contradiction between them, he forthwith begins to abolish it; and if the will does not rise
to the reason, the reason must be degraded to the will.
This is no other than that "giving over of men to a
reprobate mind," by which " the truth of God is changed
into a lie."

It is needless to point out the several devices by which
practical unfaithfulness contrives to bring about speculative
unbelief.   They are almost as various as the individual
minds producing them : and agree only in their result; viz.
the loss of all moral earnestness ; the decline of any feeling
of reality about the higher ends of life; the disinclination
to any thing that interrupts the easy play of self-love;
and the subsidence of the mighty wind of resolution which
should sweep direct and steady through the true man's
course, into fitful airs of affectation and puffs of caprice.
It is not the failure of this or that doctrinal conviction, that
we need in itself lament ; of this sort we could part perhaps with a good deal of helpless trying to believe, without
being at all the worse : but it is the loosening of moral
faith ; the fluctuating state of the boundary between right
and wrong, or even the suspicion of its non-existence ; the
absence from men's minds of any thing worth living and
dying for ; the lawyer-like impartiality, consisting of an in-
discriminate advocacy, for hire or favor, of any cause irre-
spective of its goodness, — this it is that marks how we are
drifting away from our proper anchorage.   We seem to
have reached an age of soft affections and emasculated con-

science, full of pity for pain and disease, of horror at blood and death; but doubting whether any thing is wicked that is not cruel, and reconciling itself even to that on sufficient considerations of advantage. Does the complaint appear too strong and eager? It is, however, solemn and deliberate: for when I look back over a few years, I find there is no sort of personal libertinism, or domestic infidelity, of mercantile dishonesty; no breach of faith in states, no mean dishonor in officials, no shuffling expediency in public life; no kindling of national malignity, no outrage of military atrocity, no extreme of theological jesuitry,—which we have not heard excused by amiable laxity, and shrugged off into the dark; or palliated in books enjoying disgraceful popularity; or defended and admired by statesmen who should elevate and not deprave a nation's mind. Is it then too much to fear, that the new generation may grow up with bewildered vision; without the clear and single eye of conscience full of light; and therefore without the resolute and hardy will of one who plainly sees what he is to avoid and what attain? There is a remarkable intellectual subtlety engaged now-a-days in perplexing men's moral convictions. On the one hand, there is the celebrated doctrine of happiness, ingeniously spun into a logical texture, to entangle those who are neither fine enough to pass through its meshes, nor strong enough to rend them:—the doctrine which assures you that enjoyment is the great end of existence, and is the only real element of worth in the objects of our choice. Of this I will say no more at present, than that it plainly makes all duty a matter of taste, and reduces the distinction between evil and good to the difference between pills and peaches: and that it puts an end to the spirit of moral combat in human life, and metamorphoses the "good soldier of Jesus Christ" into one knows not what strange sort of mock-heroic insincerity. At the feet of Epicurus a man must needs lay the Christian armor down: for one can hardly fancy the most logical of mortals

tying on a breastplate of faith, seeking the battle-field, and
fighting — *to be happy*. But there is a more insidious doctrine than this, largely infused, from the philosophy of a
neighboring country, into the literature of the age ; a doctrine not of the appetites, but of the imagination ; not the
utilitarian, but the æsthetic, contrary of the true faith of
duty. This would persuade us, that the moral faculty is all
very well as *one* of the elements of human nature ; is highly
respectable in its proper place among the rest, and could not
be absent without leaving a grievous gap, interruptive of
the symmetry of the man : but that it must aspire to no more
than this modest participation with its companions in the
perfection of our being ; that it must not presume to meddle
with what does not belong to it, or refuse to make liberal
concessions to the demands of beauty, expediency and self-
love ; and that it would be very narrow-minded, or, in fash-
ionable phrase, very *one-sided*, to try every thing before the
tribunal of this solitary power. Here also, only under more
artful disguise, is a complete denial of all responsibility.
Something, it is true, appears to be allowed to conscience ; a
part is given it to play ; and the point professedly disputed
is not its *existence* with an appropriate function, but its exclusive pretensions and absolute *authority*. Unhappily,
however, when this much is discarded, it is only in semblance
that any thing remains. A moral faculty with a merely concurrent jurisdiction, or from whose decisions there is some
appeal, is a palpable self-contradiction. As well might we
propose to frame a government without any one highest.
Conscience *is* authority, — divine authority, — universal authority ; or it is nothing. It is a right-royal power, that
cannot stoop to serve : dethrone it, and it dies. Not even
can it consent to be acknowledged as a " citizen-king,"
chosen by the suffrages of equals, open to their criticism,
and removable at their pleasure. Either it must be owned
as bearing a sacred and underived sovereignty, against
which argument is impiety, and dreams of redress incur

the penalties of treason; or it will decline the earthly
sceptre and retire to heaven. It reigns not by the ac-
quiescent will of other powers, but is supreme by nature
over all will : nor rules according to any given law, being
itself the fountain of all law, the guardian of order, the
promulgator of right. Its prerogatives are penetrating and
paramount, like God. In the noble words of an old writer,
" Of (moral) Law there can be no less acknowledged, than
that her seat is the bosom of God, her voice the harmony
of the world : all things in heaven and earth do her homage,
the very least as feeling her care, the greatest as not exempted from her power : both angels and men, and creatures of what condition soever, though each in different
sort and manner, yet all with uniform consent, admiring
her as the mother of their peace and joy."*

Let none then prevail with us to think, that there is any
period of life, or any sphere of our activity, or any hour of
our rest, which can escape the range of right and wrong,
and be secluded from the eye of God. Not that we need
grow stiff with the posture of unnatural vigilance, or assume
the circumspection of a scrupulous and anxious mind ; *that*
would only show that the formal and obedient will was yet
hard and dry ; that it was chiselled still into fitting shapes
by the severe tool of care, instead of flowing down into the
graceful moulds of a loving and trustful heart. The rule
of a divine spirit over our whole nature is, in truth, of all
things the most natural ; natural as the blossom that crowns
the tree, without which it would miss half its beauty, and
all its fruit. Nothing can be more offensive to a good mind
than the eagerness to claim, for some portions of our time,
a kind of holiday-escape from the presence of duty and the
consecration of pure affections; to thrust off all noble
thoughts and sacred influences into the most neglected
corner of existence; and drive away religion, as if it were
a haggard necromancer that must some time come, instead

* Hooker's Ecclesiastical Polity : end of B. I.

of a guardian-angel that must never go. It were shameful
to sanction the low-minded sentiment which so often says
of *early life,* that it is the time for enjoyment, and makes
this an excuse for dispensing with every thing else, and
declining all demands upon the hardness of the "good
soldier of Jesus Christ." According to the canons of this
wretched criticism, life would have no secret unity : it
would be no sacred epic, sung throughout by any constant
inspiration ; but a monster of incongruity; its first volume,
a jest-book; its second, a table of interest; and its last, a
mixture of the satire and the liturgy. For my own part, I
can form no more odious image of human life, than a youth
of levity and pleasure, followed by a maturity and age of
severity and pietism. *Both* sights, in this succession, are
alike deplorable : a young soul without wonder, without
reverence, without tenderness, without inspiration : with
superficial mirth, and deep indifference : standing on the
threshold of life's awful temple, with easy smile, without
uncovered head, or bended knee, or breathless listening! Is
that the time, do you say, for enjoyment? Yes; — and for
enthusiasm, for conviction, for depths of affection, and de-
votedness of will : and if there be no tints of heaven in that
morning haze of life, it will be vain to seek them in the
staring light of the later noon. And therefore is that other
sight most questionable, of religion becoming conspicuous
first in mid-life, and presenting itself as the mere precipitate
from the settling of the young blood. Every one may have
noticed examples of men, long spending their best powers,
the mellow heart, the supple thought, the agile will, in the
service of themselves, — at length, with the retreating juices
of nature and sin, baked by the drying heats of life into the
professing saint; — like the rotting-tree, simply decaying
into the grotesque semblance of something human or ghostly,
which is no product of its proper vitality, and does but
mimic other natures when the functions have departed from
its own. Who can avoid looking .on such cases with a

somewhat suspicious eye? If indeed the youth has been intrinsically noble, it is not for us to deny, that some under-current thence, after seeming loss in dark caverns of the earth, may reappear to fertilize the meadows, and raise the sweet after-grass of autumnal life. But it is not often that truth can allow the interpretation thus suggested by hope and charity. Usually, the religion thus embraced is taken up, less because it is heartily believed and trusted, than because a distrust has arisen of every thing else. It is the penance of an uneasy mind; — a memorial for pardon ad-dressed as to an enemy, not the quest of shelter with an Eternal Friend. Vainly shall we attempt to get the wages of a campaign that has not been fought, and seize the crown of mastery, without having "contended lawfully." The repose of honest victory can only follow the strife of noble conflict: and the true peace of God is the appointed pension of "the good soldier of Jesus Christ"

XXXIV.

THE REALM OF ORDER.

———◆———

1 CORINTHIANS XIV. 33.

GOD IS NOT THE AUTHOR OF CONFUSION, BUT OF PEACE, AS IN ALL
CHURCHES OF THE SAINTS.

In the production and preservation of order, all men recognize something that is sacred. We have an intuitive conviction that it is not, at bottom, the earliest condition of things; that whatever is, rose out of some dead groundwork of confusion and nothingness, and incessantly gravitates thitherwards again; and that, without a positive energy of God, no universe could have emerged from the void, or be suspended out of it for an hour. There is no task more indubitably divine than the creation of beauty out of chaos, the imposition of law upon the lawless, and the setting forth of times and seasons from the stagnant and eternal night. And so, the Bible opens with a work of arrangement, and closes with one of restoration; looks round the ancient firmament at first, and sees that all is good, and surveys the new heavens at last, to make sure that evil is no more. Far back in the old eternity, it ushers us into God's presence: and he is engaged in dividing the light from the darkness, and shaping the orbs that determine days and years; turning the vapors of the abyss into the sweet breath of life, teaching the little grass to grow, and trusting the forest tree with the seed that is in itself, to be punctually dropped upon the earth; filling the mountain slope, the sedgy plain, the open air, the hidden deep, with various creatures kept by happy instincts within the limits of his will; and setting over all, in likeness of himself, the adapting intellect, the affectionate spirit, and mysterious conscience, of lordly and reflective man. The birth of order was the first act of God, who rested not till all was blessed and sanctified. And far forward in the eternity to come, we are brought before his face again for judgment. The spoiling of his works, the wild wandering from his will, he will bear no more : the disorder that has gathered together, shall be rectified : he will again divide the darkness from the light; and confusion and wrong, — all that hurts and destroys, — shall be thrust into unknown depths; while wisdom and holiness shall be as the brightness of the firmament and as the stars for ever and ever. As it was when he was Alpha, so will it be when he is Omega. He is one that "loveth pureness" still : and the stream of Providence, — the river that went out of Eden, — however foul with the taint of evil while it takes its course through human history, shall become the river of the water of life, clear as crystal, that nurtures the secret root of all holy and immortal things.

This divine regard for order proceeds from an attribute in which we also are made to participate, and which puts us into awful kindred with God's perfections. Intelligent free-will, — a self-determining mind, — is the only true, originating cause of which we can even conceive; the sole power capable of giving law where there was none before, and of *creating the necessity* by which it is thenceforth obeyed. There was a *will*, before there was a *must*. Nothing else, we feel assured, could avail, amid a boundless primeval unsettledness, to mark out a certain fixed method of existence and no other, and make it to be; could draw forth an actual, defined, and amenable universe from the sphere of infinite possibilities. The indeterminate, the chaotic, lies in our thought behind and around the determinate and constituted ; and to sketch a positive system and bid its vivid lines of order shine on the dark canvas of negation, is the special

office of the free self-moving spirit, whereby God lifts us up
above nature into the image of himself. Hence we too, in
proportion as we approach him, shall put our hand to a like
task ; shall organize the loose materials that, touched by a
creative ˙will, may cease to be without form and void ;
shall set out our expanse of years into periods ruled by the
lights of duty, and refreshed by the shades of prayer ; shall
mould every shapeless impulse, subdue every rugged difficulty, fill every empty space of opportunity with good, and
breathe a living soul into the very dust and clod of our
existence. As " God is not the author of confusion, but of
peace," so the service of God infuses a spirit of method and
proportion into the outward life and the inward mind ; and
pure religion is *a principle of universal order*.

No two things indeed can be more at variance with each
other than a *devout* and an *unregulated* life. Devotion ˙is
holy regulation, guiding hand and heart ; a surrender of
self-will, — that main source of uncertainty and caprice, —
and a loving subordination to the only rule that cannot
change. Devotion is the steady attraction of the soul towards one luminous object, discerned across the passionless
infinite, and drawing thoughts, deeds, affections, into an
orbit ́silent, seasonal, and accurately true. In a mind submitted to the touch of God, there is a certain rhythm of
music, which, however it may swell into the thunder or sink
into a sigh, has still a basis of clear unbroken melody. The
discordant starts of passion, the whimsical snatches of appetite, the inarticulate whinings of discontent, are never
heard : and the spirit is like an organ, delivered from the
tumbling of chance pressures on its keys, and given over to
the hand of a divine skill. Nay, so inexorable is the demand of religion for order, that it shrinks from any one
allowed irregularity, as the musician from a constant mistake in the performance of some heavenly strain. Its perpetual effort is to prevail over all things loose and turbid ;
to swallow up the elements of confusion in human life ; and

banish chance from the soul, as God excludes it from the universe. It is quite impossible that an idle, floating spirit can ever look with clear eye to God; spreading its miserable anarchy before the symmetry of the creative Mind; in the midst of a disorderly being, that has neither centre nor circumference, kneeling beneath the glorious sky, that everywhere has both; and from a life that is *all* failure, turning to the Lord of the silent stars, of whose punctual thought it is, that "not one faileth." The heavens, with their everlasting faithfulness, look down on no sadder contradiction, than the sluggard and the slattern at their prayers.

To maintain the sacred governance of life is to recognize and preserve the due *rank* of all things within us and without. For there *is* a system of ranks extending through the spiritual world of which we form a part. The faculties and affections of the single mind are no democracy of principles, each of which, in the determinations of the will, is to have equal suffrage with the rest; but an orderly series, in which every member has a right divine over that below. The individuals composing the communities of men do not arrange themselves into a dead level of spirits, in which none are above and none beneath; but there are centres of natural majesty that break up the mass into groups and proportions that you cannot change. And man himself, by the highest will, is inserted between things of which he is lord, and obligations which he must serve. In short, the hierarchy of nature is episcopalian throughout: and in conforming to its order, the active part of our duty consists in this: that we must rule and keep under our hand whatever is beneath us; assigning to every thing its due place.

The whole scheme of our voluntary actions, all that we do from morning to night of every day, is beyond doubt entrusted to our control. No power, without our consent, can share the monarchy of this realm, or constrain us to lift a hand or speak a word, where resolution bids us be still and silent. And from our inmost consciousness we do know, that, whenever we will, we can *make ourselves* execute whatever we approve, and strangle in its birth whatever we abhor. To-morrow morning, if you choose to take up a spirit of such power, you may rise like a soul without a past; fresh for the future as an Adam untempted yet; disengaged from the manifold coil of willing usage, and with every link of guilty habit shaken off. I know indeed that you *will not;* that no man ever will; but the hindrance is with yourself alone. The coming hours are open yet, — pure and spotless receptacles for whatever you may deposit there; pledged to no evil, secure of no good; neither mortgaged to greedy passion, nor given to generous toil. There they lie in non-existence still; ready to be organized by a creative spirit of beauty, or made foul with deformity and waste. Perhaps it is this thought, this secret sense of moral contingency, that gives to so simple a thing as the beat of a pendulum, or the forward start of the finger on the dial, a solemnity beyond expression. The gliding heavens are less awful at midnight than the ticking clock. Their noiseless movement, undivided, serene, and everlasting, is as the flow of divine duration, that cannot affect the place of the eternal God. But these sharp strokes, with their inexorably steady intersections, so agree with our successive thoughts, that they seem like the punctual stops counting off our very souls into the past; — the flitting messengers that dip for a moment on our hearts, then bear the pure or sinful thing irrevocably away; — light with mystic hopes as they arrive, charged with sad realities as they depart. So passes, and we cannot stay it, our only portion of opportunity: the fragments of that blessed chance which has been travelling to us from all eternity, are dropping quickly off. Let us start up and live: here come the moments that cannot be had again; some few may yet be filled with imperishable good.

There is no conscious power like that which a wise and Christian heart asserts, when resolved to absorb the dead matter of its existence, and from the elements of former waste and decay to put forth a new and vernal life. The accurate economy of instants, the proportionate distribution of duties, the faithful observance of law, as it is an exercise of strength, so gives a sense of strenuous liberty. Compared with this, how poor a delusion is the spurious freedom which is the idler's boast! He says that he has his time at his disposal: but in truth, he is at the disposal of his time. No novelty of the moment canvasses him in vain: any chance suggestion may have him; whiffed as he is hither and thither like a stray feather on the wandering breeze. The true stamp of manhood is not on him, and therefore the image of godship has faded away: for he is lord of nothing, not even of himself; his will is ever waiting to be tempted, and conscience is thrust out among the mean rabble of candidates that court it. The wing of resolution, mighty to lift us nearer God, is broken quite, and there is nothing to stay the downward gravitation of a nature passive and heavy too. And so, first a weak affection for persons supplants the sense of right: to be itself, in turn, destroyed by a baser appetite for things. This woful declension is the natural outgoing of those who presume to try an unregulated life. A systematic organization of the personal habits, devised in moments of devout and earnest reason, is a necessary means, amid the fluctuations of the spirit, of giving to the better mind its rightful authority over the worse. Those only will neglect it, who either do not know their weakness, or have lost all healthy reliance on their strength.

It is a part then of the faithfulness and freedom of a holy mind, to keep the whole range of outward action under severe control: to administer the hours in full view of the vigilant police of conscience; and to introduce even into the lesser materials of life the precision and concinnity which are the natural symbols of a pure and constant spirit. And it belongs to the humility of a devout heart, not to trust itself to the uncertain ebb and flow of thought, and float opportunity away on the giddy waters of inconstancy; but to arrange a method of life in the hour of high purpose and clear insight, and then compel the meaner self to work out the prescription of the nobler. Yet this, after all, though an essential check to our instability, is but the beginning of wisdom. The mere distribution of action in quantity, however well proportioned, does not fulfil the requisites of a Christian order. This surveyor's work,— this partitioning out the superficies of life, and marking off the orchard and the field, the meadow and the grove,— will make no grass to grow, will open no blossom and mature no seed. The seasonal culture of the soul requires all this; yet may yield poor produce, when this is done. Without the deeper symmetry of the spirit, the harmonious working of living powers there, the boundaries of action, however neat, will be but a void framework, enclosing barrenness and sand. Despise not the ceremonial of the moral life; it is our needful speech and articulation; but oh! mistake it not for the true and infinite worship that should breathe through it. Mere mechanism, however perfect, has this misfortune, that it cannot set fast its own loose screws, but rather shakes them into more frightful confusion; till the power, late so smooth, works only crash and ruin, and goes headlong back to chaos. And so it is where there is nothing profounder than the systematizing faculty in the organiza-tion of a man's life. Destitute of adaptive and restorative energy, with no perception of a spiritual order that may remain above disturbance and express itself through ob-structions all the more, interruptions bewilder and upset him. Ill health in himself or the afflictions of others, that stop his projects and give him pause by a touch on his affections, irritate and weary him; he grows dizzy with the inroads on his schemes, gives up the count so hopefully begun, and runs down in rapid discords. The soul of Christian order has in it something quite different from this; more like the blessed force of nature that consumes its withered leaves as punctually as they fall, and so makes the *spread* of decay a thing impossible : that has so unwearied an appetite for the creation of beauty and productiveness, that it makes no complaint of rottenness and death, but draws from them the sap of life, and weaves again the foliage and the fruit. No *less* a vital spontaneity than this is needed in the Christian soul ; for in human life, as in external nature, the elements of corruption and disorder are always accumulating; and unless they are to breed pestilence, must be kept down and effectually absorbed. As in science, so in practical existence, our theory or ideal must ever be framed upon assumptions only partially true. The conditions required for its fulfilment will never be present *all at once and all alone:* so that the realization will be but approximate ; and a constant tension of the soul is needed to press it nearer and nearer to the ultimate design. For want of a religious source, an exact apparent order in the life may coexist with an essential disorder secreted within. Are we not conscious that so it is, whenever the toil of our hands, though punctually visited, receives no consent of our hearts ; when the spirit flies with heavy wing from reach to reach of time, and, like Noah's dove, seeing only wave after wave of a dreary flood, finds no rest for the sole of its foot, till it gets back to the ark of its narrow comforts? Is it not a plain inversion of the true order of things, when we do our work for the sake of the following rest, instead of accepting our rest as the preparative for work ? And while this continues to be the case, there will be a hidden aching, a dark corroding speck within the soul, which no outward method or proportion can ever charm away. Nor can the precision of the will be even sustained at all without the symmetry of the affections. As well might you think to set your broken compass right by hand :

if it be foul and stiff, swinging and trembling no more in obedience to its mysterious attraction, its blessed guidance is gone; and after the first straight line of your direction, you sail upon the chances of destruction.

To prevent this evil, of method just creeping up the lower part of life, and passing no farther, no positive rule, from the very nature of the case, can well be given. We can only say that, besides subjecting whatever is beneath us, there is also this passive part of Christian order, that we must surrender ourselves entirely to what is above us; and having put all lesser things into their place, we must then take and keep our own. Could indeed this proportion of the affections invariably remain, it would supersede all our mechanism, and take care of the outward harmony: and we should have no need to apply the rules of a Franklin to the spirit of a Christ. But even short of this blessed emancipation, we should rise into a higher atmosphere; escaping the wretched thraldom of reluctant duties; and should yield a free consent, through love, to that which else were irksome; quietly depositing ourselves on every work that brings its sacred claim, and moving in it, instead of writhing to get beyond it. They tell you that habit reconciles you in time to many unwelcome things. Let us not trust to' this alone. Custom indeed sweetens the rugged lot when the cheerful soul *is in it:* it does but embitter it the more, when the soul *stays out of it.* But when harshnesses are borne, and even spontaneously embraced, for the sake of God who hints them to our conscience, a perfect agreement ensues between the spirit and the letter of our life. We feel no weariness; delivered now from the intolerable burthen of flagging affections. We are disturbed by no ambitions; conscious of no jealousies of other men; for competition has no place in things divine: and even in lower matters, it is, to the thoughtful and devout, but a quiet interrogation of Providence; and the true heart that prefers the question cannot be discontented with the answer. We cease to desire a change : we feel that life affords no time for restlessness ; that in persistency is our only hope : and a blessed conservatism of spirit comes over us, that claims nothing but simple leave to go on serving and loving still. And so existence, to the devout, becomes, not confused, but peaceful, like a service in the churches of the saints.

23

XXXV.

CHRISTIAN DOCTRINE OF MERIT.

Luke xvii. 10.

SO LIKEWISE YE, WHEN YE SHALL HAVE DONE ALL THOSE THINGS WHICH
ARE COMMANDED YOU, SAY, "WE ARE UNPROFITABLE SERVANTS; WE
HAVE DONE THAT WHICH WAS OUR DUTY TO DO."

To a thoughtful interpreter of human nature, nothing so
plainly reveals the hidden principle of a man's life, as the
estimation in which he holds himself. Whether the standard which guides him be conventional, moral, or divine;
whether the invisible presence that haunts him be that of
the world's opinion, or his own self-witness, or the eye of
God, — may be seen in the contented self-delusion, or intelligent self-knowledge, or noble self-forgetfulness, which
reveal themselves through his natural language and de-
meanor. Too often you meet with a man who manifestly
looks at himself with the eyes of others; and those too, not
the wise who are above him, but the associates on the same
level or the inferiors beneath it, to whom he may be supposed an object of conspicuous attention. He stands well
with himself, because he stands well with them : and nothing
would make him angry with himself, except the forfeiture
of his position among them. Their expectations from him
being satisfied, or somewhat more, he thinks his work is
done, and turns loose into a holiday life, to do as he likes
at his own unlicensed will. Their sentiments are the mirror
by which he dresses up his life; as his self-complacency is
but the reflection of their smiles, his self-reproach is but an
imitation of their frowns, — mere regret for error, not re-

morse for wrong;—overheard in the cry of vexation, "Fool that I am!" not in the whisper of penitence, "God be merciful to me a sinner!" He every way impresses you with the conviction that, if nothing were demanded of him, nothing would be given; that he simply comes into the terms imposed by men as conditions of peace and good fellowship; and, did all men resemble him, the cynic's theory would be not far wrong, that morality is but the conciliation of opinion, and society a company for mutual protection.

However, if all men were such as he, and brought no strictly moral element into human affairs, it is plain that this much-vaunted power of "public opinion" could never get formed. Till somebody has a conscience, nobody can feel a law. Accordingly, we everywhere meet with a higher order of men, who not only comprehend the wishes, but respect the rights, of others : who are ruled, not by expectation without, but by the sense of obligation within : who do, not the agreeable, but the just; and, even amid the storm of public rage, can stand fast, with rooted foot and airy brow, like the granite mountain in the sea. Noble however as this foundation of uprightness always is, there may arise from it a self-estimate too proud and firm. If the stern consciousness of right have no softening of human affection and kindling of diviner aspiration, it will give the lofty sense of personal merits that makes the stoic, and misses the saint. To walk beneath the porch is still infinitely less than to kneel before the cross. We do nothing well, till we learn our worth; nothing best, till we forget it. And this will not be till, besides being built into the real veracious laws of this world, we are also conscious of the inspection of another: till we live, not only fairly among equals, but submissively under the Most High; and while casting the shadow of a good life on the scene below, lie in the light of vaster spheres above. Virtue, feeling its deep base in earth, lifts its head aloft : sanctity, conscious of its far-off glimpse at heaven, bends it low. And yet, outwardly, they are not different, but the same: one visible character may correspond with either; only standing amid relations incomplete in the one case, completed in the other. They are but as the different aspects of the granite isle of which we spake. Let clouds roof out the heaven and shut a darkness in, and its gray crags *look down*, with the grandeur of a gloomy monarch, sheltering the thunder and defying the flood. Sweep the rack away, and throw open the hemisphere of morning air, and it lies low in the soft light and sleeps with *upturned* gaze, like a sunny child of deep and sky, cradled on the summer sea.

How is it that minds, equally engaged in the outward service of duty, think of themselves so differently? Whence the self-reliance, bordering on self-exaggeration, of a Zeno, a Franklin, a Bentham?—the divine humility of a Pascal, a Howard, a Channing, and of the Master whose lineaments they variously reflect? The answer will present itself spontaneously, if we inquire into the true doctrine of *merit*. This word, which has its equivalent in every language, expresses a meaning familiar, I suppose, to all men; and by referring to a few common modes of speech and thought, the contents of that meaning may be unfolded and defined.

There is no merit in *paying one's debts*. To make such an act a ground of praise infallibly betrays a base mind and a dishonest community. This cannot well be denied by any clear-thoughted man, free from the influence of passion. Whatever be the practice of society with respect to the insolvent, surely it is a mean perversion of the natural moral sense to imagine that his temporary inability, or length of delay, can cancel one iota of his obligation: these things only serve to increase its stringency; tardy reparation being a poor substitute for punctual fidelity. I am far from denying that circumstances of special and blameless misfortune may justify him in accepting the voluntary mercy of friends willing to "forgive him all that debt." But whoever avails himself of mere legal release as a moral exemption, is a candidate for infamy in the eyes of all uncorrupted men. The law necessarily interposes to put a period to the controversy between debtor and creditor, and prohibit the further struggle between the arts of the one and the cruelty of the other: but it cannot annul their moral relation. Obligation cannot, any more than God, grow old and die: till it is obeyed, it stops in the present tense, and represents the eternal *now*. Time can wear no duty out. Neglect may smother it out of sight: opportunity may pass, and turn it from our guardian angel into our haunting fiend : but while it yet remains possible, it clings to our identity, and refuses to let us go. It was the first sign of the rich publican's change from the heathen to the Christian mind that he "restored four-fold" the gains that were not his. And our conversion yet remains to be wrought, until, instead of applauding as of high desert the man who repairs at length the mischief he has done, we condemn to shame every one who can buy an indulgence with an unpaid debt.

Again, there is no merit in *speaking or acting the simple truth ;* in keeping one's promissory word, and doing one's stipulated work. In this there is no more than all men are entitled to expect from us. It is their manifest right : and if, instead of respecting its demands, we give them falsehoods with our lips and life, we not merely lose all claim to their praise, but, sinking far from innocence, become obnoxious to their reproach. From this rule there are, no doubt, many apparent departures in the practical conduct of human affairs ; and we often make it a theme for public eulogy that a citizen has lived among us with unbroken pledge and faithful achievement. This, however, is hardly an example of the strict and unmixed judgment of conscience, but rather a concession from that pity and fear with which we look on human nature tried with so long a

strife.   It springs up on the retrospect of an *entire life* with
its visible temptations prostrated and its strength triumphant; and would be put to silence by a single instance of
evident bad faith.   Moreover, in cases of such unviolated
truth, there is always something more than simple absti-
nence from wrong.   They imply, by their very persistency,
a force of character, which cannot have spent itself in mere
standing still, however firm.   The man who, under all
deflecting importunities, can keep an immovable footing
against the wrong, has a life within him that, when the assault is over, will push on the victories of right: and we
justly accept the negative strength, as symptomatic of the
positive power of conscience.   On this account it is that we
honor him who never lies, nor cheats, nor stoops to mean
evasions; not that it would be otherwise than shameful if
he did; but to be throughout clear of all such shame is the
sign that he has not a passive, but a productive, soul: and
we praise him for what he is, rather than for what he is
not.

Once more : there is no merit in *restraining the appetites
from excess ;* in the avoidance of intemperance and waste;
in freedom from wild and self-destructive passions, that bear
the soul away on a whirlwind it cannot rule.   We expect
of every man, that he shall remain master of himself ; and
we feel that he does not reach the natural level of his humanity, unless he governs what he knows to be beneath
him, and, as "a faithful and wise steward," manifests a
moral prudence in administering the domain of his own
spirit.   A well-ordered economy of the personal habits
brings so evident a return of value to those who practise it,
and is so fit a consequence of the natural rights of reason
over the will, that it is rather the assumed ground and
indispensable condition, than the actual essence, of any
excellence we can honor and revere.   If ever we bestow
upon it more than a cold commendation, it is in cases where
it may be taken as a pledge of something further, that does

not directly meet the eye : where it appears, for instance, amid examples of guilty license, and inducements to a low and lax career ; and can only have grown up by the triumph of pure and divine energy within, under the obstructions of circumstance and the contradictions of men. But except when we thus find some saint amid the brood of Circe, we deem it but poor praise to a human soul, that it is not like the brutes, the creature of impulse and slave of chance affection.

From these instances it is easy to collect one of the essential characteristics of all merit. There is no room for it in the sphere of personal and prudential conduct : it can arise only in the case of duty to others. And *there* it obtains no admission, so long as we merely satisfy the claims of justice, and comply with that which law or honor have written in the bond. Failing in this, we incur guilt and demerit; *not* failing, we are entitled to no praise. The first entrance of merit, according to the sentiments of all men, is where our performance *goes beyond the acknowledged rights of another ;* and we spontaneously offer what human obligation could not ask.

There is a second characteristic admitted to be essential to every meritorious act. It must be *all our own*, the spontaneous product of our individual will and affection. If in the delirium of fever, or the fancies of somnambulism, you are led, by the command of some guide who wields you at his word, to put forth a deed of outward charity, you will take no more credit for it, than for the heroic achievements you may accomplish in your dreams. You had no more to do with the act than with the sin of Lucifer. You were not the agent in the case ; you were only the stage on which the phenomenon took place. And show me, in any instance, that a man is not the originating cause of his own apparent deed, but, in this manifestation of him, only an effect of some extraneous power ; show me that he would never have done the kindly thing, had he not been put up to it by a force that pulls the wires of his obedient mind; show me even, that he had some personal end in view, and proposed to make an investment in generosity; — and it is in vain that you ask for my admiration: as soon could I respect the industry of a clock, or the energy of a galvanized limb. If the prompter once peeps out, I know the whole to be a piece of acting, and the illusion of reality is instantaneously gone; only, instead of the avowedly fictitious, I have the insidiously false, and am the dupe, not of professed entertainment, but of real deception. *Spontaneity* then is an essential to each man's good desert; and in precise proportion to the partnership there may be in his agency, will be the diminution of his share,

Here then we have the two requisites and characteristics of every meritorious act: it must overlap the limits of mere justice, and go beyond the strict rights of the being to whom it is directed: and it must be all our own. Take away either of these properties, and merit disappears.

Now it is the characteristic of all moral systems, as such, that they allow the reality of human merit; of all religious systems, as such, and of the simply religious heart that has no system at all, that they disown it. The different forms of faith, however, do this in different ways; and the following distinction is to be carefully observed: — the spurious representations of Christianity take away all demerit at the same time; while the true have in them this mystery, that while they remove the lustre of merit, the shadow of demerit remains.

Every Fatalist or Predestinarian scheme destroys merit by denying that our actions are our own, and referring them wholly to powers of which we are not lords but slaves. We are ourselves, it is contended, true creators of nothing; but creatures, absolutely disposed of by mightier forces, like clay whirled upon the potter's wheel, and moulded by his hand; — determinate products turned out from the great workshop of the universe, with functions purely mechanical, like a more complex kind of tool. That we *seem* to have a self-moving power, to put forth spontaneous and underived effort belonging wholly to our personality, is, in the view of this doctrine, an illusion of our short-sightedness, due only to our ignorance or forgetfulness of the prime mover of our energies. All this, like the heaving of a steam-engine, or the laboring of a ship at sea, is done *for* and *upon* us, not *by* us: and when, in our remorse for the past, and our resolves for the future, we assume that we are in a responsible trust for our own spiritual state, we are dupes of an ignorant delusion, at which philosophic spirits stand by and smile. Fast locked within the series of natural effects, we are the ground on which phenomena appear for their display, but not their cause; the inventor and exhibitor stands behind the scenes, and shows us off. Life, in short, is but the long phantasm of the sleep-walker; replete with the consciousness of nimble thoughts, and vivid passions, and precarious glories, and strenuous deeds, — a perfect conflict of awful forces to him that is within it; but to the eye of waking truth outside, still and passive as the sculptured slumber of a marble image; a casket of mimic battles and ideal woes. With the particular sources of fallacy in this scheme, I have not now any direct concern. I merely wish to point out that, as it is destructive of any proper *agency* in the human being, it annihilates at once merit and de-merit; sinks man from a *person* into a *thing;* loses all moral distinctions, by representing character as an incident in one's lot, like health or disease, the color of the hair or the robustness of the limbs; and renders *obligation* altogether impossible. And so, along with the inflation of self-righteousness, which it certainly excludes, this scheme carries away also the healthful sorrows of remorse. Its humility is not the moral consciousness of unworthiness of character, but the physical sense of incapacity of nature; and the disciple looks on himself, not as the fallen angel, but as the ennobled animal.

Now, with all this Christianity appears to me to stand in strongest contrast. It annihilates merit, not by reducing obligation to nothing, but by raising it to infinitude. Leaving us the originating causes of our own acts, as we had always supposed ourselves to be, — confirming us fully in the partnership we thus enjoy with the creative energy of God, — it resists all encroachment on our responsibility. But then, it takes away from us the *other* element of merit: It renders it impossible for our performance ever to overlap and exceed the claims upon our will. For it changes the relations in which, with a conscience simply looking round over the level of our equals, we had felt ourselves to stand. Putting us *under heaven* as well as *upon the earth*, within the presence and sanctuary of God, while we are at the hearths of our friends and in the streets with our fellows, it swallows up our duties to them in one immense sphere of duty to him. Into all our transactions with them, it introduces a new and awful partner, to whom we cannot say, "Thou hast no business between them and us; if we satisfy each other, stand thou aloof!" As the holy prompter of *our* conscience, and guardian of *their* claims, he must be omnipresent with his interpositions. To him therefore our religion makes over all their rights; and thereby not only consecrates and preserves them, but gives them boundless extension. Instantly, we discern as a true demand upon us a thousand things which before we had fancied to be at our discretion, and to redound to our praise, if we conceded them. Charity merges into justice; love and pity are offerings that may not be withheld; and every former gift becomes a debt. All good that is not impossible is a thing now due, and is to be performed, not like eye-service unto men, but as to God: a solemn transfer of responsibilities has taken place, and all our doings are with the Highest now: and beyond his acknowledged rights we can never go, so as to deserve any thing of him. Towards him, obligation is strictly infinite: it covers all our *possibilities of achievement:* for, the very circumstance of any good and noble thing *being possible,* and *revealed to our hearts as such,* constitutes and creates it a duty. Thus suggested, it is one of the trusts committed to us by God, — the work which he, the great spiritual Artificer, puts into his true laborer's hands to execute; to keep the material, and not weave the texture, of his designs, were a false and unfaithful thing. Nor, when we have completed it, can we establish any title to even the most insignificant reward. For what are wages after all? Are they not, in effect, the laborer's share of the produce created, only paid in anticipation of the finished task, — *an advance* founded on his right to subsist while he toils? And do they not cancel all his claim to participate afterwards in the product of his skill? This perpetual loan by which he lives, and which he works off by exertion ever renewed, he cheerfully accepts in discharge of all his rights. And what recompenses are ever prepaid so freely as those of God? He waits not for a week's, not even for a moment's industry, but is beforehand with us every way. We have never earned *the living* which he gives us in this world; we cannot plead that we have a right to be. The field and the faculty of work are alike furnished forth by him. A little while ago, and we were not here; a little while again, and we shall be gone from our place: and have we not then been wholly set up at our post in this universe by our great Taskmaster? and does he not, by the fact of existence itself, make us his perpetual debtors? Yes: the successive moments, as they pass, are the counters of his constant payment; which we can neither reckon nor refuse, but only hasten to seize and to employ. And so, it is impossible for us ever to overtake his advances. With our fastest speed they fly before us still, like the shadow which his light behind us casts, only lengthening as we go, till it stretches over the brink of time, and covers the abyss of eternity. Resign we then every high pretension, and stand with

bended and uncovered head of self-renunciation; grateful
for every blessing God may send; eager for all the work
he may appoint; but saying, when all is done, " we are unprofitable servants; we have done that " alone, — and alas!
far less, — " which was our duty to do."

XXXVI.

THE CHILD'S THOUGHT.

1 Corinthians XIII. 11.

WHEN I WAS A CHILD, I SPAKE AS A CHILD, I UNDERSTOOD AS A CHILD, I THOUGHT AS A CHILD ; BUT WHEN I BECAME A MAN, I PUT AWAY CHILDISH THINGS.

The noblest prophets and apostles have been children once; lisping the speech, laughing the laugh, thinking the thought of boyhood. Undistinguished as Paul then was amid the crowd, unless by more earnest and confiding eye, there was something passing within him of which, it would seem, he preserved, in the kindling moments of his manly soul, the memory and the trace. And there are few men, I suppose, who do not at times send back a gentle glance into their early days; not only looking upon faces vanished now, and listening to voices that have become as distant music to the mind; but remembering the throbbing pulse of their own hopes, the strain of heroic purpose, and the awful step of wonder unabated yet. Between ourselves and the apostle, however, there is an expressive difference here. We usually turn from the past with a sigh, and a secret sense of irrevocable loss; he, with hands clasped in thanksgiving, as in the glory of an infinite gain. We envy our own children, and would fain put back the shadow on our dial, to feel again the morning sun that shines so softly upon them; he springs with glad escape out of hours too recent from the night, and welcomes the increasing glow of an eternal day. To us, the chief beauty, the only sanctities of life, are apt to appear in

the shelter of our early years : they are like a home that we
have deserted, a love that we have lost, a faith cheated from
our hearts. As we ascend the mountain-chain of life, so
long a towering mystery to our uplifted eye, they lie beneath
as the green hollow of the Alpine valley; to whose native
fields return is cut off for ever; whence the incense of our
faith went up straight to heaven, like the first smoke from
the village hearths into the clear, calm air; whose sunny
grass thaws the very heart of us, nipped by the glacier's
keenest breath ; whose stately trees, still dotting the ground
with points of shade, seem to leave us more exposed amid
the scant and stunted growths of this wintry height; and
whose church-peal, floating faintly on the ear, makes us
shudder all the more at the bleak winds near, booming in
icy caverns, or whispering to the plains of silent snow. But
Paul, though not untouched perhaps by the poetry of childhood, regarded it without regret. With him, its inspiration
had risen, not declined ; its unconscious heaven had not
retreated, but pressed closer on his heart, till it had mingled
with his nature, and articulately spoken there. He was not
going up into life to lose himself amid the relentless elements, and get buried by the avalanche of years in chasms
of fate; but, to conquer Nature and look down ; to stand
upon her higher and higher watch-towers, till he found a
way clear into the climate of the skies; and, like Moses on
Mount Nebo, with " his eye not dim," could discern, at the
pointing of God, " the whole land " of life " unto the utmost
sea ; " — and then pass where no horizon bounds the view.
We, too often, in putting away childish things, part with
the wrong elements; losing the heavenly insight, keeping
the earthly darkness. We put away the guileless mind, the
pure vision, the simple trust, the tender conscience; and
reserve the petty scale of thought, the hasty will, the love
of toys and strife. Paul put away only the ignorance and
littleness of childhood, bearing with him its freshness, its
truth, its God, into the grand work of his full age, And

hence, while our religion lies somewhere near our cradle, and is a kind of sacred memory, his lived on to speak for itself instead of being talked about. It fought all his conflicts: it took the weight out of his chains: it condensed the lightning of his pen; and kindled the whole furnace of his glorious nature.

There is a natural difference between the religion of childhood, of youth, and of maturity, which appears to be very much overlooked in our expectations and practices with regard to each. The human mind is not the same in all periods of its history : its wants, its faculties, its affections, shift their relative proportions, as that history proceeds: and a power, which, like religion, is to hover over it continually, and to lift it by a constant attraction, must not always suspend itself over the same feelings, and offer one invariable representation. Its resources are infinite : its beauty is inexhaustible; its truth dipped in every color into which the light of heaven is broken by the prism of thought: and it must adapt itself to the characteristics of every period which needs its sway. Nor is there the least art or cunning policy implied in this; but only a soul of natural sympathy, to take on it at will the burdens of the child, the youth, the man; to see their love, their fear, their admiration; to doubt their doubts, and pray their prayers; and simply to avoid the cruelty of offering the garment of grief to the spirit of joy, and singing songs to the heavy heart. Some features belonging to the early period of life, which should be borne in mind in the conduct of religious education, I would briefly indicate.

Childhood is emphatically the period of safe instincts ; permitting it to try for awhile the unreflective life of creatures less than human. Only the ingenuity of artificial corruption can spoil them. In themselves, they are incapable of excess, and offer few temptations to wrong, that are not adequately counteracted by some balancing affection. They simply ask to be let alone, and suffer no perversion :

give them room to open out; use no premature compression
to drive them back; and they will check each other, and
find a fairer proportion than can be given by your rules.
In these shrewd days, in which it has become the cleverest
thing to suspect the Devil everywhere, and God nowhere, it
is thought romantic to believe in the innocence of childhood; pardonable perhaps in a woman, but an intolerable
softness in a man. And possibly it is, if applied to the
actual children, once born in the image of God, but long
ago twisted into our miserable likeness, by the sight of our
luxuries, the contagion of our selfishness, the hearing of our
lies: possibly it is, if applied to those whom the church
teaches to blaspheme their own nature, to confess a sham
guilt, and prate of an unreal rescue from an unfelt danger.
For the world is often right in fact, though wrong in truth:
and the church has acted with a cunning theology in this
matter; having first spoiled all the children with its inani-
ties, and then produced them in its court in evidence of
original depravity. But if both world and church will
only learn what the child's simple presence may teach,
instead of teaching what he cannot innocently learn, the
truth may dawn upon them, that he seldom requires to. be
led, — only not to be *misled*. A reform in the nursery will
change the creed of Christendom; no hierarchy can stand
against it; and the pinafore of the child will be more than
a match for the frock of the bishop and the surplice of the
priest. If it be romance to look with something of reverent
affection at the being not yet remote from God, it is at least
a romance that has come to us on a voice most full of grace
and truth: it breathes fresh from the hills of Nazareth; and
its emblem is that wondering infant in the arms of Christ,
visible thence over all the earth, as the chosen watch at the
gate of heaven. Whatever be thought of this doctrine, it
cannot be denied that there is, in early years, an openness
to habit, which, while it quickly punishes our neglect, as
quickly answers to our care. No ready-made obstruction,

no ruined work, is given us to undo. Wise direction alone is needed; and such frame-work and moulding for the life as we may advisedly construct, will receive the growing nature as its silent occupant. Nay, this is largely true, not only of the acts of the hand, but of the methods and persuasions of the mind : for childhood has a *ready faith*, that may be most blessedly used or most wickedly abused; a faith so open to the sense of God, that almost unspoken, and as by look of holy sympathy, it may be given ; so eager, that it will seize on all the aliment of thought within its reach ; so trustful, that it feels no difficulty, and will cause you none. Your problem of guidance will therefore be, not so much to evade present embarrassments, as to prevent the shock of *future* perplexities, that *must* arise, when finite thought attempts to grasp an infinite faith, and reason descends to find its own ground, which it ever carries with it as it dives. Nor is there any positive way of avoiding such a crisis of the soul. Only, there is a negative wisdom in not shutting up the faith ; in *leaving a place* for future acquisitions, and verge enough for the larger operations of the mind. Meanwhile, one thing is to be immediately and always observed. Through the susceptibility of the religious principle, you may make the child *believe in* any God, from the Egyptian cat to the inspirer of Christ. But there is only one God that can really possess him with an awful love ; namely, such a one as seems to him the highest and the best. And of this there can be no constant conception through life; it changes as experience deepens, and affections open and die away. Yours cannot be the same as his : and if you speak without sympathy, if you forget your different latitude of mind, you may repel rather than instruct, and give root to a choking thorn of hatred, instead of a fruitful seed of love. If the name of God is to be sweet and solemn to young hearts, it must stand for *their* highest, not for *ours:* and many a phrase, rich and deep in tone to us, must be shunned as sure to jar on spirits differ-

24

ently attuned. Oh how many obstructions have not veracious men to remove ere they can find their true religion !
How long do they say their prayers, before they pray, and
hear and speak of holy things without a touch of worship !
How many years did we look up into only damp, uncom-
fortable clouds, that did but wet and darken life, ere the
pure breeze set in, and swept the curtain from the eternal
sky, and mingled us with the genuine night, and set us eye
to eye with the watchful stars ! If when I thought as a
child, I had also dared to speak as a child, should I not
have said, "Talk to me no more; I hate the name of God"?
— yet, not the God that ever lives and loves, but the stiff
idol of the catechism, looking rigorous from the narrow
niche of a decaying Puritanism. Not the God, whose kiss
is in the light, whose gladness on the riding sea, whose
voice upon the storm ; who shapes the little grass, and
hides in the forest, and rustles in the shower; who bends
the rainbow, and blanches the snow: for children delight
in nature, and from wonder at its beauty easily slide into
adoration of its Lord. Not the God, who moulded the orbs
that Newton weighed, and traced the curves he measured,
and blended the colors he untwined; who was on the earth
when no man was, and buried the tribes now dug from the
mountains and the plains; who thinks at this moment every
thought that science shall develop, and reads the folded
scroll of future history : for children delight in knowledge,
and will kneel with joy to Him, with whom it is at once
concentred and diffused. Not certainly the God, who
looked out upon our life and death, our strife and sorrow,
through the soul of Christ; who can no more abide the
hypocrite and the unjust that walk the streets to-day, than
Jesus the whited sepulchres of old ; who lets no widow's
mite escape his eye, no grateful heart, though of the leper
and the heretic, go without its praise: for children love
justice, mercy, and truth, and will trust themselves freely to
Him in whom they dwell beyond degree.

Nor is it only in its conception of God, that the faith of the child must differ from that of the man. Its moral element is also peculiar. To him religion, applied to life, presents itself exclusively as a *law*, — and a law that there is no serious difficulty in *perfectly obeying*. Prescribing a clear scheme of duty, and a natural and delightful state of affection, it seems to him so simple and practicable, that he is full of courage, goes forth with joyous step, and with confiding look gazes straight upon the open countenance of the future. He cannot understand the penitential strains that float from the older world around him : what have these people been about, that they have so much evil to bewail ? They appear to him very worthy, nay altogether faithful and meritorious, Christians ; and it is very strange they should speak so grievously to God, and stand before him with a culprit air and streaming tears. In all this, though it has no shadow of pretence, he cannot join ; it comes of a deeper truth of nature than he yet has reached. His circle of life is narrow, and his idea of life lies quiet within it : the thing which he thinks in his conscience in the morning, he can do with sedulous hand before night. His conception of duty is legal and human only, not spiritual and divine : it has not yet burst into transcendent aspiration, whose infinite glory in front spreads the inseparable shadow of sorrow and ill behind. Sin therefore remains to him a dreadful image from some foreign world ; a spectre of horrid witchery, whose incantations overflow from the cursing lips of bad men, and whose fires gleam from their impure eyes. But it is a thing that is preternatural still : he looks at it outside his nature, as haunting history and the world ; it is not yet a sorrowful reality within. His religion therefore is a *cheerful reverence ;* and with its sweet light no tinge should mix from the later solemnity and inner conflicts of faith. Let him take his vow with a glad voice : if you drive him prematurely to the confessional, you make him false. The matin-hymn of life to God is brilliant with hope and praise :

and, without violence to nature, you cannot displace it for the deep, low-breathing, vesper-song: the rosy air of so fresh a time was never made to vibrate to that strain. Even from the stony heart of old Memnon on the waste, beams vivid as the morning wrung a murmur of *happy* melody: and only at the dip of day did a passing *plaint* float through the desert's stately silence. It is, I am persuaded, a fatal thing, when we men and women, who make all the catechisms, and shape all the doctrines, and invent all the language of Christian faith, force our adult religion, with its meditative depth, upon the heart of childhood, not yet capacious enough to take it in. Puritanism,— fit faith for the stalwart devotion of earnest manhood in grim times,— cannot be adapted to the childish mind; and the attempt to do so will inevitably produce distaste, and occasion reaction. This indeed we can hardly doubt is one great and permanent cause of the alternations observable from age to age in the faith and spirit of communities; alternations from enthusiasm to indifference, from scepticism to mysticism, from the anxieties of moral law to the fervor of devout love, from a religion of excessive inwardness to one of outward rites or daily work. These changes, though often long in openly declaring themselves, really and at heart take place by generations. The true seat of the revolution is in the nursery and the school: the children being unable to receive what their fathers insist upon giving; getting gradually loosened from a thing that never held them in the hollow of its hand, but only detained them by the skirts of the garment; and obliged at last to begin anew, and try the power of faith's neglected pole.

As childhood merges into youth, the characteristics I have described undergo a rapid and momentous change. The early security is gone. The stronger powers demand a sterner police of conscience to maintain their peace and harmony. The whole soul displays,— in its intellect, its desires, its sentiments of duty,— the great transition from the natural to self-conscious and reflective existence. A greater openness to beauty, a more spontaneous quickness of affection, a more plenary enthusiasm for goodness, combine to waken up unutterable aspirations, and put upon the countenance of life, as it gazes into the young eyes, an expression of divinest glory. New conditions are reached under which the simple, light-hearted piety cannot longer stay. Duty is more than the child's task-work now. So grand and awful does it rise, that it makes the actual deeds that lie beneath look small, like the cultured garden at the Andes' base. Hence, to even the most brave and buoyant spirit, the sigh that seemed once so strange is not unknown. There is an incipient experience of that sad interval between conception, now so rich, and execution still so poor, which traces the lines of deepest care upon the face of men; — not however settled yet into that steady and wonderful shadow of guilt, which has spread over the purest and most strenuous souls of Christendom; but coming fitfully and vanishing again; taking its turn with the bold young faith that nothing worthy can be hard to good resolve; and only dashing the familiar joy with new longings and repentances. Amid the fiercer struggle that sets in, the great thing needed is strength of moral *denial*, the courage to say *no* to all questionable men and unquestionable fiends. Meanwhile, the very faculties of thought are changing too. The appetite for *facts* is passing into an eagerness for *truth*, full also of deep anxieties. Sometimes this noble passion degenerately tends to a disagreeable dogmatism, from the mind's having lost its childish source of trust, and not yet having gained the manly, and for awhile holding the faith neither in weak dependence on authority, nor in genial repose on the universal reason and conscience, but by the little personal tenure of private argument. And, sometimes, it is productive of dark agonies of doubt and loneliness, drearier than death; leaving the soul exposed upon the field of conflict, without a God to strive for, or a weapon

for the fight. Happily, however, the moral struggle of this
period comes before the mental; and is well over with the
faithful, ere the needed strength is broken; and oftener
than is guessed, I am convinced, it is the issue of the earlier
battle of the conscience, that really determines how the
later strife of the intellect shall end. Men that have lived
a few years of hardness for God's sake, are rarely left by
him to roam the wilds of doubt alone.

It is not much perhaps that direct and purposed teaching
can contribute to the efficacy of the religious sentiments.
But its happy avail, whatever it be, depends on its con-
formity with the conditions we have traced. If only we
will not hinder, God has a providence most rich in help.
Judge not the child's mind by your own; nor fancy that
you have a religion to create against some powerful resistance, which skill is needed to evade or proof to overcome.
His spirit, if unspoiled, is with you, not against you, when
you speak of God. Faith is the natural and normal state
of the human heart; doubt is its feverish disease: and that
which may be the fit remedy for your sickness, may be the
poison of his health. He needs but the fresh air and pure
nourishment of life; give him not the pharmacopœia of
theology, instead of the bread of heaven. Disturb him not
with unprofitable "Evidences:" they are burdensome as
the statutes-at-large to the heart of spontaneous justice;
— misplaced as a court of chancery in heaven. He has
already the truth which, at best, they can only have pre-
vented you from losing : it is not the tenure, but the scope,
of his belief that is given you to improve. And in your
efforts to enlarge it, it is well to proceed outwards rather
than inwards; to awaken apprehension of facts, more than
reflection upon feelings; to glorify for the young disciple's
eye the world around him, by lifting the veil from what
is beautiful in nature and great in history; and not drive
devotion back upon self-wonder and self-scrutiny. The
attempt to elicit a religion by interrogating his conscious-

ness, and to find in his heart all the mysteries of a metaphysical and moral experience, will end only with affectation
in the appearance, and unsoundness at the very core, of his
nature. The green fruit may be sweetened by confectionery
arts ; but the fermentation of the oven is not like the ripening of the sun; if it hastens the relish of the moment, it
kills the seed of future hope. Scarcely need the child *know*
that he has a soul; it is ours to take care that, when at
length he finds it, it shall be a noble and august discovery;
full of admirations never to be superseded, and of love that
shall bring no repentance. For this end, his teaching should
be mainly external and objective ; given with an eye ever
fixed on the true good which he most readily discerns to
be great and sacred. Let Palestine be to him, as to so many
ages it has been, a Holy Land ; and Jesus, in his gentle
majesty, the fixed and realized representative of God ; and
the high deeds and souls of the past be claimed as the expressions of his will; and opening glimpses be afforded into
that natural universe which he rules in the spirit of the
divine Nazarene. Yet withal, the exigencies of a more
advanced age, though not anticipated, need not be forgotten. Some prospective regard may be had to the reflective
years which will bring their wants at length ; and without
teaching any present theory of religion, its future demands
may be remembered in a thousand ways. If you would
prepare, not a mere baby-house, but a right noble structure
of faith, in which the soul shall have a life-interest, you will
not only lay the foundation broad and deep, but avoid filling
in with mean and perishable materials the parts, of which
the childish eye may see the surface, but which only the
manly thought can build in strength. The unnoticed outline of system may be so drawn, that painful and deforming
erasures hereafter may be spared; and by mere expansion
of the old boundary, and insertion of new beauty and new
wealth, the earnest veracity of the philosopher may be but
the glorified piety of the child. As larger views of the uni-

verse and life are opened out, a Providence will be felt to
abide there still : the laws which are detected, the unsus-
pected grandeur that is revealed, will be entered in some
orderly manner, as parts of the mighty scheme; and, instead
of subverting the central and divine authority, will be but
a province added to its sway.   And as the years of deep
and subjective religion come, and the mind sinks in wonder
before its own mysteries, the self-consciousness, as it wakes
and starts up, will on the instant see God standing in the
midst.   Such at least is the *tendency* of instruction wisely
given.   Still we must remember, that religion is after all
beyond the range of mere tuition.   It is not a didactic thing
that words can give, and silence can withhold.   It is a spirit ;
a life ; an aspiration ; a contagious glory from soul to soul ;
a spontaneous union with God.   Our inward unfaithfulness
is sure to extinguish it; our outward policy cannot produce
it.   To love and to do the holy will is the ultimate way,
not only to know the truth, but to lead others to know it
too.

XXXVII.

LOOKING UP, AND LIFTING UP.

——◆——

ROMANS xv. 1, 3.

WE THEN THAT ARE STRONG OUGHT TO BEAR THE INFIRMITIES OF THE
WEAK, AND NOT TO PLEASE OURSELVES:— FOR EVEN CHRIST PLEASED
NOT HIMSELF.

In the grouping of nature, dissimilar things are invariably
brought together, and by serving each other's wants and
furnishing the complement to each other's beauty, present
a whole more perfect than the sum of all the parts. The
world we live in is not a cabinet of curiosities, in which every
kind of thing has an assortment of its own, labelled with its
exclusive characters, and scrupulously separated from objects
of kindred tribe. The free creative hand distributes its
riches by other order than the formal arrangements of a
museum; and, for the happy life and action of the universe,
blends a thousand things, which, for ends of knowledge
only, would be kept apart. A single natural object may
be the focus of all human studies, and present problems to
puzzle a whole congress of the wise. A tropical mountain,
for instance, is a seat for all the sciences; and from the
snows of its summit to the ocean at its base, ranges through
every realm of the physical world, and presents samples of
the objects and forces peculiar to each. Its granite masses
stand up as the monumental trophy of nature's engineering;
while each successive stratum piled around their pedestal
is as a notch on the score and chronicle of her operations.
Its melting glaciers and its poised clouds keep her chemical

register; showing the temperature of her laboratory, and marking the dew-point every hour. And from the lichen and the moss that paint its upper rocks, through the fields and forests of its slope, to the sea-weeds that cling around its roots, it carries gradations of vegetable and animal life more various than can be told by the most accomplished physiologist. And perhaps from some platform on its side the observatory may be raised; whence the astronomer obtains his glimpse at other regions of creation, surveys the lordly estate of the sun of whom our holding is, and espies the realm of space beyond, where worlds lie thick as forest-leaves. In this, we have only a representation of the harmonizing method of creation everywhere, which combines the most unlike things into a perfect unity. The several *kingdoms* of nature, as we term them, are not like our political empires, enclosed with jealous boundaries, thick with commercial barriers, and bristling with military posts. They pervade and penetrate each other: they form together an indissoluble economy; the mineral subduing itself into a basis for the organic, the vegetable supporting the animal, the vital culminating in the spiritual; weak things clinging to the strong, as the moss to the oak's trunk, and the insect to its leaf; death acting as the purveyor of life, and life playing the sexton to death. Mutual service in endless gradation is clearly the world's great law.

In the natural grouping of human life, the same rule is found. It is not *similarity* but *dis*similarity, that constitutes the qualification for heartfelt union among mankind: and the mental affinities resemble the electric, in which like poles repel, while the unlike attract. A family, — than which there is no more genuine type of nature's method of arrangement, — is throughout a combination of *opposites ;* the woman depending on the man, — whose very strength however exists only by her weakness; the child hanging on the parent, — whose power were no blessing, were it not compelled to stoop in gentleness; the brother protecting

the sister, — whose affections would have but half their
wealth, were they not brought to lean on him with trustful
pride : and even among seeming equals, the impetuous
quieted by the thoughtful, and the timid finding shelter
with the brave. That there " are diversities of gifts " is
the reason why there " is one spirit :" and it is because one
is reliable for knowledge, and another for resolve, and a
third for the graces of a balanced mind, that *all* are held in
the bonds of a pure affection.

The same principle distinguishes natural society from
artificial association. The former, springing from the impulse of human feeling, brings together elements that are
unlike : the latter, directed to specific ends, combines the
like. The one, completing defect by redundance, and com-
pensating redundance by defect, produces a real and living
unity : the other, multiplying a mere fraction of life by
itself, retires further and further from any integral good,
and results only in exaggerated partiality. I do not suppose
that society arises, as some philosophers represent, from the
sense of individual weakness, and the desire for consolidated
strength ; but, it must be owned, the instinctive propensities
of mankind create nearly the same natural classes, as if it
were so. The first social group would contain a selection
of the elements least able to subsist apart, and most compact when thrown into a system. We all look with involuntary admiration on the gifts and excellences which
are wanting in ourselves : and so, ignorance is drawn to
knowledge, and artlessness resorts to skill ; thought is astonished at the achievements of action, and action wonders
at the mysteries of thought ; the irresolute trust the cour-
ageous, and all find a refuge in the noble and the just. So
long as personal qualities and spontaneous attractions determine the sorting of mankind, they will dispose themselves
in classes, containing each, in rugged harmony, the elementary materials of our humanity. And when discord arises,
it is from the presence of too many similar elements, which

have no respect for one another, no mutual want, no re-
ciprocal helpfulness, and which cannot therefore coexist
without risk of dissension. Say what you will, nature is
no democrat, but filled throughout with the most indisputa-
ble ranks: and it is only in proportion as we recede from
the natural affections, and enter upon the life of isolated
self-will, that dreams of social equality take the place of
the reality of social obedience.

Now the assortments of an old civilization follow a law
precisely the reverse of that which we have ascribed to the
Providential rule. It unites all elements that are like, and
separates the unlike. Instead of throwing men into harmonious groups, it analyzes them into distinct classes; con-
ferring upon each sort of human being a kind of charter
of incorporation; giving them something of a collective
will, a feeling for their order, and a conscious pursuit of its
special ends. The mutual dependence of differently endowed men is not indeed destroyed or even lessened; but
it is shifted from the individual to the class. Where, before,
person was helpful to person, nation now supplies the want
of nation, and one mass of labor fills up the deficiency of
another. This makes the greatest difference in the whole
moral structure of human life. The contact of the dissimilar
elements, I need not say, is much less close: vast circles,
embracing collections of men, hang upon one another; but
not the people within them, taken one by one. The daily
life of each is passed in the presence, not of his *unequals*,
but of his *equals*. He lives within his class: he mixes with
those who have much that he possesses, and little that he
wants: and who in their turn want little that he can give,
and much of which he is empty. He finds his own feelings
repeated, his own tastes confirmed, his own judgments defended, his own type of wisdom reproduced; and becoming
an adept in the characteristics of his order, he misses the
perfection of his nature. He is esteemed in proportion as
he exaggerates the peculiarities of his class; and he ceases

to be its model and its idol, the moment he seeks to infuse into it the elements of some foreign wisdom, and treats with respect the depositary of some opposing truth. How completely this association by sympathy has taken place of association by difference, is plain to all who look upon the world with open eyes. Only those who are of the same sect, of equal rank, of one party, of kindred pursuit, of pretty equal knowledge, and concurrent tastes, are found often in the same society. In education, the graduated distribution of nature is entirely broken up; all the boys collected into one set, all the girls into another; and the several ages, combined in the system of Providence, are separated by the arrangements of man. Everywhere, mechanism and economy are substituting, over our world, the classifications of an encampment for the organism of a home.

I am far from supposing that all this is entirely evil. It is a noble distinction of civilized above barbarous man, that he can bear the habitual presence of others like himself, without a coercion always suspended over his passions; can sympathize with them, and join in hearty fraternity for common ends of good. To live among our equals teaches, without doubt, the twofold lesson of self-reliance and self-restraint: it enforces a respect for others' rights, and a vigilant guardianship of our own: it substitutes prudence for impulse; and trains the sentiments of justice and veracity. But, while it invigorates the energies of purpose, it is apt to blight the higher graces of the mind; and, in confirming the moralities of the will, to impair the devoutness of the affections. A man always among his equals is like the schoolboy at his play; whose eager voice, and disputatious claim, and bold defiance of the wrong, and merciless derision of the feeble, betray that self-will is wide awake, and pity lulled to sleep. But see the same child in his home: and the genial laugh, the deferential look, the hand of generous help, the air of cheerful trust, show how, with

beings above and others beneath him, he can forget himself
in gentle thoughts and quiet reverence. And so it is with
us all. The world is not given to us as a play-ground or
a school alone, where we may learn to fight our way upon
our own level, and leave others scope for a fair race; but
as a domestic system, surrounding us with weaker souls for
our hand to succor, and stronger ones for our hearts to
serve. If the one set of relations is needful for the formation of manly qualities, it is the other that gives occasion
to the divine. And if in our own day and our own class,
the moral and intellectual elements of character have become completely and deplorably ascendant over the religious;
if, in our honor for truth and justice as realities, we have
got to think all piety a dream; if life, in becoming a vigorous work, has ceased to be a holy worship; if its tasks are
done, and its mysteries forgotten, and in being occupied by
our will it is emptied of our God: if, in the better rule of
our finite lot, we forget to serve its Infinite Disposer; — it
is, in part, because we live too exclusively with our equals;
the weak herding with the weak, the strong meeting with
the strong; the rich surrounding themselves with the rich,
and the taught fearing the more taught. We associate
with those who think our thought, feel our feelings, live our
life; we read the books which repeat our tastes, justify our
opinions, confirm our admirations; we encourage each other
in laughing at the excellence to which we are blind, and
disbelieving the truth to which we have never opened our
reason, and shuffling away from the affections and obligations to which we have a distaste. And thus our existence
shrinks into a miserable egoism: the theatre on which we
stand is surrounded by mirrors of self-repetition; and we
render it impossible to escape the monotonous variety of the
poor personal image.

Now, to break this degrading moral illusion, we have only
to study and adopt the grouping of the Christian life; which
corrects the classifications of our artificial state, by restoring

the arrangements of nature. The faith of Christ throws
together the unlike ingredients which civilization had sifted
out from one another. Every true church reproduces the
unity which the world had dissolved; and for the precarious
cohesion of similar elements substitutes again the attraction
of dissimilar. This is done not merely by placing us all, as
responsible agents, in the same venerable relations, and
so strengthening the bonds of earnest brotherhood. This
also is a noble and humanizing thing. But Christianity has
other influences operating to the same end. The moment
a man becomes a *disciple,* his exclusive self-reliance vanishes :
the rigid lines of his mere manly posture become softened :
he trusts another than himself : he loves a better spirit than
his own; and, while living in what is human, aspires to
what is divine. And in this new opening of a world above
him, a fresh light comes down upon the world beneath him:
the infinite glory of the heaven reveals the infinite sadness
there is on earth. Standing no longer on his own level, as
if that were all, he feels himself in the midst, between a
higher existence to which he would attain, and a lower to '
which he would give help. Aspiration and pity rush into
his heart from opposite directions : he forgets himself : the
stiff strong footing taken by his will gives way; and he is
mellowed into the attitudes of *looking up* and *lifting up.*
These, it always appears to me, are the two characteristic
postures of the Christian life; without which our minds,
whatever their opinions, are empty of all religious element,
and our hearts, though still humane, lie withered in atheistic
death. If there were no *ranks* of souls within our view;
if all were upon a platform of republican equality; if there
were but a uniform *citizenship* of spirits, and no royalty
of goodness, and no slavery to sin; if nothing unutterably
great subdued us to allegiance, and nothing sad and shameful roused us to compassion; — I believe that all divine
truth would remain entirely inaccessible to us, and our
existence would be reduced to that of intelligent and ami-

able animals : the noblest chamber of the soul, the vault
of its hidden worship, remaining locked, the corresponding
region of the universe, the hiding place of thunder — the
secret dwelling of the Almighty, — would be closed against
our most penetrating suspicions. And as the arrangements
by which we stand — members of a graduated series, —
with beings above and beings below, is the origin of faith ;
so is the practical recognition of this position the great
means of feeding the perpetual fountains of the Christian
life.

A great German poet and philosopher was fond of de-
fining religion as consisting in a reverence for *inferior* beings. The definition is paradoxical : but though it does not
express the *essence* of religion, it assuredly designates one
of its *effects*. True, there could be no reverence for lower
natures, were there not, to begin with, the recognition of a
Supreme Mind : but the moment that recognition exists, we
certainly look on all that is beneath with a different eye. It
becomes an object, not of pity and protection only, but of
sacred respect ; and our sympathy, which had been that of
a humane fellow-creature, is converted into the deferential
help of a devout worker of God's will. And so, *the loving
service of the weak and wanting* is an essential part of the
discipline of the Christian life. Some habitual association
with the poor, the dependent, the sorrowful, is an indispensable source of the highest elements of character. If we
are faithful to the obligations which such contact with infirmity must bring ; if we gently take the trembling hand
that seeks our guidance, and spend the willing care, and exercise the needful patience ; — why, it makes us descend
into healthful depths of sorrowful affection which else we
should never reach : it first teaches us what it is to wear
this nature of ours, and shows us that we have been men
and have not known it. It strips off the thick bandages of
self, and the grave-clothes of custom ; and bids us awake to
a life which first reveals to us the death-like insensibility

from which we are emerging. Yes; and even if we are unfaithful to our trust; if we have let our negligence have fatal way; if sorrows fall on some poor dependent charge, from which it was our broken purpose to shield his head; — still, it is good that we have known him, and that his presence has been with us. Had we hurt a *superior*, we should have expected punishment from him: had we offended an *equal*, we should have looked for his displeasure ; and, these things once endured, the crisis would have been passed. But to have injured the *weak*, who must be dumb before us, and look up with only the lines of grief which we have traced ; — this strikes an awful anguish into our hearts : a cloud of divine justice broods over us, and we expect from God the retribution which there is no man to give. The rule of heavenly equity gathers closer to us than before ; and we that had neglected mercy are brought low to ask it. Thus it is that the weak, the child, the outcast, they that have none to help them, raise up an Infinite Protector on their side, and by their very wretchedness sustain the faith of justice ever on the throne.

The other half of Christian discipline is of a less sad and more inspiring kind; and yet scarcely more welcome to the vain and easy and self-complacent heart. There are those who pass through life with no greater care than to keep in good humor with themselves ; who dislike the spectacle of any thing that greatly moves or visibly reproaches them ; who therefore shun those that know more, see deeper, aim higher, than themselves ; who are ever on the search, not for correction of their errors, but for confirmation of their prejudices ; not for rebukes to their littleness, but for praises of their greatness ; and who hurry away from the uneasiness of self-confession, if it ever begins to flow, amid the mists of self-justification. This form of selfishness may not be utterly inconsistent with the duty on which I have insisted, of lifting up the beings beneath us : but it is the direct contrary of the other portion of the devout life, which consists in

25

looking up to all that is above us. It is the more needful
to guard against the approach of such a temper, because
aspiration is more easily stifled than compassion. Its faint
breathings subside through mere forgetfulness :* but the
paroxysms of pity can be quelled only by an active selfishness : and admiration may die from dearth of objects,
while sympathy is in danger rather of exhaustion by their
multitude. The intercourse with suffering which sustains
the natural spirit of mercy is so near our doors, as hardly
to be avoided without compunction : the intercourse with
excellence which keeps resolution at its height is a privilege
so rare as not to be attained without an effort. Yet, without it, the higher elements of the Christian life must fatally
decline. The soul cannot from its own fuel permanently
feed its nobler fires : it needs at least some stream of pure
air from aloft to kindle the smouldering thoughts, and make
the clouds of doubt and heaviness burst into a flame. Only
the fewest and sublimest natures, — bordering almost on the
perfectness of Christ, — can remain in the perpetual presence, though for ends of genuine mercy, of infirm or
depraved humanity, without a lowering of the moral conceptions, and a depression of hope and faith. And by a
natural retribution, through which God rebukes every partial unfaithfulness, and forbids any spiritual grace permanently to grow without the concurrent culture of them all,
the tone of pity itself must gradually sink under this deterioration ; and every loss from the enthusiasm of a just
devotion brings a duller shade on the light of human love.
Hence, the anxiety of every one, in proportion to the noble
earnestness with which he looks on life, to hold himself in ·
unbroken communion with great and good minds ; never to
depart long from the touch of their thought and the witness
of their career ; but to intermingle some divine light of
beauty thence with the prosaic story of his days. He knows
that the upper springs of his affections must soon be dry, unless he asks the clouds to nourish them. He finds that the

near inspection and familiar converse of wise and holy men is the appointed way by which the infinite God lifts us to himself, and draws us upward with perpetual attraction. They are the mediators between the earth and heaven, between human realities and divine possibilities, between the severities of duty and the peace of God ; compelling us to own, how glorious when done are the things most difficult to do ; how surely the dreams of conscience may become the fixed products of history ; and how from the sighs of achievement may be composed the hymn of thanksgiving. If, therefore, " there be any virtue, if there be any praise," whoever would complete the circle of the Christian life will " think on these things : " will thrust aside the worthless swarm of competitors on his attention ; in his reading will exclusively retain, in his living associations will never wholly lose, his close communion with the few lofty and faithful spirits that glorify our world : and, above all, will at once quench and feed his thirst for highest wisdom, by trustful and reverent resort to Him in whom sanctity and sorrow, the divine and the human, mingled in ineffable combination.

XXXVIII.

THE CHRISTIAN TIME-VIEW.

1 Corinthians vii. 29, 31, 32.

BUT THIS I SAY, BRETHREN, THE TIME IS SHORT:—THE FASHION OF THIS WORLD PASSETH AWAY.—I WOULD HAVE YOU WITHOUT CAREFULNESS.

PAUL said this with a meaning which cannot now be restored to the words, and which makes them one of the grandest expressions of the true Christian mind. In no vague indeterminate sense, such as ours, did he declare the remainder of this life "*short:*" and we should much misunderstand his feeling here, if we took it for a commonplace sigh over the brief lodgement permitted to man on earth. It was not that he thought the natural term of our presence upon this scene too slight for earnest pursuit and resolute achievement; not that he preached any sickly and selfish indifferentism, esteeming our days too transient for love, and our generation too perishable for faithful service. He had no idea that the natural term would be completed, or the generation run itself out. Yet he felt assured that he and his disciples would be survivors of its destruction; and so urges on them pursuits of immeasurable amplitude, love of a passionless depth, and the service of none but eternal obligations. Instead of thinking, as any man might do, " Frail tenants are we of this solid globe, — phantoms that come and vanish; leaving nothing permanent but the forms of human things, which remain while the beings change, and the scene over which we are passed like troops of successive apparitions; " — the Apostle says, " My friends, we should be of quiet heart; we alone are immortal amid perishable

things, and among the vain shows of creation remain, the
realities of God: this world, though it seems like rooted
adamant, is melting, like a painted cloud, away; the forms
of human life, the structure of communities, the instinctive
relations of mankind, which alone appear unchangeable, are
alone about to cease; and our individual being, of all things
seeming the most precarious, is alone incapable of death."
Paul actually looked around him with the persuasion, that
the stable products of history by which he was environed,
the gigantic institutions, the proud traditions, the accumulated wealth, the disciplined force, the heartless slavery,
that lay within the grasp of Roman power, existed by a
feebler tenure than the sickliest infant's life: he looked to
see them all, and the mighty arm that held them, crumble
into sand before his eyes. A strange and wondrous expectation this, seen from our point of view! Afloat upon the
tide of human things, in that poor frail skiff of a Christian
Church which he took to be an ark of 'God, how could he
look at such frowning skies, and hope to ride the storm
alone? But, in truth, it was no common tempest that he
thought to see : rather did he sail on in the belief, that the
very seas of time beneath him were about to sink and flee
away; bearing with them the mighty fleet of human things
into nothingness and night; and leaving only that sacred
ark suspended in the mid-heaven of God's protection, to
grow into a diviner world. Well might he exhort his
disciples to disentangle themselves from the elements about
to perish; to disregard the perils, and forget the toils, and
transcend the anxieties, that beset them. Well might he
remind them that they were living upon a scale, that made
it shameful to brood on these things like an eager and way-
ward child ; that they might live in obedience to their largest thoughts, and compute their way as through the first
spaces of an infinite perspective; and that, to minds so
placed, nothing was so fitting as a serene spirit of power ;
quiet, not from the extinction, but from the doubling of

emotion, gathering into the same instant the feelings of
opposite times, and making "those that weep as though
they wept not, and those that rejoice as though they rejoiced
not, and those that use this world as though they used it
not;" and all, reposing "without carefulness" on the will
of God, seeing how soon "the fashion of this world passeth
away."

This was the Apostle's manner of regarding life : and
though we may say his expectation was false, we may doubt
whether any man since has had one half as true. It is, at
all events, unlike the error of our lower spirits, and arises
from a mind, not too *short-sighted*, but too *far-seeing*, for the
conditions of our mortal state. It rightly answers the great
problem between true and false religion, — I should rather
say between religion and no religion, — "*Which* is the permanent reality, life, or the scenery and receptacle of life;
the soul, or the physical objects of the soul?" Whoever
deeply feels that one of these is eternal, must see the other
to be evanescent: for the duration of either is simply
relative to the other, which is its only measure: the elonga-
tion of the one is to us the abbreviation of the other; and
he who takes an absolute stand of faith on the stability of
either, beholds the other passing into nought. To dull and
heavy souls, — nay, to the lower minds of all men, — nothing seems so *real* as the objects of the senses, nothing so
secure as the material forms of nature, to which from the
first every human life has stood related ; and in proportion
as physical science confirms this habit of thought, in proportion as masses and weights and mechanism engage us, or
the laws of organization, or the outward conditions of social
life, are we oppressed by the solid sameness of these things;
individual existence seems the sport of a dead fatalism,
swallowed up by the hunger of an insatiable necessity. To
souls like that of Paul, not passive and recipient, but vivid
and productive, — souls that put all things into different
attitudes by a pure act of meditation, and feel how the uni-

verse approaches or recedes before the changing eye of thought, — its constancy, nay its reality, seems purely relative : it lies submissive at the feet, like storm and calm before the eye of Christ: the primary force of God's creation appears to be the free spontaneous soul ; whose existence is the great miracle and mystery of heaven ; whose tendency is ever towards a higher life ; which communes through the screen of outward things with the inner mind of God, feeling both spirits immortal, and only the veil between condemned to drop away. And just in proportion as the worshipper stands up before eternity face to face, and feels it there, must this earth and its time-relations shrink beneath his feet, till he rests upon a point that soon will vanish. Paul, wholly absorbed in the immensity of existence, could by no means measure the objects of existence by our finite rules : the depth of his perspective put even distant things into his foreground ; and if this be chronological error, it comes in with the shadow of religious truth : the delusion is scarce distinguishable from the inspiration of the prophet, and is even akin to the perception of God. No one could thus look the earthly into nothing, but by filling all things with the divine.

It was not then, I conceive, the historical misapprehension about the end of the world, that led to the belief of human immortality : it was the intensity of the belief in immortality, that produced the idea of the approaching end of the world. This is apparent in a way by which you may always distinguish a primitive from a derivative doctrine : the former is everywhere assumed, and appears as an all-pervading and unconscious *faith ;* the latter is frequently argued and expounded, and appears as an avowed *opinion.* The combination of the two, however, has had important effects on the development of our religion ; and it may be doubted whether, without it, Christendom could ever have taken to heart that solemn sense of the infinite scale of human life, which is the great characteristic of its theory of existence.

Paul kept a whole generation of the church in awful and breathless suspense; listening for the approaching peal of doom, till earthly sounds fell as faint unrealities upon their ear; straining their vision aloft, as through a long watch-night, for the sign of the Son of Man in heaven; till their footing seemed loosened beneath them, and the landscape sank into the dark away. Thus alone, I believe, could the invisible world be raised into the great reality to man. The first age of Christendom, sequestered from all else, and spent on its very front, obtained a divine insight that has not been lost. The heavenly breath that swept across the margin, made it felt how the heats of the present should be cooled, and the fever of the passions purified. Our poor minds can take in only one great conception at a time, and must be left alone with it for a full lifetime, if it is to be incorporated with the character, and ennoble the history, of succeeding ages. Moreover, great religious faiths must be the visible basis of practical life to one period, ere they can be rooted in the acceptance of another: and had not the early Christians watched their hour for Christ, their fellow-disciples ever after would have fallen asleep in the fatigues of this world, deaf to the voice of its divinest sorrows, and missing the angels of preternatural strength. The superstition therefore of one age may become the truth and guidance of all others.

That Christianity did really give an infinite enlargement to the scale of human life, and that this is one of its great features, is conspicuous enough on comparing it with the religions it supplanted. It was not indeed that Pagan societies were without the conception of a future: but Christianity first got it cordially believed. Even the meditative philosophy of Greece can present no clear instances of hearty and deep conviction, except in Plato and his master; and, whatever we may think of the rhetorical leanings of Cicero in the same direction, the practical earnestness of Rome was wholly given up, for want of

higher thoughts, to material interests and outward magnificence. The faint and spectral fancies of a possible future,
that floated before the mind of the people, scared away
no crime, tranquillized no passion, disenchanted no instant
pleasure. They lay fevered and restless beneath the broad,
burning orb of this immediate life, drunk with hot indulgence, and asleep to the midnight hemisphere of faith which
is open to the vigils of the purer soul. Throughout Christendom, on the other hand, this boundless night-scene of
existence has been the great object of contemplation ; has
swallowed up the day ; has reduced the meridian glare of
life to an exaggerated starlight, truly seen as such from
more central positions where the apparent does not distort
the real. The difference between the ancient and modern
world is this : that in the one the great reality of being was
now ; in the other it is *yet to come.* If you would witness
a scene characteristic of the popular life of old, you must
go to the amphitheatre of Rome, mingle with its 80,000
spectators, and watch the eager faces of senators and people : observe how the masters of the world spend the wealth
of conquest, and indulge the pride of power : see every wild
creature that God has made to dwell from the jungles of
India to the mountains of Wales, from the forests of
Germany to the deserts of Nubia, brought hither to be
hunted down in artificial groves by thousands in an hour :
behold the captives of war, noble perhaps and wise in their
own land, turned loose, amid yells of insult more terrible
for their foreign tongue, to contend with brutal gladiators
trained to make death the favorite amusement, and present
the most solemn of individual realities as a wholesale public
sport : mark the light look with which the multitude, by
uplifted finger, demands that the wounded combatant be
slain before their eyes : notice the troop of Christian martyrs
awaiting hand in hand the leap from the tiger's den : and
when the day's spectacle is over, and the blood of two
thousand victims stains the ring, follow the giddy crowd

as it streams from the vomitories into the street, trace its
lazy course into the forum, and hear it there scrambling for
the bread of private indolence doled out by the purse of
public corruption; and see how it suns itself to sleep in the
open ways, or crawls into foul dens till morning brings the
hope of games and merry blood again; — and you have an
idea of that imperial people, with their passionate living
for the moment, which the gospel found in occupation of
the world.   And if you would fix in your thought an image
of the popular mind of Christendom, I know not that you
could do better than go at sunrise with the throng of toiling
men to the hillside where Whitefield or Wesley is about
to preach.   Hear what a great heart of reality in that hymn
that swells upon the morning air, — a prophet's strain upon
a people's lips!   See the rugged hands of labor, clasped and
trembling, wrestling with the Unseen in prayer!   Observe
the uplifted faces, deep-lined with hardship and with guilt,
streaming now with honest tears, and flushed with earnest
shame, as the man of God awakes the life within, and tells
of him that bare for us the stripe and cross, and offers the
holiest spirit to the humblest lot, and tears away the veil
of sense from the glad and awful gates of heaven and hell.
Go to these people's homes, and observe the decent tastes,
the sense of domestic obligations, the care for childhood,
the desire of instruction, the neighborly kindness, the conscientious self-respect; and say, whether the sacred image
of duty does not live within those minds: whether *holiness*
has not taken the place of *pleasure* in their idea of life:
whether for them too the toils of nature are not lightened
by some eternal hope, and their burden carried by some
angel of love, and the strife of necessity turned into the
service of God.   The present tyrannizes over their character
no more, subdued by a future infinitely great: and hardly
though they lie upon the rock of this world, they can live
the life of faith; and while the hand plies the tools of earth,
keep a spirit open to the skies.

There is something very ennobling to human character in the possession of a large *time-view :* and its effects are visible in many cases not directly religious. Next to having a noble future before us, is it well to have a wide and worthy past. This it is that renders the old man venerable. His actual momentary life is often poor and sad enough : the windows of sense and soul shut on the light and stir of the world without, and the avenues choked up through which the interests and passions of the hour should vibrate to his heart. But, while shaded from the dazzle of the instant, the tranquil light of half a century is spread beneath his eye. Many a gaudy bubble he has seen rise, and glitter, and burst ; — many a modest good take secret root and grow. Every game of hope and passion he has seen played out, and for every passage presented on the living stage can find a parallel scene in the old drama whose curtain never drops. The heroes and the wise of the past age, ideal to others, were real to him ; his familiars are among the dead,. dear yet to many hearts ; and as he explores again that silent past, and climbs once more its consecrated heights, and loses himself in its sweet valleys, and rebuilds its fallen fragments, he feels something of an historic dignity, which sustains the trembling steps, and gives courage to the sorrowful decline. And so is it too with *family recollections.* To have had forefathers renowned for honorable deeds, to belong by nature to those who have bravely borne their part in life and refreshed the world with mighty thoughts and healthy admiration, is a privilege which it were mean and self-willed to despise. It is as a security given for us of old, which it were false-hearted not to redeem : and in virtues bred of a noble stock, mellowed as they are by reverence, there is often a grace and ripeness, wanting to self-made and bran-new excellence. Of like value to a people are *heroic national traditions*, giving them a determinate character to sustain among the tribes of men, making them familiar with images of great and strenuous life, and kindling them with faith in glorious possibilities. No material interests, no common welfare, can so bind a community together, and make it strong of heart, as a history of rights maintained, and virtues uncorrupted, and freedom won : and one legend of conscience is worth more to a country than hidden gold and fertile plains. It is but an extension of the same influence that we discern in the Christian theory of life : only that it opens out our time-view alike in the future and the past. It makes both our lineage and our destiny divine ; proclaims us *sons* of God, and *heirs.* No tie can so fasten on us the feeling, that we belong not to the present, and that we degrade our nature whenever we live for the passing moment only ; that we are not our own, but the great Father God's. Our lot is greater than ourselves, and gives to our souls a worth they would not else have dared to claim. Hence the humbleness there always is in Christian dignity. The immortal lot infinitely transcends our poor deserts : how we are to grow into the proportions of so high a life, it is wonderful to think. And yet, though it be above us always,—nay, even *because* it is above us, — there is something in it true and answering to our nature still : so that, having once lived with it, we are only half ourselves — and that the meaner half — without it. The infinite burden of duty which good hearts are constrained to bear, is tolerable only to an immortal's strength. The unspeakable, imploring homage with which we look on truth and wisdom and greatness in other souls, is but sorrow and servitude, except to a spirit freed with an eternal love. The Christian hope gives peace and power by restoring the broken proportions of the mind ; and tranquillizes the restlessness of a spirit unconsciously " cabined, cribbed, confined." It is this truthfulness to our best and deepest nature, — the power we receive from it, the quiet we find in it, — that gives to the Christian estimate of life its most irresistible persuasion upon the heart. For my own part, I confess it is the only evidence that seems to give me true, serene,

absolute faith ; and when, in lower moods of thought, I am
driven to cast about for a limited, intellectual ground of
trust, and become a disciple according to argument, I sometimes doubt whether I do more than fancy I believe.

With what temper then does this great faith send us forth
to our immediate work ? — With the assurance that the true
life is not yet ; that nobler forms of being and affection are
in reserve for faithful minds ; that the present derives its
chief interest and value, not from itself, but from its relations. To live, in short, consists not in enjoying the day
and forgetting in the night ; but in a waking conscience, a
self-forgetful heart, an ungrudging hand, a thought ever
earnest for the truth ; in a perpetual outlook of hope from
our lower point upon an upper and infinite glory. We need
not let the present be so eclipsed by the future, — we need
not look upon its scenes or upon ourselves as so mean beneath that ulterior resplendence, — that life now should be
darkened by the contrast, instead of cheered by the connection. It is no sad lot of expiation that we suffer, no penance that our years on earth perform, purifying by tears and
mortification, a natural disqualification for any higher state.
On the contrary, the germs of the immortal growth are
within us now, and will spring up, not by the bruising and
crushing of our nature, but by its glorious opening out. We
are here to try and train our faculties for great achievements and harmonious residence within the will of God.
Nor is the theatre unworthy of our best endeavors. Only
let us not, in action or in suffering, sink down upon the
present moment, as if that were all. Amid the strife and
sorrow that await us, let us remember, that the ills of life
are not here on their own account, but are as a divine chal-
lenge and godlike wrestling in the night with our too reluctant wills ; and since, thus regarded, they are truly evil no
more, let us embrace the conflict manfully, and fear no defeat to any faithful will. When all is well with us in this
world, let us not forget that its enjoyments also are not here

on their own account: the cup is not to be tossed off in careless draughts. They too stand in relation to the affections and character of the soul, and thence derive their truest worth: it were sin to take them to our selfish sensibilities alone; and they must warm us with a grateful and a generous mind, more trustful in the love of God, more prompt with a true pity for man. And when we best and most strenuously follow the obligations of our career, we can permit no flutter of self-gratulation to disturb the quiet meekness of the heart. For only look up on that which we dare to hope, and how are our mightiest achievements dwarfed. All insufficient in themselves, — poor spellings-out of the mere alphabet of eternal wisdom, — they are but signs of willing pupilage, — the upturned look of a disciple sitting at the feet. As symbols of faith and service, God will be graciously pleased to accept them from us; and discern in them the early essays of a soul that shall assume at length dimensions more divine.

XXXIX.

THE FAMILY IN HEAVEN AND EARTH.

EPHESIANS III. 14, 15.

OUR LORD JESUS CHRIST, — OF WHOM THE WHOLE FAMILY IN HEAVEN AND
EARTH IS NAMED.

JESUS was never so much one with his disciples, as when
he was no longer with them : they were never so widely
severed from him, as when, with unawakened and dim-dis-
cerning heart, they lingered around him, with eyes so holden
that they did not know him. The nearest in person may
clearly be the furthest in soul: they may eat at the same
table, and morning and night exchange the greeting and the
parting look, yet each remain outside the spirit of the other,
— severed even by an impassable chasm, to which the earth's
diameter would be less than an arm's length. But where
the inner being, rather than the mere outer, has been passed
together, and we have found in some fraternal heart the
appointed confessional for the doubts and strife and sorrowful resolves of our existence, no amount of land or water
can break the mutual affiliation : the reciprocation of pity
and of trust, the placid memories, the joint courage to bear
well the solemn weight of life, which enrich a present love,
may consecrate the absent too. Nay, distance may even
set a human life in truer and more affectionate aspect before us, by stripping off its trivialities, and bringing out its
essential features, and urging our thought to conceive it
as a whole from its beginning to its close : and in the want
of any lighter union, we fold ourselves in the embrace of

the same divine laws, and compassion for the same mortal lot.

With the boldness of a true and inspired nature, the Apostle Paul gives an immeasurable extension to this thought; and speaks, with incidental ease of one *"family,"* distributed between heaven and earth. There is, it seems, a domesticity that cannot be absorbed by the interval between two spheres of being; — a love that cannot be lost amid the immensity, but finds the surest track across the void; — a home-affinity that penetrates the skies, and enters as the morning or the evening guest. And it is Jesus of Nazareth who has effected this; — has entered under the same household name, and formed into the same class, the dwellers above and those beneath. Spirits *there*, and spirits *here*, are gathered by him into one group; and where before was saddest exile, he has made a blest fraternity. Let us observe in what instances, and by what means, the spirit of Christ draws into one circle the members of some human society separated else by hopeless distance.

Members of the same home cannot dwell together, without either the memory or the expectation of some mutual and mortal farewell. Families are for ever forming, for ever breaking up; and every stroke of the pendulum carries the parting agony through fifty homes. There is no one of mature affections from whose arms some blessing of the heart, — parent, sister, child, — has not died away, and slipped, not as once into extinction, but (chief thanks to the Son of Man) into eternity. All we who dwell in this visible scene can think of kindred souls that have vanished from us into the invisible. These, in the first place, does Jesus keep dwelling near our hearts; making still one family of those in heaven and those on earth.

This he would do, if by no other means, by the prospect he has opened, of actual restoration. Hopeless grief for the dead, in being passionate, is tempted to be faithless too : for it has no remedy but in suffering remembrance to fade

away, and employing the gaudy colors of the present to
paint over the sacred shadows of the past. On the other
hand, the most distant promise of a renewed embrace is
sufficient to keep alive an unforgetful love. Come where
and when it may, after years or ages, in the nearest or the
furthest regions of God's universe, it passes across our minds
the vision of reunion : it opens a niche in the crypt of the
affections, where the images of household memory may
stand, and gaze with placid look at the homage of our sorrow, till they light up again with life, and fall into our arms
once more. It matters little at what point in the perspective of the future the separation enforced by death is
thought to cease. Faith and Love are careless time-keepers :
they have a wide and liberal eye for distance and duration :
and while they can whisper to each other the words " Meet
again," they can watch and toil with wondrous patience, —
with spirit fresh and true, and, amid its most grievous loneliness, unbereft of one good sympathy. And since the grave
can bury no affections now, but only the mortal and familiar
shape of their object, death has changed its whole aspect
and relation to us ; and we may regard it, not with passionate hate, but with quiet reverence. It is a divine message
from above, not an invasion from the abyss beneath ; not
the fiendish hand of darkness thrust up to clutch our gladness enviously away, but a rainbow gleam that descends
through tears, without which we should not know the various beauties that are woven into the pure light of life.
Once let the Christian promise be taken to the heart ; and
as we walk through the solemn forest of our existence, every
leaf of love that falls, while it proclaims the winter near,
lets in another patch of God's sunshine, to paint the glade
beneath our feet, and give " a glory to the grass." Tell me
that I shall stand face to face with the sainted dead ; and,
whenever it may be, shall I not desire to be ready, and to
meet them with clear eye and spirit unabashed ? Shall I
not feel, that to forget them were a mark of a nature base

26

and infidel? — that under whatever pleasant shelter I may
rest, and over whatever wastes I may wander as a wayfarer
in life, I must bear their image next my heart; — like the
exile of old, flying with his household gods hidden in his
mantle's secret folds? That the gospel leaves undetermined
the period and place of restoration; — that we call it "hereafter" and know not when it is; that we call it "heaven"
and know not where it is; — detracts nothing from its power
to unite into one family the living and the departed. It
is the office of pure religious meditation to thin away the
partitions of time till they vanish, and cast a zone around
space and enclose it all within the mind; to feel that whatever is certain must be soon, and whatever is real must be
near at hand. And hence, it is the characteristic of Christianity to be indifferent as to the time and locality of the
events in which it excites our faith. Content with scatter-
ing great and transforming ideas, it allows every kind of
misplacement in these accidental relations; for, if *true* portions of the invisible are given to our belief, what matters
the disposition into which our thoughts may throw them?
Early or late, near or far, are alike in the eye of God, and
may well be left open to mutable interpretation from the
wants and affections of men. Jesus himself spake much,
before his crucifixion, of his reunion with his disciples. It
was his favorite topic throughout that parting night; — the
subject, now of promise, now of prayer; — the vision from
which, in that hour of anguish, he could never, for many
moments, bear to part. He leaves the impression that it
would be very speedy; and so thought the apostles ever
after. And as to place, his expressions fluctuate somewhat
between *here* and *there;* though his hearers thenceforth
looked, and looked in vain, for him to come back to be with
them. But of what concern was this? For were they not
ready to meet him, be it where it might? Did not that
hope keep alive within their hearts the divine and gracious
image of their Lord, and, at the end of forty years of vari-

ous toil, still evoke it, beaming and breathing as though it
were of yesterday? Worlds above and worlds below; —
mansions are they all of the great Father's house : and the
disciples' greeting would be equally blessed, whether the
immortal Galilean descended to the embrace on this vestibule of finite things; or summoned them rather across its
threshold into the presence-chamber of the Infinite. And
no less indifferent to our affections are the localities beyond
the grave. Having faith that the lost will assuredly be
found, our souls detain them lovingly in the domestic circle
still, and own one family in heaven and on earth. We may
cease to ask, in *which* of the provinces of God may be the
city of the dead ; a guide will be sent, when we are called
to go.

Such and so much encouragement would Christianity
give to the faithful conservation of all true affections, if
it only assured us of some distant and undefinable restoration. But it appears to me to assure us of much more than
this ; to discountenance the idea of any, even the most temporary, extinction of life in the grave ; and to sanction our
faith in the absolute immortality of the mind. Rightly understood, it teaches not only that the departed *will* live, but
that they *do* live, and indeed have never died, but simply
vanished and passed away. It opens to our view the diviner
sphere of Christ's ascension, wherever it may be, not as a
celestial solitude, where he spends the centuries alone ; but
as the ever-peopling home of men and nations, where predecessors waited to give him welcome, and disciples go to
call him blessed. It is a great thing, thus totally to abolish
the idea of any annihilation, however momentary, in death,
and to reduce it to simple separation. For it is a perilous
and even fatal concession to the power of the grave, to admit that it holds any thing in non-existence, and absolutely
cancels souls ; swallowing up every trace of their identity,
and necessitating the creation of another, though corresponding, series. Once let an object of deep love drop

into that abyss and sink in its privative darkness, and how shall I recover it again? Faith stands trembling on the awful brink, and with vain cries and broken supplications, owns herself unequal to the task: for, between *being* and *no being*, who can fathom the infinite depth? The very creature that has really fallen through it, scarcely can Omnipotence bring back; though it produce another like in every feature, giving us the phantasm and not the essence. But neither to God's power nor to our faith, does death present any serious perplexity, if it be only the migration of a spirit that does not cease to live. Thus regarded, it interposes nothing but physical distance between us and the objects of our affectionate remembrance. While we poor wayfarers still toil, with hot and bleeding feet, along the highway and the dust of life, our companions have but mounted the divergent path, to explore the more sacred streams, and visit the diviner vales, and wander amid the everlasting Alps, of God's upper province of creation. The memorial which our hand affectionately raised when they departed, is no monument to tell what once had been and is no more; it is no symbol of hopeless loss; but the landmark from which we measure off the miles of our solitary way, and reckon the definite, though unknown, remnant of our pilgrimage : and as the retrospect is lengthened out, the prospective loneliness is shortening to its close. And so we keep up the courage of our hearts, and refresh ourselves with the memories of love, and travel forward in the ways of duty with less weary step, feeling ever for the hand of God, and listening for the domestic voices of the immortals whose happy welcome waits us. Death, in short, under the Christian aspect, is but God's method of colonization; the transition from this mother-country of our race to the fairer and newer world of our emigration. What though no other passage thither is permitted to all the living, and by neither eye nor ear we can discover any trace of that unknown receptacle of vivid and more glorious life? So might the dwellers in any other sphere make complaint respecting our poor world. Intensely as it burns with life, dizzy as our thought becomes with the din of its eager passions, and the cries of its many woes, yet from the nearest station that God's universe affords, — nay, at a few miles beyond its own confines, — all its stormy force, its crowded cities, the breathless hurry and ferment of its nations, — the whole apparition and chorus of humanity, is still and motionless as death; gathered all and lost within the circumference of a dark or illumined disk. And silent as those midnight heavens appear, well may there be, among their points of light, some one that thrills with the glow of our lost and immortal generations; busy with the fleet movements, and happy energies, of existence more vivid than our own; where, as we approach, we might catch the awful voices of the mighty dead, and the sweeter tones, lately heard in the last pain and sorrow, of our own departed ones.

But it is not merely the members of the same literal home that Christ unites in one, whether in earth or heaven. He makes the good of every age into a glorious family of the children of God; and inspires them with a fellow-feeling, whatever the department of service which they fill. Discipleship to Christ is not like the partisanship of the schools, — an exclusive devotion to partial truth, an exaggeration of some single phase of human life. Keeping us ever in the mental presence of the divinest wisdom and in veneration of a perfect goodness, it accustoms us to the aspect of every grace that can adorn and consecrate our nature; trains our perceptions instantly to recognize its influence or to feel its want. It looks with an eye of full and clear affection over the wide circle of human excellence. Had we not been followers of one, whose thoughts were often deep and mystic, showing how simplicity touches upon wonder, and wonder elevates simplicity; we might have overlooked the high problems of our life, and held in light esteem the souls agitated by their grandeur, perhaps lost in their profundity. Had we not sat at the feet of One, before whose gentle tones and patient looks the shrinking child and the repentant woman might feel it a safe and healing thing to stand, we might have despised that faith of love which, in being feminine, does not cease to be manly, and have allowed no recess of honor in our hearts to the apostles of meekness and mercy. Had we not heard, from a Master's lips, the blighting severities before which Phari-sees and hypocrites flinched and stood aghast, we might have softened unworthily the austere claims of truth and justice, have lost the healthy horror at sin, and refused our thanksgiving to the patriots and prophets, whose flashing zeal has purified the atmosphere of this world. And were it not for the words so infinitely graceful, and prayers of deepest aspiration, that fell from the Man of Sorrows, the very soul of Christendom would have been steeped in colors far less fair : we might never have felt how soon the kindred fountains of sanctity and beauty blend together ; and have denied to the poet, as the priest of nature, his fit alliance with the priest of faith. But thrown as we are into rever-ence for no disproportioned and unfinished soul, we cannot but contract a catholic sympathy for every noble form as-sumed by our humanity. Philosophy and art, the statesman and the bard, the reformer and the saint, all take their place before us in the Providential sphere, and in proportion as they are faithful to their trust, draw from us an admiring recognition. We see in them selections from the exhaust-less inspiration of the infinite wisdom ; streaks of divine illumination, rushing in through the cloud-openings of our world. No genuine disciple can be sceptical as to the ex istence, or fastidious in the acknowledgment, of any true worthiness. We owe it largely to the Author of our faith, that we cannot encounter the great and good in the genera-tions of the past, without affectionate curiosity, and even strong friendship. Christ, himself the discerner of the Sa-maritan's goodness and the alien's faith, has called the noble dead of history to a better life than they had before, even in this world: their memory is dearer; their example, more productive; their spirit, more profoundly understood. Thus is there a fraternity formed that disowns the restrictions of place and time; a Church of Christ that passes the bounds of Christendom: and though, in the general chorus of great souls, disciples only can well apprehend the theme and put in the words, yet the glorious voices of Socrates and Plato, of Alcæus and Pindar, of Aristides and Scipio, of Antoninus and Boethius, richly mingle as preluding or supporting instruments, filling the melody, though scarce interpreting the thought. Nor is this brotherhood confined even by historic bounds: it spreads beyond this sphere and makes one family in heaven and earth. The very faith that the honored men of old still live, and carry on elsewhere the appointed work of faithful minds, unspeakably deepens our interest in them; forbids us to sigh after them as irrecoverable images of the past; enrolls them among our contemporaries; and from the lights of memory transfers them to the glories of hope. If Pascal's "thoughts" are not half published yet, but are pondering for us the secrets of sublimer themes: if Shakspeare's genial eye is withdrawn from the stage of life only that it may read the drama of the universe: if Paul, having testified for what a Christ he lived, shall yet tell us with what a gain he died : if Isaiah's harp is not really silent, but may fill us soon with the glow of a diviner fire ; — with what solemn heart, what reverential hand, shall we open the temporary page by which, meanwhile, they speak with us from the past! Such hope tends to give us a prompt and large congeniality with them ; to cherish the healthful affections which are domestic in every place and obsolete in no time; to prepare us for entering any new scene, and joining any new society where goodness, truth, and beauty dwell.

Even this wide friendship need not entirely close the circle of our fraternity. Beyond the company of the great

and good, a vast and various crowd is scattered round : no
line must be drawn which they are forbid to pass; some
span of sympathy must embrace them too. No proud
mysteries, no secret initiation, guards the entrance to the
Christian brotherhood; even wandering guilt must be sought
for and brought home; and penitence that sits upon the
steps must be asked to come within the door. Christ will
not remain at the head of the " whole family," if its forlorn
and outcast members are simply put away in selfish shame,
and no gentle care is spent to smooth the pathway of return.
He gives to some a present joy in one another : he denies
to none a hope for all. The alliance of our hearts is itself
founded on the kindred in our being : and is but the actual
result of affections not impossible to any. The affinities
of nature lie deeper than the sympathies of taste; and
should be accepted as guarantees for the equal tenderness
of God, amid the alienations of our foolish passions. And
whoever will take to heart, how the same human burthen
is laid on all, and the divine relief so nobly used by some
is for awhile so sadly missed by more; how much resemblance lurks under every difference between man and man ;
how small a space may often separate the decline into
grievous failure and the ascent into glorious success; must
surely feel the yearnings of a fraternal heart towards all
who have borne the earthly mission : must look on the
apparition and disappearance of generation after generation
on this scene with an almost domestic regret and household
pity for his kind : consoled and elevated by the trust, that
men and nations who have performed the parts of shame
and sorrow here are trained to nobler and more natural
offices elsewhere.

XL.

THE SINGLE AND THE EVIL EYE.

—◆—

MATTHEW VI. 22, 23.

THE LIGHT OF THE BODY IS THE EYE: IF THEREFORE THINE EYE BE
SINGLE, THY WHOLE BODY SHALL BE FULL OF LIGHT; BUT IF THINE
EYE BE EVIL, THY WHOLE BODY SHALL BE FULL OF DARKNESS. IF
THEREFORE THE LIGHT THAT IS IN THEE BE DARKNESS, HOW GREAT IS
THAT DARKNESS!

GREAT indeed! because it not only hides realities, but produces all kinds of deceptive unrealities; to the blinding
character of all darkness, adding the creative activity of
light; suppressing the clear outline and benign face of
things, and throwing up instead their twisted and malignant
shadows. This is the difference, so awfully indicated by
the greatest of Seers in the words just cited, between the
evil eye, and *no eye at all*. The latter only misses what
there is: the former surrounds itself by what is not. The
one is an innocent privation, that makes no pretence to
knowledge of the light: the other is a guilty delusion, proud
of its powers of vision, and applying its blind organ to every
telescope with an air of superior illumination. The one is
the eye simply closed in sleep: the other, staring with night-
mare, and burning with dreams; whose strain the gloom of
midnight does not relieve, and whose trooping images the
dawning light does not disperse. He whose very light has
become darkness, treats the privative as positive, and the positive as privative; he sees the single, double, and the double,
single: with him nothing is infinite, and the infinite is nothing. The great spectrum of truth is painted backward, and

the rainbow of promised good is upside down : and while he cannot espy the angel standing in the sun, he can read the smallest print by the pit-lights of Tophet, that threaten to blind the spirits, and smoke out the stars. To the evil eye the universe is not simply hidden, but reversed.

This will not appear strange to any one who considers that two things are requisite for perception of any sort; viz., an *object*, and an *instrument*, of perception ; — an outward thing, and an inward faculty. Sunshine is of no use in an eyeless world ; and the most sensitive retina is wasted in the dark. The impressions we receive are the result of a *relation* between the scene by which we are environed, and the mind with which we survey it : take away either term of this relation, and the other disappears. In like manner, *alter* the character of either term, and the relation ceases to be the same. The sweet may become bitter, not only by chemical changes in the substance, but by the sick palate of the taster. And if it were the Creator's will to paint afresh the spectacle of his works visible from this earth, and make the heavens green and the grass like fire, he might work the miracle, either by revising the laws of light and color, or by fitting up our visual power anew, and tingeing its glass with different shades. Nor could we ever, in such case, tell *which* it was ; our consciousness commencing with the effect and not reaching back to the cause. Just as it would be, if all our measures of time were to be simultaneously accelerated to a double speed. Under such conditions, an apparent revolution would take place in the duration of all phenomena. It would seem, that human life had resumed its patriarchal length, and all recent history would appear as through a diminishing medium. Nor indeed is it any idle fancy that such changes are possible. We even feel the warning touch of them day by day : and their faint breath, like a passing chill trespassing from the invisible, sweeps by and leaves an awe on thoughtful hearts. If self-forgetful activity, or the lively commerce of mind with mind, can dwindle hours into minutes, while a dull and heavy sorrow may protract a night into an age; if the dream of a few instants can comprise the history of years; — how evident is it that our apparent time, which is our real life, stretches or shrinks with the variable moods of the mind; that not only does the way we go become as the moist meadow or the parched desert, according as we gaze through the cool lens of a pure health, or the throbbing eye of fever, but by the quicker or slower pace of thought, we may be made to fly across the soft grass of our refreshment, or crawl over the hot sands of our torture; that, by only such shifting of our time-measures as occurs in each night's sleep, a thousand years might become to us also as one day, or one day as a thousand years; that thus the smallest element of joy or woe might be multiplied into infinite value, and a heaven or hell be constructed from the feeling dropped by a moment's passing wing! Here, at least, the veil of tender mercy becomes transparent, which alone screens us from a lot more terrible than death.

So far however as our views of things are determined by the endowments conceded to our nature, we accept them with a calm content. We know indeed that God might have made us otherwise, and so have set quite a different universe before us: nor have we the smallest power of comparing that possible system of phenomena with this actual, so as to demonstrate which of them may best agree with the truth of things. This is a matter which, like all the foundations of our being, must rest on faith: it is one of our very roots, which we cannot manufacture for ourselves in the dry light; — which we cannot even scrape up to look at, how it lives; — but which insists on growing down into the darkness, and spreading its fibres through the subsoil of nature. It is plain, that if our faculties were in themselves incapable and deceptive; or if they were hopelessly vitiated by secret and resistless causes, — there would be no help for us. We could no more lift ourselves above our illusions and perversions, than the ape could raise himself into a man, or the man into an angel. We cannot issue from ourselves, and alight upon a station outside our own nature: that nature is with us when we judge it, and does but pass sentence on itself. We cannot think of the laws of thought, but by remaining within them; or estimate what we know, except as an element of knowledge. However often the drop may turn itself inside out, and circulate its particles from centre to surface, and from pole to pole, it remains the same constant sphere, reflecting the same vault that hangs over it, and yielding to the same attractions stirring within it. And while there would be no help for such human incapacity, there could be no consciousness of it. To be conscious of it, would be to escape it, — to have a rule of judgment exempted from its operation; for he who sees that he has missed the truth, misses it no more. Faith therefore in our own faculties, as God has given them, is at the very basis of all knowledge and belief, on things human or divine ; — an act of primitive religion, so inevitable that without it scepticism itself cannot even begin, but wanders about through the inane, in fruitless search for a point on which to hang its first sophistic thread. And each one of our natural powers is to be implicitly trusted within its own sphere, and not beyond it: the senses, as reporters of the outward world ; the understanding, in the ascertainment of laws and the interpretation of nature ; the reason and conscience, in the ordering of life, the discernment of God, and the following of religion. Whoever tries to shake their authority, as the ultimate appeal in their several concerns, though he may think himself a saint, is in fact an infidel. Whoever pretends that any thing can be above them, — be it a book or a church, — is secretly cutting up all belief by the roots. Whoever tells me that prophet or apostle set himself above them, and contradicted, instead of reverently interpreting and rendering audible, the whispers of the highest soul, is chargeable with fixing on the messengers of

God the sure sign of imposture or of wildness. To tell me,
with warnings against my erring faculties, that a thing is
divine which offends my devoutest perception of the true
and holy; — as well might you persuade me to admire the
sweetness of a discord by abusing my sense of hearing, or
to prefer a signboard to a Raphael by enumerating optical
illusions and preaching on the imperfections of sight. Amid
the clamor of dissonant theologies, let us sit then, with a
composed love, at the feet of him who pointed to the way,
— which no doubt can darken and no knowledge close, —
of seeing God through purity of heart. That clear and
single eye, filling the soul with light; — what is it but the
open thought and conscience by which the truth of heaven
streams in? And does not Jesus appeal to this as our only
rescue from utter darkness and spiritual eclipse? If so,
then men can see for themselves in things divine. They
are not required to take on trust a rule of life and faith, in
which they would discern no authority and feel no confidence, were it not for the seal it professes to carry, and the
affidavit with which it is superscribed. A system, indeed,
befriended on the mere strength of its letters of recom-
mendation misses every thing divine. A rule which cannot
authorize itself is no rule of duty, no source of obligation;
but, at best, only a maxim of policy and instruction to self-
interest. Till it touches us with its internal sanctity and
excellence, and we can no longer neglect it without shame
and remorse as well as fear, our adoption of it is not moral,
but mimetic: we imitate the things which may be duty to
persons who have a conscience, but which are no duty to
us. If Christ alone had personal and first-hand discernment
of the truth and authority of Christianity, and all other men
have to take it solely on his word, then Christianity wholly
ceases to be a religion, and the compliance with it becomes
a mere simial observance of the movements of a great
posture-master of the soul. It is as if God had sent one
solitary being gifted with eyesight into a world of the blind.

to teach them to act *as though they could see;* groping about in dark places and shading their faces in a blaze: in which case, the actions, proceeding from no vision, would have no meaning, and though displaying docility, would border on foolishness and hypocrisy. Turn the matter as we may, it will appear that the fullest, most unqualified admission of a moral and rational nature in man, whose decisions no external power can overrule, and which constitutes God's ever open court for trying the claims of scripture and prophecy, no less than of philosophy, is the prime requisite of all devout faith; without which, duty loses its sacredness, revelation its significance, and God himself his authority.

Though, however, our first act of faith must be an implicit trust in the powers through which alone divine things are apprehensible by us, it must be a trust in the intrinsic nature which God has given them, not in the actual state to which we may have reduced them. They are liable to the same law as the inferior endowments which connect us with material things; attaining clearness and precision with faithful use; vitiated and discolored by abuse; benumbed and confused by disuse. The eye that had been long closed in privation opened at first with so little discernment as to see " men like trees, walking." And the soul shut up from earnest meditation, and drowsy amid the heavenly light to which it should direct its patient gaze, is likely to see God, like Fate, sleeping; or, like a ghost, unreal; or, like the master-builder, retreating from the ship he has launched upon the waves; or, like the spectrum of the sun, a patch of darkness perforating the heavens, where once looked forth a glorious orb, " of this great world both eye and soul." Surely it is a truth of personal experience, that our views of God, of the life we live, of the world we occupy, materially change according to the caprices of our own mind. When the spirits are sinking, and the press of the world arises in its strength; when the will trembles and faints beneath its load, and the hours seem to dash exulting by and leave us at a cruel distance; when the presence of more energetic and devoted souls fills us with a sorrowing reverence, and humbles us to the dust with self-reproach; when the silent shadow of lost opportunity sits cold upon us, and the memory of misspent moments drips upon the sad heart, like rain-drops from the wintry boughs; — then, no peace of God, no tranquil order of life, no free and open affection, seems possible again : the bow of hope has fled from heaven, and the green sod of the earth is elastic to our feet no more : the very universe seems stricken with a rod of disappointment that has turned it into lead : and Providence either vanishes utterly from our view, or appears to us as a hard taskmaster, that lashes a jaded strength, and lays on us a burden greater than we can bear. At other times, when perhaps some affliction casts us down, or some call of arduous duty startles us, we have clearness enough left to pray with a mighty and uplifted heart. God seems to behold the silence of our surrender, and snatches us up into his infinite deliverance. The soul retreats within, and sees his light : it spreads without, and feels his power. We can put our heel on toil and fear, and move over them with the spring of resolution. A glory spreads over the clouds of sorrow, that makes them majestic as the serene and open sky : they hang over us as a canopy of heavenly fire, the hiding-place of a thunder that terrifies us not ; or as the piled mountains of a sublimer world, in whose awful valleys we would abide, though threatened by the roar of the avalanche, and the advancing glacier of inevitable death. The things so huge to the microscopic eye of care retreat into infinite littleness before the sweep of a more comprehensive vision. Whole floods of trouble, peopled with terrors, become as dew-drops on the grass : and the very earth itself, with its crowd of struggling interests, appears as a calm orb floating in the deeps of heaven. Moments like these occur in the history of all tried and faithful minds; and comprise

within them a larger portion of existence than years of the
eating, drinking and sleeping, the bargaining and book-
keeping, which men call life. They are the beacons and
landmarks of our spiritual way, often remaining visible over
long reaches of our career. Nor do they stand alone, to
show how our own mood affects, for better or worse, the
views we take of things above us. Let a man go suddenly
from the meal of luxury to the deathbed of selfishness,
where no love lingers and tears only pretend to flow : let
him pass from the sense of animal enjoyment to the spectacle of animal extinction ; — and he will inevitably believe in
annihilation. The saintly words of everlasting hope will be
as a strange jargon in his ears : the death-rattle on the bed
will put out all the silent possibilities of eternity : he will
shake off the remembrance of them as the remnants of a
troubled dream; and return, with a shrug, to the table of
his enjoyment, to " eat and drink, since to-morrow he dies."
But only let the heart beat with love, and the eye look upon
the scene through the perspective of an infinite sorrow : let
it be the child, catching the last accents of a parent venerated for richness of wisdom and greatness of life ; or the
parents, resigning the child whose infancy is the most graceful picture in their memory, to whose opening wonder they
have held the guiding hand, whose expanding reason they
have sought to fill with order and with light, whose deepening earnestness of duty and trust of pure affection has
revived their fainting will, and refreshed them with a thankful mind : and do you think that any doubt will linger
there? Do you suppose that that father or that child will
be buried in the earth or sea ? — can be hidden from the
eyes by mountains of dust, or the waves of any unfathomable ocean? Ah no! All matter becomes transparent to
inextinguishable light like this : and soil, and air, and water,
and time, and the realm of death, must let this lamp of God
shine through : and we follow it as it recedes in the holy
darkness: till we too await the divine hand, and hope, with

that help, to overtake it once again. Nay, can any one deny, that it is often possible to foreknow a man's moral and religious faith by mere acquaintance with the general temper of his mind? — that even his outward professions themselves go for little with us, if they are violently at variance with this natural expectation? It is useless to tell me, of a libertine and Epicurean, that he believes in the divine rule, and is a devout worshipper at church. I know him to be an atheist by a surer mark than words and post-ures, — by a necessity of corrupted nature, which can only be reversed by a renovated life. Nor need you try to per-suade me that a soul pure, tender, merciful, has any real faith in a relentless hell, where the cry of penitence can avail no more. Such things may stand written in creeds which those gentle lips may still repeat: but let the heretic friend or son die away from her arms, and she will find some divine excuse for keeping the torment far away. The eye of love is too clear and single, to allow of the light that is in it becoming so dread a darkness as that impossible faith.

Such then as the man is, such is his belief: and the faith to which he bears his testimony, testifies in return of him. He sees such things as his soul is qualified to show him; nor can he describe the prospect before him without betraying the direction to which his window turns. Let it not be supposed that truth and falsehood are thus rendered arbi-trary and precariously distinguished; that, as there is a different interpretation of life and discernment of God for every temper of the mind, all are probable alike, and none deserving of our trust. It would be so, if we were always imprisoned in the same temper, and unable to compare it with another; or if, on the admission of such comparison, we could perceive no ground of difference, no reason of preference. But we are ever passing from mood to mood of thought; and it is not hidden from us which are sound and worthy, which are corrupt and mean. We know our shameful from our noble hours; and we cannot honestly pretend to confide in the insinuations of the one, as we do in the inspirations of the other. Who can affect unconsciousness of the times when the climate of his soul is dull and stagnant, and thick with fog ; and when it is clear and fresh, and eager to transmit the light? Who can presume to compare the murky doubts and damp short-sightedness of the one, with the sunny outlook and far horizon of the other; or ask, in good faith, "how do I know which of these views is true ?" So long as the cloud does not fixedly close upon the heart, but light enough darts in to show us the intermediate darkness, excuse is shut out, and hope remains. The slightest opening left may be enlarged ; heaven will look in, and may melt the margin as it passes through. Whoever will reverence the glimpses of his better mind shall find them multiplied ; and even whilst they pass, they may be rich in revelations. Faithfully used, the momentary transit may expound an everlasting truth ; and by predicting, may procure, the recurrence of like happy instants. Ashamed of no pure love, distrustful of no worthy aspiration, forgetful of no clear insight once granted to the soul, we shall find the weight of gloom and fear fast break away, and beneath the open hemisphere of faith shall bend in the worship of joy, and say, "Thou art light, and in thee is no darkness at all."

XLI.

THE SEVEN SLEEPERS.

Isaiah xlvi. 9, 10.

REMEMBER THE FORMER THINGS OF OLD. FOR I AM GOD, AND THERE IS
NONE ELSE: I AM GOD, AND THERE IS NONE LIKE ME; DECLARING THE
END FROM THE BEGINNING, AND FROM ANCIENT TIMES THE THINGS
THAT ARE NOT YET DONE! SAYING, MY COUNSEL SHALL STAND.

THE fictions of popular piety are usually inconstant and
local. But there is a legend of the early Christianity, whose
ready acceptance within a few years of its origin is not
less remarkable than its wide diffusion through every country from the Ganges to the Thames; — a legend which has
spread over West and East from the centres of Rome and
Byzantium; which you may hear in Russia or in Abyssinia;
and which, having seized on the ardent fancy of Moham-
med, is found in the Koran, and is as familiar to the Arab
and the Moor, as to the Spaniard and the Greek.

In the middle of the fifth century, the resident proprie-
tor of an estate near Ephesus was in want of building-stone
to raise some cottages and granaries on his farm. His fields
sloped up the side of a mountain, in which he directed his
slaves to open a quarry. In obeying his orders they found
a spacious cavern, whose mouth was blocked up with masses
of rock artificially piled. On removing these, they were
startled by a dog, suddenly leaping up from the interior.
Venturing further in, to a spot on which the sunshine, no
longer excluded, directly fell, they discovered, just turning
as from sleep, and dazzled with the light, seven young men
of dress and aspect so strange, that the slaves were terri-

fied, and fled. The slumberers, on rising, found themselves
ready for a meal; and, the cave being open, one of them
set out for the city to buy food. On his way through the
familiar country (for he was a native of Ephesus) a thousand surprises struck him. The road over which yesterday's
persecution had driven him was turned; the landmarks
seemed shifted, and gave a twisted pattern to the fields:
on the green meadow of the Cayster had sprung up a circus
and a mill. Two soldiers were seen approaching in the
distance: hiding himself till they were past, lest they
should be emissaries of imperial intolerance, he observed
that the accoutrements were fantastic, the emblems of Decius were not there, the words that dropped from their talk
were in a strange dialect, and in their friendly company
was a Christian presbyter. From a rising ground, he
looked down the river to the base of Diana's hill; and
lo! the great temple, — the world-wide wonder, — was nowhere to be seen. Arrived at the city, he found its grand
gate surmounted by a cross. In the streets, rolling with
new-shaped vehicles filled with theatrical-looking people, the
very noises seemed to make a foreign hum. He could suppose himself in a city of dreams; only that here and there
appeared a house, all whose rooms within he certainly
knew; with an aspect, however, among the rest, curiously
dull and dwindled as in a new window looks an old pane,
preserved for some line scratched by poet or by sage. Before his errand is quite forgot, he enters a bread-shop to
make his purchase; offers the silver coin of Decius in payment; when the baker, whose astonishment was already
manifest enough, can restrain his suspicions no longer; but
arrests his customer as the owner of unlawful treasure,
and hurries him before the city court. There he tells his
tale: that with his Christian companions he had taken
refuge in the cave from the horrors of the Decian persecution; had been pursued thither, and built in for a cruel
death; had fallen asleep till wakened by the returning sun,

let in again by some friendly and unhoped-for hand; and crept back into the town to procure support for life in their retreat. And there too, in reply, he hears a part of the history which he cannot tell: that Decius had been dethroned by death nearly *two* centuries ago, and paganism by the truth full *one :* that, while heaven has wrapped him in mysterious sleep, the earth's face, in its features physical and moral, had been changed : that the empire had shifted its seat from the Tiber to the Bosphorus : that the temple had yielded to the church; the demons of mythology to the saints and martyrs of Christendom ; and that he who had quitted the city in the *third* century, returned to it in the *fifth,* and stood under the Christian protection of the second Theodosius. It is added, that the Ephesian clergy and their people were conducted by the confessor to the cave, exchanging wonders as they conversed by the way ; and that the seven sleepers, having attested in their persons the preserving hand of God, and re-told the story of their life, and heard snatches of the news of nearly two hundred years, gave their parting blessing to the multitude, and sank in the silence of natural death.

For the purpose of mental experiment, fable is as good as fact. To reveal our nature to itself, it is often more effectual for the imagination to go out upon a fiction, than for the memory to absorb a chronicle. When the citizens and the sleepers met, each was awe-struck at the other; yet no one had been conscious of any thing awful in himself. The youths, startled by the police of paganism, had risen up from dinner, leaving their wine untasted ; and on arriving breathless at their retreat, laid themselves down, dusty, weary, ordinary creatures enough. They resume the thread of being where it hung suspended ; and are greeted everywhere with the uplifted hands, and shrinking touch, of devout amazement. And the busy Ephesians had dressed themselves that morning, and swept their shops, and run down to the office and the dock, with no idea that they

were not the most commonplace of mortals, pushing through
a toilsome and sultry career. They are stopped mid-day to
be assured, that, their familiar life is an incredible romance,
that their city is steeped in visionary tints, and they themselves are as moving apparitions. And they are told this,
when they cannot laugh at it, or brush it, like Sunday memories, away. For who are they that say such things, gazing
into them with full, deep eyes? Counterparts in their looks
of all the marvels they profess to see ; — proofs that the old,
dead times were once alive, warm with young passions, noble
with young faith ; astir with limbs that could be weary, and hiding sorrows whose sob and cry might be overheard. Would
not the men, returning to their homes, be conscious of understanding life anew? Would they not look down upon
their children, and up at the portraits of their ancestors,
with a perception from which a cloud had cleared away?
Would the fashion of the drawing-room, the convention of
the club, the gossip of the exchange, retain all their absorbing interest ; and the wrestlings of doubt and duty, the
sighs of reason, the conflicts of affection, the nearness of
God, spoken of by prophets in the trance of inspiration, and
by the church in its prayer of faith, appear any more as
idle words? No ; the revelation of a reality in the past,
would produce the feeling of an unreality in the present.
Many invisible things would shape themselves forth, as with
a solid surface, reflecting the heavenly light, and sleeping in
the colors of pure truth : many visible things would melt in
films away, and retreat like the escaping vista of a dream.
When the people's anthem went up on the Sabbath morning, " O God of our fathers ! " that grave, historic cry would
not seem to set his spirit far, but to bring it overhanging
through the very spaces of the dome above. When the
holy martyrs were named with the glory of affectionate
praise, their silent forms would seem to group themselves
meekly round. And when the upper life of saints and
sages — of suffering taken in its patience and goodness in

its prime, of the faithful parent and the Christ-like child —
was mentioned with a modest hope, it would appear no
fabled island, for which the eye might stretch across the
sea in vain, but a visible range of everlasting hills, whose
outline of awful beauty is already steadfast above the
deep.

Now whence would spring an influence like this? what
source must we assign to the power which such incident
would have exerted over its witnesses? The essence of it
is simply this : the past stood up in the face of the present,
and spake with it : and they found each other out: and
each learned, that he beheld the other with true eye, and
himself with false. The lesson is not set beyond our reach.
No miracle indeed is sent to teach it ; no grotesque extracts
from bygone centuries walk about among us. But our ties
with other days are not broken; fragments of them stand
around us ; notices of them lie before us. The recesses of
time are not hopelessly dark ; opened by the hand of labor,
and penetrated by the light of reason, their sleeping forms
will rise and re-enter our living world, and in showing us
what they have been, disclose to us what we are. The
legendary youths are but the impersonations of history;
and their visit to the Ephesians, but a parable of the relation
between historical perception and religious faith.

The great end, yet the great difficulty, of religion is, so
to analyze our existence for us, as to distinguish its essential
spirit from its casual forms, the real from the apparent, the
transient from the eternal. Experience mixes them all up
together, and arranges nothing according to its worth. The
dress that clothes the body, and the body that clothes the
soul, appear in such invariable conjunction, and become so
much the signs of one another, that all run into one object,
and tempt us to exaggerate the trivial and depreciate the
great. That which a man *has*, and that which he *is*, move
about together, and live in the same house ; till our fancy
and our faith grow too indolent to separate them ; we

fasten him to his possessions, and when they are dropped
in death, think that he has gone to nought. It is the business of faith to see all things in their intrinsic value: it is
the work of experience to thrust them on us in accidental
combinations: and hence the flattering, sceptical, blinding
influence of a passive and unresisted experience. Hence it
is that time is apt to take away a truth for each one that
he gives, and rather to change our wisdom than to increase
it; and while foresight assuredly comes to the man, insight
will often tarry with the child. When the eye first looks
on life, it is not to study its successions, but to rest upon its
picture: its loveliness is discerned before its order: its
aspect is interpreted, while its policy is quite unknown.
Our early years gaze on all things through the natural glass
of beauty and affection, which in religion is the instrument
of truth. But soon it gets dimmed by the breath of usage,
which adheres to all except natures the most pure and fine:
and a cold cloud darkens the whole universe before us.
Day by day, the understanding sees more, the imagination
less, in the scene around us; till it seems all made up of soil
to grow our bread, and clay to build our house: and we
become impatient, if any one pretends to find in it the depth
which its atmosphere has lost to us, and the grandeur which
has faded from our view. We dwell in this world, like dull
serfs in an Alpine land; who are attached indeed to their
home with the strong instincts of men cut off from much
intercourse with their kind, and whose passions, wanting
diffusion, acquire a local intensity; who therefore sigh in
absence for their mountains, as the Arab for his desert; but
in whom there is no sense of the glories amid which they
live; who wonder what the traveller comes to see; who in
the valleys close by the glacier, and echoing with the torrent, observe only the timber for their fuel, and the paddock
for their kine. We are often the last to see how noble are
our opportunities, to feel how inspiring the voices that call
us to high duties and productive sacrifice: and while we

loiter on in the track of drowsy habit, esteeming our lot common and profane, better hearts are looking on, burning within them to stand on the spot where we stand, to seize its hopes, and be true to all its sacredness. It is an abuse of the blessings of experience, when it thus stupefies us with its benumbing touch, and in teaching us a human lesson, persuades us to unlearn a divine. The great use of custom is to teach us what to expect, to familiarize us with the order of events from day to day, that we may compute our way aright, and know how to rule whatever lies beneath our hand. This is the true school for the active, working will. But for the thoughtful, wondering affections, a higher discipline is needed; an excursion beyond the limits where the senses stop, into regions where usage, breathless and exhausted, drops behind; where the beaten ways of ex-pectation disappear, and we must find the sun-path of faith and reason, or else be lost. Only by baffled anticipation do we learn to revere what is above our hand : and custom must break in pieces before us, if we are to keep right the everlasting love within us, as well as the transient life with-out. Surrendering itself to habit alone, the mind takes step by step right on, intent on the narrow strip of its own time, and seeing nothing but its linear direction. But brought to the untrodden mountain-side, it is arrested by the open ground, and challenged by the very silence, and compelled to look abroad in space, and see the fresh, wide world of God; where all roads have vanished, except the elemental highways of nature, — the sweep of storm-felled pines, and the waving-line where melted waters flow. Now, in shaking off the heavy dreams of custom, and waking us up from the swoon so fatal to piety, religion receives the greatest aid from history; and though they seemed to be engaged in opposite offices, they only divide between them the very same. Religion strips the costume from the life that *is:* History restores the costume to the life that *was:* and by this double action we learn to feel sensibly, where the mere dress ends and the true life begins; how much thievish time may steal, and corroding age reduce to dross; and what treasure there is, which no thief approacheth or moth corrupteth. Those who are shut up in the present, either by involuntary ignorance, or by voluntary devotion to its immediate interests, contract a certain slowness of imagination, most fatal both to wisdom and to faith. Restrained in every direction by agglutination to the type of personal experience, their thought cannot pass beyond vulgar and material rules; cannot believe in any aspect of existence much different from things as they are; in any beings far removed from those that walk the streets to-day; in any events that would look absurd in the newspaper, or affect sagacious politicians with serious surprise. Their feeling can make nothing of the distinction between the mortal and the immortal, the spirit and the form of things. If they moralize on human affairs, it is only to say one of the two things which, since the days of Ecclesiastes, have always fallen from Epicurism in its sentimental mood: that all things continue as they were, and there can be nothing new under the sun; or that nothing can continue as it is, and all that is sublunary passes as the shadow; and as this dieth, so dieth that. A mind, rich in the past, is protected against these mean falsehoods; can discriminate the mutable social forms, from that permanent humanity, of whose affections, whose struggles, whose aspirations, whose Providential course, history is the impressive record; and thus trained, finds it easy to cast an eye of faith upon the living world, and discern the soul of individuals and of communities beneath the visible disguise, so deceitful to the shallow, so suggestive to the wise. The habit of realizing the past is essential to that of idealizing the present.

But, besides this general affinity between historical thought and the religious temper, a more direct influence of knowledge upon faith is not difficult to trace. The great objects of our belief and trust cannot be conceived of, except in the poorest and faintest way, where all is blank beyond mere personal experience. A man to whom the present is the only illuminated spot, closely pressed by outlying darkness all around, will vainly strive to meditate, for example, on the eternity of God. What sort of helpless attempt even can he make towards such a thing? He knows the measure of an hour, a day, a year : and these he may try to multiply without end, to stretch along the line of the infinite life. But this numerical operation carries no impression : it has no more religion in it, than any other long sum. The mere vacant arithmetic of duration travels ineffectually on ; glides through without contact with the Living God ; and gives only the chill of a void loneliness. Time, like space, cannot be appreciated by merely looking into it. As in the desert, stretching its dreary dust to the horizon, all dimensions are lost in the shadowless sunshine ; so, over a mere waste of years the fancy strains itself only to turn dizzy. As, in the one, we want objects to mark the retreating distance, the rising spire, the sheltered green, the swelling light on headland slope ; so, in the other, we need visible events standing off from view to make us aware of the great perspective. And for the ends of faith, they must be *moral* vicissitudes, the deeply-colored incidents of *human* life : or, the vastness which we see we shall not love : we shall traverse the infinite, and never worship. Science, as well as history, has its past to show :— a past, indeed, much larger ; running, with huge strides, deep into the old eternity. But its immensity is dynamical, not divine ; gigantesque, not holy ; opening to us the monotonous perseverance of physical forces, not the various struggles and sorrows of free-will. And though sometimes, on passing from the turmoil of the city, and the heats of restless life, into the open temple of the silent universe, we are tempted to think, that there is the taint of earth, and here the purity of heaven ; yet sure it is, that God is seen by us through man, rather than through nature : and that without

the eye of our brother, and the voices of our kind, the winds
might sigh, and the stars look down on us in vain. Nor is
the Christian conception of the second and higher existence
of man heartily possible to those who are shut out from all
historic retrospect. At least the idea of other nations and
other times, the mental picture of memorable groups that
have passed away; the lingering voices of poets, heroes,
saints, floating on the ear of thought; are a great, if not an
indispensable aid to that hope of the future, which. can
scarcely maintain itself without attendant images. That
old, distant, venerable earth of ours, with its quaint people,
lies silent in the remote places of our thought: and is not so
far from the scene of scarcely more mysterious life, where
all now abide with God : the same perspective embraces
them both; it is but the glance of an eye from below to
above : and as the past reality of the one does not prevent
its being now ideal, so the present ideality of the other is
no hindrance to its reality. The two states, — that in the
picture of history, and that on the map of faith, — recede
almost equally from our immediate experience; and the
conception of the one is a sensible help to the realization of
the other. Indeed there is not a truth of religion in reference to the future and the unseen which the knowledge of
the·past does not bring nearer to our minds. And when we
invoke this aid to faith, we give it an ally, not, as might
seem, accessible to learning only, but singularly open to the
resources of ordinary men. Happily, the very fountains
and depositories of our religion are historical; and records
of human affairs, not theories of physical nature, are supplied in the sacred writings, from which we learn the lessons
of Providence. Apart from all questions of inspiration,
there is no grander agent than the Bible in this world. It
has opened the devout and fervid East to the wonder and
affection of the severer West. It has made old Egypt and
Assyria more familiar to Christendom than its own lands :
and to our people at large the Pharaohs are less strange

than the Plantagenets, and Abraham is more distinct than Alfred. The Hebrew prophet finds himself in the presence of the English tradesman, or domesticated in the Scotch village; and is better understood when he speaks of Jordan, than the poet at home who celebrates the Greta or the Yarrow. Scenes of beauty, pictures of life, rise on the people's thought across the interval of centuries and continents. Pity and terror, sympathy and indignation, fly over vast reaches of time, and alight on many a spot else unclaimed by our humanity, and unconsecrated by the presence of our God. It is a discipline of priceless value; securing for the general mind materials of thought and faith most rich and varied; and breaking that servile sleep of custom, which is the worst foe of true belief and noble hope. From the extension of such discipline, according to opportunity, whosoever is vigilant to keep a living faith will draw ever fresh stores ; and, that he may better dwell in heart with Him "who declareth the end from the beginning," will "remember the former things of old."

XLII.

THE SPHERE OF SILENCE.

I. MAN'S.

—♦—

LUKE VI. 45.

OF THE ABUNDANCE OF THE HEART, THE MOUTH SPEAKETH.

IT is often assumed, as if implied in these words, that whatever is a fit subject for thought is necessarily the fit subject
of conversation. As language is but the expression of the
mind, it seems natural to suppose that the mind must appear
through its medium; that the matters which occupy the lips
must be those which engage the heart; and that no deep
and powerful interest can fail to overflow, in its full proportion, on our communications with each other. *That*
about which silence is the habit, and speech the exception,
— which, even in the sweet counsel of friends, glides in but
for the moment and flits away, — cannot, it is affirmed, have
any strong and constant hold upon men; and by its tran-
siency confesses itself to be an evanescent interest. Many
there are who apply this rule to religion; and who would
measure the reality and force of its influence on the character by the frequency and explicitness of its appearance in
our intercourse. If we are truly penetrated with the same
highest concerns; if we are standing in the same attitude
before God; if the same solemnity of life covers us with its
cloud, and the same glory of hope guides us by its fire; —
how can we do otherwise than always speak together of a
lot so awful and a faith so high? May it not be fairly
doubted, whether those who are drawn by no experience,

inspired by no joy, melted by no sorrow, to break their
reserve on these things, have any devout belief of them
at all?

There seems to be a show of reason in this: and when it
is urged on the modest and self-distrustful, they often gather
from it a lesson of inward reproach, and know not how to
answer. Yet the appeal has always failed to gain its end.
It has not unsealed the lips of men to converse of divine,
as they would of human, things: a certain loneliness, which
cannot be removed, still hangs over their loftiest relations;
and they are stricken, as with dumbness to one another,
before God. There is, indeed, a foundation in our unperverted nature for this repugnance to mingle talk and worship, to look into another's eye and say the thought of
inward prayer; and it is a harsh and false interpretation to
take such repugnance as the sign of irreligion. Many an
earnest and devout heart, too lowly to teach others, too
quiet to proclaim itself, you may find watching the scene
of human things through a constant atmosphere of piety;
recognizing a holy light on all; touching each duty with a
gentle and willing love; yet saying not a word, because
unable to make a special tale of that which is but the truth
of nature. And many a family group may be observed,
gathering round the decline of some venerated life, well
knowing whither it fast tends : and he who discerns nothing
beneath the surface, may think it but a worldly thing, that
all the care seems spent in providing outward alleviation,
and sheltering from inward shock, and keeping some glow
of tempered cheerfulness about the slackening pulse and
deepening chill of life. But an eye less obtuse may often
read a secret meaning in all this, and recognize in it the
symbol of an unspoken mystery : the sacred hope, the perfect trust, the will laid low, the love raised high, make their
confession by faithful act, and learn the right of a holy
silence. And, assuredly, he to whose ready speech the
sanctities most quickly come, who has no difficulty in run-

ning over everlasting things, and never pauses at the awful
name, and can coin the words for what is most dear and
deep, is not often the most truly devout. The sects and
classes, moreover, who make the greatest point of bringing
their Christianity into the drawing-room, the street, or the
senate, after beguiling you into respect and perhaps admiration, continually let out the other half of the truth by some
surprising coarseness, or some selfish intolerance. Yet, in
spite of these appearances, it is altogether true that "of the
abundance of the heart, the mouth speaketh."

Language has two functions, easily distinguished, yet
easily forgotten. It is an instrument of communication
with one another; and an instrument of thought within
ourselves. Plato used to say that thought and speech are
the same : only that thought is the mind's silent dialogue
with itself.* It need not however be always silent: in its
higher moods it presses for utterance: it cannot go on to
rise without casting away the burthen of its words; and
outbursts of song and pulses of prayer are as successive
strokes of the ever-beating wing of aspiration. But in this
we want no one to hear us: we could bear no watchful
human presence: the voice is but the relief to the spirit
overcharged; and our nature could not thus revolve in its
own circuit, except in the loneliness which shelters it from
foreign attractions. Speech therefore assumes two forms;
converse, and soliloquy: the one intended to convey our
thought abroad; the other to detain it at home : the one,
opening what we wish; the other, what we hide: the one,
the common talk of life; the other, equivalent to silence,

---

* The definition is so apposite that I am tempted to subjoin it : —

ΞΕ. Οὐκοῦν διάνοια μὲν καὶ λόγος ταὐτόν· πλὴν ὁ μὲν ἐντὸς τῆς ψυχῆς
πρὸς αὐτὴν διάλογος ἄνευ φωνῆς γιγνόμενος τοῦτ' αὐτὸ ἡμῖν ἐπωνο-
μάσθη, διάνοια;

ΘΕΑΙ. Πάνυ μὲν οὖν.

Sophista 263. E. The same thought is more fully presented in the
Theætetus, 189. E. 190. A.

except to those who may overhear. Of the latter only did Jesus say, that "out of the abundance of the heart, the mouth speaketh." He knew that what men utter face to face is often far different from the real thought of their minds; that they are no less ashamed of their best feelings than of their worst : and that, by watching the coin of words that passes between them in the open commerce of life, you can ill judge of the secret wealth or insolvency of their souls. To estimate them aright, you must wait till the company disperse ; and linger near them when they speak, amid the silence of God, not to others, but from themselves. Nor does this divergence of their private thought from their public conversation imply the slightest approach to artfulness and duplicity : on the contrary, it is possibly the most artless of whom it is most true. The false man has lost the half of himself which makes this variance. The double-dealer has but a single nature : but in the pure and guileless, there are two souls; of which the one comes forward amid human things with quick and genial speech, while the other ever sits with finger on the lips. The one achieves its end, with energy and stir like that of the city's industry; the other noiselessly, like the spring growth of forest and of field : the one opens gladly out, the other shrinks, as if scorched, within, at the light of the human eye. Our nature is as a flower that shines of itself with one color by night, and reflects from the sun another by day; and those who see only its borrowed gayety at noon know nothing of its own fainter beauty beneath the stars. The truth is, the presence of our fellows, and the exchange of looks and words with them, are the great instruments of self-consciousness, and are suitable for all those parts and faculties of a man which are improved by study and attention. But there are elements of our being that were never meant for this; which change their character by being breathed upon; or which vanish in the sound that utters them. They will insist on flowing unobstructed in their natural bed : and if

28

gossip will arrest and dam them up, they are turned from the torrent of health into the marsh of pestilence.

There are things too low to be spoken of; which indeed become low by being spoken of. The appetites are of this kind. They were meant to be the beginnings of action, not the end of speech : and under the dropping of words, they are as wholesome food analyzed into constituent poisons. God lights that fire, and does not want our breath to blow it, or the fuel of our thought to feed it. The inferior impulses in man are glorified by being placed at the natural disposal of higher sentiments ; they are submitted to the transforming power of generous aspiration and great ideas. Wielded by these, they are far above the level of sense ; and are not only controlled by conscience, but dignified by the light of beauty, and ennobled by the alliance of affection. Their just action is secured far less by repressive discipline against them, than by nourishing the strength of the humanities that use them ; by keeping them wholly inattentive to themselves ; by breaking every mirror in which their own face may be beheld. Purity consists, not in the ascetic abnegation of the lower, but in a Christian merging of the lower in the higher ; in the presence of a divine perception so quick to recoil from degradation, that avoidance aforethought need not be studiously provided. And purity of mind is forfeited, less by exceeding rules of moderation, than by needing them ; — by attention to the inferior pleasures, as such. There might be less of moral evil in the rude banquet of heroic times, marked perhaps by excess, but warmed by social enthusiasm, and idealized by lofty minstrelsy, than in many a meal of the prudent dietitian, setting a police over his sensations, and weighing out the scruples of enjoyment for his palate. Not rules of quantity, but habits of forgetfulness, constitute our emancipation from the animal nature. You cannot make any good thing of the voluptuary's mind, regulate it as you may. It may be covered over with an external disguise : it may be strengthened by self-restraint for social use; but with all its wise ways, what trace can God behold there of his own image? He sees at best Aristotle's "rational animal," not one of Christ's "children of the Highest." Most futile is the attempt so prevalent in our days, to base the morality of the appetites on physiology; to open the way to heaven with the dissecting knife; to give up the Prophets for the "Constitution of Man;" and with a gospel of digestion to replace the Sermon on the Mount. Let us indeed accept such help as may come from this source also : but let us rate it at its worth and assign it to its place. Good for the remedy of bodily disease, it is not good for the formation of character; and it is odious as the substitute for religion. Who ever found himself nearer God by inspecting drawings of internal inflammation? There may be those, to whom the check of abjectness and fear may be of service, and who must walk a hospital before they can respect a law. But as an element of education this kind of teaching is fatally misplaced. The ideas it communicates cannot co-exist with the high, devout affections, which are the natural guides and safeguards of a pure heart: they can occur only in uneasy succession with them, and are repelled by them with unconquerable antipathy. Indeed, in good minds, not needing recovery from fall, all mere physical and prohibitive morality is liable to be a source of direct contamination. By simply talking about your rules, you may turn innocence into guilt. The mere discussion of a habit necessarily converts it into a self-conscious indulgence or privation; and thereby totally alters its real character and its moral relations; and may make that evil which was not evil before. And thus, the very cure of outward excess may sometimes be attended with the creation of inward corruption; and what was harmless till you mentioned it, becomes sinful by being named. So are words great powers in this world; not only telling what things are, but making them what else they would not be: and they cannot encroach upon the sphere of silence, without desecrating the sanctuary of nature, and banishing the presence of God.

There are also things too high to be spoken of: and which cease to be high, by being made objects of ordinary speech. Language occupies the mid-region of our life, between the wants that ground us on the earth, and the affections that lift us to the skies. If we were all animal, we could not use it : if we were as God, we should give it up, and lapse, like him, into eternal silence. It is the instrument of business, of learning, of mutual understanding, of common action; the tool of the intellect and the will; the glory of a nature more than brutal, the mark of one less than the divine ; as truly the characteristic of labor in the mind, as the sweat of the brow of the body's toil; emblem at once of blessing and of curse ; recalling an Eden half remembered, while we work in the desert that can never be forgot. When we try to raise it to higher functions, it only spoils the thing it cannot speak; which becomes, like an uttered secret, a treasure killed and gone. Religion in the soul is like a spirit hiding in enshadowed forests : call it into the staring light, it is exhaled and seen no more; or as the whispering of God among the trees; peer about behind the leaves, and it is not there. Men in deep reverence do not talk to one another, but remain with hushed mind side by side. Each one feels, though he cannot tell how it is, that words limit what faith declares unlimited ; that they divide and break to pieces what it comprehends and embraces as a whole; that they distribute into dead members what it discerns as a life of beauty indivisible ; that they reduce to successive propositions what it adores as a simultaneous and everlasting reality. The whole operation of the mind in communicating by speech is the direct opposite of that which bends in worship; the one laboring after definite conceptions and scientific reasoning ; the other intuitively evading both, and bursting the fetters which the provinces of nature own, but the infinity of God rejects.

Hence it is that men lower the voice as they distantly approach these things, and deem it fit to let their words be few. Spoken reverence passes into cant: or, in more elaborate forms, into philosophy. I do not say that there may not be an intermediate period, when earnest men are able to establish a mutual language of religion which, in their day, is true to them: but from the moment of its first freshness it begins to fade; and the hour of its birth is the beginning of its death. And soon the devoutest spirits will be those that say the least; and the currency, once priceless, now debased, will remain chiefly with Pharisees and professional divines. True, there is a sceptic as well as a devout silence on the highest things. But who is there that cannot tell at a glance the difference between the shrinking of unbelief, and the shrinking of reverence? Look only at their eye; and the shallow gloss of the one is not like the deep light of the other. The one pushes the matter externally away; the other hides it internally from view. The one is averse to take the divine ideas into the mind; the other recoils from putting them out. The one yields to the repulsion of dislike; the other exercises the shelter of an ineffable love. There was truth, and not absurdity, in the Friends' silent meeting before God; — a truth indeed too great and high for a permanent institution addressed to our poor nature, but affording an infallible memorial of the genuine inspiration that once breathed through that noble people. And what even were the whining voice and tremulous speech, but the instinctive attempt to escape from the vulgarities of life, and reach the strange music, broken, dissonant, and sweet, in which divine and human things conflict and reconcile themselves? Nor is it essentially different in any worship: for, though we meet together, it is not to speak with one another: it is not even to be spoken to and taught; for that could produce nothing but theology: if it is not for absolute silence of devotion (which were best, if it were possible), it is only for soliloquy; which is but the thought before God, of one, for the guidance of a silence before God, of all. It is to Him we lay ourselves open, and not to our neighbor : only, the sense of brethren near who have concerns like our own that bring them hither, who feel with us his mystic touch, and look up to his heavenly hope, and remember the healing sorrows of his mercy, and expect his early call, and trust his everlasting shelter, — is a mighty help to those deep realities which are too great except for the consentaneous grasp of our collective soul. Prayer, like poetry, can never be any thing but thought aloud : if ever it is " said for the sake of them that stand by," it is a mockery and a pretence, from which every soul that is akin to Christ will shrink with abhorrence and with awe ; and which none who had been altogether steeped in his spirit could ever ascribe to him. Nor let any one say that this makes the office of religion one of uncertain imagination, transient as the colors of beauty, and vague as the impressions of a dream. Never do we more completely deceive ourselves, than when we fancy that the work of the understanding is durable, while that of our richer genius is evanescent; that what we know is solid, what we aspire after and adore in thought is unsubstantial : that the achievements of physical discovery are the fixed products of time, while the visions of poetry are but the adornments of a passing age. How plainly does historical experience contradict this estimate! Of no nation, of no period, within the limits of known and transmitted civilization, does the most advanced science remain true for us : while of none has the genuine poetry perished : Thales and Archimedes have been obsolete for centuries ; while old Homer is fresh as ever, and delights the modern·schoolboy only less than he did the Greek hero. The acuteness of the Athenian intellect has left us no account of any law of nature, which the greatest masters of ancient knowledge deciphered as we do now: but the strains of Job and the rapt song of Isaiah will never be worn out, while a human soul is on the earth, and a divine heaven above it. The readings of philosophy, the creeds of theology, are alike transitory: but the discernment of sacred truth and beauty is perpetual, and without essential change. Never knowing but *in part*, we find all our knowledge successively vanishing away : but in adoring the grandeur, feeling the solemnity, and aspiring to the perfection of the whole, the inspirations of genius and the yearnings of faith are consentaneous and eternal.

XLIII.

THE SPHERE OF SILENCE.

II. GOD'S.

———◆———

JOHN I. 1 & 14.

IN THE BEGINNING WAS THE WORD: AND THE WORD WAS WITH GOD;
AND THE WORD WAS GOD. AND THE WORD WAS MADE FLESH, AND
DWELT AMONG US (AND WE BEHELD HIS GLORY, — THE GLORY AS OF
THE FATHER'S ONLY-BORN) FULL OF GRACE AND TRUTH.

HUMAN speech, it has already been observed, is employed
in two different ways, issuing from states of mind distinct
and almost opposite. We speak to impart information;
and we speak in confession of ourselves; in intentional
address to the minds of others, or in unconscious revelation of our own; drawn by an external end which we wish
to compass, or propelled by internal feeling which we
cannot but express. In the one case, we begin with our
purpose, and then lay, with such skill as we can command,
our train of approach towards its realization: in the other,
we start from the emotion that occupies us, and advance
along a line of tendency, never lawless, yet ever unforeseen.
The one discloses the policy at which our action aims; the
other, the affection whence it issues. In the one, we teach,
we expound, we report the past, we predict the future: in
the other, we remember, we hope, we paint the soul's immediate vision, and own its everlasting faith. In the one, we
talk and reason: in the other, we meditate and sing. History and science are the birth of the one; art and religion,
of the other; morals and philosophy, of both.

But man is not the only being that has this two-fold voice. God also puts to a double engagement his silent instruments of expression. He too lives amid a company of minds; and to them he has to say something of what already he has done, and of what he yet designs to do, — to communicate the order of the scene on which they stand, and put into the hand of expectation a clew of faithful guidance. But he also *is* a Mind, reserving within himself infinite powers, ever awake and moving; thought, large as space and deep and solemn as the sea; holiness, stern as the mountains, and pure as the breath that sighs around them; a mercy, quick as the light, and gentle as the tints that make it. It is not for these to remain inert and repressed, as though they were not. They must have way, and reach their overflow: and if only we place our spirits right, we may catch the blessed flood, and find it as the waters of regeneration. Beyond and behind every definite end of which it is needful to apprise us, there actually exists in the divine nature an indefinite affluence of living perfection, which cannot go for nothing in the universe. It may have not a word to say to others; but whispers will escape it on its own account : it may not be heard; and yet articulately overheard : and, could we only find the focus of those stray tones, we should understand more than any knowledge can tell : we should learn the very prayers that Heaven makes for only Heaven to hear; and should catch the soliloquy of God. And not only can we find it, but we are ever in it; and beneath the dome of this universe, which is all centre and no circumference, we cannot stand where the musings of the eternal mind do not murmur round us, and the visions of his lonely, loving thought, appear.

Works of science and history are the medium in which men speak to us; works of poetry and art, that in which they speak from themselves. With these the heavenly dialects precisely correspond ; being in fact the great originals, whereof these are but faint echoes. The *outward objects*

of science and history, — the phenomena recorded by the
one, and the events narrated by the other, — all the calculable *happenings* of the frame and order of things, are God's
didactic address, in which he gives us the information we
most need about his ways. And that which awakens poetry and art, the invisible light that bathes the world — the
nameless essence that fills it, — the devout, uplifted look of
all things, — is the personal effusion of God's spirit, by which
the secret spreads of what he is. In the *system* of nature
and life he teaches us his *will:* in the *beauty* of nature and
life, he meditates from *himself*. If we and all similar beings were away, the former would become unmeaning; and
the busy movements, the mighty forces, the mechanical successions, the breathless haste of moments, the patient roll of
ages, would seem to be superseded, and to be a mere sense-
less stir, were they not in sympathy with teeming life, and
a discipline of countless minds. But, in our presence or our
absence, the everlasting beauty would still remain: all that
lay beneath the eternal eye would sleep in the serene light,
and wait no leave from us. *That* is a thought which God
has writ only for himself: a *Word* of his that asks no audience. Yet he cares not to hide it from us : and he has
made us so like himself, that a glance suffices to interpret,
and to fill us with his blessed inspiration.

God is related to his works and ways, just as genius to
the creations of poetry or art that issue from it : and both
must be apprehended in the same manner, — by the softened
gaze of reverence, not by the dry sharpsightedness of knowledge. All our acute study of such things is but a delusion
and a flattery, if we suppose it really to open to us the
sources from which they come. You may analyze, if you
will, the dramas of Shakspeare, the paintings of Raphael,
the music of Beethoven; you may disengage for separate
inspection, action, character, sentiment and costume; grouping and colors ; theme and treatment; and you may thus
know each composition at every turn ; discern its structure ;

recognize its proportions; lay your finger on its happiest lights. But do you reproduce the state of mind that first created it? Do you get upon the traces of the author's way of work? Are your rules and laws, when you have drawn them out, a faithful representation of the soul from whose expression you have deduced them? Can they spread, beneath any other view, the many-clustered plain of life, as it lay beneath the player's large and genial eye: or fill the world again with the rich tints and noble forms that reflected their repose upon the painter's face: or send through any second heart the wild night-winds that sighed and sung through the deaf musician's soul? This, you will own, your criticism cannot do. At best, it does but sketch an artificial method, which, if it could be perfectly obeyed, might be a substitute for the natural one. Only, it cannot be obeyed; and when the attempt is made, it produces not a living likeness, but a dead imitation; human nature turned into wax, and the heavens flattened to the canvas, and the passion of melody reduced to an uneasiness among the strings. The canons of taste, so far from being an approach to the mind of the artist, are the extreme point of departure from it; being the expression of a dissecting self-conscious ness, the intrusion of which would have been fatal to his work.

Now this principle appears to me to be rigorously applicable to our contemplation of the works and ways of God. What we call *science* is nothing but our critical interpretation of nature; our reduction of it into intelligible pieces or constituents, that we may view successively what we cannot grasp at once. And it no more exhibits to us the real sources from which creation sprang, or the modes of its appearing, than the critic's system shows us the poet's soul. The supposition is as derogatory to God in the one case, as it is insulting to genius in the other. The books which repeat to us the laws of the physical world usually mislead us on this matter. They enumerate certain forces, with which they pretend to be on the most intimate footing, and which are able to do great things in the universe; and by putting them together, in this way and that, they show what events would come about: they then point out, that such events do actually occur; and think it proved that the real phenomena are manufactured after their pattern, and truly spring from the causes in their list. Thus Newton is said to have detected the powers that determine the planetary orbits. He found them, we are assured, to be but *two; one*, the primary impulse that commenced the motion of each globe, and sent it careering on its way; the *other*, the constant attraction that curves it ever to the sun. So fixed is this representation in our thoughts by the exposition of astronomers, that it is generally accepted as a true picture of the *fact:* and, in order to trace the ellipse of our Earth or Mars, the two forces are supposed to have been, once upon a time, actually put together, and, like the separate parts of a machine, brought to co-operate. Yet, fondly as this image clings to our fancy, no thoughtful man can seriously hold to so gross an error. Was there then really a certain moment in the past, when the divine hand shot forth the globes, and then condensed into the sun the power to bend them into their ever-circling course? Is it an historic fact in the universe, that this artillery of the skies was once played off, and might be seen by any spirit-witness passing by? No: the planets are not a mere set of bowls; nor was the great court of the zodiac bounded and made plane for such a game as that! No one can well believe that this is an account of what actually occurred: travel through the past with the most vigilant eye, you nowhere arrive at such event. The imagination of it is a pure fiction which begins and ends with the mind that thinks it. What then, you will say, has Newton done? He has done this: he has found or defined two forces which, *if they were to operate under the conditions prescribed, would* produce just such phenomena as we observe. He has discovered a way

in which the same thing *might be done;* has detected, not
the actual causes, but a system of equivalents that will serve
the end as well. By laying these before us, he fulfils the
aim of knowledge : he gives us a rule by which to compute
the course of nature, and from the present to foretell the
approaching attitudes of things. He draws a true picture
for us of all the future, and of all the past, that lies within
the existing order : but of the source of that order, or the
posture of affairs before it rose, he cannot afford the faintest
glimpse. And so is it throughout the sciences. Whenever
they give you a report of *causes*, they tell you, not the real
process, but its equivalent : that by which *we should work*,
not that by which *God does work.* The optician enumerates
the several colors of which light is made : but who can think
that thus we learn the order of God's creation, —and that
first he provided the yellow, red, and blue, and then put them
together to form the one white ray ? The chemist will give
you a list of what he finds in the bursting seed, the shooting
plant, the growing animal ; but do you suppose that the divine
hand really measures these doses of hydrogen and carbon ;
that in bringing out the gentle grass, and shedding its glory
on the forest tree, and tracing the dear human face; and putting a strange depth into the eye, God works by the pharmacopœia or the scale of chemical equivalents ? Ah no ! else
were he not the Creator, but the manufacturer,* of this universe ; a mixer of ingredients ; a worker in wood and iron :
little more than a Vulcan, Neptune, or Æsculapius, with another name. To be chief artificer, chief dyer, chief engineer ;
to be able to construct a world, to tincture the drapery of
clouds, and poise the clustered stars ; — this is not to be the
everlasting God. The steps by which we slowly understand
are not the order in which he instantly discerns and eternally executes. The laws which we extract are but the
patient alphabet in which he spells out successively to us the
tendencies of his spontaneous thought. They are the rules

* Not ποιητής, but δημιουργός.

which our criticism draws from the analysis of his pro-
ductions: but like the precepts taken from the study of
ancient art, they express our afterthought, not his forethought; and though they are a true light to our knowledge,
they are a false shadow on our religion. In one sense, no
doubt, they are the voice of God. As men talk to us and
tell us what they have been doing and what they still in-
tend to do; yet shelter from us, perhaps almost from themselves, their inmost love and worship; so here does God
adopt our speech, address himself to our instruction, and
teach us the outward purpose of his will; but opens not
the infinite well-spring whence all the power and the order
flow.

Is this then the only voice of His that comes to us from
the physical world? It is the only voice in which he
directly accosts us, and commands our obedience. But we
are always in his presence; and there would seem to be
when he forgets that we are by; and his own nature confesses itself through all the loneliness of space; and we
may apprehend its essence rather than its act. To do this,
we have but to look on creation as a picture, instead of
examining it as a machine. It must fix our eye as a work
of beauty, not as a structure of ingenuity. The simplest
impressions from nature are the deepest and most devout:
and to get back to these, after spoiling the vision with the
artificial glasses of science, is the difficult wisdom of the
pure heart. The modest flower, nestling in the meadow
grass; the happy tree, as it laughs and riots in the wind;
the moody cloud, knitting its brow in solemn thought; the
river, that has been flowing all night long; the sound of the
thirsty earth, as it drinks and relishes the rain; these things
are as a full hymn, when they flow from the melody of
nature, but an empty rhythm, when scanned by the finger
of art. The soul, as it sings, cannot both worship and beat
time. The rainbow, interpreted by the prism, is not more
sacred, than when it was taken for the memorandum of

God's promissory mercy, painting the access and recess of his thought. The holy night, that shows us how much more the sunshine hides than it reveals, and warns us that the more clearly we see what is beneath our feet, the more astonishing is our blindness to what is above our heads, is less divine, when watched from the observatory of science, than when gazed at from the oratory of private prayer. To the one it is the ancient architecture, to the other the instant meditation of the Most High. And so is it with all the common features of our world. The daily light, fresh as a young child every morning, and dignified as the mellowness of age at even; the yearly changes, less fair and dear to our infancy than to our maturity, — the weariness of nature as she drops her leaves, the glee with which she hangs them out again, — the silver mists of autumn, the slanting rains of spring, the sweeping lines of drifted snow; all are as the natural language of God, — the turns of his almighty thought, — to the spirit that lies open to their wonder: to others, they are but a spinning of the earth, an evaporation of the waters, an equilibrium in the winds.

It is the same in the case of human life, as in that of the outward world. There also our knowledge does not represent God's ways; our knowledge being a critical deduction of rules which his ways indeed have furnished but did not follow. There also we should think of him, not as constructing mechanically for an end, but as creating spontaneously from himself. In our review of ancient or modern nations, we are anxious to account for the peculiarities that mark them, and the influence they have had upon mankind; and we search their climate and geography, their inheritance of language and tradition, their relative position and experience, for the causes of their special genius and institutions. And such enumeration is invaluable in its fruits of practical and political wisdom. Only let us not imagine that God works by the sort of composition of causes, which our poor intellect is obliged to fancy to itself. He did not

model the Hebrew, or fabricate the Greek, after the fashion
of our historical analysis, saying to himself " This climate
will do, but then it must have that organization, and be
mixed with such and such sort of memories." It were contemptible to think that he thus moulds and serves up the
nations, like one that holds a receipt-book in his hand.
And so too with the individual mind. Philosophy, justly
curious to observe the structure of our faculties, and the
nature of those wondrous operations by which man alone,
of all creatures, has acquired a history, endeavors to untwine
the finished web of thought, and lay out the variegated
filaments, — the warp of constant nature, and the woof of
flying experience, — from which the texture seems to have
been composed. And this also is well: opening to us the
deepest problems and yielding many useful lessons. Only
we must not suppose that God makes men after the pattern
of Locke's or Mill's human nature; providing the raw
material of so many simple ideas, with measured lots of
pleasure and pain, to be mixed up into a Plato, or fused
down into a Channing. Nor ought we to think that he
preconceives a particular task to be accomplished for the
world, and then proceeds to make and move men, like fitting
puppets, to perform it. The souls of the sons of God are
greater than their business; and they are thrown out, not
to do a certain work, but to be a certain thing; to bear
some sacred lineaments, to show some divine tint, of the
Parent Mind from which they come. The mighty spirits
of our race are as the lyric thoughts of God that drop and
breathe from his almighty solitude; — transient chords flying forth from the strings as his solemn hand wanders over
the possibilities of beauty. One only finished expression
of his mind, one entire symmetric strain, has fallen upon
our world. In Christ, we have the overflowing Word, the
deep and beautiful soliloquy, of the Most High; not his
message and his argument, — for in that there were no
religion, — but the very poetry of God, which could not

have been told us face to face, but only cast in meditation upon the silence of history. Not more certainly do we discern in the writings of Shakspeare the greatest manifestation of human genius, than in the reality of Christ the highest expression of the Divine. Not more clearly does the worship of the saintly soul, breathing through its window opened to the midnight, betray the secrets of its affections — than the mind of Jesus of Nazareth reveals the perfect thought and inmost love of the All-ruling God. Were he the only-born, — the solitary self-revelation, — of the Creative Spirit, he could not more purely open the mind of Heaven : being the very Logos, — the apprehensible nature of God, — which, long unuttered to the world, and abiding in the beginning with him, has now come forth, and dwelt among us full of grace and truth.

www.ingramcontent.com/pod-product-compliance
Lightning Source LLC
Chambersburg PA
CBHW030041130726
47901CB00005BA/1427